The Gen X' Series

SCIENCE OLYMPIAD 9

Useful for Science Olympiads Conducted at School, National & International Levels

Author
Preeti Agarwal

Peer Reviewer
P. Lalita

Strictly According to the Latest Syllabus of Science Olympiad

V&S PUBLISHERS

Published by:

F-2/16, Ansari road, Daryaganj, New Delhi-110002
☎ 23240026, 23240027 • *Fax:* 011-23240028
✉ info@vspublishers.com • 🌐 www.vspublishers.com

 Online Brandstore: amazon.in/vspublishers

Regional Office : Hyderabad
5-1-707/1, Brij Bhawan (Beside Central Bank of India Lane)
Bank Street, Koti, Hyderabad - 500 095
☎ 040-24737290
✉ vspublishershyd@gmail.com

Follow us on:

BUY OUR BOOKS FROM: | AMAZON | FLIPKART

© Copyright: *V&S* PUBLISHERS
ISBN 978-93-579404-8-1
New Edition

DISCLAIMER

While every attempt has been made to provide accurate and timely information in this book, neither the author nor the publisher assumes any responsibility for errors, unintended omissions or commissions detected therein. The author and publisher makes no representation or warranty with respect to the comprehensiveness or completeness of the contents provided.

All matters included have been simplified under professional guidance for general information only, without any warranty for applicability on an individual. Any mention of an organization or a website in the book, by way of citation or as a source of additional information, doesn't imply the endorsement of the content either by the author or the publisher. It is possible that websites cited may have changed or removed between the time of editing and publishing the book.

Results from using the expert opinion in this book will be totally dependent on individual circumstances and factors beyond the control of the author and the publisher.

It makes sense to elicit advice from well informed sources before implementing the ideas given in the book. The reader assumes full responsibility for the consequences arising out from reading this book.

For proper guidance, it is advisable to read the book under the watchful eyes of parents/guardian. The buyer of this book assumes all responsibility for the use of given materials and information.

The copyright of the entire content of this book rests with the author/publisher. Any infringement/transmission of the cover design, text or illustrations, in any form, by any means, by any entity will invite legal action and be responsible for consequences thereon.

Publisher's Note

General Trade and Mass Appeal books across various genres have helped **V&S Publishers** to gain widespread popularity. In a short span of 10 years, we have successfully published more than 1000 titles across 9 languages in our 50 subject categories. Being into the publishing business for about 40 years, we have always been a dynamic publishing house, with a massive distribution network, across India; including E-commerce platforms.

Understanding the need of inculcating knowledge and developing a spirit of healthy competition amongst students to make them ready for the world outside schools and colleges; we created Olympiad Series under the **GEN X SERIES Imprint** which, owning to its rich content and unique representation became popular amongst students, in no time. The motivation is not to improve marks in terms of numbers, but is to make sure that the students are already prepared to face competitive environment with respect to college admissions and cracking various entrance examinations, while ensuring their conceptual clarity.

Published for classes 1-10 across subjects English, Mathematics, Science, Computers, General Knowledge, the books are unlike any other in the market and are written in a guidebook pattern and exhaustively include examples and Multiple-Choice Questions.

Here, we present the latest Edition of **SCIENCE OLYMPIAD CLASS 9.**

Unique Features of the book are as follows:

- Authored by Subject Matter Experts' and Peer reviewed by School Principals and HOD's for the respective subjects
- Books based on principles of Applied Psychology and Bloom's Taxonomy
- Suited for Olympiad Examinations held at School level, National level & International Level irrespective of organizing body.
- The only Olympiad Book in India written in Guidebook Pattern with Concise Theory, images and illustrations.
- Exhaustively include Examples, MCQs, Subjective Questions, and HOTS with Answer Keys & Solutions.
- Multiple Model Papers for thorough practice also given inside the book with solutions.
- OMR sheets appended at the end of the book for simulating exam environment.

Besides, we are also planning to launch an App very soon for the Olympiad preparation which further testifies our constant endeavor to keep up with student demands. We have made sure to closely follow syllabus patterns of not only Olympiad conducting bodies but also education boards & organizations like CBSE and NCERT, to make sure that our books prove useful to students; helping them to boost their academic performance in schools as well.

P.S. While every care has been taken to ensure the correctness of the content, if you come across any error, howsoever minor, do not hesitate to discuss with teachers while pointing that out to us in no uncertain terms.

We wish you All the Best!

DISTINCTIVE

WHY OLYMPIADS?

Olympiads are just like competitive exams; conducted by various bodies at national and international levels. The aim is to experience a competitive examination at the school level and also to help students to discover their interest acrss subjects like English, Mathematics, Science and General Knowledge.

WHY V&S OLYMPIADS?

We at V&S Publishers aim to build an avid-reading student audience. Hence, our resolve is to follow an innovative pedagogic pattern which would help students to navigate through the book with utmost ease and comfort. Crisp theory practical examples and illustrations keep our book interactive and comprehensive.

01 LEARNING OBJECTIVES
They list the whole chapter as subtopics, helping the teachers to guide children in a step-by-step manner.

02 DID YOU KNOW
Enhance your knowledge by getting acquainted with some amazing facts across various subjects like science, Mathematics and English.

03 MULTIPLE CHOICE QUESTIONS
MCQs act as an excellent learning aid, helping you to understand and work on your mistakes.

04 THINGS TO REMEMBER
A quick recap of the chapter in a summarized format helps in faster revision along with conceptual clarity.

05 HOTS
The High Order Thinking Questions aim to help the student to solve Application-based questions and gain practical understanding of the subject.

FEATURES

SUBJECTIVE QUESTIONS — 06
Help to place the knowledge gained in orderly fashion by using **"WH"** questions, mostly in the form of bullet points.

ACHIEVER'S SECTION — 07
Offers a quick revision of the book along with some new facts for the students to discover.

A SET OF OMR SHEETS — 08
To allow the student to practice question in an exam-like format which would help them to get the "feel" of how Olympiad exams take place.

MODEL TEST PAPERS — 09
Two model test papers are provided at the end of each book, which help the student to test the knowledge which they have gained after thorough reading of all chapters.

ANSWER KEY & SOLUTIONS — 10
Detailed Answer Key along with explanations aid the pupil to indentify, understand the mistakes they make during the course of Olympiad preparation.

COMPLEMENT SCHOOL SYLLABI

The syllabi across all Olympiad examination closely follow the pattern of academic books. Hence, they not only provide a competitive examination experience, but also help to revise topics for school examinations as well, while strengthening conceptual precision.

ENHANCEMENT OF ANALYTICAL & LOGICAL REASONING

Practicing analytical ability questions, not only helps in developing intellectual ability but also plays a vital role in building critical thinking ability which helps an individual to think about a question or a crisis like situation in day to day life; from all aspects and directions.

Note to Parents

Dear Parents,

Olympiad examinations come with a plethora of advantages. First and foremost among such advantages is the application of knowledge studied, in the form of multiple-choice questions. It helps the child not only to step away from rote learning, but also helps them to exhibit their competencies across various subjects.

In addition to this, Olympiads help the student to understand the importance of revision and practice, and to imbibe upon these practices; which also prove useful in academic performance of the child.

The Olympiads are conducted across multiple subjects, and help the child to recognize their field of interest, thereby encouraging the students to make a career in the field where they can excel the most.

However, cognitive development of a child is not just limited to the four walls of classroom. Following steps can be encouraged by you, to ensure their ward is able to grasp various concepts with ease or lesser difficulty:

- **Eat a balanced diet:** Ensure intake of vitamins and minerals to keep you active. Include fruits and super foods like millet in your diet to ensure healthy functioning of organs. Huge intake of junk food should be avoided.
- **Indulge in outdoor activities:** Outdoor games break the monotony of life. Play your heart out in greenery to keep yourself alert, active and fit.
- **Sleep well:** A sound sleep of 7-8 hours refreshes the brain and makes it ready to understand new topics with more clarity. A sleep derived person faces difficulty in doing even the simplest tasks of day to day life.
- **Reduce your Screen time:** More screen time leads to not only weakening of eyesight but decreases concentration span. Regulated Screen time should be encouraged
- **Do not hesitate to raise a hand:** Having a doubt in class? Do not hesitate to ask your parents or teachers. This ensures more Conceptual Clarity and hence leads to Application based understanding of various subjects and topics.
- **Teach and Learn:** No need to do rote-learning. Once you understand a topic teach or explain it to your friends, siblings and parents. It brings clarity and ensures the child does his revision this way.
- **Keep smiling:** A positive attitude promotes a growth mindset and encourages the child to be more inquisitive and try to learn something new, everyday!

HAPPY LEARNING!

Contents

SECTION 1 : SCIENCE

1. Motion — 9
2. Force and Laws of Motion — 22
3. Gravitation — 31
4. Work and Energy — 42
5. Sound — 53
6. Matter in Our Surroundings — 63
7. Is Matter Around us Pure — 74
8. Atoms and Molecules — 88
9. Structure of Atom — 101
10. Cell–The Fundamental Unit of Life — 111
11. Tissues — 122
12. Diversity in Living Organisms — 137
13. Why do We Fall Ill — 158
14. Natural Resources — 169
15. Improvement in Food Resources — 182

SECTION 2 : LOGICAL REASONING

1. Analogy — 194
2. Classification — 197
3. Series Completion — 201
4. Coding and Decoding — 204
5. Number, Ranking, and Time Sequence Test — 208
6. Alphabet Test — 212
7. Blood Relation Test — 217
8. Mathematical Operations — 222
9. Arithmetical Reasoning — 226
10. Inserting the Missing Character — 231
11. Series — 236
12. Paper Cutting — 242
13. Mirror Images — 247
14. Water Images — 251
15. Cubes and Dice — 255

SECTION 3 : ACHIEVERS' SECTION

Achivers' Section — 260
Model Test Paper - 1 — 266
Model Test Paper - 2 — 271

ANSWER KEYS (Access Content online on Dropbox) — 277
APPENDIX — 286

SECTION 1
SCIENCE

Motion

Learning Objectives : In this chapter, students will learn about:
- concept of motion
- distance and displacement
- different types of motion
- the terms – velocity, acceleration and retardation

CHAPTER SUMMARY

A body is said to be in motion when its position changes continuously with respect to a stationary object, taken as a reference point. For example, when a car changes its position with respect to a stationary object like traffic signal (see fig. 1.1), we say that the car is in motion. Hands of clock, pendulum of a clock, merry-go-round, moving blades of mixer are some of the examples of motion observed around us in our daily life.

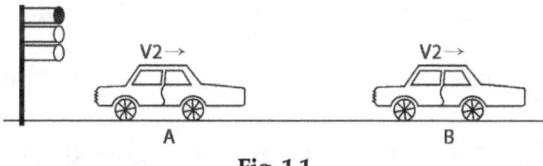

Fig. 1.1

Distance and Displacement

The concept of distance travelled and displacement of an object can be understood by an example. Suppose a man lives at a place, say A and he has to reach his office located at C, but first he has to take his medicine from a shop located at a place, say B. The path travelled by him is drawn in the fig. 1.2.

Distance from A to B = 5 km

Distance from B to C = 4 km

Length of the path ABC travelled by the man = 5 + 4 = 9 km. Then the actual distance travelled by the man in reaching from A to C, is given by, distance travelled, AB + BC = 9 km.

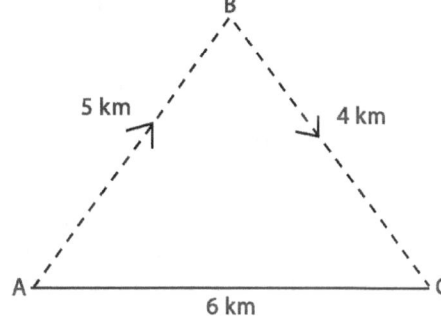

Fig: 1.2

If we want to know how far the man is from his starting point A, then we have to find the shortest distance between point A and point C. To do this we draw a straight line joining A and C whose length is 6 km. This distance AC is called the displacement of the man from point A to the point C.

This displacement in is the East direction. Thus,

Distance travelled refers to the actual length of the path travelled by an object during motion.

Displacement refers to the shortest path between the initial and the final position of an object during motion.

Note: Distance has only magnitude but displacement has magnitude as well as direction. Thus, Distance is a scalar quantity and displacement is a vector quantity.

Can the displacement of a body be zero?

Yes, the displacement of a body can be zero, when it traces along a closed loop path and its final and initial positions are at the same point. For example, a boy takes a path along the border of a square park whose each side is 1 km long, and comes back to its starting position A. He travelled along the path AB→BC→CD→DE; Distance travelled = 1 + 1 + 1 + 1 = 4 km

Displacement (from A to A) = 0

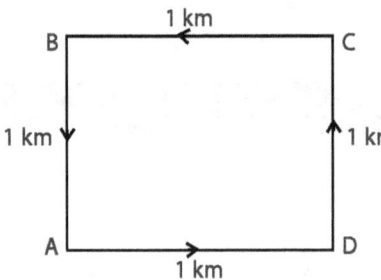

Fig. 1.3

Example 1: A boy travels a distance of 1 km towards East, then 3 km towards South and finally moves 5 km towards East. Find the total distance travelled and the resultant displacement.

Sol.

Total distance travelled
= AB + BC + CD
= 1 + 3 + 5 = 9 km

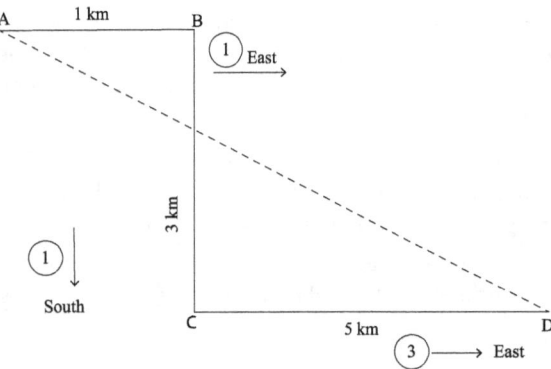

Fig. 1.4

To measure displacement, join points A and D by a straight line. Suppose 1 cm represents 1 km. Using this scale draw AB = 1 cm, BC = 3 cm and CD = 5 cm on a page. Now measure the length AD which is 7.2 cm thus 7.2 cm = 7 km is the final displacement.

> **TRIVIA**
> Tooth enamel is stronger than bones. The lining of our teeth is the hardest substance in the human body.

Types of Motion

(i) **Linear motion:** The motion of an object along a straight line is called linear or rectilinear motion. For example, a boy running on a 100 m straight track on a ground, the motion of a bus on a straight highway etc

(ii) **Circular motion:** The motion of an object on a circular path is called circular motion. For example, an athlete running on a circular path around the field.

(iii) **Rotatory Motion:** The motion of an object along its axis on a fixed point is called the rotatory motion. For example, motion of a top, motion of a globe, motion of a ceiling fan, etc.

(iv) **Vibratory Motion:** The to-and-fro motion of a body about the mean position along the same path is called vibratory motion. For example, the motion of a pendulum in a clock.

Uniform Motion and Non-Uniform Motion

Uniform Motion

A body moves in a uniform motion if it travels equal distances in equal intervals of time. For example, a car running at speed of 15 meters per second will always cover 15 meters in every one second of its motion.

Start time	Distance (km)	Time Period (hr)
9:00	2 km	1
10:00	2 km	1
11:00	2 km	1
12:00	2 km	1

From the above table, we observe that an athlete runs a marathon 8 km long, starting at 9:00 AM. He covers 2 km in every 1 hour, thus covering the whole distance in 4 hours.

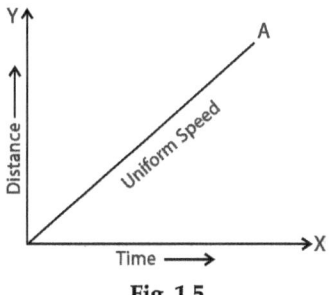

Fig. 1.5

Note: The distance-time graph for uniform motion is a straight line.

Non-Uniform Motion

A body moves in a non-uniform motion if it travels unequal distances in equal intervals of time. For example, a car travels 15 km in one hour due to heavy traffic, but 25 km in the next one hour due to less traffic, and then 35 km on the road in city outskirts where there is no traffic at all. Thus, total distance covered is 75 km in 3 hours.

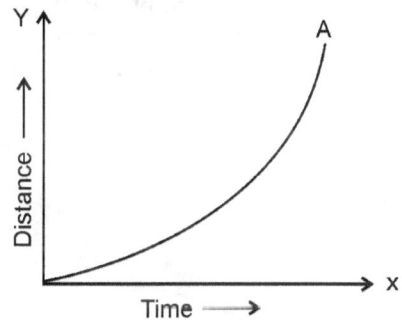

Fig. 1.6

Start time	Distance (km)	TimePeriod (hr)
9:00	15	1
10:00	25	1
11:00	35	1

Note: The distance time graph for a body having a non-uniform motion is a curved line. The non-uniform motion is also called accelerated motion.

Speed, Velocity and Acceleration

The motion of a body can be described by three terms: speed, velocity and acceleration.

Speed

The distance travelled by an object in unit time is called **speed**. It can be measured by dividing the distance travelled by the time taken to travel this distance. It is a scalar quantity.

$$\text{Speed} = \frac{\text{Distance travelled (in meters)}}{\text{Time taken (in seconds)}}$$

If a body travels a distance d in time t, then its speed v is given by:

$$v = \frac{d}{t}$$

The SI unit of speed is metres per second written as ms^{-1}.

Average speed: The average speed of a body is given by the total distance travelled divided by the time taken to cover this distance.

$$\text{Average speed} = \frac{\text{Total distance travelled}}{\text{time}}$$

Example 2: An athlete runs 200 m in 25 seconds and another 300 m in 35 seconds. What is the average speed of the athlete?

Sol.
Total distance travelled by the athlete
$= 200 \text{ m} + 300 \text{ m} = 500 \text{ m}$
Total time taken $= 25 \text{ s} + 35 \text{ s} = 60 \text{ s}$

$$\text{Average speed} = \frac{500 \text{ m}}{60 \text{ s}} = 8.33 \text{ ms}^{-1}$$

Example 3: A car travels a distance of 30 km at a speed of 40 km/hr and the next 30 km at a speed of 20 km/hr. Find its average speed.

Sol.
First 30 km travelled at the speed of 40 km/hr. Let time taken during this journey be

$$t_1 = \frac{\text{distance travelled}}{\text{speed}}$$

$$= \frac{30}{40} = \frac{3}{4} \text{ hrs}$$

Next 30 km travelled at the speed of 20 km/hr

$$\text{Time taken } t_2 = \frac{\text{distance}}{\text{Speed}} = \frac{30}{20} = \frac{3}{2} \text{ hours}$$

Total distance travelled
$= (30 + 30) \text{ km} = 60 \text{ km}$

Total time taken $= \frac{3}{4} \text{ hr} + \frac{3}{2} \text{ hr} = \frac{9}{4} \text{ hrs}$

Motion

Average speed = $\dfrac{\text{Total distance travelled}}{\text{Total time taken}}$

$= \dfrac{60}{9/4} = \dfrac{240}{9}$

$= 26.6 \text{ km/hr}$

Velocity

Velocity of a moving body is the distance travelled by it per unit time in a given direction, denoted by the symbol v

If a body travels a distance d in time t in a given direction, then its velocity v is given by

$$\boxed{V = \dfrac{d}{t}}$$

d = distance travelled in a given direction = displacement, thus, velocity of a body is the displacement produced per unit time. The SI unit of velocity is same as that of speed, namely m/s or ms^{-1}. Velocity is a vector quantity.

Note: The direction of velocity is same as the direction of displacement of the body.

Can average velocity of an object be zero?

In most cases, the bodies move in a single straight line without changing direction. The values of speed and velocity will be same in these cases. In case the body changes its direction at some point of time, then speed and velocity may be different.

Though average speed of a moving body can never be zero, the average velocity of a moving body can be zero.

Example 4: A bus travels a distance of 200 km from Delhi to Agra towards East in 3 hours in the afternoon and returns to Delhi in West covering the same distance in 3 hours again at night. Find its average speed and average velocity for the whole journey.

Sol.

Average speed = $\dfrac{\text{Total distance travelled}}{\text{Total time taken}}$

$= \dfrac{(200 + 200)}{(3 + 3) \text{ hrs}}$

$= \dfrac{400}{6} = 66.6 \text{ (km/hr)}$

Average speed $(v) = \dfrac{\text{Total displacement}}{\text{Total time taken}}$

Total displacement = Distance travelled in East − distance travelled in West

$= 200 \text{ km} - 200 \text{ km} = 0$

∴ Average velocity = $\dfrac{0 \text{ km}}{6 \text{ km}} = 0 \text{ km/h}$

Thus, the average velocity of the bus for the whole journey is 0 km/h. Direction cannot be stated in the case of zero velocity.

Average velocity: Average velocity can also be calculated by taking the average of the initial velocity, represented by u and the final velocity, represented by v.

Average velocity, $v_{av} = \dfrac{u + v}{2}$

Distance – time graph for uniform speed

The graph for an object moving at uniform speed (covering equal distances in equal time periods) is a linear graph.

Distance – time graph for a non-uniform speed

Case 1: When the speed of a moving object increases with time, the graph will exhibit an upward curve.

Case 2: When the speed of a moving object decreases with time, the graph will exhibit a downward curve.

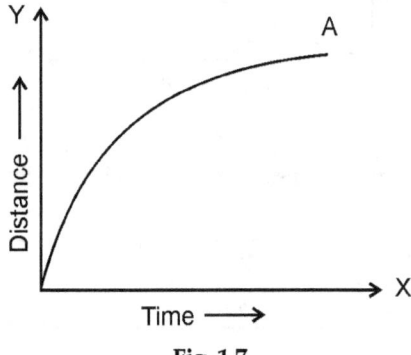

Fig. 1.7

Acceleration

When an object starts, its velocity is zero. Gradually, it increases and then decreases to halt. The rate at which the velocity of the object changes with time is called *acceleration*, it is denoted by a.

Acceleration = $\dfrac{\text{Change in velocity}}{\text{Time taken}}$

Change in velocity = Final velocity – Initial Velocity
= v − u

$$a = \frac{v}{t}$$

t is the time taken for the change in velocity.
The SI unit of acceleration is m/s² or ms⁻².

Note: When a body is moving with uniform velocity, its acceleration will be zero as $v = u$ i.e, change in velocity is zero.

Uniform Acceleration

If a body travels in a straight line and its velocity increases by equal amounts in equal intervals of time, the body is said to be in **uniform acceleration**. The motion of a freely falling body or the motion of a ball rolling down on an inclined plane is an example of uniformly accelerated motion.

The velocity–time graph of a body having uniformly accelerated motion is a **straight line**.

Non-uniform Acceleration

A body is said to be in non-uniform acceleration if its velocity increases by unequal amounts in equal intervals of time i.e. its velocity changes at a non-uniform rate. The velocity–time graph for a body having non-uniform acceleration is a curved line.

Retardation or Negative Acceleration

Acceleration takes place when the velocity of a body changes. This change can be increasing or decreasing. Thus, acceleration can be classified into two categories.

Positive acceleration: When a car runs down on an inclined plane, the velocity of the car increases and it is said to be moving with positive acceleration, which we usually call **acceleration**.

Negative acceleration: When a car runs upwards on an inclined plane, the velocity of car decreases and it is said to be running with negative acceleration, which we generally call **retardation** or **deceleration**. A ball thrown vertically upwards is also an example of negative acceleration. Parachute is also example of deceleration.

Zero acceleration: A bus standing at the bus stop and a bus moving on a straight road with a constant speed of 40 km/hr are the examples of zero acceleration. In both cases, velocity is constant i.e; $\Delta v = 0$.

Example 5: A driver decreases the speed of a car from 45 m/s to 25 m/s in 5 seconds. Find the acceleration of the car.

Sol.
Initial velocity, $u = 45$ m/s;
Final velocity, $v = 25$ m/s;
Time taken, $t = 5$ seconds

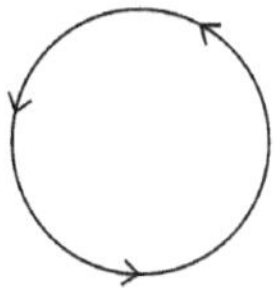

Fig. 1.8

$$a = \frac{v-u}{t} = \frac{25-45}{5} = \frac{-20}{5} = -4 \text{ m/s}^2$$

The negative sign of acceleration means that it is retardation; so, we can say that the car is decelerating at the rate of 4 m/s².

Equations of Uniformly Accelerated Motion

There are equations for the motion of those bodies which travel with a uniform acceleration these equations give the relationship between initial velocity (u), final velocity (v), time taken (t), acceleration (a) and distance travelled (s) by the bodies.

First equation of motion: It gives the velocity acquired by a body in time t moving with acceleration a.

$$a = \frac{v-u}{t}$$

$$\boxed{v = u + at}$$

Second equation of motion: It gives the distance travelled (s) by a body, moving at an initial speed of u, in time t

$$\boxed{s = ut + \frac{1}{2}at^2}$$

Third equation of motion: It gives the velocity (v) acquired by a body in travelling a distance (s)

$$\boxed{v^2 = u^2 + 2as}$$

Note:
1. If a body starts from rest, initial velocity, $u = 0$
2. If a body comes to rest, its final velocity, $v = 0$
3. If a body moves moves with uniform velocity, its acceleration, $a = 0$

Motion

Example 6: A bus acquires a velocity of 36 km per hour in 10 seconds just after the start. Calculate the acceleration of the bus.

Sol.

$$36 \text{ km/hr} = 36 \times \frac{1000}{3600} = 10 \text{ m/s}$$

$u = 0, v = 10, t = 10$

$v = u + at$

$10 = 0 + a \times 10$

$10a = 10 \Rightarrow a = 1 \text{ m/s}^2$

Example 7: A motor bike has a uniform acceleration of 4 m/s². What distance will it cover in 10 seconds after the start?

Sol.

$u = 0, a = 4, t = 10$

$s = ut + \frac{1}{2}at^2$

$= 0 \times 10 + \frac{1}{2} \times 4 \times 10^2 = 200 \text{ m}$

Thus, the distance covered by the bike in 10 s is 200 m.

Example 8: A scooter moving at a speed of 10 m/s is stopped by applying brakes which produce a uniform acceleration of –0.5 m/s². How much distance will be covered by the scooter before it stops?

Sol.

$u = 10 \text{ m/s}, v = 0$ (scooter stops);

$a = -0.5 \text{ m/s}^2, v^2 = u^2 + 2as$

$(0)^2 = (10)^2 + 2(-0.5) \times s$

$0 = 100 - s$,

$s = 100 \text{ m}$.

Uniform Circular Motion

When a body (or any object) moves along a circular path, its direction of motion keeps changing continuously. This we can understand with the concept of motion along an octagonal track. While running along the octagonal track, the athlete changes his direction of motion eight times at the eight corners A, B, C, D, E, F, G and H of this track. If we increase these directions to a greater number, it gets converted into a circular track so, if an athlete moves with a constant speed along a circular path, then the velocity of the athlete will not be constant because velocity is the speed in a specified direction and here the direction of speed changes continuously. **Since the velocity changes (due to continuous change in direction), the motion along a circular path is said to be accelerated.**

When a body moves in circular path with uniform speed (constant speed), its motion is called uniform circular motion.

Examples:

(i) Artificial satellites moving in their orbits in space

(ii) Moon moving around the earth

(iii) Toy train moving on a circular track

(iv) Tip of the needle of a clock.

Speed of a body in uniform circular motion: When a body takes one round of a circular path, it travels a distance of $2\pi r$, where r is the radius of the circular path.

$$\text{Speed } v = \frac{\text{Distance travelled (circumference)}}{\text{Time taken}}$$

$$\boxed{v = \frac{2\pi r}{t}}$$

$$\pi = \frac{22}{7} = 3.14$$

Example 9: A cyclist goes around a circular track once every 2 minutes. If the radius of the circular track is 105 m, calculate his speed.

(given $\pi = \frac{22}{7}$)

Sol.

$$v = \frac{2\pi r}{t} = \frac{2 \times \frac{22}{7} \times 105}{2 \times 60} = 5.5 \text{ m/s}$$

MUST REMEMBER

- A body is said to be in motion when its position changes continuously with respect to a stationary object, taken as a reference point.
- Distance has only magnitude but displacement has magnitude as well as direction. Thus, Distance is a scalar quantity and displacement is a vector quantity.
- The displacement of a body can be zero, when it traces along a closed loop path and its final and initial positions are at the same point.
- The motion of an object along a straight line is called linear or rectilinear motion.
- The motion of an object on a circular path is called circular motion.
- The motion of an object along its axis on a fixed point is called the rotatory motion.
- The to-and-fro motion of a body about the mean position along the same path is called vibratory motion.
- A body moves in a uniform motion if it travels equal distances in equal intervals of time.
- A body moves in a non-uniform motion if it travels unequal distances in equal intervals of time.
- The average speed of a body is given by the total distance travelled divided by the time taken to cover this distance.
- Velocity of a moving body is the distance travelled by it per unit time in a given direction.
- The rate at which the velocity of the object changes with time is called acceleration.
- If a body travels in a straight line and its velocity increases by equal amounts in equal intervals of time, the body is said to be in uniform acceleration.
- The velocity–time graph of a body having uniformly accelerated motion is a straight line.

MULTIPLE CHOICE QUESTIONS

1. What remains constant in uniform circular motion?
   (a) Speed
   (b) Direction
   (c) Both (a) and (b)
   (d) None of these

2. The quantity which is measured by the area occupied under the speed-time graph is _____.
   (a) Velocity
   (b) Distance travelled
   (c) Time taken
   (d) None of these

3. If a body moves 6 m towards South and then turns towards East and moves 8 m, the displacement of the body is _____.

   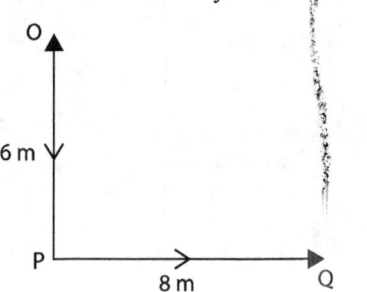

   (a) 12 m   (b) 8 m
   (c) 10 m   (d) 6 m

4. A man travels a distance of 2 m towards East, 6 m towards South and finally 6 m towards East. The resultant displacement is _____.
   (a) 10 m   (b) 8 m
   (c) 12 m   (d) 14 m

5. The motion in which a body has a constant speed but not constant velocity is called _____.
   (a) Uniform linear motion
   (b) Uniform circular motion
   (c) Rotatory motion
   (d) Vibratory motion

6. What does the slope of a velocity-time graph indicate?
   (a) Speed
   (b) Distance travelled
   (c) Velocity
   (d) Acceleration

7. What can you say about the motion of body if its speed-time graph is a straight line parallel to the time axis?
   (a) Speed of the body is zero
   (b) Speed of the body is increasing at a constant rate
   (c) Speed of the body is uniform i.e., constant
   (d) None of these

8. A car travels first 40 km at the speed of 55 km/h and next 20 km at the speed of 50 km/h. Find the total time taken by the car to reach its destination _____.
   (a) 1.34 hours   (b) 1.2 hours
   (c) 1.72 hours   (d) 1.127 hours

9. What can you say about the motion of a body whose distance–time graph is a straight line parallel to time axis?
   (a) Body is moving at same speed
   (b) Body is at rest
   (c) Both body and time are at rest
   (d) None of these

10. What conclusion can you draw about the acceleration of a body from the speed–time graph shown below?

    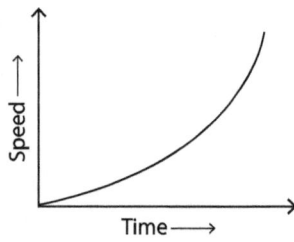

    (a) Positive acceleration
    (b) Deceleration
    (c) Non-uniform acceleration
    (d) Uniform acceleration

11. It is possible for an object to accelerate but not to change its speed if it moves ———.
    (a) In a circular track
    (b) On a sloppy hill
    (c) On a straight path
    (d) To and fro

12. Find the acceleration of a cyclist whose speed changes from 30 m/s to 45 m/s in 3 seconds.
    (a) 3 m/s²   (b) –3 m/s²
    (c) 5 m/s²   (d) –5 m/s²

13. Which of these, decides the direction of motion of the body?
    (a) Speed   (b) Velocity
    (c) Distance   (d) Acceleration

14. The figure shows distance-time graphs of two cars A and B running at different speeds. Which car is running with a greater speed in comparison to the other car?

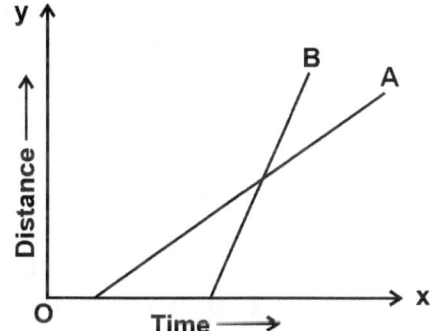

    (a) Car A is running faster than B
    (b) Car B is running faster than A
    (c) Both A and B have same speed
    (d) None of these

15. A bus increases its speed from 36 km/h to 72 km/h in 10 seconds. Its acceleration is ———.
    (a) 5 m/s²   (b) 2 m/s²
    (c) 3.6 m/s²   (d) 1 m/s²

16. A bus moving along a straight line at 15 m/s undergoes an acceleration 2.5 m/s². After 2 seconds, its speed will be ———.
    (a) 20 m/s   (b) 26 m/s
    (c) 25 m/s   (d) 30 m/s

17. The area under a speed-time graph represents a physical quantity which has the unit ———.
    (a) m   (b) ms
    (c) ms⁻¹   (d) ms⁻²

18. If the displacement of an object is proportional to the square of time, then the object is moving with

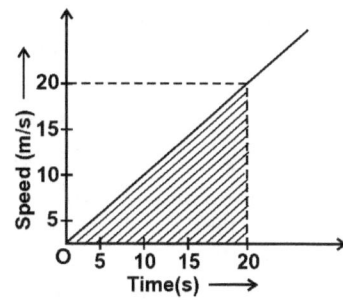

    (a) Uniform velocity
    (b) Uniform acceleration
    (c) Increasing acceleration
    (d) Decreasing acceleration

19. What is the distance covered by a particle during the time interval of 20 seconds, for which the speed-time graph is shown in the adjacent figure?
    (a) 400 m   (b) 100 m
    (c) 200 m   (d) All of these

20. Four cyclists A, B, C, and D are cycling on a levelled straight road. Their distance-time graphs are shown in the given figure. Which of the following is correct regarding the motion of these cyclists?

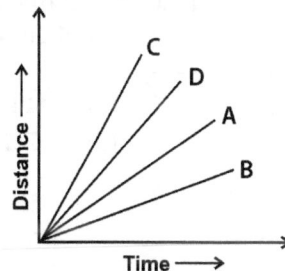

    (a) Cyclist A is faster than D
    (b) Cyclist B is the slowest
    (c) Cyclist D is faster than C
    (d) Cyclist C is the slowest

21. A car of mass 1000 kg is moving with a velocity of 10 ms⁻¹. If the velocity-time graph for this car is a horizontal line parallel to the time-axis, then the velocity of car at the end of 25 s will be _____.
    (a) 10 ms⁻¹   (b) 25 ms⁻¹
    (c) 125 ms⁻¹   (d) 40 ms⁻¹

22. An object moving with a velocity of 30 m/s decelerate at the rate of 1.5 m/s². Find the time taken by the object to come to rest _____.
    (a) 10 seconds   (b) 20 seconds
    (c) 15 seconds   (d) 30 seconds

23. A car accelerates from 15 km/h to 60 km/h in 300 seconds. Find the distance travelled by the car during this time _____.
    (a) 3.35 km   (b) 3.1 km
    (c) 4.33 km   (d) 5 km

24. A motor cycle is being driven at a speed of 20 m/s when a brakes are applied to bring it to rest in five seconds. The deceleration produced in this case will be _____.
    (a) +4 m/s²   (b) −4 m/s²
    (c) +0.25 m/s²   (d) −0.25 m/s²

25. An artificial satellite is moving in a circular orbit of radius 32,000 km. If it takes 30 hours to complete one revolution around the earth, then find the velocity of the satellite _____.
    (a) 9428 km/h   (b) 9500 km/h
    (c) 6704 km/h   (d) 7295 km/h

26. A cyclist takes 3 minutes to complete one round of the circular track. If the radius of the circular track is 45 metres, then the speed of the cyclist is _____.
    (a) 1.57 m/s   (b) 3.14 m/s
    (c) 4.25 m/s   (d) 5.67 m/s

27. A sprinter is running along the circumference of a big stadium with a uniform speed. Which of the following is changing in this case?

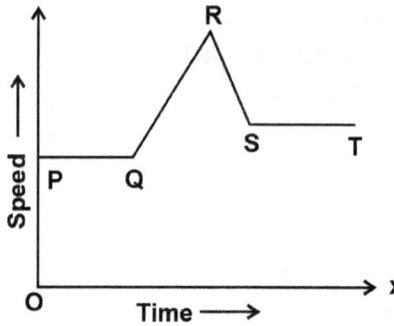

    (a) Magnitude of acceleration being produced
    (b) Distance covered by the sprinter per second
    (c) Direction in which the sprinter is running
    (d) Centripetal force acting on the sprinter

28. In the speed-time graph for a moving object shown here, the part which indicates uniform deceleration of the object is _____.
    (a) ST   (b) QR
    (c) RS   (d) PQ

29. Which one of the following is most likely not a case of uniform circular motion?
    (a) Motion of the earth around the sun
    (b) Motion of a racing car on a circular track
    (c) Motion of a toy train on a circular track
    (d) Motion of hours' hand on the dial of a clock

30. A train starting from rest attains a velocity of 72 km/h in 5 minutes. Assuming that the acceleration is uniform, find the distance travelled by the train for attaining this velocity.
    (a) 5 km   (b) 7 km
    (c) 6 km   (d) 3 km

HOTS

1. **Statement 1:** Displacement of a body along circular path is zero whereas its distance travelled is $2\pi r$.
   Statement 2: The straight line distance between initial and final positions will be zero.
   (a) Statement 1 is true but statement 2 is false
   (b) Statement 2 is true but statement 1 is false
   (c) Both statement 1 and statement 2 are true but statement 2 is not the correct reason for statement 1
   (d) Both statement 1 and 2 are true and statement 2 is correct reason for statement 1.

Direction (2–5): Fill in the blanks with the correct option:

2. The motion of an object along a straight line is called _____.
   (a) Uniform motion
   (b) Non-uniform motion
   (c) Linear motion
   (d) None of these

3. The motion of an object on a circular path is called _____.
   (a) Uniform motion
   (b) Non-uniform motion
   (c) Circular motion
   (d) Linear motion

4. The motion of an object along its axis on fixed point is called _____.
   (a) Rotatory motion
   (b) Linear motion
   (c) Uniform motion
   (d) None-uniform motion

5. The motion of a body travelling equal distances in equal intervals of time is called _____.
   (a) Linear motion
   (b) Uniform motion
   (c) Non-uniform motion
   (d) Vibratory motion

6. The velocity of a car at 10.50 am is 60 km/hr and at 10.52 am it is 80 km/hr. Assuming constant acceleration in the given period, the car is accelerating at _____.
   (a) 650 km/hr^{-2}
   (b) 600 km/hr^{-2}
   (c) 450 km/hr^{-2}
   (d) 350 km/hr^{-2}

7. A planet is moving along a circular orbit of radius 200 km with a uniform speed. The ratio of the distance covered and the displacement of the planet in half revolution is _____.
   (a) 2π
   (b) π
   (c) $\dfrac{\pi}{2}$
   (d) 0

8. A missile is projected vertically upwards from the top of a building reaches the ground in 't_1' seconds. If it is projected vertically downwards from the same place with the same velocity, it reaches the ground in 't_2' seconds. If it falls freely from the top of building, the time taken to reach the ground is _____.
   (a) $\sqrt{t_1 t_2}$
   (b) $\sqrt{t_1 + t_2}$
   (c) $\sqrt{\dfrac{t_1 t_2}{2}}$
   (d) $\sqrt{t_2 - t_1}$

9. Three boxes B_1, B_2 and B_3 of masses 10 kg, 2 kg and 3 kg respectively are attached by a light inextensible string and they are moved on a smooth horizontal plane. If a force of 36N is applied to the string connected to the box B_3, find the ratio of the tensions T_1 and T_2 in the string.

   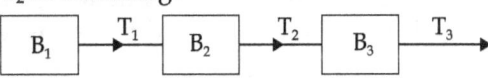

   (a) 10:3
   (b) 3:10
   (c) 13:10
   (d) 10:13

10. A bullet of mass 'm' moving with a speed 'v' strikes a wooden block of mass M and gets embedded in it. The speed of this embedded block will be _____.
    (a) $\left(\dfrac{m}{M+m}\right)^v$
    (b) $\left(\dfrac{m}{M-m}\right)^v$
    (c) $\left(\dfrac{m}{M}+1\right)^v$
    (d) $\left(\dfrac{M+m}{m}\right)^v$

SUBJECTIVE QUESTIONS

1. What are different types of speed?

Ans.

There are mainly four types of speed:

Uniform speed: An object is said to be moving with uniform speed if it covers equal distances in equal time intervals.

Non-uniform speed: An object is said to be moving with variable speed or non-uniform speed if it covers equal distances in unequal intervals of time or vice-versa.

Average speed: When we travel in a vehicle, the speed of the vehicle changes from time to time depending upon the conditions existing on the road. In such a situation, the speed is calculated by taking the ratio of the total distance travelled by the vehicle to the total time taken for the journey. This is called the average speed.

Instantaneous speed: When we say that the car travels at an average speed of 60 km/h, it does not mean that the car would be moving with the speed of 60 km/h throughout the journey. The actual speed of the car may be less than or greater than the average speed at a particular instant of time.

The speed of a moving body at any particular instant of time is called instantaneous speed.

2. A block of wood is kept on a table top. The mass of wooden block is 5 kg and its dimensions are 40 cm × 20 cm × 10 cm. Find the pressure exerted by the wooden block on the table top if it is made to lie on the table top with its sides of dimensions.
   (a) 20 cm × 10 cm and (b) 40 cm × 20 cm

Ans.

The mass of the wooden block 'm' = 5 kg

Area of a side = length × breadth = 20 cm × 10 cm = 0.02 m²

Thrust = mg = 5kg × 9.8 ms^{-2} = 49 N

$$\text{Pressure} = \frac{\text{Thrust}}{\text{Area}} = \frac{49}{0.02} = 2450 \text{ Nm}^{-2}$$

When the block lie on its side of dimensions 40 cm × 20 cm, it exerts the same thrust.

Area = l × b = 40 cm × 20 cm = 0.08 m²

$$\text{Pressure} = \frac{49}{0.08} = 612.5 \text{ Nm}^{-2}$$

3. Give an example of a body which may appear to be moving for one person and stationary for the other.

Ans.

The passengers in a moving bus observe that the trees, buildings as well as the people on the roadside appear to be moving backwards. Similarly, a person standing on the roadside observes that the bus (along with its passengers) is moving in forward direction. But, at the same time, each passenger in a moving bus or train observes, his fellow passengers sitting and not moving. Thus, we can tell that motion is relative.

4. How can we describe the location of an object?

Ans.

To describe the position of an object we need to specify a reference point called the origin. For example, suppose that a library in a city is 2 km north of the railway station. We have specified the position of the library with respect to the railway station i.e., in this case, the railway station acts as the reference point.

5. What do you mean by average speed? What are its units?

Ans.

Average speed is defined as the average distance travelled per unit time and is obtained by dividing the total distance travelled by the total time taken. The unit of average speed is the same as that of the speed, that is, ms^{-1}.

6. What is the difference between uniform velocity and non-uniform velocity?

Ans.

An object with uniform velocity covers equal distances in equal intervals of time in a specified direction, e.g., an object moving with speed of 40 km h^{-1} towards west has uniform velocity.

When an object covers unequal distances in equal intervals of time in a specified direction, or if the direction of motion changes, it is said to be moving with a non-uniform or variable velocity, e.g., revolving fan at a constant speed has variable velocity.

7. Differentiate between distance and displacement.

Ans.

Distance	Displacement
It is the length of the actual path covered by an object, irrespective of its direction of motion.	Displacement is the shortest distance between the initial and final positions of an object in a given direction.
Distance is a scalar quantity.	Displacement is a vector quantity. Displacement may be positive negative or zero.
Distance between two given points may be same or different for different path chosen.	Displacement between two given points is always the same.
Distance covered can never be negative. It is always positive or zero.	Displacement between two given points is always the same.

8. What are the uses of a distance-time graph?

Ans.

The various uses of a distance-time graph are as follows:

(a) It tells us about the position of the body at any instant of time.
(b) From the graph, we can see the distance covered by the body during a particular interval of time.
(c) It also gives us information about the velocity of the body at any instant of time.

9. A cyclist cycles for t second at a speed of 3 m/s and then for the same time at a speed of 5 m/s along a straight road due north. What is the average speed of the cyclist?

Ans.

You may compute arithmetic mean to compute average speed.

Alternately,

Total Time taken = 2t seconds

Total Distance covered = 3t + 5t = 8t m

$$\text{Avg. Speed} = \frac{\text{Total Distance}}{\text{Total Time}}$$

$$= \frac{8t}{2t}$$

$$= 4 \text{ m/s}$$

10. A bus starting from rest moves with a uniform acceleration of 0.1 ms^{-2} for 2 minutes. Find (a) the speed acquired, (b) the distance travelled.

Ans.

Given,

Initial speed (u) = 0 m/s

Acceleration of bus (a) = 0.1 ms^{-2}

Time taken (t) = 2 min = 2 × 60 = 120 s

Final velocity = ?

Distance Covered (S) = ?

∴ $v = u + at$

$= 0 + 0.1 \times 120$

$= 12$ m/s

∴ $S = ut + ½ at^2$

$= 0 + (0.1 \times 120^2)/2$

$= 0.1 \times 14400/2$

$= 720$ m

Force and Laws of Motion 2

Learning Objectives : In this chapter, students will learn about:
- ✓ concept of force and its effects
- ✓ balanced and unbalanced forces
- ✓ Newton's Laws of Motion
- ✓ momentum and conservation of momentum
- ✓ applications of the law of momentum

CHAPTER SUMMARY

It is believed that rest is the natural state of an object. We put in some effort like pushing, pulling, stretching, pressing, hitting, etc. in order to set the object at rest into motion. The objects move because we apply a force on them.

For example, a force is used when we push the door to open it; we use force in pulling the drawer of a table; a force is used in lifting a heavy box; a force is used when we squeeze out water by twisting wet clothes; dry leaves from trees fly away because the force of wind pushes them.

Effects of Force

We cannot see force. A force can be judged only by the effects produced by it. A force can produce the following effects.
(i) A force can move a stationary object.
(ii) A force can stop a moving object.
(iii) A force can change the direction and speed of a moving body.
(iv) A force can change the shape and size of a body.

TRIVIA

Pure hydrogen can kill you. Pure hydrogen gas acts as a chemical asphyxiant. If you walk into a room with no oxygen, you won't be able to breathe.

Balanced and Unbalanced Forces

If the resultant of all the forces acting on a body is zero the forces are called **balanced forces**. A heavy box placed on the table is pushed from the left side in order to move it. The four forces acting on the box are as mentioned below.

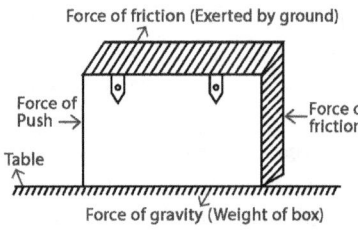

Fig. 2.1

i. Force of push.
ii. Force of friction (which opposes the push and does not allow the box to move).
iii. Force of gravity or weight of box (which pulls the box downwards).
iv. Force of reaction exerted by the ground on the box (upwards which balances the force of gravity).

Even after application of these four forces, the box does not move at all. Thus, we can conclude that the resultant of all the forces is zero.

In a tug of war, if the two teams have equal strength and apply equal force in opposite directions, the rope will not move in either direction.

Note:
(i) If a number of balanced forces act on a stationary body, the body continues to remain in its stationary position.
(ii) If a number of balanced forces act on a body in uniform motion, the body continues to be in its state of uniform motion.

If the resultant of all the forces acting on a body is not zero, the forces are called **unbalanced forces**.

Unbalanced forces can move a stationary body or they can stop a moving body.

In case of a toy car, again four forces of push, friction, gravity and reaction are applied. Force of gravity on the car acting downwards and the force of reaction of ground acting upwards are equal and opposite, so they balance each other. Due to the wheels of the toy car, the opposing force of friction is much less than the force of our push. The resultant of all the forces is not zero causing an unbalanced force acting on the toy car which makes the car move from its position of rest.

Newton's Laws of Motion

Sir Isaac Newton gave three laws of motion to describe the motion of bodies. These laws give a precise definition of force and establish a relationship between the force applied on a body and the state of motion acquired by it.

Newton's First Law of Motion

A body at rest will remain at rest, and a body in motion will continue to be in motion in straight line with a uniform speed, unless it is compelled by an external force to change its state of rest or uniform motion.

Inertia

The tendency of a motionless body to remain at rest, or if moving, to continue moving in a straight line, is called inertia. Newton's first law states that every body has some inertia. Inertia is that property of a body due to which it resists a change in its state of rest or uniform motion.

Note: Mass is a measure of the inertia of a body. Heavier objects have more inertia and require more force to move as compared to lighter objects.

Momentum

The force required to stop a moving body is directly proportional to the mass and velocity of that body. A cricket ball requires more force than a tennis ball to be stopped from moving in air. Thus, the quantity of motion in a body depends on the mass and the velocity of the body. This quantity was introduced by Newton as momentum, denoted by P. It is the product of mass and velocity.

Momentum = mass × velocity

$$\boxed{P = m \times v}$$

If a body is at rest, its velocity is zero, hence momentum is zero. The SI unit of momentum is kg m/s. Momentum is a vector quantity.

Note: Every moving body possesses momentum.

Example 1: What is the momentum of a man of weight 70 kg when he walks with a uniform velocity of 3 m/s?

Sol.
$$\text{momentum, } P = m \times v$$
$$= 70 \times 3$$
$$= 210 \text{ kg ms}^{-1}$$

Newton's Second Law of Motion

According to Newton's second law of motion, the *rate of change of momentum of a body is directly proportional to the applied force, and takes place in the direction in which the force acts.*

The force necessary to change the momentum of an object depends on the time taken at which the momentum is changed.

$$\text{Force} \propto \frac{\text{Change in momentum}}{\text{Time taken}}$$

or $$F \propto \frac{mv - mu}{t}$$

or $$F \propto m \frac{(v-u)}{t}$$

$$\boxed{F \propto ma}$$

Thus the force acting on a body is directly proportional to the product of 'mass' of the body and the 'acceleration' produced in the body by the action of the force, and it acts in the direction of acceleration.

$$F = k \times m \times a$$

In SI units, value of constant k is 1. So the equation becomes

$$F = ma$$

Putting $m = 1$ kg and $a = 1$ m/s^2, F becomes 1 Newton.

Note: A Newton is that force which when acting on a body of mass 1 kg produces an acceleration of 1 m/s^2 in it, represented by 1N.

Force and Laws of Motion

Applications of Newton's second law
(i) A cricket fielder moves his hands backwards on catching a fast running cricket ball, in order to increase the time taken to reduce the momentum of ball to zero.
(ii) A high jumping athlete is provided either a cushion or a heap of sand on the ground to fall upon. This cushion or sand, being soft reduces the athlete's momentum more gently.

Example 2: Calculate the force required to impart to a car, a velocity of 30 m/s in 10 sec, starting from rest. The mass of the car is 1500 kg.

Sol.
$u = 0, v = 30$ m/s, $t = 10$ s.
$$a = \frac{v-u}{t} = \frac{30}{10} = 3 \text{ m/s}^2$$
$F = ma = 1500 \times 3 = 4500$ N

Newton's Third Law of Motion
Newton's third law of motion describes the relationship between the forces that come into play when the two bodies interact with one another. According to this law,

Whenever one body exerts a force on another body, the second body exerts an equal and opposite force on the first body. It can also be written as 'To every action, there is an equal and opposite reaction.'

Note: Action and reaction are just forces acting on two different bodies, and they act simultaneously.

Application of third law
(i) The box exerts 'action' (force of its weight) in downward direction on the ground. The ground is exerting an equal and opposite force, upward, on the box, which we called 'reaction'.
(ii) Same way, when a gun is fired, it exerts a forward force on the bullet. The bullet exerts an equal and opposite reaction force on the gun which makes the gun recoil back.
(iii) In another case, as the sailor jumps from the boat in forward direction towards the shore, the boat moves backward in water.

All these examples prove the Newton's third law of motion.

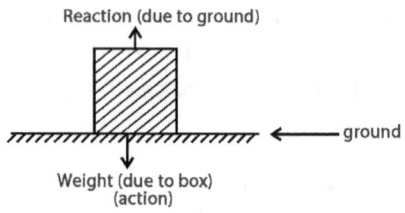
Fig. 2.2

Conservation of momentum
According to the law of conservation of momentum, 'when two (or more) bodies collide with one another, their total momentum remains constant (or conserved) provided no external forces are acting.'

It means that whenever one body gains momentum, then the other body must lose an equal amount of momentum so that total momentum of the two bodies remains same. Thus, the law states that 'Momentum is neither created nor destroyed.' suppose two bodies, a truck (of mass m_1 and speed u_1) and a car (of mass m_2 and speed u_2) are moving in the same direction. Then,

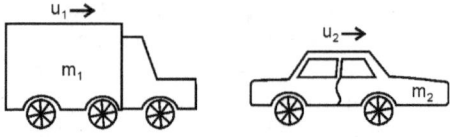
Fig. 2.3

Momentum before collision = $m_1u_1 + m_2u_2$

Fig. 2.4. *Truck collided with the car*

After collision, they again move in the same direction but with new velocities, m_1 with v_1 and m_2 with v_2 due to forces acting on each other.

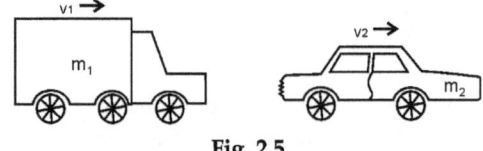
Fig. 2.5

Momentum after collision = $m_1v_1 + m_2v_2$
According to this law
$$\frac{\text{Total momentum}}{\text{Before collision}} = \frac{\text{Total momentum}}{\text{after collision}}$$

$$\boxed{m_1u_1 + m_2u_2 = m_1v_1 + m_2v_2}$$

Applications of the law of conservation of momentum

(i) The chemicals inside the rocket burn and produce high velocity blast of hot gases passing through the tail nozzle of the rocket in the downward direction. The rocket moves up to balance the momentum of gases.

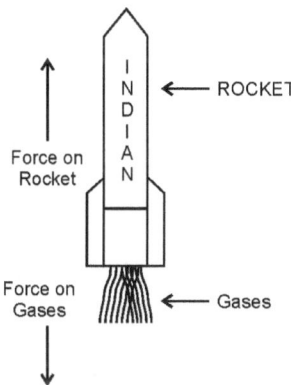

Fig. 2.6

Although the mass of gases emitted is comparatively small, they have a very high velocity and hence a very large momentum. An equal momentum is imparted to the rocket in the opposite direction, so that, in spite of its large mass, the rocket goes up with a high velocity.

Example 3: A bullet of mass 10 g is fired from a gun of mass 6 kg with a velocity of 300 m/s. calculate the recoil velocity of the gun.

Sol.

According to the law of conservation of momentum,

momentum of bullet = momentum of gun

$\dfrac{10}{1000}$ kg × 300 m/s = 6 kg × v

(let the recoil velocity of gun be v m/s)

$3 = 6v \quad v = 0.5$ m/s

Example 4: The car A of mass 1500 kg, running at the speed of 25 m/s collides with another car B of mass 1000 kg travelling at the speed of 15 m/s in the same direction. After collision the velocity of car A becomes 20 m/s. Calculate the velocity of car B after collision.

Sol.

Total momentum of car A and car B before collision

= 1500 × 25 + 1000 × 15

= 52,500 kg.m/s

Total momentum of car A and car B after collision

= 1500 × 20 + 1000 × V

(After collision let car B moves with the speed V)

= 30,000 + 1000 V

Now, according to the law of conservation of momentum

Total momentum before collision = Total momentum after collision

52,500 = 30,000 + 1000 v

⇒ 1000 V = 525000 − 30000

⇒ 1000 V = 22500

⇒ V = 22.50 m/s

Thus, the car B after colliding with car A travelled at the speed of 22.5 m/s gaining 7.5 m/s velocity.

MUST REMEMBER

➡ If the resultant of all the forces acting on a body is zero the forces are called balanced forces.
➡ If the resultant of all the forces acting on a body is not zero, the forces are called unbalanced forces.
➡ Heavier objects have more inertia and require more force to move as compared to lighter objects.
➡ Newton's third law of motion describes the relationship between the forces that come into play when the two bodies interact with one another.

Force and Laws of Motion

MULTIPLE CHOICE QUESTIONS

1. The physical quantity which makes it easier to accelerate small car than a large car is measured in the unit of _____.
   (a) m/s   (b) kg
   (c) kg. m/s   (d) kg. m.s^2

2. The rocket works on the principle of conservation of _____.
   (a) Mass   (b) Energy
   (c) Velocity   (d) Momentum

3. Assume that you were in the space in a weightless environment, will it require a force to set an object in motion?
   (a) Yes
   (b) Both (a) and (b) partly correct
   (c) No
   (d) None of these

4. A motor cycle and a car are moving on a horizontal road with the same velocity. If they are brought to rest by the application of brakes, which provide equal retardation, then _____.
   (a) Motor cycle will stop at shorter distance
   (b) Car will stop at a shorter distance
   (c) Both will stop at the same distance
   (d) Nothing can be predicted

5. Which physical quantity corresponds to the rate of change of momentum?
   (a) Energy   (b) Acceleration
   (c) Force   (d) Mass

6. If the mass of a body and the force acting on it are both doubled, what happens to the acceleration?
   (a) It get doubled
   (b) It is halved
   (c) It remains same
   (d) It becomes four times increased

7. The amount of force required to keep a 5 kg object moving in the right direction with a constant velocity of 2 m/s is _____.
   (a) 0 N   (b) 0.4 N
   (c) 2 N   (d) 10 N

8. Andy spends his holiday at rest on the sofa, watching cricket match and eating junk food. What effect does this practice have upon his inertia?
   (a) Decreases
   (b) Increases
   (c) No effect
   (d) None of these

9. A force of 5N is applied on a body of mass M to produce an acceleration of 10 ms^{-2}. The same force when applied on another body of mass 'm' produces acceleration of 20 ms^{-2}. Find the acceleration produced by the force when both the masses are combined together
   (a) 6.6 ms^{-2} (b) 2.66 ms^{-2}
   (c) 3.66 ms^{-2} (d) 4 ms^{-2}

10. A girl weighing 45 kg is standing on the floor, exerting a downward force of 200 N on the floor. The force exerted on her by the floor is _____.
    (a) Greater than 200 N
    (b) Less than 200 N
    (c) Equal to 200 N
    (d) no force exerted

11. Newton's second law of motion can be written as _____.
    (a) Force = mass × acceleration
    (b) Force = rate of change of momentum
    (c) Both (a) and (b)
    (d) neither (a) nor (b)

12. A girl of mass 20 kg having velocity 2 m/sec jumps on stationary cart of mass 2 kg. Find the velocity of the girl when the cart starts moving _____.
    (a) 2 m/s   (b) 54 m/s
    (c) 0.95 m/s   (d) 1.81 m/s

13. A bullet of mass 20 g is horizontally fired with a velocity of 150 m/s from a pistol of mass 2 kg. What is the recoil velocity of the pistol?
    (a) –1.25 ms^{-1} (b) –1.5 ms^{-1}
    (c) 1.5 ms^{-1} (d) 2.5 ms^{-1}

14. The property of matter due to which a body continues in its state of rest or of uniform motion unless an external force is applied on it is called _____.
    (a) Momentum
    (b) Elasticity
    (c) Inertia
    (d) Gravitational pull

15. A constant force acts on an object of mass 5 kg for a duration of 2 seconds. It increases the object's velocity from 3 m/s to 7 m/s, find the magnitude of the force applied on the object.
    (a) 10 N (b) 20 N
    (c) 25 N (d) 30 N

16. Which body would require a greater force – accelerating a body of mass 2 kg at 5 ms^{-2} or a body of mass 4 kg at 2 ms^{-2}?
    (a) Body of mass 4 kg
    (b) Body of mass 2 kg
    (c) Both requires equal force
    (d) Can't say

17. The sparks produced during sharpening of a knife against a grinding wheel leaves the rim of the wheel tangentially. This is due to _____.
    (a) Inertia of direction
    (b) Inertia of motion
    (c) Inertia of rest
    (d) Force applied

18. An object of mass 5 kg is sliding with a constant velocity of 10 m/s on a frictionless horizontal table. The force required to keep this object moving with the same velocity is _____.
    (a) 8 N (b) 4 N
    (c) 2 N (d) 0 N

19. For a stationary body _____.
    (a) There is no force acting on it
    (b) The body is in vacuum
    (c) The force acting on it is not in contact with it
    (d) The combination of forces acting on it balances each other

20. A batsman hits back a ball straight in the direction of the bowler without changing its initial speed of 12 m/s. If the mass of the ball is 0.15 kg, the impulse imported on the ball is _____.
    (a) 4.2 Ns
    (b) 2.8 Ns
    (c) 3.6 kg m/sec
    (d) 1.6 Ns

21. According to the third law of motion, action and reaction _____.
    (a) Always act on different bodies in opposite directions
    (b) Always act on the same body but in opposite directions
    (c) Have same magnitudes and direction
    (d) Act on either body at normal to each other

22. A force of 5 N gives a mass M_1, an acceleration equal to 8 ms^{-2} and m_2 an acceleration of 24 ms^{-2} What is the acceleration if both the masses are tied together?
    (a) 3 ms^{-2} (b) 4 ms^{-2}
    (c) 6 ms^{-2} (d) 12 ms^{-2}

23. A body of mass 50 kg standing on ground exerts a force of 500 N on the ground. The force exerted by the ground on the body will be _____.
    (a) 50 N (b) 25000 N
    (c) 10 N (d) 500 N

24. A sports car, a matador, a bus and a truck are all running at the same speed of 70 km/h under identical conditions. If all these car are hit from behind with the same force and they continue to move forward, the maximum acceleration will be produced in _____.
    (a) Truck (b) Matador
    (c) Sports car (d) Bus

25. A player stops a football weighing 0.5 kg which comes flying towards him with a velocity of 10 m/s. If the impact lasts for $\frac{1}{50}$ th second and the ball bounces back with a velocity of 15 m/s, then the average force involved is _____.
    (a) 625 N (b) 525 N
    (c) 425 N (d) 325 N

Force and Laws of Motion

26. The acceleration produced by a force of 5 N acting a mass of 20 kg in m/s² is _____.
    (a) 4 (b) 100
    (c) 0.25 (d) 2.5

27. For years space travel was believed to be impossible because there was nothing which rockets could push off in space in order to provide the propulsion necessary to accelerate. This inability of a rocket to provide propulsion is because _____.
    (a) Space is void of air and so there is no air resistance in space
    (b) Rockets do accelerate in space and have been able to do so for a long time
    (c) Gravity is absent in space
    (d) Space is void of air, so the rockets have nothing to push off

28. A ball of mass m is thrown vertically upwards. What is the rate at which the momentum of the ball changes?
    (a) Zero
    (b) Infinity
    (c) mg
    (d) Data is not sufficient

29. A fielder pulls his hands backward while catching the fast running cricket ball This enables the fielder to _____.
    (a) Exert a larger force on the ball by increasing time to catch
    (b) Reduce the force exerted by the ball by increasing the time to catch
    (c) Increase the rate of change of momentum
    (d) keep the ball in hands frimly.

30. Calculate the change in momentum of a body weighing 10 kg when its velocity decreases from 20 m/s to 0.2 m/s.
    (a) –198 Ns (b) 204 Ns
    (c) +198 Ns (d) –204 Ns

HOTS

1. **Statement 1:** A cricket fielder moves his hands backwards on catching a fast running cricket ball to increase the momentum of ball to maximum.
   Statement 2: The rate of change of momentum of a body is directly proportional to the applied force, and takes place in the direction in which the force acts.
   (a) Statement 1 is true but statement 2 is false.
   (b) Statement 2 is true but statement 1 is false
   (c) Both statement 1 and statement 2 are true but statement 2 is not the correct reason for statement 1
   (d) Both statement 1 and statement 2 are true and statement 2 is the correct reason for statement 1.

2. The distance 'd' covered in time 't' by a body having velocity 'v_0' and having a constant acceleration 'a' is given by $d = v_0 + \frac{1}{2}at^2$. This result follows from _____.
   (a) Newton's First Law
   (b) Newton's Third Law
   (c) Newton's Second Law
   (d) None of these

3. When the speed of an object is doubled, the ratio of its kinetic energy to its momentum _____.
   (a) gets doubled
   (b) remains the same
   (c) becomes half
   (d) becomes four times

4. A force of 10 N displaces an object through 20 cm and does work of 1 J in the process. Find the angle between the force and displacement _____.
   (a) θ = 60° (b) θ = 30°
   (c) θ = 35° (d) θ = 45°

5. A plot of velocity versus time is shown in figure. A single force acts on the body. The correct statement is _____.

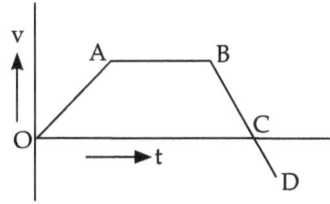

(a) In moving from C to D, work done by the force on the body is positive.

(b) In moving from O to A, work is done by the body and is negative.
(c) In moving from B to C, work done by the force on the body is positive.
(d) In moving from A to B, the body does work on the system.

SUBJECTIVE QUESTIONS

1. If action is always equal to reaction, explain how a horse can pull a cart.

Ans.
The horse pulls the cart with a force (action) in the forward direction. Since every action has an equal and opposite reaction, so the cart also pulls the horse with an equal force (reaction) in the backward direction. As a result of which the two forces get balanced. But while pulling the cart the horse also pushes the ground with its feet in the backward direction. The reaction of the earth moves it in forward direction along the cart. This is how the horse applies force and pulls the cart.

2. Explain how Newton's second law of motion can be used to derive a quantitative definition of force.

Ans.
Suppose a force F acts on a body of mass m, and change its velocity from u to v in t seconds. Then,
Initial momentum of the body, $p_1 = mu$
Final momentum of the body, $p_2 = mv$
Change in momentum = $p_2 - p_1 = m(v - u)$
Time taken = t

Rate of change in momentum = $\dfrac{m(v-u)}{t} = ma$,

where a is the acceleration of the body.
According to Newton's second law of motion, the rate of change of momentum of a body is directly proportional to the applied force. So,
$F \propto ma$
Or $F = kma$ (k is constant)

The unit of force is so chosen that k is equal to one i.e., if $m = 1$, $a = 1$ and $F = 1$, then $k = 1$
Therefore, $F = ma$.
So, a unit of force is that force which produces unit acceleration in a body of unit mass. The SI unit of force is Newton. From the above formula we can say that one Newton is that force which produces an acceleration of 1 m/s² in a body of mass 1 kg. Thus, the Newton's second law of motion gives us a method to measure force.

3. State the difference in balanced and unbalanced force.

Ans.

Balanced force	Unbalanced force
Forces acting on a body from the opposite directions are same.	Forces acting on a body from two opposite directions are not same.
It does not change the state of rest or of motion of an object.	It change the state of rest or of motion of an object.

4. What change will force bring in a body?

Ans.
Force can bring following changes in the body:
- It can change the speed of a body.
- It can change the direction of motion of a body,
- It can change the shape of the body.

5. When a motorcar makes a sharp turn at a high speed, we tend to get thrown to one side. Explain why?

Force and Laws of Motion

Ans.
It is due to law of inertia. When we are sitting in car moving in straight line, we tend to continue in our straight-line motion. But when an unbalanced force is applied by the engine to change the direction of motion of the motorcar. We slip to one side of the seat due to the inertia of our body.

6. For an athletic races why do athletes have a special posture with their right foot resting on a solid supporter?

Ans.
Athletes have to run the heats and they rest their foot on a solid supports before start so that during the start of the race the athlete pushes the support with lot of force and this support gives him equal and opposite push to start the race and get a good start to compete for the race.

7. Why do you think it is necessary to fasten your seat belts while travelling in your vehicle?

Ans.
While we are travelling in a moving car, our body remains in the state of rest with respect to the seat. But when driver applies sudden breaks or stops the car our body tends to continue in the same state of motion because of its inertia. Therefore, this sudden break may cause injury to us by impact or collision. Hence, safety belt exerts a force on our body to make the forward motion slower.

8. What is the relation between Newton's three laws of motion?

Ans.
Newton's first law explains about the unbalanced force required to bring change in the position of the body.
Second law states/explains about the amount of force required to produce a given acceleration.
And Newton's third law explains how these forces acting on a body are interrelated.

9. A bullet of mass 20 g is horizontally fired with a velocity 150 m/s from a pistol of mass 2 kg. What is the recoil velocity of the pistol?

Ans.
For Bullet
$m_1 = 20g = 0.02$ kg
$u_1 = 0$
$v_1 = +150$ m/s
Pistol
$m_2 = 2$ kg
$u_2 = 0$
$v_2 = ?$
Total momentum of the pistol and bullet before firing, when the gun is at rest
$= m_1u_1 + m_2u_2$
$= (0.02 \times 0) + (2 \times 0)$
$= 0$ kg m/s
Total momentum of the pistol and bullet after it is fired
$= m_1v_1 + m_2v_2$
$= (0.02 \times 150) + (2 \times v)$
$= 3 + 2v$

10. State all 3 Newton's law of motion. Explain inertia and momentum.

Ans.
Newton's 1st law of motion: An object remains in a state of rest or of uniform motion in a straight line unless acted upon by an external unbalanced force.

Newton's 2nd law of motion: The rate of change of momentum of an object is proportional to the applied unbalanced force in the direction of the-force.

Newton's 3rd law of motion: To every action, there is an equal and opposite reaction and they act on two different bodies.

Inertia: The natural tendency of an object to resist a change in their state of rest or of uniform motion is called inertia.

Momentum: The momentum of an object is the product of its mass and velocity and has the same direction as that of the velocity. Its S.I. unit is kgm/s. $p = m \times v$

Gravitation

Learning Objectives : In this chapter, students will learn about:
- the universal law of gravitation
- the equations of motion of freely falling body
- mass and weight
- Kepler's laws of planetary motion
- the Archimedes' principle
- terms density and relative density

CHAPTER SUMMARY

It was **Sir Isaac Newton** who first gave the term 'gravitation' when he saw an apple falling from a tree and thought, 'why an apple falls towards the earth and does not go upwards.' Later, he realised that it is because the earth attracts every object towards itself with a force called the **gravitational force**.

Universal Law of Gravitation

According to this law, 'Every body in the universe attracts every other body with a force which is directly proportional to the product of their masses and inversely proportional to the square of the distance between them.'

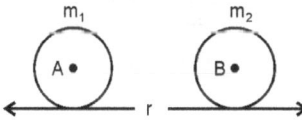

Fig. 3.1

The direction of force is along the line joining the centres of the two bodies. Suppose that the two objects A and B of masses m_1 and m_2 are lying at a distance r from each other, then the gravitational force,

$$F = G \frac{m_1 \times m_2}{r^2}$$

Where, G is a constant known as 'universal gravitational constant.' Newton's law of gravitation is universal because it is applicable to all the bodies having mass; whether the bodies are big or small, terrestrial or celestial such as star, planets, rocket etc.

Gravitational Constant, G

$$F = G \frac{m_1 \times m_2}{r^2}$$

$$\Rightarrow G = F \times \frac{r^2}{m_1 \times m_2}$$

If $m_1 = m_2 = 1$ kg and $r = 1$ m, $F = G$.

Thus, the gravitational constant G is numerically equal to the force of gravitation which exists between two bodies of unit mass kept at a distance of 1 metre from each other. The value of G has been found to be 6.67×10^{-11} Nm²/kg². The gravitational force is a vector quantity and it acts along the line joining the centres of mass of the two bodies. SI unit is Nm² kg⁻². The value of G does not depend on the medium between the two bodies, mass or distance between the two bodies.

Example 1: Calculate the force of gravitation due to the earth on a ball of mass 1 kg lying on the ground. (Mass of the earth = 6×10^{24} kg, Radius of earth = 6.4×10^3 km, G = 6.7×10^{-11} Nm²/kg²)

Sol.
$r = 6.4 \times 10^3$ km = 6.4×10^6 m
$m_1 = 1$ kg, $m_2 = 6 \times 10^{24}$ kg

$$F = G \frac{m_1 m_2}{r^2}$$

$$= \frac{6.7 \times 10^{-11} \times 1 \times 6 \times 10^{24}}{(6.4 \times 10^6)^2}$$

F = 9.8 Newtons

Fig. 3.2

Thus, the earth exerts a gravitational force of 9.8 N on a ball and attracts it towards itself when dropped from a height.

Applications of Law of Gravitation
(i) Force of gravitation binds us with earth.
(ii) The motion of moon around the earth is due to the gravitational force.
(iii) It also helps the planets to revolve around the sun.
(iv) Regular eruption of tides in the ocean and sea is due to gravitational force.

Acceleration Due to Gravity g
When an object is dropped from some height, a uniform acceleration is produced in it by the gravitational pull of the earth, and this acceleration does not depend on the mass of the falling object.
'The uniform acceleration produced in a freely falling body due to the gravitational force of the earth is known as acceleration due to gravity.' It is denoted by g and has a value of 9.8 m/s². When a body is dropped freely, it falls with an acceleration of 9.8 m/s² and when a body is thrown vertically upwards, it undergoes a retardation of 9.8 m/s².

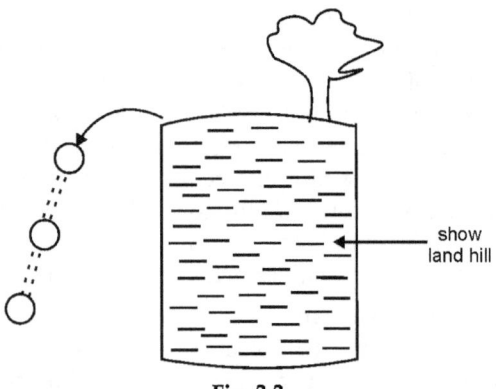

Fig. 3.3

The force between a ball of mass m and the earth of mass M_e, is given by

$$F = G \frac{m M_e}{R_e^2} - (i), R_e = \text{radius of the earth.}$$

The force due to earth's gravity is given by

$$F = ma = mg - (ii) \quad (g = \text{gravity})$$

Equating equations (i) and (ii), we get

$$mg = \frac{m M_e}{R_e^2}$$

$$\Rightarrow g = G \frac{M_e}{R_e^2}$$

$G = 6.7 \times 10^{-11}$ Nm²/kg², $M_e = 6 \times 10^{24}$ kg, $R_e = 6.4 \times 10^6$ m

Substituting, these values in the above equation, we get $g = 9.8$ m/s²

Note: Since the earth is not perfectly spherical, the radius increases from poles to the equator. Hence the value of g decreases from pole to equator as g is inversely proportional to square of the radius of the earth.

TRIVIA
The ocean contains 20 million pounds of gold. Gold in the ocean waters is so dilute that it would be like looking for sugar grains in a gallon of unstirred coffee. Gold ores can also be found in the depths of the seafloor, but these deposits are encased layers upon layers of rock. Currently, there is no efficient way to retrieve these gold deposits from the ocean.

Equations of motion of body falling freely under gravity
For freely falling bodies, the acceleration due to gravity is g. The horizontal distance of the freely falling bodies is known as height h. The three equations of motion are:

$$v = u + gt$$

$$h = ut + \frac{1}{2} gt^2$$

$$v^2 = u^2 + 2gh$$

(i) When a body is falling vertically downwards, its velocity is increasing, so the acceleration due to gravity, g is taken as *positive*.
(ii) When a body is thrown vertically upwards its velocity is *decreasing* so the acceleration due to gravity g is taken as *negative*.
(iii) When a body is dropped freely from a height, u = zero.
(iv) When a body is thrown. vertically upwards, its final velocity, v = zero.

(v) The time taken by a body to rise to the highest point is equal to the time it takes to fall from the same height.

Example 2: A stone takes 2 seconds to touch the water surface of the river, when it is dropped freely from the bridge. What is the height of the bridge above the water level?

Sol.

Initial velocity of stone, $u = 0$

Time taken to cover distance h is 2 seconds

$$h = ut + \frac{1}{2}gt^2$$

$$= 0 \times 2 + \frac{1}{2} \times 9.8 \times (2)^2$$

$$h = 19.6 \text{ m}$$

Mass and Weight

Mass of a body is the total quantity of the matter contained in it. It is a scalar quantity which has only magnitude but no direction. The SI unit of mass is kilogram (kg). Mass of an object is same everywhere, whether on earth or on moon or in space.

The weight of a body is defined as the force with which a body is attracted towards the centre of the earth. In other words, the force of earth's gravity acting on a body is known as its **weight**. Thus,

W = force = $m \times g$

Since, g is constant everywhere, therefore at a given place $W \propto m$, i.e, weight of a body is directly proportional to its mass.

Thus, the weight of 1 kg mass is 9.8 Newtons. Weight is a vector quantity having downward direction.

In space, force of gravity, $g = 0$ thus all the bodies feel weightlessness. Thus, the weight of a body in space is zero.

Note: Whatever be the weight of a body on the surface of the earth, its weight will becomes zero when it is taken to the centre of the earth. (because the value of g is zero at the centre and maximum at poles.)

Weight of the object on moon

Let M_m be the mass of the moon, and R_M be the radius of the moon. Let us consider an object of mass 'm' placed on the surface of the moon. Then, the weight of the object on the surface is given by,

$$W_m = g\frac{M_m \times m}{R_m^2} \quad \ldots(i)$$

Weight of the same object on the surface of the earth is given by

$$W_e = g\frac{M_e \times m}{R_e^2} \quad \ldots(ii)$$

Taking the ratio of both the weights, we get

$$\frac{W_m}{W_e} = \frac{M_m}{M_e} \times \frac{R_e^2}{R_m^2}$$

Mass of earth, $M_e = 6 \times 10^{24}$ kg

Mass of moon, $M_m = 7.4 \times 10^{22}$ kg

Radius of earth, $R_e = 6400$ km

Radius of moon, $R_m = 1740$ km

Putting these values in the ratio, we get

$$\frac{W_m}{W_e} = \frac{7.4 \times 10^{22} \times (6400)^2}{6 \times 10^{24} \times (1740)^2} = \frac{1}{6}$$

Thus, weight of an object on the moon is one-sixth its weight on the earth.

Kepler's Laws of Planetary Motion

Johannes Kepler established three laws which defined the motion of planets around the sun.

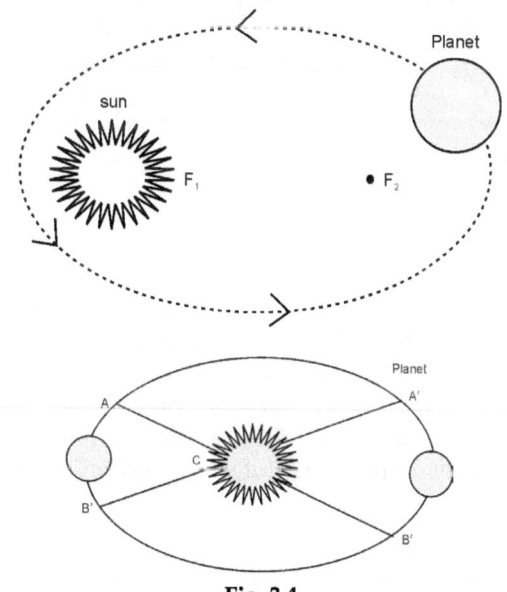

Fig. 3.4

Gravitation

First Law: Kepler's first law states that the planets move in elliptical orbits around the sun, with the sun at one of the two foci of the elliptical orbit.

Second Law: Kepler's second law states that each planet moves around the sun in such a way that the line joining the planet to the sun sweeps over equal areas in equal intervals of time. It means that a planet moves faster when it is closer to the sun, and it moves slowly when it is farther from the sun.

Area ABC = Area A' B' C, covered in equal time intervals.

Third Law: Kepler's third law states that 'the cube of the mean distance of a planet from the sun is directly proportional to the square of time it takes to move around the sun'.

$$r^3 \propto T^2$$

Let A and B be the two planets whose time period are T_1 and T_2.

If r_1 and r_2 be their distance from the sun, then

$$\frac{T_1^2}{T_2^2} = \frac{r_1^3}{r_2^3}$$

Thrust and Pressure

Thrust is the force acting on the body perpendicular to the surface. Its unit is same as that of force. When you apply a force on the head of the drawing pin to enable it to get inserted into the board, you are applying thrust on the pin. SI unit of thrust is **Newton**. Pressure is the thrust (force) applied normal to the surface per unit area. It is given by

$$P = \frac{\text{Force}}{\text{Area}} = \frac{F}{A}$$

The unit of pressure is N/m^2 or pascal. 1 Pa = 1 N/m^2. Thus, the effect of a force depends on the area of the object on which it acts. The same force can produce different pressures depending on the area over which it acts. Force applied on a smaller surface area produces larger pressure as compared to the same force applied on a larger surface area.

Example 3: A force of 100 N is applied on an object of area 2 m^2. Calculate the pressure.

Sol.
$$F = 100 \text{ N}, A = 2 \text{ m}^2$$
$$\text{Pressure} = \frac{F}{A} = \frac{100 \text{ N}}{2 \text{ m}^2} = 50 \text{ N/m}^2 \text{ or } 50 \text{ Pa}.$$

Applications of Pressure

(i) School bags have wide straps so that the weight of bag may fall over a large area of the shoulder of the child, producing less pressure.
(ii) A sharp knife cuts better as force is applied over a very small area of the object produces larger pressure.

Pressure in Fluids: The substances which can flow easily are called fluids. All liquids and gases are fluids. Water and air are the two most common fluids. Fluids have weight, so they exert pressure on the container in which they are enclosed in all directions – downward, upward and lateral.

Atmospheric Pressure: It is the pressure exerted by air on the surface of earth. It can be measured using **barometer**. 1 Atmospheric pressure is equal to 760 mm of mercury.

Buoyant Force

When an object is immersed in a liquid, it experiences an upward force called the **buoyant force** which makes the object appear less heavy in the liquid than its actual weight in air. The buoyant force is also known as up thrust. It is due to the buoyant force exerted by water that we are able to swim in water. Ships float in water due to the same reason.

The magnitude of this buoyant force acting on an object immersed in a liquid depends on the volume of the solid object immersed and the density of the liquid in which it is immersed.

Archimedes' Principle

When a solid object is immersed in a liquid, an upward 'buoyant force' acts on the object. The magnitude of this force is given by Archimedes' Principle. According to this principle:

"When an object is wholly or partially immersed in a liquid, it experiences a buoyant force (or up – thrust) which is equal to the weight of liquid displaced by the object."

For example, if a stone, on being immersed in water, displace 10 N weight of water, then the buoyant force acting on this stone will be equal to 10 Newtons.

Example 4: When an iron ball is immersed in water, it displaces 7 kg of water. How much is the buoyant force acting on the iron ball, in Newtons? [Given g = 10 m/s²]

Sol.

Weight of water displaced = buoyant force acting on the ball

$$W = m \times g$$
$$= 7 \text{ kg} \times 10 \text{ m/s}^2$$
$$= 70 \text{ kg m/s}^2 = 70 \text{ N}$$

Density

Some materials appear to be heavy whereas other are light. For example, iron is heavier than aluminium and oil is heavier than water. We describe this heaviness of different materials by the word, '**Density**', which is defined as mass of the substance per unit volume.

$$\text{Density} = \frac{\text{Mass}}{\text{Volume}}$$

- The SI unit of density is kg/m³ or kg m⁻³. In smaller units, it can by measured in g cm⁻³.
- If the density of substance is more than the density of water then the substance will be heavier than water and hence sink in water.
- If the density of a substance is less than the density of water, then the substance will be lighter than water and hence float on water.

Example 5: The mass of 3m³ of steel rod is 15000 kg. Calculate the density of steel rod in SI unit.

Sol.

$$\text{Density} = \frac{\text{Mass}}{\text{Volume}} = \frac{15000 \text{ kg}}{3 \text{m}^3} = 5000 \text{ kg/m}^3$$

Relative Density

The relative density of substance is the ratio of its density to that of water.

$$\text{Relative Density of a substance} = \frac{\text{Density of the substance}}{\text{Density of water}}$$

If we take equal volumes of the substance and water, the relative density of a substance is the ratio of the mass of any volume of the substance to the mass of an equal volume of water.

Relative density has no units.

Example 6: The relative density of silver is 10.8. If the density of water be 1.0×10^3 kg m⁻³, calculate the density of silver in SI units.

Sol.

$$\text{Relative Density of a substance} = \frac{\text{Density of the substance}}{\text{Density of water}}$$

$$10.8 = \frac{\text{Density of silver}}{1.0 \times 10^3}$$

$\Rightarrow$ Density of silver = 10.8×10^3 kg m⁻³

Gravitation

MUST REMEMBER

- Newton's law of gravitation is universal because it is applicable to all the bodies having mass; whether the bodies are big or small, terrestrial or celestial.
- The uniform acceleration produced in a freely falling body due to the gravitational force of the earth is known as acceleration due to gravity.
- Mass of a body is the total quantity of the matter contained in it.
- Mass of an object is same everywhere, whether on earth or on moon or in space.
- Weight of an object on the moon is one–sixth its weight on the earth.
- Kepler's first law states that the planets move in elliptical orbits around the sun, with the sun at one of the two foci of the elliptical orbit.
- Kepler's second law states that each planet moves around the sun in such a way that the line joining the planet to the sun sweeps over equal areas in equal intervals of time.
- Kepler's third law states that 'the cube of the mean distance of a planet from the sun is directly proportional to the square of time it takes to move around the sun'.
- When an object is immersed in a liquid, it experiences an upward force called the buoyant force which makes the object appear less heavy in the liquid than its actual weight in air.

MULTIPLE CHOICE QUESTIONS

1. A truck falls from a bridge into the river in 0.5 s. let g = 10 ms^{-2}, what is the height of the bridge from the surface of water?
   (a) 1 m   (b) 1.25 m
   (c) 2 m   (d) 2.25 m

2. SI unit of gravitational constant is _____.
   (a) Nm^2 kg^2 (b) Nm^2 kg^{-2}
   (c) Nm kg^2 (d) Nm^{2}s^{-2}

3. If the distance between two bodies is doubled, the force of attraction F between them will be _____.
   (a) 1/4 F   (b) 1/2 F
   (c) 3/2 F   (d) F

4. The force of gravitation between two bodies in the universe does not depend on _____.
   (a) The distance between them
   (b) Product of their masses
   (c) The total of their masses
   (d) The gravitationl constant

5. The fundamental force which holds the planets in their orbits around the sun is _____.
   (a) Gravitational pull of earth
   (b) Nuclear force of attraction
   (c) Electrostatic force of attraction
   (d) Gravitational force of attraction

6. Two objects of mass 200 kg and 800 kg are separated by a distance of 50 m. Find the gravitational force between the two bodies.
   (a) 4.26 × 10^{-9} N   (b) 2.4 × 10^{-8} N
   (c) 2 × 10^{-9} N   (d) 4.2 × 10^{-11} N

7. When an object is thrown up, the force of gravity _____.
   (a) Is opposite to the direction of motion
   (b) Is in the same direction as to the direction of motion
   (c) Becomes zero at the highest point
   (d) Increases as it rises up

8. A ball is dropped from a certain height. Find the speed of the ball at the end of 2 seconds.
   (a) 9.8 m/s   (b) 19.6 m/s
   (c) 28.4 m/s   (d) 29.6m/s

9. A ball is thrown upward with the speed of 19.6 m/s, find the speed of ball after 3 seconds.
   (a) −8.8 m/s   (b) 6.2 m/s
   (c) 9.8 m/s   (d) −9.8 m/s

10. The mass of moon is about 0.012 times that of earth and its diameter is about 0.25 times that of earth. The value of G on the moon will be _____.
    (a) Less than that on the earth
    (b) Same as that on the earth
    (c) More than that on the earth
    (d) About one-sixth of that on the earth

11. The value of g on the surface of the moon _____.
    (a) Is the same as on the earth
    (b) Is more than that on the earth
    (c) Is less than that on the earth
    (d) Keeps changing day by day

12. What is the final velocity of a body moving against gravity when it attains the maximum height?
    (a) Zero   (b) $\dfrac{u^2}{2g}$
    (c) $\dfrac{h}{t}$ (d) 2gh

13. A stone is dropped from a cliff. Its speed after it has fallen 100 m is _____.
    (a) 9.8 m/s   (b) 44.2 m/s
    (c) 19.6 m/s   (d) 98 m/s

14. Find the value of acceleration due to gravity on the surface of the moon, given mass of the moon = 7.4 × 10^{22} kg; radius of the moon = 1740 km; and G = 6.7 × 10^{-11} Nm^2/kg^2
    (a) 24 m/s^2 (b) 1.56 m/s^2
    (c) 1.63 m/s^2 (d) 1.84 m/s^2

15. When a ball is thrown vertically upwards, it goes through a distance of 19.6 m. Find the initial velocity of the ball.
    (a) 9.8 m/s   (b) 19.6 m/s
    (c) 28.4 m/s   (d) 37.2 m/s

Gravitation

16. If acceleration due to gravity on the earth is 10 m/s², then the acceleration due to gravity on moon is _____.
    (a) 1.66 m/s²   (b) 16.6 m/s²
    (c) 10 m/s²   (d) 0.166 m/s²

17. The second equation of motion for a freely falling body starting from rest is _____.
    (a) $h = ut + \frac{1}{2}gt^2$ (b) $h = -\frac{1}{2}gt^2$
    (c) $h = ut - \frac{1}{2}gt^2$ (d) $h = \frac{1}{2}gt^2$

18. The acceleration due to gravity is zero at _____.
    (a) The equator
    (b) Poles
    (c) Sea level
    (d) The centre of the earth

19. A feather and a coin released simultaneously from the same height do not reach the ground at the same time because of the _____.
    (a) Resistance of the air
    (b) Force of gravity
    (c) Force of gravitation
    (d) Difference in mass

20. The weight of an object of mass 15 kg at the centre of the earth is _____.
    (a) 147 N   (b) 147 kg
    (c) Zero   (d) 150 N

21. A ball is thrown up with a speed of 15 m/s. How high will it go before it begins to fall (g = 9.8 m/s²)?
    (a) 7.5 m   (b) 11.4 m
    (c) 22.8 m   (d) 24 m

22. A body whose weight is 120 kg on the earth. Find its weight on the surface of moon.
    (a) 10 kg   (b) 15 kg
    (c) 20 kg   (d) 25 kg

23. A rectangular wooden block has length, breadth and height of 50 cm, 25 cm and 10 cm, respectively. This wooden block is kept on ground in three different ways, turn by turn. Which of the following is the correct statement about the pressure exerted by this block on the ground?
    (a) The maximum pressure is exerted when the length and breadth form the base.
    (b) The maximum pressure is exerted when the length and height form the base.
    (c) The maximum pressure is exerted when the breadth and height form the base.
    (d) None of these

24. A metal in which iron can float is _____.
    (a) Sodium   (b) Magnesium
    (c) Mercury   (d) Manganese

25. Four balls A, B, C and D displace 10 ml, 24 ml, 15 ml and 12 ml of a liquid α respectively when immersed completely. The ball which will undergo the maximum apparent loss in weight will be _____.
    (a) A   (b) B
    (c) C   (d) D

26. A solid block of density 900 kg/m³ floats in oil. The oil floats on water of density 1000 kg/m³. The density of oil in kg/m³ could be _____.
    (a) 850   (b) 1050
    (c) 950   (d) 900

27. An object weight 10 N in air, when immersed fully in a liquid it weighs only 8 N. The weight of the liquid displaced by the object will be _____.
    (a) 2 N   (b) 8 N
    (c) 10 N   (d) 12 N

28. How much would a man, whose mass is 120 kg weigh on the moon?
    (a) 98 N   (b) 196 N
    (c) 600 N   (d) 120 N

29. The relative densities of four liquids P, Q, R and S are 1.26, 1.0, 0.84 and 13.6, respectively. An object is floated in all these liquids one by one. In which liquid the object will float with its maximum volume submerged under the liquid?
    (a) P   (b) Q
    (c) R   (d) S

30. The SI unit of relative density of any substance is _____.
    (a) g/cm³   (b) kg/m³
    (c) kg/m²   (d) None of these

HOTS

1. Match column I with column II and choose the correct option.

Column I	Column II
(a) When a body is falling vertically downward	(i) Acceleration due to gravity is taken as negative
(b) When a body is thrown vertically upward	(ii) Initial velocity is zero
(c) When a body is dropped freely from a height	(iii) Acceleration due to gravity is taken as 5 positive

   (a) (a)-(i), (b)-(iii), (c)-(ii)
   (b) (a)-(iii), (b)-(i), (c)-(ii)
   (c) (a)-(ii), (b)-(iii), (c)-(i)
   (d) (a)-(ii), (b)-(i), (c)-(iii)

2. Two bodies 'A' and 'B' having masses 'm' and '2m' respectively are kept at a distance 'd' apart. A small particle is to be placed so that the net gravitational force on it, due to both the bodies, is zero. Its distance from the mass A should be _____.

   (a) $x = \dfrac{d}{\sqrt{6}-1}$
   (b) $x = \dfrac{d}{\sqrt{3}}$
   (c) $x = \dfrac{d}{1+\sqrt{2}}$
   (d) $x = \dfrac{d}{1-\sqrt{2}}$

3. The height at which a body has one fourth of its weight when it is on the surface of the earth is _____.

   (a) at a height 2r where r is the radius of the earth.
   (b) at a height r where r is the radius of the earth.
   (c) at a height $\dfrac{r}{2}$ where r is the radius of the earth.
   (d) at a height $\dfrac{r}{4}$ where r is the radius of the earth.

4. Read the two statements and choose the correct option.

   Statement 1: The value of acceleration due to gravity of earth does not depend upon mass of the body.

   Statement 2: Acceleration due to gravity is a constant quantity.

   (a) Both statements 1 and 2 are true and statement 2 is the correct explanation of statement 1.
   (b) Statement 1 is true but statement 2 is false.
   (c) Both statements 1 and 2 are true but statement 2 is not the correct explanation of statement 1.
   (d) Both statements 1 and 2 are false.

5. Which of the following is true when a Mango falls from a Mango Tree?
   (a) Only the Earth attracts the Mango.
   (b) Only the Mango attracts the Earth.
   (c) Both Mango and Earth attract each other
   (d) Both Mango and Earth repel each other

Gravitation

SUBJECTIVE QUESTIONS

1. A stone thrown vertically upward rises to a height of 30 m on the surface of the moon. Calculate initial velocity of the stone and the time taken to gain the maximum height, given $g_m = 1.63$ m/s² at moon.

Ans.
Maximum height $(h) = 30$ m
Final velocity $(v) = 0$ (at the maximum height, velocity becomes zero).

Acceleration due to gravity of moon,
$g_m = -1.63$ m/s²
$v^2 - u^2 = -2gh$
$0 - u^2 = -2 \times 1.63 \times 30$
$-u^2 = -2 \times 48.9$
$u = \sqrt{97.8} = 9.89$ m/s
$v = u - gt$
$0 - 9.89 - 1.63 \times t$
$t = \dfrac{9.89}{1.63} = 6.067$ s is the time taken to gain maximum height.

2. Give five differences between mass and weight.

Ans.

Mass	Weight
It is the amount of matter contained in an object.	It is the force with which an object is pulled towards the Earth.
The mass of a body is constant throughout the universe.	Weight varies from place to place as 'g' varies.
Mass can never be equal to zero.	Weight can be equal to zero.
Mass is a scalar quantity.	Weight is a vector quantity.
SI unit of mass is kg.	SI unit of weight is Newton.

3. Calculate the acceleration due to gravity on the surface of the planet X if its mass and radius are half that of the earth.

Ans.
The acceleration due to gravity on earth is given by the equation.

$g_e = \dfrac{GM_e}{R_e^2}$ ...(i)

where M_e is the mass of the earth having radius R_e.

let R_x and M_x be the radius and mass of planet X, respectively.

$\therefore g_x = \dfrac{GM_x}{R_x^2}$

Given $M_x = \dfrac{M_e}{2}$ and $R_x = \dfrac{R_e}{2}$

$\Rightarrow g_x = \dfrac{G\left(\dfrac{M_e}{2}\right)}{\left(\dfrac{R_e}{2}\right)^2} = 4\dfrac{GM_e}{2R_e^2}$

$\Rightarrow g_x = \dfrac{2GM_e}{R_e^2}$ ...(ii)

Dividing equation (i) by equation (ii), we get

$= \dfrac{g_e}{g_x} = \dfrac{GM_e}{R_e^2} \times \dfrac{2R_e^2}{2GM_e} = \dfrac{1}{2}$

$\Rightarrow g_x = 2g_e = 19.6$ m/s² (as $g_e = 9.8$ m/s²)

4. The relative density of gold is 19.3. The density of water is 103 kg/m³? What is the density of gold in S.I. unit?

Ans.
Relative density of gold = 19.3
Relative density of gold = Density of gold/Density of water

∴ Density of gold = Relative density of gold × Density of water

= 19.3 × 10³ kg/m³

= 19300 kg/m³

5. **What are fluids? Why is Archimedes' principle applicable only for fluids? Give the application of Archimedes' principle.**

Ans. Fluids are the substances which can flow e.g., gases and liquids are fluids. Archimedes' principle is based on the upward force exerted by fluids on any object immersed in the fluid. Hence it is applicable only for fluids.

Applications of Archimedes' principle:

i. It is used in designing of ship and submarine.

ii. It is used in designing lactometer, used to determine the purity of milk.

iii. To make hydrometers, used to determine the density of liquids.

Work and Energy

Learning Objectives : In this chapter, students will learn about:
- different types of energy
- the law of conservation of energy
- the concept of power as a unit of energy

CHAPTER SUMMARY

In our day-to-day life, we consider any useful physical or mental activity as work. Activities like reading a book, singing a song, pushing a car although it does not move, are all forms of work. But in scientific terminology, these tasks are not work.

Two necessary conditions for considering work to be done are:

(a) a force must be applied on an object.

(b) the object must be displaced.

If any of the above conditions are not satisfied, work is not done. Thus in science we can define work as

'Work is done when a force applied on an object produces motion'

Examples are a bullock pulling the cart, an engine moving the train, a man pushing the rickshaw, a coolie lifting the luggage from the ground to his head and walking, a man climbing the stairs of a house – these all are different forms of work.

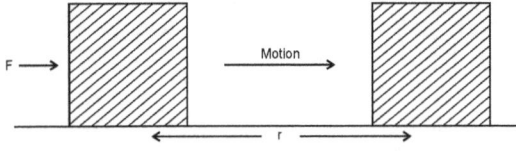

Fig. 4.1

Work done in moving a box by the distance "s" by applying a force "F" on it can be expressed as:

Work = Force × Displacement

$W = F \times s$

It should be noted that when a body is moved on the ground applying force, work is done against friction (which opposes the motion of the body). We can use the term displacement for distance moved.

Force is expressed in Newtons and displacement in metre.

1 Newton × 1 metre = 1 Joule = 1 Nm

The SI unit of work is **Joule** denoted by the letter J. Work is a **scalar quantity**.

Work done against gravity

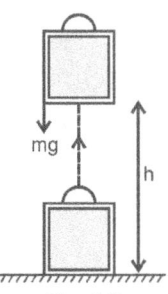

Whenever work is done against gravity (which is acting downwards), the amount of work done is equal to the product of weight of the body and the vertical distance through which the body is lifted. Suppose a coolie lifted a suitcase of mass m kg from the ground to his head, and his height is h metre.

Fig. 4.2

Work done = weight of body × vertical distance

$W = m \times g \times h$

Example 1: Calculate the work done in lifting a bucket of 25 kg of water through a height of 5 metres (assume $g = 10$ m/s^2).

Sol.

$w = mgh$
$= 25 \text{ kg} \times 5 \text{ m} \times 10 \text{ m/s}^2$
$= 1250 \text{ Nm} = 1250 \text{ J}$

Work done when force acts obliquely on the body

In case when a child pulls a toy with a rope tied to it, the force applied is along the string at an angle θ to the direction of motion.

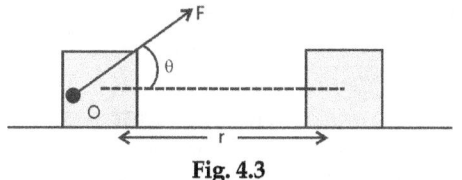

Fig. 4.3

In such cases, the work done in pulling the body will be equal to the product of horizontal component of force (F cos θ) and distance moved by the body (s).

$$W = F \cos \theta \times s$$

Example 2: A child pulls a toy car though a distance of 10 m on a smooth, horizontal floor. The string held in child's hand makes an angle of 60° with the horizontal surface. If the force applied by the child is 5N, calculate the work done by the child in pulling the toy car.

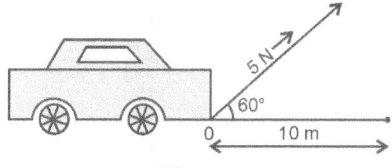

Fig. 4.4

Sol.

$W = F \cos \theta \times s$
$F = 5\,N,\ \theta = 60°,\ s = 10\,m$
$W = 5 \times \cos 60° \times 10\,m$
$= 5 \times \dfrac{1}{2} \times 10 = 25\,J$

Note: When the displacement of the body is perpendicular to the direction of force, θ = 90°, no work is done as cos 90° = 0. A man carrying. Suitcases horizontally does no work with respect to gravity; though he may be doing some work against the force of friction and air resistance.

Work done when force acts opposite to direction of the motion

When we kick a football at rest on the ground, the football starts moving. The force of our kick has same direction as that of the movement of the ball. Here, force is positive.

But when a player kicks the ball in opposite direction to get it reversed in the opponent's court, the force acts opposite to the direction of motion. Here, the force becomes negative.

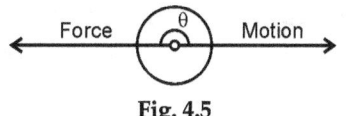

Fig. 4.5

$W = - F \times s$
Because θ = 180°, cos 180° = –1
∴ $W = F \cos 180° \times s = -Fs$

Work done is positive when F and s are in same direction.

Work done is zero when F and s are perpendicular to each other.

Work done is negative when F and s are in opposite direction.

Energy

Energy is the ability to do work. The amount of energy possessed by a body is equal to the amount of work it can do when its energy is released. Whenever some work is done, energy is consumed. Energy is a scalar quantity, its SI unit is also Joules (J). The larger unit of energy is kilojoule (1 kj = 1000 J)

Different forms of energy are:
(i) Kinetic Energy
(ii) Potential Energy
(iii) Chemical Energy
(iv) Electrical Energy
(v) Light Energy
(vi) Nuclear Energy

In this chapter we will discuss only about Kinetic Energy.

Kinetic Energy (K.E.): The energy of a body possessed by it due to its motion is called **Kinetic Energy**. The Kinetic Energy of a moving body is measured by the amount of work it can do before coming to rest.

A body of mass m moving with a velocity v has the capacity of doing work equal to $\dfrac{1}{2}mv^2$ before it stops.

$$\text{Kinetic Energy} = \dfrac{1}{2}mv^2$$

Work and Energy

Since K. E. of a body depends on its mass and velocity, heavy bodies moving with high velocities have more kinetic energy (they can do more work), than slow moving bodies of small mass.

Potential energy (P.E.): It is defined as the energy possessed by a body by virtue of its shape and position. The energy of body due to its position above the ground is called gravitational potential energy, and the energy of a body due to a change in its shape and size is called elastic potential energy. A body may possess energy even when it is not in motion, called the **potential energy**.

Suppose a body of mass m is raised to a height h above the surface of the earth, against the force of gravitational pull ($m \times g$), the work done (force × distance) against this force gets stored up in the body as potential energy.

$$\text{Potential energy} = m \times g \times h$$

(i) A stationary stone at top of hill possess only P.E.
(ii) A rolling stone. Has both P.E. and K.E.
(iii) When the stone reaches the bottom of the hill, it has only K.E.

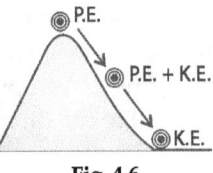
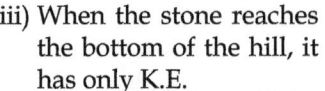

Fig. 4.6

Law of Conservation of Energy

According to the law of conservation of energy, energy can neither be created, nor destroyed. It can only be transformed from one form to another.

When a body falls from a certain height, its P.E. changes into K.E. but the total energy always remains same. Thus, there is no loss or no gain of energy.

During the conversion of energy from one form to another, some energy may be wasted. But the total energy of the system remains the same.

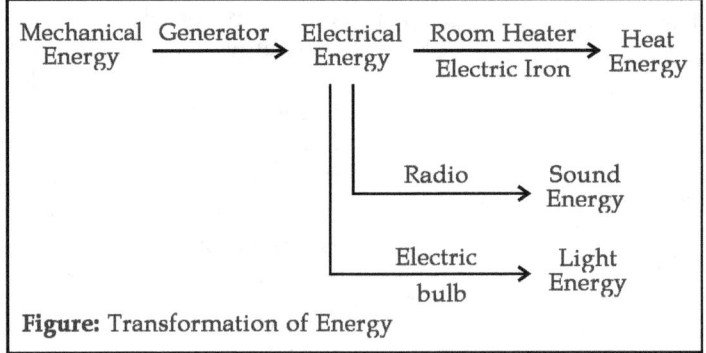

Figure: Transformation of Energy

Power

Power is defined as *the rate of doing work*. We can also define it as the rate at which energy is utilised (consumed) in doing some work.

$$\text{Power} = \frac{\text{work done}}{\text{time taken}}$$

Or

$$\Rightarrow \quad P = \frac{W}{t}$$

$$\text{Power} = \frac{\text{energy consumed}}{\text{time taken}}$$

$$P = \frac{E}{t}$$

The SI unit of power is watt denoted by symbol W.

1 watt is the power of an appliance which does work at the rate of 1 joule per second, or which consumes energy at the rate of 1 joule per second (1 kilowatt kw = 1000 w)

Note: Another unit of power is 'horse power' which is equal to 746 watts. Thus, 1 h.p. = 746 w ≃ 0.75 kw.

Example 3: What is the power of the electric bulb that consumes 7.2 kj of electrical energy in 2 minutes?

Sol.

$$\text{Power} = \frac{\text{energy consumed}}{\text{time taken}}$$

$$= \frac{7.2 \times 1000 \, j}{2 \times 60 \, s} = \frac{7200}{120}$$

$$= 60 \, J/s = 60 \, w$$

TRIVIA

A 5th-grader accidentally created a new molecule in 2012. During a class activity, 10-year-old Clara Lazen presented her teacher with a randomly constructed molecule diagram. Instead of dismissing it, Mr. Kenneth Boer took a photo and sent it to a chemist for analysis. Turns out, it was a new, explosive molecule called Tetranitratoxycarbon.

Commercial unit of energy

The commercial unit of energy is kilowatt-hour (kwh), which is used as domestic unit of electrical energy consumed by the households. One kilowatt-hour is the amount of the electrical energy consumed when an electrical appliance of 1000 W is used for one hour.

$$1 \text{ KWH} = 3.6 \times 10^6 \text{ J}$$

MUST REMEMBER

- The SI unit of work is Joule denoted by the letter J. Work is a scalar quantity.
- The amount of energy possessed by a body is equal to the amount of work it can do when its energy is released.
- Power is defined as the rate of doing work.
- One kilowatt-hour is the amount of the electrical energy consumed when an electrical appliance of 1000 W is used for one hour.

Work and Energy

MULTIPLE CHOICE QUESTIONS

1. The work done in lifting a 50 kg of bag from the ground to the head, height of coolie is 200 cm, by the coolie is (assume g = 10 m/s²) _____.
   (a) 500 J (b) 1000 J
   (c) 2000 J (d) 10,000 J

2. A coolie carries a load of 50 N to a distance of 100 m. The work done by him is _____.
   (a) 10 N (b) 0
   (c) 5000 Nm (d) $\frac{1}{2}$ J

3. A child pull a toy car by applying force of 15 N at an angel of 60°. Find the work done in pulling the toy by a distance of 20 metres.
   (a) 150 J (b) 120 J
   (c) 130 J (d) 140 J

4. The P. E. of a body at a certain height is 200 J. The K.E. possessed by it when it just touches the surface of the earth is _____.
   (a) > P.E. (b) < P. E.
   (c) = P.E. (d) can't be known

5. Find the Kinetic energy of a body of mass 2 kg moving with velocity of 0.1 metre per second.
   (a) 0.1 J (b) 1.0 J
   (c) 0.01 J (d) 10.0 J

6. An object of mass 12 kgs is at a certain height above the ground. If the P.E of the object is 480 J, find the height at which the object is with respect to the ground. Given, g = 10 ms⁻².
   (a) 12 m (b) 4 m
   (c) 8 m (d) 20 m

7. Two objects of masses 1×10^{-3} kg and 4×10^{-3} kg have equal momentum. What is the ratio of their kinetic energies?
   (a) 4 : 1 (b) 2 : 1
   (c) 16 : 1 (d) $\sqrt{2}$: 1

8. If the speed of an object is doubled, then its kinetic energy is _____.
   (a) Doubled (b) Tripled
   (c) Quadrupled (d) Remains same

9. A man of mass 100 kg jumps to a height of 50 cm. His potential energy at the highest point is (g = 10 m/s²) _____.
   (a) 50 J (b) 500 J
   (c) 1000 J (d) 0

10. The type of energy possessed by a simple pendulum, when is it at the mean positions?
    (a) K.E (b) P.E
    (c) K.E. + P. E. (d) Sound energy

11. Find the energy possessed by a ball of mass 550 g rolling on the surface with a speed of 25 m/sec.
    (a) 130.896 J (b) 138.875 J
    (c) 171.875 J (d) 160.472 J

12. A batsman hits the ball of mass 250 g with his bat and the ball leaves the bat with a speed of 10 m/s. Find the work done by the bat on the ball.
    (a) 10.25 J (b) 12.5 J
    (c) 1.25 J (d) 125 J

13. An iron sphere of mass 30 kg has the same diameter as an aluminium sphere whose mass is 10.5 kg. The spheres are dropped simultaneously from a cliff. When they are 10 m from the ground, they have the same _____.
    (a) Acceleration
    (b) Momentum
    (c) Kinetic energy
    (d) Potential energy

14. A 1 kg mass has a kinetic energy of 1 joule when its speed is _____.
    (a) 0.50 m/s (b) 1.24 m/s
    (c) 4.4 m/s (d) 1.4 m/s

15. If air resistance is negligible, the sum total of potential and kinetic energies of a freely falling body _____.
    (a) Increases
    (b) Decreases
    (c) Becomes zero
    (d) Remains the same

16. Work done by a string when a stone is tied to it and whirled in a circle is ―――――.
    (a) Positive   (b) Negative
    (c) Zero   (d) None of these

17. A car is accelerated on a travelled road and acquires a velocity 4 times of its initial velocity. During this process, the potential energy of the car ―――――.
    (a) Does not change
    (b) Becomes twice that of the initial P.E.
    (c) Decomes four times that of the initial P.E.
    (d) Becomes 16 times that of the initial P.E.

18. A car is accelerated on a levelled road and attains a speed of 4 times its initial speed. In this process, the K.E. of the car ―――――.
    (a) Does not change
    (b) Becomes 4 times that of initial P.E.
    (c) Becomes 8 times that of initial P.E.
    (d) Becomes 16 times that of initial P.E.

19. In case of negative work, the angle between the force and displacement is ―――――.
    (a) 0°   (b) 45°
    (c) 90°   (d) 180°

20. Two unequal masses posses the same momentum, then the Kientic energy of the heavier mass is ――――― than the Kinetic energy of the lighter mass.
    (a) More   (b) Less
    (c) Equal   (d) Insufficient data

21. A copper ball of mass 10 kg has the same diameter as an aluminium ball of mass 3.5 kg. Both the balls are dropped simultaneously from a tower. When they are 10 m above the ground, they have the same ―――――.
    (a) Acceleration
    (b) Momentum
    (c) Potential energy
    (d) Kinetic energy

22. The work done on an object does not depend on the ―――――.
    (a) Displacement
    (b) Force applied
    (c) Angle between force and displacement
    (d) Initial velocity of the object

23. An electric bulb of 60 w is used for 6 h per day. Calculate the 'units of energy consumed in one day by the bulb ―――――.
    (a) 0.60 'units'
    (b) 0.36 'units'
    (c) 0.45 'units
    (d) 0.24 'units'

24. If the speed of a motor car becomes six times, then the kinetic energy becomes ―――― times.
    (a) 6
    (b) 12
    (c) 36
    (d) Remains the same

25. The momentum of a bullet of mass 20 g fired from a gun is 10 kg. m/s. The kinetic energy of this bullet in kJ will be ―――――.
    (a) 5   (b) 1.5
    (c) 2.5   (d) 25

26. In which of the following situations will the potential energy of the spring be minimum?
    (a) Compressed
    (b) Extended
    (c) In its original shape
    (d) None of these

27. Each of the following statement describes a force acting. Which of these forces is causing work to be done?
    (a) The weight of a book at rest on a table
    (b) The pull of a moving railway engine on its coaches
    (c) The tension in an elastic band wrapped around a parcel
    (d) The push of a person's feet when standing on the floor

28. When a stone is thrown upward with a certain speed, then its kinetic energy at the highest point is ―――――.
    (a) Maximum
    (b) Minimum
    (c) Zero
    (d) None of these

Work and Energy

29. A girl weighing 400 N climbs a vertical ladder. If the value of g be 10 ms^{-2}, the work doen by her after climbing 2 m will be _____.
    (a) 200 J   (b) 80 J
    (c) 2000 J   (d) 800 J

30. Which of the following energy change involves frictional force?
    (a) Chemical energy to heat energy
    (b) Kinetic energy to heat energy
    (c) Potential energy to sound energy
    (d) Chemical energy to kinetic energy

HOTS

1. The bulb glows because of electricity. Identify the energy conversion in this process.
   (a) Light energy into electrical energy
   (b) Electrical energy into light energy
   (c) Chemical energy into heat energy
   (d) Light energy into heat energy

2. A ball is released from certain height. Which of the following statement is correct about this example?
   (a) Kinetic energy decreases at each second.
   (b) Potential energy decreases at each second.
   (c) Total energy decreases at each second.
   (d) All of these

3. In which of the following examples does the work done not be zero?
   (a) The stone is rolling on frictionless surface with constant velocity.
   (b) A small child pushes a truck but truck remains stationary.
   (c) Moon revolve around earth because of gravitational force exerted by earth.
   (d) None of these

4. The stone of mass 3.5 kg is height of 165 cm. Calculate potential energy contained in that stone.
   (a) 52.6 J   (b) 54.6 J
   (c) 56.6 J   (d) 58.6 J

5. A bulb of rating 52 watt is on for 2 hours. Calculate energy consumed by the bulb.
   (a) 374.4 KJ   (b) 372.4 KJ
   (c) 370.4 KJ   (d) 368.4 KJ

SUBJECTIVE QUESTIONS

1. Calculate the kinetic energy of a ball of mass 10 g and momentum 1000 g cm/s.

Ans.
Momentum of the ball = 1000 g cm/s
$= 1000 \times \dfrac{1}{1000} \text{ kg} \times \dfrac{1}{100} \text{ m/s} = 0.01 \text{ kg m/s}$
Mass of the ball = 10 g = 0.01 kg
$\therefore$ kinetic energy $= \dfrac{p^2}{2m} = \dfrac{(0.01)}{2 \times (0.01)} = \dfrac{1}{200}$
= 0.005 J.

2. An electrical heater is rated 1200 W. How much energy does it use in 10 hours?

Ans.
Electrical energy = Power × time taken
= 1.2 × 10
= 12 kWh

3. If an electric appliance is rated 1000 W and is used for 2 hours. Calculate the work done in 2 hours.

Ans.
Work done = Energy consumed
Energy = Power × Time taken
= 1000 W × 2 hour
= 2000 W-hr or 2 kW-hour or 2 kWh

4. A man of mass 62 kg sums up a stair case of 65 steps in 12 s. If height of each step is 20 cm, find his power.

Ans.
m = 62 kg, g = 10 m/s²
h = 65 × 20/100 = 13 m
P.E. = mgh
P.E. = 62 × 10 × 13
= 8060 J
Power (P) = (P.E.)/t
= 8060/12
= 671.67 W

5. How is work done by a force measured? A porter lifts a luggage of 20 kg from the ground and puts it on his head 1.7 m above the ground. Find the work done by the porter on the luggage. (g = 10 m/s²)

Ans.
Work done is product of force and displacement
W = F × s
m = 20 kg
g = 10 m/s²
h = 1.7 m
The work done by the porter = mgh
= 20 × 10 × 1.7 = 340 J

6. (a) Under what conditions work is said to be done?
(b) A porter lifts a luggage of 1.5 kg from the ground and puts it on his head 1.5 m above the ground. Calculate the work done by him on the luggage.

Ans.
(a) (i) Force should be applied.
(ii) Body should move in the line of action of force.
(iii) Angle between force and displacement should not be 90°.
(b) Mass of luggage, m = 15 kg and displacement, s = 1.5 m.
Work done, W = F × s = mg × s
= 15 × 10 × 1.5 = 225 J

7. Four persons jointly lift a 250 kg box to a height of 1 m and hold it.
(i) Calculate the work done by the persons in lifting the box.
(ii) How much work is done for just holding the box?
(iii) Why do they get tired while holding it? (g = 10 ms²)

Ans.
(i) F = 250 × 10 = 2500 N
s = 1 m
W = F × s
= 2500 × 1 |
= 2500 J
(ii) Zero, as there is no displacement.

Work and Energy

(iii) To hold the box, men are applying a force which is opposite and equal to the gravitational force acting on the box. While applying the force muscular effort is involved, and so they feel tired.

8. A boy is pulling a cart by supplying a constant force of 8 N on a straight path of 20 m. On a round about of 10 m diameter he forgets the path and takes 1½ turns and then continues on the straight path for another 20 m. Find the net work done by the boy on the cart.

Ans.
F = 8N
Work done, W = F × s
W_1 = 8 × 20 = 160 J
D = 10 m
So radius,
D/2 = 10/2 = 5m
Circumference of a circle = 2πr
= 2 × 22/7 × 5
= 31.43
Distance in 1/2 circle = πr
= 22/7 × 5 = 15.71
Total distance for 1½ circle
= 31.43 + 15.71 = 47.14 m
W_2 = F × s
= 8 × 47.14 = 376 J
W_3 = 20 × 8 = 160 J
Total work done = 160 + 376 + 160 = 696 J

9. Calculate the electricity bill amount for a month of 30 days, if the following devices are used as specified:
(i) 2 bulbs of 40 W for 6 hours.
(ii) 2 tubelights of 50 W for 8 hours.
(iii) A TV of 120 W for 6 hours.

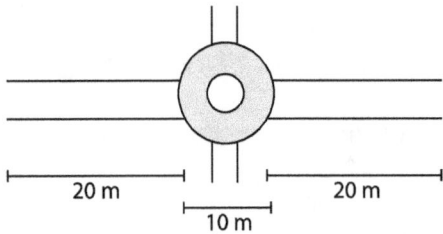

Given the cost of electricity is ₹2.50 per unit.

Ans.
Given the cost of electricity is ₹2.50 per unit.
(i) 2 bulbs of 40 watts for 6 hrs.
Energy consumed by Bulbs E_1
= 2 × 40 × 6 = 480 W = 0.48 kWh
(ii) Energy consumed by 2 tubelights E_2
= 50 × 8 × 2 = 0.800 kWh
(iii) Energy consumed by TV E_3
= 120 × 6 = 0.720 kWh
Total Energy = 0.48 + 0.80 + 0.72
= 2.00 units rate
= 2.50 per unit
Cost per day = 2 × 2.50 = 5.00
Cost 30 days = 5.00 × 30 = 150

10. A boy pushes a book by applying a force of 40 N. Find the work done by this force as the book is displaced through 25 cm along the path.

Ans.
Here, force acting on the book, F = 40 N
distance through which book is displaced,
s = 25 cm = 0•25 m
Work done by the force, i.e., W = F × s
= (40 N) (0•25 m)
= 10 J

11. A ball of mass 1 kg thrown upwards, reaches a maximum height of 4 m. Calculate the work done by the force of gravity during the vertical displacement. (g = 10 m/s²).

Ans.
Here, force of gravity on the ball,
F = mg = (1 kg) (10 m/s²) = 10 N
vertical displacement of the ball, s = 4 m
Since the force and the displacement of the ball are in opposite directions, work done by the force of gravity, i.e., W = F × s
= 10 × 4
= 40 J
Obviously, work done against the force of gravity = 40 J

12. An engine pulls a train 1 km over a level track. Calculate the work done by the train given that the frictional resistance is 5 × 10⁵ N.

Ans.
Here, frictional resistance, $F = 5 \times 10^5$ N
distance through which the train moves,
$$s = 1 \text{ km} = 1000 \text{ m}$$
Work done by the frictional force, i.e.,
$$W = Fs = (5 \times 10^5) \times 1000 = 5 \times 10^8 \text{ J}$$
(F and s are in opposite directions)
Obviously, work done by the train is 5×10^8 J

13. A man weighing 70 kg carries a weight of 10 kg on the top of a tower 100 m high. Calculate the work done by the man. ($g = 10$ m/s²).

Ans.
Here, force exerted by the man,
$$F = (70 + 10) = 80 \text{ kg wt}$$
$$= 80 \times 10 = 800 \text{ N}$$
vertical displacement, $s = 100$ m
Work done by the man, i.e.,
$$W = F \times s$$
$$= (800 \text{ N})(100 \text{ m}) = 80000 \text{ J}$$

14. A player kicks a ball of mass 250 g at the centre of a field. The ball leaves his foot with a speed of 10 m/s, Find the work done by the player on the ball.

Ans.
The ball, which is initially at rest, gains kinetic energy due to work done on it by the player.
Thus, the work done by the player on the ball, W = kinetic energy (Ek) of the ball as it leaves his foot, i.e., $W = E_k = mv^2$
Here, $m = 250$ g $= 0\bullet25$ kg,
$v = 10$ m/s
$W = (0\bullet25) \times (10)^2$
$= 12\bullet5$ J

15. A bullet of mass 20 g moving with a velocity of 500 m/s, strikes a tree and goes out from the other side with a velocity of 400 m/s. Calculate the work done by the bullet in joule in passing through the tree.

Ans.
Here, mass of the bullet, $m = 20$ g $= 0\bullet02$ kg
initial velocity of the bullet, $u = 500$ m/s
final velocity of the bullet, $v = 400$ m/s

If W is the work done by the bullet in passing through the tree, then according to work-energy theorem
$$W = mu^2 - mv^2$$
$$= m(u^2 - v^2)$$
$$= (0\bullet02)[(500)^2 - (400)^2]$$
$$= 900 \text{ J}$$

16. A body of mass 4 kg is taken from a height of 5 m to a height 10 m. Find the increase in potential energy.

Ans.
Here, mass of the body, $m = 4$ kg
increase in height of the body, $h = (10 - 5) = 5$ m
Increase in potential energy,
$$E_p = mgh$$
$$= 4 \times 10 \times 5$$
$$= 200 \text{ J}$$
Initial potential energy of the body,
$$E_{pi} = mgh$$
$$= 4 \times 10 \times 5$$
$$= 200 \text{ J}$$
Final potential energy of the body,
$$E_{pf} = mgh_f$$
$$= 4 \times 10 \times 10$$
$$= 400 \text{ J}$$
Increase in potential energy,
$$E_p = E_{pf} - E_{pi}$$
$$= 400 \text{ J} - 200 \text{ J}$$
$$= 200 \text{ J}$$

17. A 5 kg ball is thrown upwards with a speed of 10 m/s.
    (a) Find the potential energy when it reaches the highest point.
    (b) Calculate the maximum height attained by it.

Ans.
(a) Here, mass of the ball, $m = 5$ kg,
speed of the ball, $v = 10$ m/s
Kinetic energy of the ball,
$$E_k = mv^2$$
$$= 5 \times (10)^2$$
$$= 250 \text{ J}$$

Work and Energy

When the ball reaches the highest point, Its kinetic energy becomes zero as the entire kinetic energy is converted into its potential energy (E_p) i.e., E_p = 250 J ....(i)

(b) If h is the maximum height attained by the ball,
$E_p = mgh$ .... (ii)
From eqn. (i) and (ii),
mgh = 250 J
$\Rightarrow h = \dfrac{250}{mg}$
$\Rightarrow h = \dfrac{250}{5 \times 10}$
$\Rightarrow h = 5$ m

18. A rocket of mass 3×10^6 kg takes off from a launching pad and acquires a vertical velocity of 1 km/s and an altitude of 25 km. Calculate its (a) potential energy (b) kinetic energy.

Ans.

Here, mass of the rocket, $m = 3 \times 10^6$ kg
velocity acquired by the rocket,
v = 1 km/s = 1000 m/s
height attained by the rocket,
h = 25 km = 25000 m

(a) Potential energy of the rocket,
$E_p = mgh$
= $(3 \times 10^6) \times (10^2) \times 25000$
= 7.5×10^{11} J

(b) Kinetic energy of the rocket,
$E_k = mv^2$
= $(3 \times 10^6) \times (1000)^2$
= 1.5×10^{12} J

19. A boy of mass 40 kg runs up a flight of 50 steps, each of 10 cm high, in 5 s. Find the power developed by the boy.

Ans.

Here, mass of the boy, m = 40 kg total height gained, h = 50 × 10 cm
= 500 cm = 5 m
time taken to climb, t = 5 s
Work done by the boy,
$W = mgh$
= 40 × 10 × 5
= 2000 J

Power developed, $P = \dfrac{w}{t} = \dfrac{2000}{5}$ = 400 W

20. What should be the power of an engine required to lift 90 metric tonnes of coal per hour from a mine whose depth is 200 m.

Ans.

Here, mass of the coal to be lifted,
m = 90 metric tonnes
= 90 × 1000 kg
= 9 × 10⁴ kg

height through which the coal is to be lifted, h = 200 m

time during which the coal is to be lifted,
t = 1 h
= 60 × 60
= 3600 s

work done to lift the coal, i.e.,
$W = mgh$
= 9 × 10⁴ × 10 × 200 m
= 18 × 10⁷ J

Power of the engine required i.e.,
$P = \dfrac{w}{t} = \dfrac{18 \times 10^7}{3600 \text{ s}}$ = 50000 W = 50 kW

Sound

Learning Objectives : In this chapter, students will learn about:
- ✓ how sound is produced and propagated
- ✓ the mechanism of echo and reverberation
- ✓ the anatomy of human ear
- ✓ applications of ultrasound

CHAPTER SUMMARY

In everyday life we hear many sounds around us. Sound is a form of energy which produces a sensation of hearing in our ears.

Production of Sound

How is sound produced by different organisms? This is the first question that comes to our mind when we study about sound. The correct answer to this question is that whenever something vibrates due to disturbance produced in the medium, sound is produced. **Vibration means a kind of rapid to and fro motion of an object**. Sound is produced whenever we speak, or whenever we strike something with the help of hard objects. In each case the sound is produced due to vibration in the medium.

The tunning fork is used to produce a specific type of sound. It is a U shape steel device with a stem at the base. Whenever it is struck against a rubber pad, the prong starts vibrating and these vibrations produce sound.

Propagation of Sound

Sound is produced by the vibration in the medium. The substance or matter through which sound is transmitted is called **a medium**. The medium may be solid, liquid or gas. When an object vibrates, it sets the particle of the medium around it into vibration. The particles do not move from their place. It's the disturbance that travels through the medium. A particle of the medium in contact with the vibrating object is first displaced from its equilibrium position. It then exerts a force on the adjacent particle. As a result of this, the adjacent particle gets displaced from its position of rest. After displacing the adjacent particle, the first particle comes back to its original position. This process continues in the medium till the sound reaches our ear.

Thus, a wave is a disturbance which travels though the medium when the particles of the medium start vibrating. The sound waves are characterized by the motion of particles in the medium and are called mechanical waves.

Air is the most common medium through which sound travels. Whenever the vibration starts, it pushes air particles in front of it and creates a region of high pressure. This region of high pressure is called **compression**. This compression starts to move away from the vibrating object. As the object moves backwards, it creates a region of low pressure, which is called the **rarefaction**. When the object moves backward and forward very rapidly, a series of compression and rarefaction are formed. Thus, sound is propagated through the medium in the form of compression and rarefaction.

Pressure is related to the number of particles of a medium in a given volume. Higher density of the particles in the medium exerts higher pressure and vice-versa.

TRIVIA

For different species such as chickens, some animals practice sperm dumping to reject the sperm of mates they don't like.

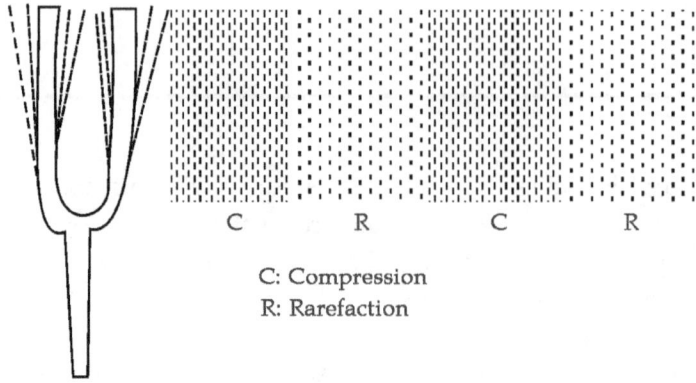

Fig. 5.1. *A vibrating object creating a series of compression (C) and rarefactions (R) in the medium*

Reflection of Sound

Sound bounces off when it strikes the solid or liquid surfaces, as a ball bounces off when it strikes the wall or the surface of the earth. Sound is reflected in the same way as light. **The laws of reflection of light are obeyed by the reflection of sound.** The laws of reflection of sound are as follows:

1. The incident sound wave, the reflected sound wave and the normal at the point of incidence, all lie in the same plane.
2. The angle of reflection of sound is always equal to the angle of incidence of sound.

There are two phenomenon of reflection of sound; (i) Echo and (ii) Reverberation

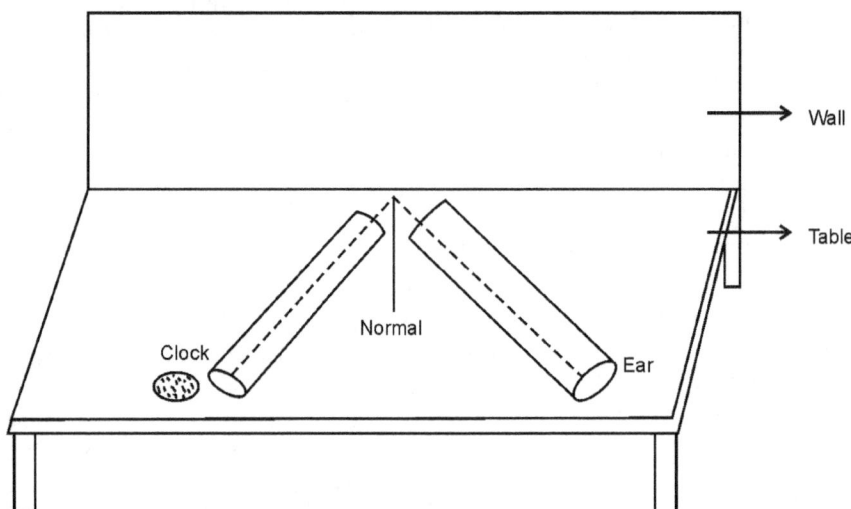

Fig. 5.2. *Reflection of Sound*

Echo

Whenever we shout or clap near a reflecting surface such as tall building or mountain or in an empty hall, we will hear the same sound again a little later. This sound which we hear is called echo, i.e., the successive reflection of sound from a number of reflecting surfaces is called an **echo**.

The sensation of sound persist in our brain for nearly 0.1 second. Thus, to hear the distinct echo, the time interval between the original sound and the reflected one must be at least 0.1 second. The speed of sound in air at 20°C is almost 344 m/sec. Hence the total distance from the point of production of sound to the target and return must be atleast $344 \times 0.1 = 34.4$ metres. Thus, for hearing distinct echoes, the minimum distance of the obstacle from the source of sound must be half of this distance, that is 17.2 metres.

This distance will change with the temperature of air. The roaring of thunder is due to the successive reflections of the sound from a number of reflecting surfaces, such as the clouds and the land.

Reverberation

'The persistence of sound in a big hall due to repeated reflections from the walls, ceiling and floor of the hall is called reverberation.'

This situation sometimes occurs in big halls, such as an auditorium, where excessive reverberation is undesirable. To reduce the reverberation of sound, the roof and wall of hall and auditorium are generally covered with sound absorbent materials like compressed fibreboard, rough plaster or draperies. The seat material are also selected on the basis of their sound absorbing properties.

Example 1: A man claps his hands near a mountain and hears the echo after 4 seconds. If the speed of sound under these conditions is 330 m/s, calculate the distance of the mountain from the man.

Sol.

Here the time taken by the sound (of clap) to go from the man to the mountain, and return to the man (as echo) is 4 Seconds. So, the time taken by the sound to go from the man to the mountain will be half of this time, which is $\frac{4}{2}$ = 2 seconds. Now,

$$\text{Speed} = \frac{\text{Distance travelled}}{\text{Time taken}}$$

So, $330 = \frac{\text{Distance travelled}}{2}$

Distance = 330×2
= 660 m

Uses of multiple reflections of sound

(i) The property of reflection of sound is used in megaphones, loudspeakers, horns, trumpets etc.
(ii) It is used in stethoscope used by the doctors to check the heart beat and impulse.
(iii) Generally, the ceilings of concert halls, conference halls and cinema halls are curved so that, sound after reflection reaches all corners of the hall, sometimes a curved soundboard may be placed behind the stage so that the sound, after reflecting from the sound board, spreads evenly across the width of the hall.

Range of Hearing

The sound is classified into three categories on the basis of their frequency. They are Audible sound, Infra sound and Ultrasound.

Audible Sound

The audible range of sound for human beings extends from about 20 Hz to 20,000 Hz. Children under the age of five and animals such as dogs can hear up to 25 kHz (1 kHz = 1000 Hz)

Infra Sound

Sounds of frequencies below 20 Hz are called infrasonic sounds or infra sounds. For example: Vibration of the wings of the bee; Rhinoceroses also communicate using infra sound of frequency as low as 5 Hz, whales and elephants produce sounds in the infrasound range.

Ultra Sound

Frequencies higher than 20 kHz are called ultrasonic sounds or ultra sounds. Ultrasound is produced by dolphins, bats and tortoises.

Moths of certain families have very sensitive hearing equipment, and can sense when a bat is flying nearby and are able to escape capture. Rats also play games by producing ultrasound.

Applications of Ultrasound: Ultrasounds are high frequency waves. Ultrasounds are able to travel along well-defined paths even in the presence of obstacles. Ultrasounds are used extensively in industries and for medical purposes:

(i) Ultrasound is used in industry for detecting flaws (cracks, etc.) in metal blocks without damaging them.
(ii) Ultrasound is used in industry to clean 'hard to reach' parts of objects such as spiral tubes, odd-shaped machines and electronic components etc.
(iii) It is used to break kidney stones into fine granules (which then get flushed out with wire).
(iv) It is used to investigate the internal organs of the human body such as liver, gall bladder, pancreas, kidneys, uterus and heart etc.
(v) Ultrasound scans are used to monitor the development of foetus (unborn baby) inside the mother's uterus.

(vi) Ultrasound is used in '**Sonar**' apparatus to measure the depth of sea (or ocean) and to locate under-sea objects like a shoal of fish, shipwrecks, submarines, sea-rocks and hidden icebergs in the sea.

(vii) Bats use ultrasound to fly at night (without colliding with other objects) and to search their prey (like flying objects).

SONAR: The word 'SONAR' stands for 'Sound Navigation And Ranging.' A sonar apparatus consists of two parts (i) a transmitter (for emitting ultrasonic waves) and (ii) a receiver (for detecting ultrasonic waves). The transmitter of sonar is made to emit pulse of ultrasonic sound with very high frequency of about 50,000 hertz. This pulse of ultrasonic sound travels down the sea water to the bottom of the sea. When this pulse strikes the bottom of the sea, it is reflected back to the ship in the form of an echo. This echo produces an electrical signal in the receiver of the sonar device. Thus, the sonar device measures the time taken by the echo to return to the ship.

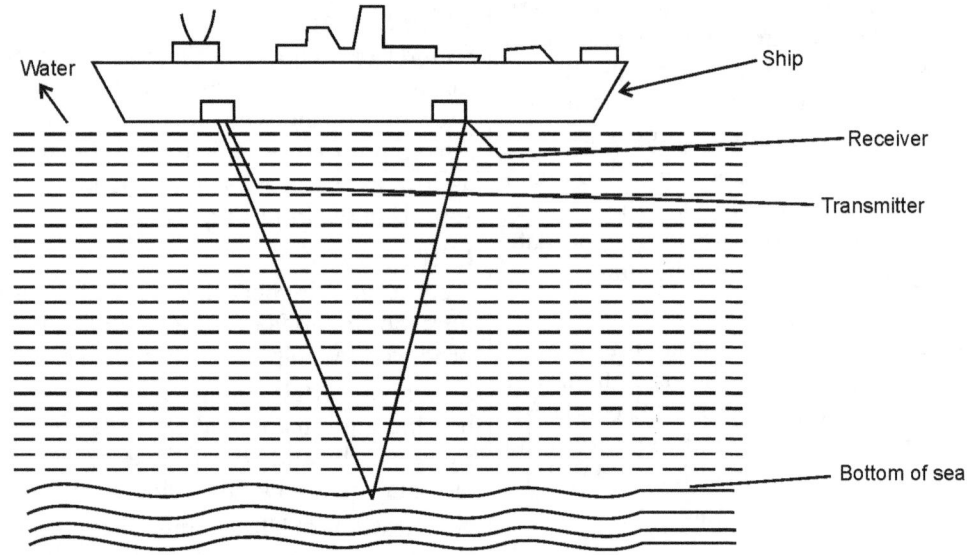

Fig. 5.3. *To Measure the Depth of a Sea by using Sonar*

The distance of the object that reflected the sound wave can be calculated by knowing the speed of sound in water and the time interval between transmission and reception of the ultrasound. Let the time interval between transmission and reception of ultrasound signal be t and speed of sound through sea-water be v. The total distance, 2d travelled by the ultrasound is then,

$2d = v \times t$

The above method is called echo-ranging.

Example 2: A sonar device attached to a ship sends ultrasonic waves in the sea. These waves are reflected from the bottom of the sea. If the ultrasonic waves take 4 seconds to travel from the ship to the bottom of the sea and back to the ship (in the form of an echo), what is the depth of the sea? (speed of sound in water = 1500 m/s)

Sol.

Time taken by the ultrasonic waves to travel from the ship to the sea-bed and back to the ship is 4 sec. So, the time taken by the ultrasonic sound to travel from the ship to sea bed will be half of this time, which is $\frac{4}{2} = 2$ seconds.

Now, speed = $\frac{\text{Distance}}{\text{Time}}$

$\Rightarrow 1500 = \frac{\text{Distance}}{2}$

$\Rightarrow$ Distance = $1500 \times 2 = 3000$ m

Thus, the depth of the sea below the ship is 3000 m.

Structure of Human Ear

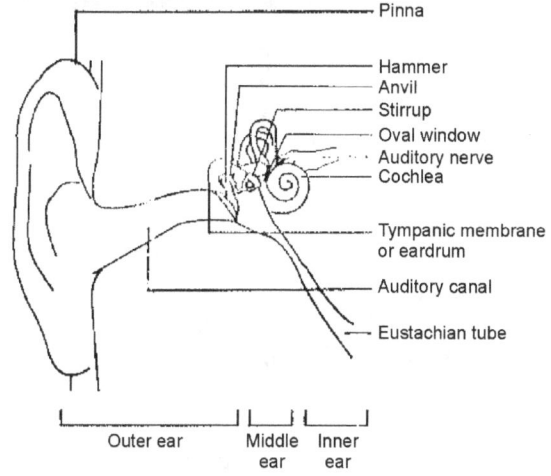

Fig. 5.4 *Auditory Parts of Human Ear*

Human ear is one of the most important sense organs which enables human to hear the sound distinctly, also to recognise the sound. The human ear is divided into three parts: outer ear, middle ear and inner ear.

The outer ear is called '**Pinna**'. It collects the sound from the surroundings and transmits it to the middle ear. The middle ear consists of eardrum and three inter connected bones called **hammer, anvil** and **stirrup**. These three bones amplify the sound several times and transmit it to the inner ear. The inner ear consists of a liquid filled coiled tube called the **cochlea**. It converts these sounds into electrical signals and then send to the brain via auditory nerve. The brain interprets the sound and reacts accordingly.

MUST REMEMBER

- Sound is a form of energy which produces a sensation of hearing in our ears.
- The substance or matter through which sound is transmitted is called a medium.
- Higher density of the particles in the medium exerts higher pressure and vice versa.
- Sound bounces off when it strikes the solid or liquid surfaces.
- The roaring of thunder is due to the successive reflections of the sound from a number of reflecting surfaces, such as the clouds and the land.
- The word 'SONAR' stands for 'Sound Navigation And Ranging.'
- The outer ear is called 'Pinna'.
- The inner ear consists of a liquid filled coiled tube called the cochlea.

MULTIPLE CHOICE QUESTIONS

1. When a wave travels through medium _____.
   (a) Energy is transferred in a periodic manner
   (b) Energy is transferred at a constant speed
   (c) Particles are transferred from one place to another
   (d) All statements are correct

2. Which of the following can produce longitudinal waves as well as transverse waves under different conditions?
   (a) Water
   (b) Slinky
   (c) T.V. transmitter
   (d) Tuning fork

3. Which of the following statements best describes frequency?
   (a) The distance travelled by a wave per second
   (b) The distance between one crest of a wave and the next one
   (c) The number of complete vibrations per second
   (d) The maximum disturbance caused by a wave

4. A boy fires a gun and hears the echo 2 seconds later. If he is 480 m away from a wall, what will be the velocity of sound in air?
   (a) 240 ms^{-1}
   (b) 480 ms^{-1}
   (c) 960 ms^{-1}
   (d) 120 ms^{-1}

5. If the speed of a wave is 340 m/s and its frequency is 1700 Hz, then λ for this wave in cm will be _____.
   (a) 0.2
   (b) 2
   (c) 20
   (d) 200

6. Which of the following vibrates when a musical note is produced by the cymbals in an orchestra?
   (a) Air coloumns
   (b) Metal plates
   (c) Stretched strings
   (d) Stretched membranes

7. A musical instrument is producing a continuous note. This note cannot be heard by a person having a normal hearing range. To hear, such notes must be passing through _____.
   (a) Wax
   (b) Vacuum
   (c) Water
   (d) Empty vessel

8. A girl claps and hears the echo after reflection from cliff which is 660 m away. If the velocity of sound is 330 m/s, the time taken for hearing the echo will be _____.
   (a) 4s
   (b) 3s
   (c) 2s
   (d) 8s

9. We can distinguish between the musical sounds produced by different singers on the basis of the characteristic of sound called?
   (a) Pitch
   (b) Timbre
   (c) Loudness
   (d) Frequency

10. What will be the frequency of a sound wave whose time period is 0.05s?
    (a) 10 Hz
    (b) 15 Hz
    (c) 20 Hz
    (d) 30 Hz

11. Which one of the following does not consist of transverse waves?
    (a) TV signals from a satellite
    (b) Light emitted by a CFL
    (c) Ripples on the surface of a pond
    (d) Musical notes of an orchestra

12. The maximum speed of vibrations which produce audible sound will be in _____.
    (a) Sea water
    (b) Ground glass
    (c) Human blood
    (d) Dry air

13. The sound waves travel faster _____.
    (a) In solids
    (b) In gases
    (c) In vacuum
    (d) In liquids

14. The frequency of a wave travelling at a speed of 500 ms^{-1} is 25 Hz. Its time period will be _____.
    (a) 0.05s
    (b) 0.04s
    (c) 20s
    (d) 25s

15. A ship on the surface of water sends a signal and receives it back after 4 seconds from a submarine inside the water. Calculate the distance of the submarine from the ship. (the speed of sound in water is 1450 ms^{-1})
    (a) 2900 m
    (b) 1450 m
    (c) 3900 m
    (d) 1950 m

16. If the sound wave produced by a vibrating tunning fork shown in the diagram, half the wavelength is represented by _____.

    (a) AB
    (b) DE
    (c) BD
    (d) AE

17. Which kind of sound is produced in an earthquake before the main shock wave begins?
    (a) Infrasound
    (b) Ultrasound
    (c) Audible sound
    (d) None of these

18. Which of the following device does not work on the multiple reflections of sound waves?
    (a) Hydrophone
    (b) Soundboard
    (c) Megaphone
    (d) Stethoscope

19. Bats detect obstacles in their path by receiving the reflected _____.
    (a) Radiowaves
    (b) Ultrasonic waves
    (c) Radio waves
    (d) Electro-magnetic waves

20. When sound travels through air, the air particles _____.
    (a) Vibrate along the direction of wave propagation
    (b) Vibrate perpendicular to the direction of wave propagation
    (c) Vibrate but not in any fixed position
    (d) Do not vibrate

21. Before playing the orchestra in a musical concert, a sitarist tries to adjust the tension and pluck the strings suitably. By doing so he is adjusting _____.
    (a) Amplitude of sound only
    (b) Intensity of sound only
    (c) Frequency of the sitar string with the frequency of other musical instruments
    (d) Loudness of sound

22. The ultrasound waves can penetrate into matter to a large extent because they have _____.
    (a) Very high frequency
    (b) Very high speed
    (c) Very high amplitude
    (d) Very high wavelength

23. An echo-sounder in a trawler (fishing boat) receives an echo from a shoal of fish 0.4 s after it was sent. If the speed of sound in water is 1500 m/s, how deep is the shoal?
    (a) 7500 m
    (b) 600 m
    (c) 150 m
    (d) 300 m

24. The vibrations of the pressure variations inside the inner car are converted into electrical signals by the _____.
    (a) Cochlea
    (b) Anvil
    (c) Hammer
    (d) Stirrup

25. Vibrations inside the ear are amplified by the three bones namely the _____ in the middle ear _____.
    (a) Hammer, anvil and pinna
    (b) Hammer, anvil and stirrup
    (c) Auditory bone, anvil and stirrup
    (d) Hammer, cochlea and stirrup

Sound

HOTS

1. **Statement 1:** The incident sound wave, the reflected sound wave and the normal at the point of incidence all lie in the same plane.
   Statement 2: The angle of reflection of sound is always equal to the angle of incidence of sound.
   (a) Statement 1 is true but statement 2 is false
   (b) Statement 1 is false but statement 2 is true
   (c) Both statement 1 and statement 2 are true but statement 2 is not the correct reason for statement 1
   (d) Both statement 1 and statement 2 are true and statement 2 is the correct reason for statement 1

   Direction (2–3): See the figure and choose the correct option.

   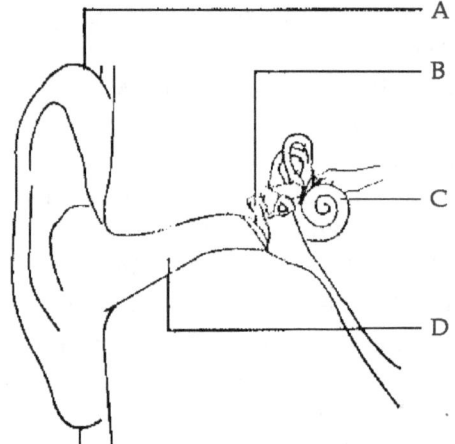

2. It collects the sound from the surrounding.
   (a) A   (b) B
   (c) C   (d) D

3. It converts the sounds into electrical signals and then send to the brain via auditory nerve.
   (a) A   (b) B
   (c) C   (d) D

   Directions (4–7): Fill in the blanks with appropriate option.

4. Sound waves do not travel through _____.
   (a) Solids   (b) Liquids
   (c) Gases   (d) Vacuum

5. The frequency which is not audible to the human ear is _____.
   (a) 5000 Hz   (b) 50000 Hz
   (c) 500 Hz   (d) 50 Hz

6. _____ can hear infrasound.
   (a) Rhinoceros   (b) Humans
   (c) Bat   (d) Dog

7. 'Note' is a sound _____.
   (a) Of a single frequency
   (b) Always unpleasant to listen to
   (c) Of a mixture of several frequencies
   (d) Of mixture of only two frequencies

8. A stone dropped from the top of a tower of height 300 m splashes into a pond of water at its base. When will the splash be heard at the top?
   (velocity of the sound = 340 ms^{-1})
   (a) 5.6 s   (b) 5.2 s
   (c) 8.7 s   (d) 7.6 s

9. The distance between a crest and the next trough in a periodic wave is _____.
   (a) $\dfrac{\lambda}{2}$ (b) $\dfrac{\lambda}{4}$
   (c) λ (d) 2λ

10. Read the given statements and choose the correct option.
    Statement 1: Echo is produced when sound is incident on hard and polished surface.
    Statement 2: Sound energy can totally be reflected by objects with soft and loose texture.
    (a) Both the statements are true and statement 2 is not the correct explanation of statement 1.
    (b) Both the statements are true and statement 2 is the correct explanation of statement 1.
    (c) Both the statements are false.
    (d) Statement 1 is true but statement 2 is false.

SUBJECTIVE QUESTIONS

1. (a) A vibrating tuning fork is placed over the mouth of a burette with water. The tap is opened and the water level gradually falls. It is observed that the sound becomes the loudest for a particular length of air column.
    (i) What is the name of the phenomenon taking place when this happens?
    (ii) Why does the sound become the loudest?
    (iii) What is the name of the phenomenon taking place when sound is produced for another length of air column and is not the loudest.
    (b) What change if any would you expect in the characteristics of a musical sound when we increase _____.
    (i) frequency?
    (ii) amplitude?

Ans.
(a) (i) The phenomenon is resonance.
(ii) When the frequency of the air column at that particular length is equal to or an integral multiple of the frequency of the tuning fork, then it starts vibrating with a large amplitude which produces a loud sound.
(iii) This phenomenon is forced vibration. Here, the air column vibrates but the amplitude is not as large as for resonance. Hence the sound is not the loudest.
(b) (i) When the frequency increases, its pitch also increases.
(ii) The loudness of the sound increases when its amplitude increases.

2. A man fires a gun and hears its echo after 5 seconds. The man then moves 310 m towards the hill and fires his gun again. This time he hears the echo after 3 seconds. Calculate the speed of sound.

Ans.
Let d be the distance between the man and the hill in the beginning. Sound, in echo, travels from man to hill and reflects back travelling the same distance again to produce echo. Speed of sound be v, distance be d.

$$\therefore v = \frac{2d}{t}$$

In the first case $t = 5$

$$\therefore v = \frac{2d}{5} \qquad \qquad ...(i)$$

He moves 310 m towards the hill

$$\therefore v = \frac{2(d-310)}{3} \qquad \qquad ...(ii)$$

Since the velocity of sound is same, equating (i) and (ii) we get:

$$\frac{2d}{5} = \frac{2(d-310)}{3}$$

$$\Rightarrow 3d = 5d - 1550$$

$$\Rightarrow d = \frac{1550}{2} = 775 \text{ m}$$

$$\therefore v = \frac{2d}{5} = \frac{2 \times 775}{5} = 310 \text{ ms}^{-1}.$$

3. Differentiate between longitudinal wave and transverse wave.

Ans.

Longitudinal Wave	Transverse Wave
It needs medium for propagation.	It may or may not need medium for propagation.
Particles of the medium move in a direction parallel to the direction of propagation of the disturbance.	Particles of the medium move in perpendicular direction of propagation of the disturbance.
Example: sound wave	Example: light wave, seismic wave

4. What is crest and trough?

Ans.
When a wave is propagated as represented below. A peak is called the crest and a valley is called the trough of a wave.

Sound

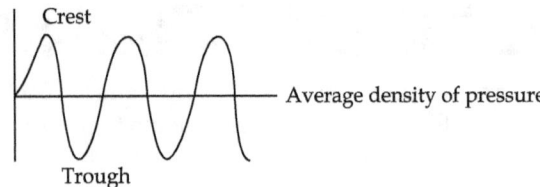

5. A sound wave causes the density of air at a place to oscillate 1200 times in 2 minutes. Find the time period and frequency of the wave.

Ans.

Frequency = 1200/2 × 60 = 10Hz

Time period = ?

Frequency = 1/T

∴ T = 1/Frequency

= 1/10

= 0.1 s

6. Give 3 uses of ultrasound.

Ans.

Use of ultrasound:
i. Ultrasound is used to detect cracks and flaws in metal blocks.
ii. It is used in 'echo-cardiography', the ultrasonic waves are made to reflect from various parts of the heart and form the image of the heart.
iii. It is used in 'ultrasonography', to detect the image of organs or to detect the abnormalities in the organs. It is also used to examine the foetus during pregnancy to detect congenital defects.

7. What is the function of middle ear?

Ans.

Middle ear consist of three small bones called hammer, anvil and stirrup. These three bones receive the sound vibrations and increase the strength of these vibrations to amplify the vibrations received by ear-drum. These amplified vibrations are furthgr passed to the inner ear.

A ship sends out ultrasound that return from the seabed and is detected after 3.42 s.

8. If the speed of ultrasound through seawater is 1531 m/s. What is the distance of the seabed from the ship?

Ans.

Time between transmission and detection t = 342 s.

Speed of ultrasound in seawater = 1531 m/s.

Distance travelled by the ultra sound = 2 × depth of sea = 2d

2d = speed of sound × time

= 1531 × 3.42

= 5236 m

∴ d = 5236/2

= 2618 m.

The distance of the seabed from the ship is 2618 m.

9. Distinguish between tone, note and noise.

Ans.

Tone: A sound of single frequency is called a tone.

Note: The sound which is produced due to a mixture of several frequencies is called a note.

Noise: The sound which is produced due to a mixture of several frequencies but is unpleasant to the ear is called noise.

10. A child watching Dussehra celebration from a distance sees the effigy of Ravana burst into flames and hears the explosion associated with it 2 sec after that. How far was he from the effigy if the speed of sound in air that night was 335 m/sec?

Ans.

Speed of sound in air = 335 m/s.

time required to reach the sound = 2 sec

distance of the source of sound = ?

∴ Speed = Distance/Time

∴ Distance = Speed × Time

= 335 × 2 sec

= 670 m.

Matter in Our Surroundings   6

Learning Objectives : In this chapter, students will learn about:
- ✓ characteristics of particles of matter
- ✓ solid, liquid and gas matter
- ✓ the process of evaporation
- ✓ factors affecting evaporation

CHAPTER SUMMARY

Anything which occupies space and has mass is called **matter**. If we look around us, we see a large number of things of different shapes, sizes and textures. Many of these things are used by us in our everyday life. For example, we eat food, drink water, breathe in air and wear clothes. The things like food, water, air, clothes, table, chair, human beings, animals, plants and trees are all examples of matter.

Air and water, hydrogen and oxygen, sugar and sand, copper and coal, carbon and sulphur are all different kinds of matter, because all of them occupy space and have mass. Matter can be classified in a number of ways. According to early Indian philosophers all the matter, living or non-living, was made up of five basic elements (panch tatva): air, earth, fire, sky and water (vayu, prithvi, agni, akash and jal). Modern-day scientists classify matter in two ways: on the basis of its physical properties and on the basis of its chemical properties. On the basis of physical properties, matter is classified into solids, liquids and gases. On the basis of chemical properties, matter is classified into elements, compounds and mixtures. In this chapter, we will study the classification of matter on the basis of its physical properties.

Physical Nature of Matter

Everything around us is made up of particles. These particles are so small that they cannot be seen even with a microscope. These particles are continuously moving *i.e.*, they are in state of constant random motion which is maximum in gases and minimum in solids.

Note: The particles of matter are very small. Their size is beyond our imagination.

Characteristics of Particles of Matter

The different characteristics of particles of matter are:

(i) **Particles of matter have space between them:** When we put sugar or salt in water, we see that after sometime it disappears. Where do these particles go?

The answer to this question is: as there is space between the particles of water molecules, the sugar or the salt molecules get into the space between the molecules of the water. Thus, we can say the particles of matter have space between them.

(ii) **Particles of matter are continuously moving:** All the particles of matter possess kinetic energy. The velocity of particles increases with increase in temperature that is why rate of diffusion increases with increase in temperature. Hence the particles start moving faster.

(iii) **Particles of matter attract each other:** There are some force of attraction between the particles of matter which bind them together. The force of attraction is known as **cohesion**. The force of attraction is different in the particles of different kinds of matter. It is maximum in particles of solid matter and minimum in the particles of gaseous matter.

Classification of Matter

On the basis of physical states, all matter can be classified into three groups solids, liquids and gases. The following is a flowchart showing classification of matter:

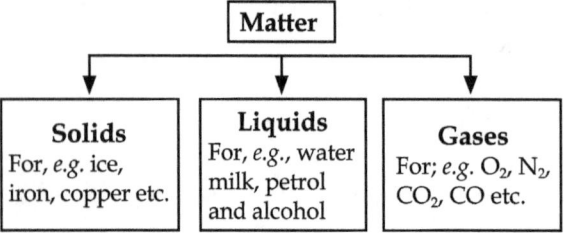

Solid State

In solids, molecules are closely packed. There is strong force of attraction between particles (atoms, ions or molecules) of solids which hold them in fixed position. In solids, molecules vibrate only about their fixed positions. If a solid is heated its particles start vibrating faster.

The space between particles of solid is very small. In solid, molecules have minimum kinetic energy (energy due to motion of particles). Solids have well defined orderly arrangement of atoms, ions or molecules.

Example of solids: Carbon, Sulphur, Sugar, Ice, Sodium Chloride etc.

Liquid State

In liquids, molecules are close together to lesser extent than solids, therefore, there is less force of attraction between molecules of liquids than solids. The molecules of liquids can move from one position to another.

In liquid, molecules have more kinetic energy than solids. There is less orderly arrangement of molecules than solids. In general we can say that 'A liquid has a fixed volume but it has no fixed shape, it takes the shape of its container'.

Example of liquids: Milk, Kerosene, Petrol, Alcohol, Blood etc.

Gaseous State

Gases have extremely weak force of attraction between atoms or molecules. That is why, they have neither a fixed shape nor a fixed volume. The force of attraction between the molecules of a gas is negligible, so molecules of gases can flow in all directions.

The molecules of gases have maximum kinetic energy due to which gases have more disorderly arrangement of atoms, ions or molecules. The molecules of gases are in state of constant random motion in all directions. They collide among themselves as well as with the walls of the container and exert pressure.

Example of gases: Hydrogen, Oxygen, Nitrogen, Fluorine, Air Carbon dioxide, Ammonia etc.

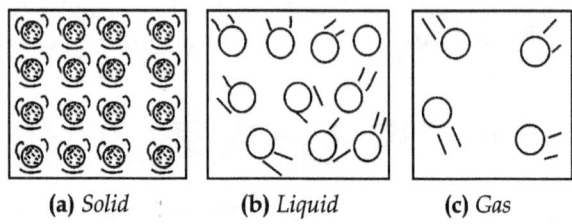

(a) Solid   (b) Liquid   (c) Gas

Fig. 6.1. *Arrangement for particles in Solids, Liquids and Gases*

Note:
CNG: It stands for compressed natural gas containing 90% CH_4. The remaining is hydrogen along with other hydrocarbons. CNG is being used as automobile fuel.

LPG: It stands for liquefied petroleum gas. It consists of mainly butane and isobutane along with small amounts of ethane and propane.

Can matter change its state?

Matter can change from one state to another. For example water can exist in three states –
(i) Solid as ice
(ii) Liquid as water and
(iii) Gas as water vapour

What happens inside the matter during this change of state? What happens to the particles of matter during the change of states? How does this change of state take place? There are many factors responsible for such changes such as temperature, pressure and evaporation.

Effect of Temperature

On increasing the temperature of solids, the force of attraction between particles decreases, therefore kinetic energy of particles will increase and ultimately it melts and thus solid changes into liquid.

'The temperature at which a solid melts to become a liquid at the atmospheric pressure is called its melting point.' 'The process of melting, that is change of solid state into liquid state is also known as **fusion**.'

We observe that during melting the temperature remains constant till the entire solid changes into liquid though we continue to heat the beaker. This heat energy is used up in changing the state by overcoming the intermolecular force of attraction. This heat is absorbed by solid without showing any rise in temperature. This hidden heat is known as **latent heat of fusion**.

Latent Heat of Fusion

Therefore 'The amount of heat energy that is required to change 1 mole of solid into liquid at atmospheric pressure without any change of temperature at its melting point is known as latent heat of fusion.'

The temperature at which liquid changes into vapours completely is called **boiling point of liquid**. The vapour pressure of liquid becomes equal to atmospheric pressure at this temperature. The boiling point of water is 100°C (373 K = 100°C + 273)

'**Latent heat of vaporisation** is defined as heat required to convert 1 mole of liquid into vapours completely at its boiling point.'

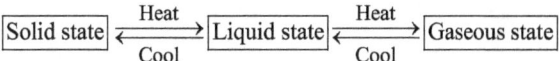

Substances around us change state from solid to liquid and from liquid to gas on application of heat. But there are some examples that change directly from solid state to gaseous state and vice versa. 'The process in which solid directly changes into vapours without becoming liquid or vice versa i.e., vapours directly changes into solid without becoming liquid is called **sublimation**.'

For example: Iodine, Camphor and Ammonium chloride.

Effect of Pressure

Pressure plays an important role in interconversion of states of matter. When we start applying pressure and compress a gas, it converts into liquid. But if we compress a liquid by applying the pressure and reducing temperature it gets converted into solid like freezing of liquid into ice.

Gases can be liquefied by applying pressure and lowering temperature:

When a high pressure is applied to a gas, it gets compressed (into a small volume), and when we also lower its temperature, it gets liquefied. So, we can also say that gases can be liquefied (turned into liquids) by compression and cooling.

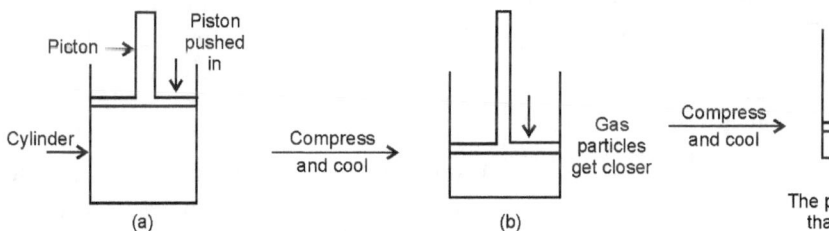

Fig. 6.2

By applying high pressure, the particles of a gas can be brought so close together that it liquifies.

Solid carbon dioxide is also known as **dry ice**. How does it change into solid? The answer is simple. When we decrease the temperature, intermolecular forces of attraction increase simultaneously. If we increase the pressure also then intermolecular forces of attraction increase to a large extent and CO_2 gas can be converted into solid.

Thus, pressure and temperature determine the state of a substance i.e. whether it will be a solid, liquid or gas.

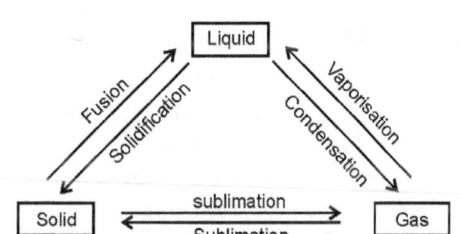

Fig. 6.3 *Inter Conversion of the Three States of Matter*

Evaporation

When a liquid is left exposed to air, its volume decreases gradually. This is due to evaporation.

Matter in Our Surroundings

We know that particles of liquid are always moving and are never at rest. These particles in liquid collide with each other. After some time the particles present on the surface of liquid gain sufficient energy to overcome the intermolecular force of attraction and break away. The particles of higher energy leave the surface and change into vapour.

Therefore 'The phenomenon of changing liquid into vapours below its boiling point is called vaporisation or evaporation.' It is a surface phenomenon. The particles at the surface gain energy and leave the surface.

Factors Affecting Evaporation

The rate of evaporation depends on the following factors:

Surface area

Evaporation is a surface phenomenon. If the surface area is increased, the rate of evaporation increases.

For example: Take some amount of alcohol or petrol or kerosene in a china dish and take same amount in a test tube and keep it near the window or fan. Measure, the volume of liquid after 1 hour. The volume of liquid left in test tube will be more than the liquid left in china dish. It shows that the rate of evaporation increases with the increase in surface area. The reason for this is that greater the surface area more will be molecules on the surface, therefore higher will be rate of evaporation. That is why we spread our clothes for drying up so as to increase the surface area.

> **TRIVIA**
>
> Tuna has the highest protein content for fish. Bluefin and yellowfin tuna are especially rich in protein. Bluefin offers 29.91 grams of protein per 100 grams of dry-cooked fish, and yellowfin provides 29.15 grams.

Temperature

The rate of evaporation increases with increase in temperature. With the increase of temperature more number of particles get enough kinetic energy to go into the vapour state.

Why we feel more cold after taking bath with hot water as compared to cold water? It is because evaporation of hot water is faster than evaporation of cold water.

Humidity

Humidity is the amount of water vapour present in air. The rate of evaporation increases with decrease in humidity. Air around us cannot hold more than a definite amount of water vapour at a given temperature. If the water vapours in air are already high, the rate of evaporation decreases.

That is why during rainy season, our clothes do not dry up easily because humidity is maximum in air.

Wind Speed

The rate of evaporation increases with increase in wind speed. It is a common observation that clothes dry faster on a windy day as compared to a dry day. With increase in speed of wind the particles are moved away with decreasing amount of vapours in atmosphere, thereby increasing the rate of evaporation.

Why do we feel coldness when we keep acetone on our palm?

It is because acetone is a volatile liquid. Acetone takes heat from our palm and surface molecules get sufficient energy to change into vapours and the remaining molecules possess lower energy and we feel coldness due to decrease in temperature.

Why do we wear cotton clothes in summer?

During summers we prespire a lot, which keeps us cool. The latent heat of vaporisation is required for water to vaporise which is taken from our body and it leads to cooling of our body.

Why do we see water droplets on the outer surface of glass containing ice or cold water?

It is because water vapours present in air on coming in contact with the cold glass lose energy and get converted into liquid state because molecules come closer to each other forming water droplets.

MUST REMEMBER

- The space between particles of solid is very small.
- The molecules of liquids can move from one position to another.
- Gases have extremely weak force of attraction between atoms or molecules.
- The molecules of gases have maximum kinetic energy due to which gases have more disorderly arrangement of atoms, ions or molecules.
- The amount of heat energy that is required to change 1 mole of solid into liquid at atmospheric pressure without any change of temperature at its melting point is known as latent heat of fusion.
- Latent heat of vaporisation is defined as heat required to convert 1 mole of liquid into vapours completely at its boiling point.
- The process in which solid directly changes into vapours without becoming liquid or vice versa i.e., vapours directly changes into solid without becoming liquid is called sublimation.
- The rate of evaporation increases with increase in temperature.
- The rate of evaporation increases with decrease in humidity.
- The rate of evaporation increases with increase in wind speed.

Matter in Our Surroundings

MULTIPLE CHOICE QUESTIONS

1. Helium gas is a matter because _____.
   (a) It has mass and occupies volume
   (b) It has no definite volume
   (c) It can be compressed easily
   (d) It has a mass

2. Which of the following is correct arrangement of decreasing order of force of attraction between particles?
   (a) Water, air, chalk
   (b) Sugar, alcohol, nitrogen
   (c) Sulphur dioxide, carbon disulphide, sulphur
   (d) Oxygen, water sugar

3. On converting 0°C, –6°C, 273°C into Kelvin, the correct sequence of temperature will be _____.
   (a) 273 K, 267 K, 546 K
   (b) 273 K, 279 K, 546 K
   (c) 273 K, 267 K, 0 K
   (d) –273 K, –279 K, 0 K

4. For any substance the temperature remains same during the change of state due to _____.
   (a) Loss of heat
   (b) Latent heat
   (c) Less supply of heat
   (d) Lattice energy

5. What will be boiling point of water at hill station?
   (a) 100°C
   (b) <100°C
   (c) >100°C
   (d) Either less than 100°C

6. The mixture of sulphur and sodium chloride can be separated by _____.
   (a) Dissolving in water followed by filtration and evaporation
   (b) Sublimation
   (c) Dissolving in alcohol followed by filtration
   (d) Crystallization

7. Which one of the following statement is correct in respect of fluids?
   (a) Only gases behave as fluids
   (b) Only liquids are fluids
   (c) Gases and solids behave as fluids
   (d) Gases and liquids behave as fluids

8. When we determine the boiling point of liquid, the thermometer _____.
   (a) Should dip into liquid
   (b) Should be above the liquid and remain vertical
   (c) Should touch the bottom of container
   (d) Should be placed slanting in the liquid

9. Which of the following statements is incorrect?
   (a) The particles of matter are very-very small
   (b) The particles of matter attract one another
   (c) The particles of all the matter have spaces between them
   (d) The particles of some of the matter are moving constantly

10. The best evidence for the existence and movement of particles in liquids was provided by _____.
    (a) Kerosene
    (b) Krypton
    (c) Carbon steel
    (d) Carbon dioxide

11. During respiration, glucose and oxygen enter our body cells whereas waste products like carbon dioxide and water leave body cells by the process of _____.
    (a) Osmosis   (b) Effusion
    (c) Diffusion   (d) Plasmolysis

12. Which of the following energy is absorbed during the change of state of a substance?
    (a) Heat capacity
    (b) Latent heat
    (c) Heat of solution
    (d) Specific heat

13. On converting 308 K, 329 K and 391 K to Celsius scale, the correct sequence of temperature will be _____.
    (a) 33°C, 56°C and 118°C
    (b) 35°C, 56°C and 118°C
    (c) 35°C, 56°C and 119°C
    (d) 56°C, 119°C and 35°C

14. Which of the following are also considered to be the states of matter?
    (i) BEC (ii) BHC (iii) plasma (iv) platelets
    (a) (i) and (ii)   (b) (i) and (iii)
    (c) (ii) and (iii)   (d) (iii) and (iv)

15. If the temperature of an object is 268 K, it will be equivalent to _____.
    (a) –5°C   (b) +5°C
    (c) –25°C   (d) 368°C

16. The boiling point of ethane is, –88°C. This temperature will be equivalent to _____.
    (a) 185 K   (b) 361 K
    (c) 288 K   (d) 285 K

17. When heat is constantly supplied by a burner to boiling water, then the temperature of water during vaporisation _____.
    (a) Rises very slowly
    (b) First rises and then becomes constant
    (c) Rises rapidly until steam is produced
    (d) Does not rise at all

18. When water at 0°C freezes to form ice at the same temperature of 0°C, then it _____.
    (a) Absorbs some heat
    (b) Release some heat
    (c) Neither absorbs nor releases heat
    (d) Absorbs exactly 3.34×10^5 j/kg of heat

19. In the following diagram ammonia gas obtained from ammonium hydroxide reacts with HCl (g) obtained from hydrochloric acid, and form white fumes of ammonium chloride. Observe the following diagram and choose the correct option.

    (a) White fumes ring will be formed at the centre
    (b) White fumes ring will be formed near 2nd end
    (c) White fumes ring will be formed near 1st end
    (d) White fumes ring will not be formed at all

20. During summer days water kept in an earthen pot (pitcher) becomes cool because of the phenomenon of _____.
    (a) Osmosis
    (b) Evaporation
    (c) Transpiration
    (d) Diffusion

21. The evaporation of water increases under the following conditions _____.
    (a) Increase in surface area, decrease in temperature
    (b) Increase in surface area, rise in temperature
    (c) Increase in temperature, decrease in surface area
    (d) Increase in temperature, increase in surface area addition of common salt

22. One of the following does not undergo sublimation. This one is _____.
    (a) Iodine
    (b) Camphor
    (c) Sodium chloride
    (d) Ammonium chloride

23. When a gas jar full of air is placed upside down on a gas jar full of bromine vapours, the red – brown vapours of bromine from the lower jar go upward into the jar containing air. In this experiment _____.
    (a) Bromine is heavier than air
    (b) Air is heavier than bromine
    (c) Coth air and bromine have the same density
    (d) Bromine cannot be heavier than air because it is going upwards against gravity

Matter in Our Surroundings

24. Ice floats on water because _____.
    (a) It is solid
    (b) It is low melting solid
    (c) It has higher density than water
    (d) It has lower density than water due to more volume

25. Seema took a 100 ml beaker and filled half the beaker with water and marked the level of water. She dissolved some salt with the help of a glass rod and recorded water level again. Choose the correct observation related to above activity.
    (a) The water level decreases
    (b) There is little increase in water level
    (c) The water level remains the same
    (d) The water level increases appreciably

26. Which of the following has minimum kinetic energy?
    (a) Particles of ice below 0°
    (b) Particles of water at 0°
    (c) Particles of water at 100°
    (d) Particles of steam at 100°

27. Which one of the following statements is not true?
    (a) The molecules in a gas exert negligibly small forces on each other, except during collisions
    (b) The molecules of a gas occupy all the space available
    (c) The molecules in a liquid are arranged in a regular pattern
    (d) The molecules in a solid vibrate about a fixed position

28. Convert the temperature of 300 K to the Celsius scale.
    (a) 30°C   (b) 27°C
    (c) 28°C   (d) 26°C

29. Which of the following process/processes release heat?
    (i) Condensation   (ii) Vaporisation
    (iii) Freezing   (iv) Melting
    (a) (i) and (ii)   (b) (i) and (iii)
    (c) only (ii)   (d) Only (iv)

30. Particles of matter are _____.
    (a) Stationary
    (b) In continuous motion
    (c) Rotating about on axis
    (d) Vibrating in one position

HOTS

1. Which of the following is not true?
    (i) On increasing the temperature of solids, the force of attraction between particles increases
    (ii) On increasing the temperature of solids, kinetic energy of particles will decrease
    (iii) Melting point is the temperature, at which a solid melts to become a liquid at the atmospheric pressure
    (a) Only (i)   (b) (i) and (ii)
    (c) (i), (ii) and (iii) (d) None of these

2. Find the increase in the temperature of 1kg of water if 1000 J of heat is supplied to it.
    (a) $\left(\frac{4186}{1000}\right)°c$ (b) $\left(\frac{1000}{4186}\right)°c$
    (c) $(1000 \times 4186)°c$ (d) $(4186 - 1000)°c$

3. It was observed during a hail storm that ice balls turned into water when they reached the ground. At what height could the rain drops have formed into ice balls? Assume that g is 10 ms^{-2}
    (a) 320 km   (b) 350 km
    (c) 334 km   (d) 343 km

4. The temperature of 104°F when measured on a Kelvin scale will give the reading of ____.
    (a) 313 K   (b) 302 K
    (c) 307 K   (d) 380 K

5. What is mean by sublimation?
    (a) change of state directly from solid to liquid without changing into gas state
    (b) change of state directly from soil to gas without changing into liquid state
    (c) change of state directly from solid to gas without changing into ice state
    (d) change of state directly from solid to gas without changing into liquid state

SUBJECTIVE QUESTIONS

1. What happens to the sugar when it dissolves in water? Where does the sugar go? What information do you get about the nature of matter from the dissolution of sugar in water?

Ans.

(a) When sugar dissolves in water, its tiny particles break off from the solid 'sugar crystals'.

(b) The sugar particles go into the spaces between the particles of water and mix with them (to form sugar solution).

(c) The dissolution of sugar in water tells us that:
   (i) The matter (here sugar and water) is made up of small particles.
   (ii) The particles of matter (here water) have spaces between them.

2. Describe Plasma and Bose-Einstein condensate states of matter.

Ans.

Plasma is a mixture of free electrons and ions. Plasma is considered the fourth state of matter. Plasma occurs naturally in the stars (including the sun). Inside the stars, the temperature is so high that the atoms break up. Some of the electrons break away from the atoms converting the rest of atoms into electrically charged particles called ions. This mixture of free electrons and ions in a star is called plasma. The sun and other stars glow because of the presence of plasma in them.

Plasma can also be made on the earth by passing electricity through gases at very low pressure taken in a glass tube (called discharge tube). The fluorescent tubes and neon sign bulbs from plasma when they are switched on. A fluorescent tube may contain helium gas (or some other gas) and a neon sign bulb contains neon gas. when electricity is passed through a fluorescent tube (or neon sign bulb), the gases present in than get ionised to form plasma. This plasma makes a fluorescent tube (or neon sign bulb) to glow.

In 1920, an Indian scientist Satyendra Nath Bose did some calculations, for the fifth state of matter. On the basis of these calculations, Albert Einstein predicted the existence of a new state of matter called Bose. Einstein condensate (BEC). The fifth state of matter called Bose-Einstein condensate was finally achieved by three scientists Cornell, Ketterle and Wieman of USA by cooling a gas of extremely low density (about one hundred thousandth the density of normal air) to super low temperatures.

3. 12 grams of potassium sulphate dissolves in 75 grams of water at 60°C. What is its solubility in water at that temperature?

Ans.

Here given that 75 grams of water dissolves 12 grams of potassium sulphate. We have to find how much potassium sulphate will dissolve in 100 grams of water.

Now, 75g of water dissolves = 12g of potassium sulphate

So, 100 g of water will dissolve = $\frac{12}{75} \times 100$ g of potassium sulphate

= 16 g of potassium sulphate

Thus, the solubility of potassium sulphate in water is 16 g at 60°C.

4. Distinguish between evaporation and boiling.

Ans.

Evaporation	Boiling
Evaporation is a natural process that occurs when the liquid form changes into the gaseous form; while causing an increase in the pressure or temperature.	Boiling is an unnatural process where the liquid gets heated up and vaporized due to continuous heating of the liquid.
Evaporation usually occurs on the surface of the liquid being heated up.	Boiling usually occurs on the entire mass of the liquid that gets heated up.

Matter in Our Surroundings

Bubbling effect is not visible in evaporation.	Bubbling effect is visible during the process of boiling.
The process of evaporation is usually slower and more carried out when compared to boiling.	The process of boiling is usually much quicker and the process happens quite rapidly as well.

5. Why is it advisable to use pressure cooker at higher altitudes?

Ans.
At higher altitudes, the atmospheric pressure is low and the water boils very fast and evaporates at faster rate therefore, the pressure is required to increase the cooking process and this is done by using pressure cooker which increases the pressure inside the container and cooks food faster.

6. The melting point of ice is 273.16 K. What does this mean? Explain in detail.

Ans.
Ice is solid at 0°C i.e., 273° K. The molecules of ice are tightly packed. These molecules have to overcome the force of attraction with which they are held and hence they gain this heat from the surrounding but the temperature remains the same as their energy is used to overcome the force of attraction between the particles. The particles have their state and starts vibrating freely and a stage reaches when the solid ice melts and is converted to liquid state at the same temperature i.e., 273 K.

7. How is the high compressibility property of gas useful to us?

Ans.
The gases have high compressibility. This property is used in the following situation:
(i) LPG (liquefied petroleum gas) is a fuel which is made up of petroleum gas. On compressing this petroleum gas it forms liquid.
(ii) Oxygen cylinders in the hospitals have compressed gas filled in it.
(iii) CNG (compressed natural gas) is a natural gas, methane, which is compressed and used as a fuel in vehicles and at home.

8. With the help of an example, explain how diffusion of gases in water is essential?

Ans.
The gases from the atmosphere diffuse and dissolve in water. Gases like oxygen and carbon dioxide diffuse in water, are essential for the survival of aquatic animals and plants.

Animals breathe in this oxygen dissolved in water for their survival and plants can use carbon dioxide dissolved in water for photosynthesis.

9. Explain giving examples the various factors on which rate of evaporation depends.

Ans.
The rate of evaporation depends on the following factors:
(i) Surface area: If the surface area is increased the rate of evaporation also increases.
   (a) To dry the clothes we spread them to dry faster.
   (b) Tea in saucer cools faster than in a cup.
(ii) Temperature: If the temperature is increased the rate of evaporation also increases. Due to increase in temperature the particles gain more kinetic energy and change their phase from liquid to gaseous. Water will evaporate faster in sun than in shade.
(iii) Humidity: It is the amount of water vapour present in air. The air can hold definite amount of water vapour, at a given temperature. If the amount of water vapour is high in the air then the rate of evaporation decreases. On hot and humid day, desert coolers are not effective as the air cannot hold any more moisture to get the cooling effect.
(iv) Wind speed: With the increase in wind speed, the rate of evaporation increases. The particles of water vapour move away with the wind, decreasing the amount of water vapour in the surrounding.

10. Shreya commutes in a CNG fitted van to school every day along with many other students. She told the van driver to get the CNG connection certified and timely checked it for any leakage or loose connection of pipes. She told the driver to be more careful during summers.
    (a) What is CNG?
    (b) Why should one be more careful with CNG cylinders during summer?
    (c) What value of Shreya is seen in the above act?

Ans.
(a) CNG is Compressed Natural Gas used as fuel.
(b) During summers, the CNG connections and cylinder need to be checked because the gas expands due to heat and if there would be any leakage then it would cause fire in the vehicle.
(c) Shreya showed the value of concerned citizen and morally responsible behaviour.

Force and Pressure

Learning Objectives : In this chapter, students will learn about:
- ✓ different types of elements
- ✓ solutions, colloids and suspensions
- ✓ separation of components of a mixture
- ✓ physical and chemical changes

CHAPTER SUMMARY

In our daily life we come across several types of matter in our surroundings. It is very difficult to say which matter is pure. Even the eatables, which we purchase from the market are not found to be pure and are adulterated with undesirable materials that are harmful to us. *The pure substance is one which is made up of only one kind of particles.*

The matter around us is of two types: Pure substance and mixtures:

Mixtures

A **mixture** is a substance which consists of two or more elements or compounds not chemically combined together or not in any fixed proportion.

Example:
(i) Air is a mixture of gases like oxygen, nitrogen, carbon dioxide and water vapour etc.
(ii) Gun Powder is a mixture of potassium nitrate, sulphur and charcoal (charcoal is a form of carbon).

All solution are mixtures.

For example: sea water, dyes, vinegar, muddy river water, milk of magnesia, hair spray, fog and mist.

Properties of Mixture
(i) The constituents of mixtures can be separated by physical methods (like filtration, sublimation, distillation, solvents, magnet etc.)
(ii) A mixture shows properties of all the constituents present in it.

(iii) Energy is usually neither given out nor absorbed in the preparation of a mixture. So, the formation of a mixture is a physical change.
(iv) The constituents in the mixtures are not present in any fixed proportion.
(v) Mixtures do not have any fixed melting and boiling points.

Types of Mixtures
Mixtures are two of types:
(i) Homogeneous mixture
(ii) Heterogeneous mixture

Homogenous Mixture
Those mixtures in which the substances are completely mixed together and are indistinguishable from one another are called **homogeneous mixtures**.

A homogeneous mixture has a uniform composition. It has no visible boundaries of separation between the various constituents. A mixture of sugar or salt in water is a homogenous mixture, sugar or salt gets dissolved completely in water and particles of sugar are not visible to our naked eyes. There are no visible boundaries of separation between various constituents and usually exist in one phase.

All the homogeneous mixtures are called **solutions**.

For example: Sugar solution, copper sulphate solution, petrol and oil mixture, soda water, soft drinks, kerosene oil etc.

Note: Petrol and kerosene are not single substances, they are mixtures of various compounds of carbon and hydrogen (called **hydrocarbons**).

Heterogeneous Mixture
Those mixtures in which the substances remain separate and one substance is spread throughout the other substance as small particle droplets or bubbles are called **heterogeneous mixtures**.

It has visible boundaries of separation between the various constituents. The mixture of sugar and sand is a heterogeneous mixture because this mixture will have different sugar-sand composition.

The suspension of solids in liquids are also heterogeneous mixtures.

For example, A suspension of chalk in water, polluted air, gunpowder, milk, ink, butter, cheese, face cream, shaving cream, hair spray, fog and mist etc.

Note: Most of the mixtures are heterogeneous, only solutions and alloys are homogenous mixtures.

Pure Substance
Substances which are made up of only one kind of particles or one kind of atoms are called **pure substances**. For example: oxygen, carbon, sodium chloride, calcium etc.

Properties of Pure Substance
(i) It has certain fixed density.
(ii) It has fixed melting and boiling points.
(iii) Normally it has viscosity.
(iv) Refractive index can be measured accurately.
(v) Pure substances are either conductors, insulators or semi-conductors.

Types of Pure Substance
On the basis of their chemical composition, substances can be classified either into elements or compounds.

Elements
An element is a substance which is made of only one kind of atoms It cannot be split into two or more simpler substances by the chemical methods. This definition was given by **Robert Boyle** in 1661 in **Britain**.

On the basis of their properties, all the elements can be divided into three groups:
(i) Metals
(ii) Non-metals
(iii) Metalloids

Metals
A metal is an element that is malleable and ductile, and conducts electricity.

All the metals are solids except mercury which is liquid at room temperature.

Properties of metals:
(i) Metals are malleable and ductile. Malleable means metals can be beaten into thin sheets with a hammer and ductile means metals can be drawn (or stretched) into thin wires.
(ii) Metals are good conductors of heat and electricity.
(iii) Metals are lustrous (or shiny)
(iv) Metals are usually strong and have high tensile strength. It means metals can hold large weights without breaking.
(v) All metals except mercury are solids at room temperature. Mercury is in a liquid state at the room temperature.
(vi) Metals generally have high melting and boiling points and high density **except sodium and potassium**.
(vii) Metals are sonorous i.e metals make a ringing sound when we strike them.
(viii) Metals usually have a silver or grey colour **except copper and gold**.

Non-metals
A non metal is an element that is neither malleable nor ductile, and does not conduct electricity.

Properties of non-metals:
(i) Non-metals are not malleable and ductile but they are brittle.
(ii) Non-metals are bad conductors of heat and electricity.
(iii) Non-metals are not lustrous (not shiny). They are dull in appearance.
(iv) They are not strong and have low tensile strength.
(v) They are generally soft except carbon (in the form of diamond).
(vi) Non-metals may be solids, liquids or gases at the room temperature.

Force and Pressure

(vii) Non-metals have low melting and boiling points except graphite which has a very high melting point (3700°C)
(viii) Non-metals have low densities except iodine.
(ix) They are not sonorous and have different colours.

Metalloids

Elements which show the properties of both metals and non-metals. They are called the **metalloids**.

For example: Boron (B), Silicon (Si) and Germanium (Ge) are some examples of metalloids.

Compounds

A compound is a substance made up of two or more elements chemically combined in a fixed proportion by mass.

For example: Water (H_2O) is a compound made up of two elements, hydrogen and oxygen, chemically combined in a fixed proportion of 1:8 by mass. Sodium chloride (NaCl), ammonium chloride (NH_4Cl), are also the example of compounds.

Note: Compounds can be further divided into three classes: acids, bases and salts, on the basis of their properties.

Properties of compounds

(i) It is a homogeneous substance.
(ii) It has fixed melting point and boiling point.
(iii) The composition of a compound is fixed, the constituents are present in a fixed proportion by mass.
(iv) The properties of a compound are entirely different from those of its constituent elements.
(v) A compound cannot be separated into its components by physical methods.
(vi) Formation of compound is associated with either evolution or absorption of heat and light.

Alloys

Alloys are homogeneous mixtures of metals and cannot be separated into their components by physical methods. An alloy is considered to be a mixture because (i) it shows the properties of its constituents and (ii) it has a variable composition.

For example: Brass is a mixture of approximately 30% Zinc and 70% copper. Brass is considered to be a mixture because:

(i) it shows the properties of its constituents i.e. copper and zinc, and
(ii) it has a variable composition. (The amount of zinc in brass can vary from 20 to 35%)

Solutions

It is a homogeneous mixture of two or more substances in which one substance is liquid. It consists of two parts, **solvent** and **solute**.

The substance which is dissolved in a liquid to make a solution is called solute and the liquid in which solute is dissolved is known as **solvent**.

For example: In a solution of salt and water, salt is the solute as it is dissolved in water and water is the solvent. Vinegar, metal alloys (brass) and air etc. are some more examples of solution.

Properties of a Solution

(i) A solution is a homogeneous mixture.
(ii) The particles of a solution cannot be seen even with a microscope.
(iii) The size of solute particles in a solution is extremely small (10^{-9} nm).
(iv) A true solution does not scatter light (This is because its particle are very small).
(v) The solute particles cannot be separated from the mixture by the process of filtration, the solute particles do not settle down when left undisturbed, i.e., a solution is stable.

Types of solution: Various types of solutions are:

(i) **Solution of solid in a liquid:** For example – sugar solution and salt solution.
(ii) **Solution of liquid in a liquid:** Vinegar is a solution of acetic acid in water.
(iii) **Solution of gas in a liquid:** Soda water is a solution of carbon-dioxide gas in water.
(iv) **Solution of gas in a gas:** Air is a solution of gases like oxygen, argon, carbon dixide and water vapour, etc. in nitrogen gas. Nitrogen is the solvent in air and all other gases are solutes.

Concentration of a Solution

The solution is basically of two types, **saturated** and **unsaturated**. Saturated solutions are those in which no more solutes can be dissolved. On the other hand, the solution in which more solutes can be dissolved are called the unsaturated solution. The amount of solute present in the saturated solution at a given temperature is called its **solubility**.

The concentration of a solution is defined as the mass of solute in grams present in 100 grams of the solution.

Types of Concentration of Solution
(i) Mass by mass percentage of a solution
$$= \frac{\text{Mass of solute}}{\text{Mass of solution}} \times 100$$
(ii) Mass by volume percentage of a solution
$$= \frac{\text{Mass of solute}}{\text{Volume of solution}} \times 100$$

Question: A solution contains 30 g of sugar dissolved in 370 g of water. Calculate the concentration of this solution.

Solution:
Mass of solute (Sugar) = 30 g
Mass of solvent (water) = 370 g
Mass of solution = Mass of solute + Mass of solvent
= 30 + 370 = 400 g
We know that –
Concentration of solution $= \frac{\text{Mass of solute}}{\text{Mass of solution}} \times 100$
$= \frac{30}{400} \times 100 = \frac{30}{4} = 7.5\%$
Thus, concentration of solution = 7.5%

Suspensions
A suspension is a heterogeneous mixture in which the small particles of solid are spread throughout a liquid without dissolving in it i.e., those substances which are insoluble in water form suspensions.

For example: Chalk-water mixture is a suspension of fine chalk particles in water, muddy water is a suspension of soil particles in water, milk of magnesia, sand particles suspended in water and flour in water are some more example of suspensions.

Properties of Suspension
(i) A suspension is a heterogeneous mixture.
(ii) The size of solute particles in suspension in a quite large, so particles of suspension can be seen by the naked eye.
(iii) A suspension scatters a beam of light passing through it because its particles are quite large
(iv) The solute particles settle down when a suspension is left undisturbed, i.e., a suspension is unstable.
(v) The particles of a suspension do not pass through a filter paper. So a suspension can be separated by filtration.

Colloidal Solutions
It is a heterogeneous mixture in which particles having size between 10^{-7} to 10^{-4} cm are dispersed in a continuous medium. The continuous medium is called dispersion medium and the particles in the medium form dispersed phase.

Colloids can be classified on the basis of the affinity of dispersed phase and dispersion medium for each other. On the basis of this it is of two types: *Lyophilic colloids and lyophobic colloids.*

The colloid which shows affinity towards the dispersion medium is called lyophilic colloids.

For example: Gelatin and starch are lyophilic colloids.

The colloid which does not show affinity towards the dispersion medium is called lyophobic colloid.

For example: Metals and their hydroxide and sulphide are lyophobic colloid.

Classification of Colloids

No.	Technical name	Dispersed phase	Dispersion medium	Examples
1.	Sol	Solid	Liquid	Ink, soap solution, starch solution most paints
2.	Solid sol	Solid	Solid	Coloured gemstone (Ruby)
3.	Aerosol	(i) Solid, (ii) Liquid	Gas, Gas	Smoke, automobile exhausts / Hairspray, fog mist, clouds
4.	Emulsion	Liquid	Liquid	Milk, butter, face cream
5.	Foam	Gas	Liquid	Fire extinguisher foam, soap bubbles, shaving cream, beer foam
6.	Solid foam	Gas	Solid	Insulating foam, foam rubber, sponge, bread
7.	Gel	Solid	Liquid	Jellies, Gelatine, Hairgel

Continuous network of solid in liquid

Properties of Colloids
(i) It is heterogeneous in nature.
(ii) The particles of colloids cannot be seen by naked eyes.
(iii) It is very unstable in nature i.e., the particles of solute settle down when left undisturbed.
(iv) The particles of colloids cannot be separated by filtration.
(v) The particle of colloids show Brownian movement.
(vi) It shows **electrophoresis** i.e., it shows the movement of particles under the influence of electric field towards the oppositely charged electrodes.
(vii) It shows tyndall effect i.e., it scatters the beam of light passing through it.
(viii) It exhibits the coagulation i.e., the colloidal particles precipitate and settle down if all the charge is removed from it.
(ix) It can be done by adding oppositely charged electrolytes.

Separating the Components of a Mixture

Many of the materials around us are mixtures. These mixtures have two or more than two substances (or constituents) mixed in them. It may not be possible to use a mixture as such in homes and in industries. We may require only one (or two) separate constituents of a mixture for our use.

So, depending upon the nature of mixture we have to use different methods for separation, such as: Evaporation, centrifugation, decantation, distillation, fractional distillation, using separation funnel chromatography and sublimation.

TRIVIA
Tungsten is the hardest metal known to man. It is used for heavy-duty industries such as space travel and ballistics.

Evaporation
This method is used to separate the dissolved material from the solvent. The process of evaporation is based on the fact that liquids vaporise easily whereas solids do not vaporise easily.

For example: We can separate the mixture of salt and water and coloured component from blue/black ink.

Centrifugation
In this method, when mixture is spun (rotated) at a high speed, the denser particles are forced to settle at the bottom and lighter particles stay at the top. Therefore can be separated from each other.

For example: We can separate cream from milk and clay particles suspended in water by the method of centrifugation.

This method is also used in dairies and home to separate butter from cream, in washing machines to squeeze out water from wet clothes, in diagnostic laboratories for blood and urine test.

Using a Separating Funnel
This method is used to separate the mixture of two liquids, which are not miscible. The separation of two immiscible liquids by a separating funnel depends on the difference in their densities.

In this method the mixture is put into the funnel and is allowed to settle. When it settles down, the lighter liquid forms the upper layers and the heavier liquid forms the lower layers. The top of the funnel is open and the lower layer is carefully drained out and thus, the liquids are separated.

This method is used to separate a mixture of petrol and water and in the extraction of iron from its ore.

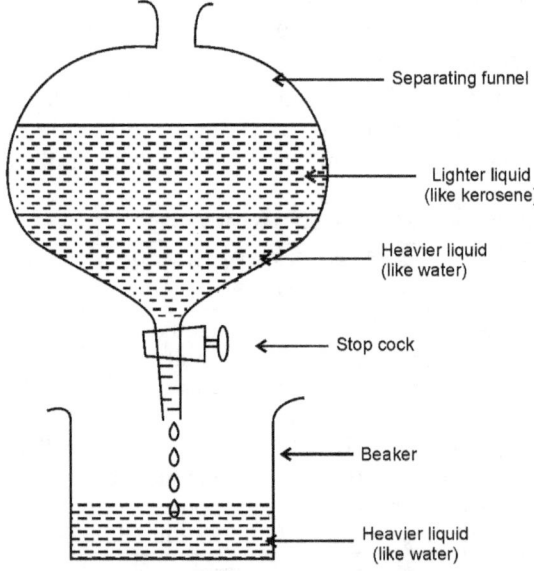

Fig. 7.1: *Separation of Two Immiscible Liquids*

Sublimation

In this method the solid directly gets vaporised without transforming into liquid, when heated. This method can be used to separate a mixture of two solids, in which one sublimes easily.

For example: The mixture of ammonium chloride and salts. The other compound which undergoes sublimation are *Camphor, iodine, Naphthalene, anthracene* etc.

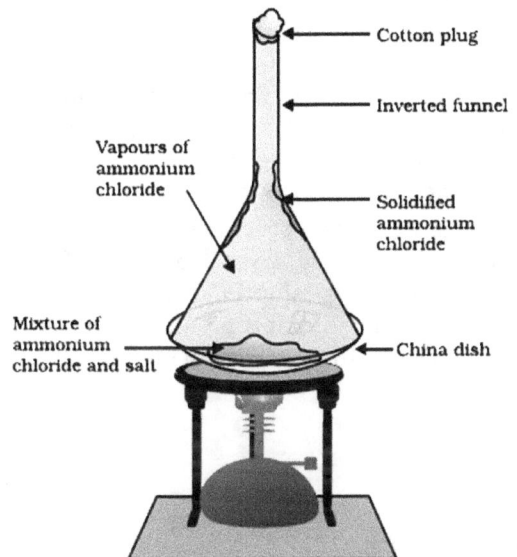

Fig. 7.2. *Separation of Ammonium Chloride and Salt*

Chromatography

This method is used to separate the mixture of solute formed by distribution of dissolved materials between two immiscible phases, in which one is movable and other is stationary. This separation is based on the fact that though two (or more) substances are soluble in the same solvent their solubilities may be different. This method is used to separate the dyes present in black ink.

Distillation

This method is used to separate a mixture of two liquids of different boiling points.

Distillation is the process of heating a liquid to form vapour, and then cooling the vapour to get back liquid. Distillation can be represented as:

$$\text{liquid} \underset{\text{Cooling}}{\overset{\text{Heating}}{\rightleftarrows}} \text{Vapours (or gas)}$$

This method is used to separate the mixture of acetone and water (two miscible liquids).

Fractional Distillation

To separate a mixture of two or more miscible liquids for which the difference in boiling points is less than 25 K, fractional distillation process is used.

For example:

For the separation of different gases from air, different fractions from petroleum products etc. The apparatus is similar to that for simple distillation except that a fractionating column is fitted in between the distillation flask and the condenser.

A simple fractionating column is a tube pocket with glass beads. The beads provide surface for the vapours to cool and condense repeatedly.

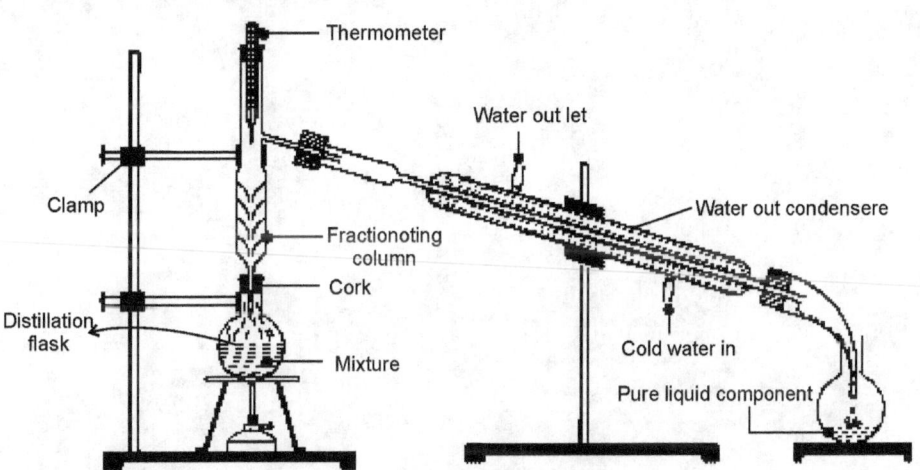

Fig. 7.3. *Fractional Distillation*

Force and Pressure

Crystallisation

The crystallisation method is used to purify solids. The process of cooling a hot, concentrated solution of a substance to obtain crystals is called **crystallisation**.

Impure copper sulphate can be purified by the method of crystallisation.

> **Note:** Crystallisation is a better technique than evaporation to dryness because of the following:
> (i) Some solids (like sugar) decompose or get charred on heating to dryness during evaporation.
> There is no such problem in crystallisation.
> (ii) The soluble impurities do not get removed in the process of evaporation. But such impurities get removed in crystallisation.

Physical and Chemical Changes

Physical changes: Those changes in which no new substances are formed are called physical changes.

In a physical change, the substances involved do not change their identity. They can be easily returned to their original form by some physical process. The physical changes are temporary change which can be reversed easily to form the original substance. Some common examples of physical changes are: Melting of ice, freezing of water, boiling of water, condensation of steam making a solution, glowing of an electric bulb and breaking of a glass tumbler, cutting or tearing a piece of paper, Tearing of cloth, and Rotation of a fan etc.

Chemical changes: Those changes in which new substances are formed, are called chemical changes. In a chemical change, the substances involved, change their identity. The new substances usually cannot be returned to their original form. Chemical changes are irreversible process.

Common examples of chemical changes are: burning of magnesium wire, burning of paper, rusting of iron, ripening of fruits, formation of curd from milk, cooking of food, growth of a plant, cutting of trees, digestion of food etc.

MUST REMEMBER

- Those mixtures in which the substances are completely mixed together and are indistinguishable from one another are called homogeneous mixtures.
- The suspension of solids in liquids are also heterogeneous mixtures.
- A metal is an element that is malleable and ductile, and conducts electricity.
- A non metal is an element that is neither malleable nor ductile, and does not conduct electricity.
- Alloys are homogeneous mixtures of metals and cannot be separated into their components by physical methods.
- The substance which is dissolved in a liquid to make a solution is called solute and the liquid in which solute is dissolved is known as solvent.
- The amount of solute present in the saturated solution at a given temperature is called its solubility.
- A suspension is a heterogeneous mixture in which the small particles of solid are spread throughout a liquid without dissolving in it.
- Distillation is the process of heating a liquid to form vapour, and then cooling the vapour to get back liquid.
- The process of cooling a hot, concentrated solution of a substance to obtain crystals is called **crystallisation**.
- Chemical changes are irreversible process.

MULTIPLE CHOICE QUESTIONS

1. Which of the following is not an element?
   - (a) Germanium
   - (b) Silica
   - (c) Carbon
   - (d) Silicon

2. Which of the following are compounds?
   - (i) CO
   - (ii) No
   - (iii) NO
   - (iv) Co
   - (a) (i) and (ii)
   - (b) (i) and (iii)
   - (c) (ii) and (iii)
   - (d) (ii) and (iv)

3. Identify the pure substance from the given material _____.
   - (a) Calcium oxide
   - (b) Wood
   - (c) Air
   - (d) All of these

4. One of the following substances is neither a good conductor of electricity nor an insulator. This substance is _____.
   - (a) Chromium
   - (b) Gallium
   - (c) Germanium
   - (d) Potassium

5. Which of the following is not a mixture?
   - (a) Kerosene
   - (b) Alcohol
   - (c) Air
   - (d) Petrol

6. Which of the following statements are true for pure substances?
   - (i) Pure substances contain only one kind of particles
   - (ii) Pure substances may be compounds or mixture
   - (iii) Pure substances have the same composition throughout
   - (iv) Pure substances can be exemplified by all elements other than nickel
   - (a) (i) and (ii)
   - (b) (ii) and (iii)
   - (c) (i) and (iii)
   - (d) (ii) and (iv)

7. Which of the following does not have a fixed melting point/boiling point?
   - (a) Ethanol
   - (b) Air
   - (c) Oxygen
   - (d) Gold

8. If 10 g of sodium hydroxide is dissolved in 150 g of water, then calculate the mass percent of sodium hydroxide in the solution _____.
   - (a) 8.2%
   - (b) 6.25%
   - (c) 5%
   - (d) 7.5%

9. Which of the following is homogeneous in nature?
   - (i) Ice
   - (ii) Wood
   - (iii) Soil
   - (iv) Air
   - (a) (i) and (ii)
   - (b) (i) and (iv)
   - (c) (ii) and (iii)
   - (d) (iii) and (iv)

10. If 110 g of copper sulphate is present in 550 g of solution, what will be the concentration of solution?
    - (a) 11%
    - (b) 20%
    - (c) 55%
    - (d) 22%

11. Milk of magnesia is _____.
    - (a) A true solution
    - (b) A colloid
    - (c) A suspension
    - (d) A homogeneous mixture

12. Which one of the following liquids will leave behind a residue on heating?
    - (a) Brine
    - (b) Mercury
    - (c) Bromine
    - (d) Alcohol

13. Which one of the following is most likely to exhibit Tyndall effect?
    - (a) Chalk powder and water mixture
    - (b) Potash alum and water mixture
    - (c) Sugar and water mixture
    - (d) Potassium permanganate and water mixture

14. Which one of the following is a solid foam _____.
    - (a) Ruby
    - (b) Shaving cream
    - (c) Bread
    - (d) Butter

15. Which one of the following will show the properties of electrophoresis?
    - (a) Hydrosols
    - (b) Carbondioxide
    - (c) Chalk in water
    - (d) Arseneous sulphide

16. Which of the following is not an emulsion?
    - (a) Butter
    - (b) Milk
    - (c) Shaving cream
    - (d) Face cream

17. One of the following represents the solution of solid in a solid. This one is _____.
    (a) Boron (b) Brass
    (c) Bread (d) Beryllium

18. Which one of the following is an aerosol?
    (a) Mist (b) Sugar solution
    (c) Egg yolk (d) Vapour

19. A solution is prepared by dissolving 80 g of salt in 500 g of water. Find the concentration of the solution.
    (a) 10% (b) 11%
    (c) 13.8% (d) 1.38%

20. Which of the following are physical changes?
    (i) Melting of iron metal
    (ii) Rusting of iron metal
    (iii) Bending of iron rod
    (iv) Drawing a wire of iron metal
    (a) (i), (ii) and (iii) (b) (i), (iii) and (iv)
    (c) (i), (ii) and (iv) (d) (ii), (iii) and (iv)

21. Tincture of iodine has antiseptic properties. This solution is made by dissolving _____.
    (a) Iodine in alcohol
    (b) Iodine in acetone
    (c) Iodine in water
    (d) Iodine in potassium iodide

22. A mixture of sulphur and carbon disulphide is _____.
    (a) Heterogeneous and shows tyndall effect
    (b) Heterogeneous and does not show tyndall effect
    (c) Heterogeneous and shows tyndall effect
    (d) Heterogeneous and does not show tyndall effect

23. Which of the following are chemical changes?
    (i) Decaying of wood
    (ii) Burning of wood
    (iii) Sawing of wood
    (iv) Hammering of nail into wood
    (a) (i) and (ii) (b) (ii) and (iii)
    (c) (i) and (iv) (d) (ii) and (iv)

24. A mixture of milk and ground oil can be separated by _____.
    (a) Sublimation
    (b) Separating funnel
    (c) Filtration
    (d) Evaporation

25. Which one of the following pair of gases cannot be separated by diffusion method?
    (a) CO_2 and NO_2 (b) CO_2 and N_2O_2
    (c) CO_2 and H_2 (d) CO_2 and N_2O

26. For removing the greasy spot from the shirt what method should we use?
    (a) Sublimation
    (b) Using suitable solvent
    (c) Evaporation
    (d) Solvent extraction

27. Naphthalene can be separated from sand _____.
    (a) By sublimation
    (b) By crystallisation
    (c) By distillation
    (d) Using suitable solvent

28. A solution contains 50 ml of alcohol mixed with 150 ml of water. Calculate the concentration of this solution _____.
    (a) 15% (b) 10%
    (c) 25% (d) 20%

29. Name the metal which is found in liquid form.
    (a) Antimony (b) Tin
    (c) Bromine (d) Mercury

30. The rusting of an iron object is called _____.
    (a) Corrosion and it is a chemical change
    (b) Corrosion and it is a physical as well as chemical change
    (c) Dissolution and it is a chemical change
    (d) Dissolution and it is a physical change

31. Which of the following mixtures cannot be separated by using water as the solvent?
    (a) Sand and sulphur
    (b) Sugar and sand
    (c) Copper sulphate and sand
    (d) Sand and potash alum

32. The best way to recover sugar from an aqueous sugar solution is ———.
    (a) Evaporation to dryness
    (b) Distillation
    (c) Filtration
    (d) Crystallisation
33. Which of the following cannot be separated from air by the process of fractional distillation?
    (a) Hydrogen   (b) Oxygen
    (c) Argon   (d) Nitrogen
34. When a mixture of iron powder and sulphur powder is heated strongly to form iron sulphide, then heat energy is ———.
    (a) Absorbed
    (b) Released
    (c) First absorbed and then released
    (d) Neither absorbed nor released
35. Which one of the following scrap metal cannot be separated by magnetic separation?
    (a) Cobalt   (b) Chromium
    (c) Steel   (d) Nickel

HOTS

1. Which of the following is not false?
   (i) Compounds are homogeneous substance.
   (ii) The composition of a compound is fixed, the constituents are present in a fixed proportion by mass.
   (iii) A compound cannot be separated into its components by physical methods.
   (a) Only (i)
   (b) (i) and (ii)
   (c) (i), (ii) and (iii)
   (d) None of these

2. Technical names of some colloids are given under column I whereas the dispersion media are under column II. Match column I with column II and choose the correct option.

   Column I   Column II
   (a) Aerosol   (i) Solid
   (b) Emulsion   (ii) Liquid
   (c) Solid Foam   (iii) Gas

   (a) (a) (i), (b) (ii), (c) (iii)
   (b) (a) (ii), (b) (iii), (c) (i)
   (c) (a) (iii), (b) (ii), (c) (i)
   (d) (a) (i), (b) (iii), (c) (ii)

3. The empirical formula of a compound is CH_2O. Its molecular weight is 90. The molecular formula of the compound is (Atomic weight of C = 12, H = 1, and O = 16)?
   (a) $C_3H_7O_3$ (b) $C_3H_6O_3$
   (c) $C_3H_4O_7$ (d) $C_2H_4O_2$

Direction (4–5): The figure given below is showing separation of ammonium chloride and salt by sublimation. Referring to this diagram, answer the questions given below:

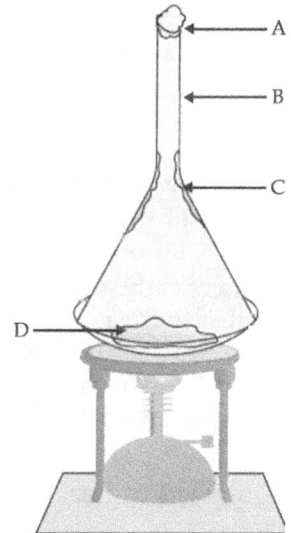

4. Which of the following is the mixture of ammonium chloride and salt?
   (a) A   (b) B
   (c) C   (d) D

5. Which of the following is showing the solidified ammonium chloride after separation?
   (a) A   (b) B
   (c) C   (d) D

SUBJECTIVE QUESTIONS

1. Explain why, air is considered a mixture and not a compound.

Ans.

Air is considered a mixture because of the following reasons:

(i) Air can be separated into its constituents like oxygen, nitrogen, etc. by the physical process of fractional distillation (of liquid air).

(ii) Air shows the properties of all the gases present in it. For example, oxygen supports combustion and air also supports combustion; carbon dioxide turns lime water milky and air also turns lime water milky though very, very slowly.

(iii) Heat and light etc. are neither given out nor absorbed when air is prepared by mixing the required properties of oxygen, nitrogen, carbon dioxide, argon, water vapour, etc.

(iv) Air has a variable composition because air at different places contains different amounts of the various gases. It does not have a definite formula.

2. About 640 ml of carbon monoxide is mixed with 800 ml of oxygen and ignited in an enclosed vessel. Calculate the total volume of gases after the burning is completed. All volumes are measured at S.T.P.

Ans.

The chemical reaction actually taking place is:
$2CO + O_2 \rightarrow 2CO_2$
2   :   1   2
640 mL   320 mL   640 ml

Volume of O_2 used = 320 ml

Volume of O_2 left = 800 – 320 = 480 ml

Volume of CO_2 formed = 640 ml

Therefore the total volume of gases after burning is
480 + 640 = 1120 ml

3. In an experiment, 1.288 g of copper oxide was obtained from 1.03 g of copper. In another experiment, 3.672 g of copper oxide gave, on reduction, 2.938 g of copper. Show that these figures, verify the law of constant proportions.

Ans.

Here we have to calculate the ratio (or proportion) of copper and oxygen in two samples of copper oxide compound. Now,

(a) In the first experiment:
Mass of copper = 1.03 g
And, mass of copper oxide = 1.288 g
So, mass of oxygen = Mass of copper oxide – Mass of copper
= 1.288 × 1.03
= 0.258 g

Now, in the first sample of copper oxide formed:
Mass of copper : Mass of oxygen
= 1.03 : 0.258
$= \dfrac{1.03}{0.258} : 1$
= 3.99 : 1 = 4 : 1

(b) In the second experiment:
Mass of copper = 2.938 g
And, mass of copper oxide = 3.672 g
So, mass of oxygen = Mass of copper oxide – Mass of copper
= 3.672 – 2.938
= 0.734 g

Now, in the second sample of copper oxide compound
Mass of copper : Mass of oxygen
= 2.938 : 0.734
$= \dfrac{2.938}{0.734} : 1 = 4 : 1$

From the above calculations, we can see that the ratio (or proportion) of copper and oxygen elements in the two samples of copper oxide compound is the same 4 : 1. So, the given figures verify the law of constant proportions.

4. Why is mixture called impure substance?

Ans.

Mixture consist of different components which retain their properties and can be easily separated by physical processes, hence it is called as impure substance.

5. Give the differences between mixture and compound.

Ans.

Mixture	Compound
Impure matter.	Pure matter.
Constituents combine in faxed ratio to form a compound.	Constituents combine in fixed ratio to form a compound.
Constituents retain their properties.	Constituents do not retain their properties as a new substance is formed.
Constituents can be separated by physical processes.	Constituents cannot be separated by physical processes.

6. Distinguish between a physical change and chemical change.

Ans.

Physical Change	Chemical Change
No new substance is formed.	New substance is formed.
It is a reversible change.	It is irreversible change.
The properties of constituents are retained.	The properties of constituents are not retained.
No new substance is formed.	Completely new substance is formed.

7. State the properties of a solution.

Ans.

Properties of a solution are:
- A solution is a homogeneous mixture.
- Particles of a solution are smaller than 1 nm and cannot be seen by naked eyes.
- Do not scatter beam of light.
- Solute particles cannot be separated from the mixture by the process of filtration and thus, solution is stable.

8. State the properties of a suspension.

Ans.

Properties of a suspension:
- Suspension is a heterogeneous mixture having particle size greater than 100 nm.
- The particles of a suspension can be seen by naked eyes.
- Particles can scatter a beam of light.
- It is unstable.

9. State the properties of colloidal solution.

Ans.

Properties of colloidal solution:
- It is a heterogeneous mixture having particle size between 1 nm to 100 nm.
- Size of particles is very small, cannot be seen with naked eyes.
- It scatters a beam of light.
- They are stable as the particles do not settle when left undisturbed.

10. Give the applications of centrifugation.

Ans.

Application of centrifugation are:
- Used in diagnostic laboratories for blood and urine test.
- Used in dairies and home to separate butter from cream.
- Used in a washing machines to squeeze out water from wet clothes.

11. Give the applications of chromatography.

Ans.

Applications of chromatography are:
- To separate colours in a dye.
- To separate pigments from natural colours.
- To separate drugs from blood.

12. **Why is air considered as a mixture and not compound?**

Ans.

Air is considered as a mixture because it exhibits following properties:
  i. Each component present in air retains its properties.
  ii. Each component can be separated by simple physical processes.
  iii. The components do not have any fixed proportion. All gases are present in different amount. Example, in greener area — more oxygen and water vapour is present; near industrial area — air consists of lot of impurities and smoke suspended in it.

13. **How can you prove that water is a compound?**

Ans.

Water is a compound because if we pass electricity through it then at two different electrodes, we get two different gases i.e., oxygen and hydrogen during electrolysis of water. The ratio of oxygen: hydrogen is 1 : 2 by number of molecules.
  i. The properties of oxygen and hydrogen gases sire entirely different from that of liquid water.
  ii. The ratio of oxygen: hydrogen combination is always constant i.e., 1: 2 by volume.
  iii. To separate the components of water, we need electrolytic cell, and it is not a simple process.

14. Classify each of the following, as a physical or a chemical change. Give reasons.

(a) Drying of a shirt in the sun.

Ans.

Drying of shirt in the sun is a physical change. Since in this change no new substance is formed.

(b) Rising of hot air over a radiator.

Ans.

Since, in rising of hot air over a radiator no new substance is formed, hence it is a physical change.

(c) Burning of kerosene in a lantern.

Ans.

While burning of kerosene in a lantern carbon dioxide, and water vapour is formed, hence it is a chemical change.

(d) Change in the colour of black tea on adding lemon juice to it.

Ans.

In this change a new substance is formed, hence it is a chemical change.

(e) Churning of milk cream to get butter.

Ans.

While churning of milk cream to get butter, no new substance is formed, hence it is a physical change.

15. (a) Define solution.
    (b) Give different types of solutions with one example each.

Ans.

(a) Solution: It is a homogeneous mixture of two or more substances. It consists of solute and solvent.

(b) Different types of solution:
   (i) Based on solvent: Aqueous and Non-aqueous. Aqueous solution has water as solvent. Example, (sugar + water). Non-aqueous solution has some other solvent but not water. Example, (sulphur + carbon disulphide).
   (ii) Depending on the amount of solute dissolved in solvent: Dilute solution and Concentrated solution.

   Dilute solution: Less amount of solute particles are present in a solvent.

Concentrated solution: Amount of solute present in its maximum capacity in a solvent.

(iii) Amount of solute present in its maximum capacity at a given temperature: Saturated and Unsaturated solution.

Saturated solution: It is a solution in which no more solute can further dissolve in a given solvent at a given temperature.

Unsaturated solution: It is a solution in which some more solute can dissolve in a solvent at a given temperature.

(iv) Depending on the size of solute particles.

True solution size is very small and particles cannot be seen through naked eyes.

Suspension size is very big and can be seen through naked eyes.

Colloid size is intermediate between true solution and suspension.

Atoms and Molecules

Learning Objectives : In this chapter, students will learn about:
- the laws of chemical combination
- Dalton's Atomic Theory
- the concept of molecules and chemical formulae
- molecular mass
- the concept of mole

CHAPTER SUMMARY

All matter is made up of small particles called atoms and molecules. Different kinds of atoms and molecules have different properties due to which different kinds of matter also show different properties. All this was based on philosophical consideration and not much experimental work to validate these ideas could be done till the eighteenth century.

By the end of the eighteenth century. **Antoine L. Lavoisier** established two important laws of chemical combination.

Laws of Chemical Combination

There are four important laws of chemical combination.

These are:
(i) Law of conservation of mass
(ii) Law of constant proportion
(iii) Law of multiple proportion
(iv) Gay Lussac's law

Law of Conservation of Mass

According to this law, matter is neither created nor destroyed in a chemical reaction. Thus, 'The law of conservation of mass states that in a chemical reaction the total mass of products is equal to the total mass of reactants'. There is no change in mass during a chemical reaction.

For example:

$$CaCO_3 \xrightarrow{Heat} CaO + CO_2$$
Calcium carbonate Calcium oxide Carbon dioxide
(100 g) (56 g) (44 g)

In this example, calcium carbonate is the reactant and it has a mass of 100 g. Calcium oxide and carbon dioxide are the products and they have a total mass of 56 g + 44 g = 100 g.

Now, since the total mass of products (100 g) is equal to the total mass of reactants (100 g), there is no change of mass during this chemical reaction. So, this example supports the law of conservation of mass.

Question: Calcium carbonate decomposes, on heating, to form calcium oxide and carbon dioxide. When 10 g of calcium carbonate is decomposed completely, then 5.6 g of calcium oxide is formed. Calculate the mass of carbon dioxide formed.

Sol.
$$CaCO_3 \xrightarrow{heat} CaO + CO_2$$
10 g 5.6 g ?

According to law of conservation of mass
  Mass of products = Mass of reactants
Or Mass of CaO + Mass of CO_2 = Mass of $CaCO_3$
  5.6 + mass of CO_2 = 10
  Mass of CO_2 = 10 − 5.6
  Mass of CO_2 = 4.4g

Law of Constant Proportion

This law was given by Proust in 1779. According to this law "A chemical compound always consists of the same elements combined together in the same proportion by mass".

For example:
(i) **Water (H_2O) is a compound** which always consists of the same two elements, hydrogen

and oxygen, combined together in the same constant proportion of 1 : 8 by mass.

(ii) **Ammonia (NH_3) is a compound.** It has been found by analysis that ammonia always consists of the same two elements, nitrogen and hydrogen combined together in the same ratio of 14 : 3 by mass.

Question: In an experiment, 1.288 g of copper oxide was obtained from 1.03 g of copper. In another experiment, 3.672 g of copper oxide gave, on reduction, 2.938 of copper. Show that these figures verify the law of constant proportion.

Sol.
To solve this problem we have to calculate the ratio (or proportion) of copper and oxygen in the two samples of copper oxide compound. Now
(a) In the first experiment
  Mass of copper = 1.03 g
  Mass of copper oxide = 1.288 g
  So, mass of oxygen = mass of copper oxide – mass of copper
    = 1.288 – 1.03
    = 0.258 g
  Now, in the first sample of copper oxide is a compound
  Mass of copper : mass of oxygen = 1.03 : 0.258
    $= \frac{1.03}{0.258} : 1$
    = 3.99 : 1
    = 4 : 1
(b) In the second experiment
  Mass of copper = 2.938 g
  Mass of copper oxide = 3.672 g
  So, mass of oxygen = mass of copper oxide – mass of copper
    = 3.672 – 2.938
    = 0.734 g
  Now in the second sample of copper oxide compound
  Mass of copper : mass of oxygen = 2.938 : 0.734
    $= \frac{2.938}{0.734} : 1$
    = 4 : 1

From the above calculation it has been proved that ratio of copper and oxygen elements in the two samples of copper oxide compound is the same, i.e. 4 : 1. So, the given figures verify the law of constant proportions.

Law of Multiple Proportion

This law states that ' if two elements form more than one compound between them, then the ratio of the masses of the two elements which combine with a fixed mass of the first element, will be in the ratio of smallest whole number.'

For example: Considering carbon monooxide and carbon dioxide : CO and CO_2, 100 grams of carbon may react with 133 grams of oxygen to produce carbon monoxide, or with 266 grams of oxygen to produce carbon dioxide. The ratio of the masses of oxygen that can react with 100 grams of carbon is 266 : 133, which is equal to 2 : 1, a ratio of small whole numbers.

Gay Lussac's Law

The ratio between the volume of the reactant gases and the products can be expressed in simple whole numbers.

This law can also be expressed as the pressure of a sample of gas at constant volume is directly proportional to its temperature in kelivn.

i.e., $\left[\frac{P_1}{T_1} = \text{constant}\right]$

or $\left[\frac{P_1}{T_1} = \frac{P_2}{T_2}\right]$

Dalton's Atomic Theory

The theory states that 'all matter is made up of very small indivisible particles called **atoms**.' Dalton put his atomic theory of matter in 1808. The various assumption of Dalton's atomic theory of matter are as follows:

(i) All matter is made up of smallest particles called atoms.
(ii) Atoms are indivisible and can neither be created, nor be destroyed.
(iii) Atoms of some elements are identical in shape, size and mass.
(iv) Atoms of different elements have different mass and chemical properties.
(v) Atoms always combine together in fixed proportion by mass to form the compound.
(vi) In a given compound the relative number and kinds of atoms are constant.

Atoms and Molecules

Merits of Dalton's Atomic Theory
(i) It can easily explain the reason for the validity of law of conservation of mass.
(ii) It also explain the laws of constant proportion.
(iii) It can also explain the difference between the atoms of elements and that of compound.

Demerits of Dalton's Atomic Theory
(i) According to Dalton's atomic theory atoms are indivisible, but under special circumstances, atoms can further be divided into still smaller particles called electrons, protons and neutrons.
(ii) This theory states that atoms of some elements are similar in shape and properties. But it is not so, as the occurrence of isotopes prove that.
(iii) This theory says that atoms of different elements have different mass, but occurrence of isobars proves that it is not so.
(iv) It also fails to explain why the atoms are together in a compound and what binding force is responsible for this.
(v) It also fails to explain Gay Lussac's law.

Atoms
Just as all the houses are made up of bricks, in the same way, all the matter is made up of atoms. Thus, atoms are the building blocks of all the matter around us. Therefore, 'an **atom** is the smallest particle of an element that can take part in a chemical reaction.' Since the atoms of elements are quite reactive, they do not exist in free state, except for noble gases. All the atoms consist of subatomic particles called electron, proton and neutron. The number of electrons and protons in an atom is always found to be the same. The electron revolves around the nucleus in a fixed orbit and the proton and the neutron are present in the nucleus of an atom.

The atoms are very small in size and cannot be seen by naked eyes. The size of an atom is indicated by its radius which is called '**atomic radius**'. Atomic radius is measured in 'nanometres' (nm)

$$1 \text{ nanometre} = \frac{1}{10^9} \text{ metre}$$

or $$1 \text{ nm} = \frac{1}{10^9} \text{ m}$$

or $$1 \text{ nm} = 10^{-9} \text{ m}$$

The radius of smallest atom, 'Hydrogen' is 0.37×10^{-10} or 0.037 nm

Symbols of Elements
The atoms are normally denoted by symbols. Dalton was the first scientist to use the symbols to represent elements in short. Some of the symbols of elements given by Dalton are shown below:

Elements	Dalton's Symbol	Elements	Dalton's Symbol
Hydrogen	⊙	Iron	Ⓘ
Carbon	●	Copper	Ⓒ
Oxygen	○	Silver	Ⓢ
Phosphorus	⊕	Gold	Ⓖ
Sulphur	⊕	Lead	Ⓛ
Platinum	Ⓟ	Mercury	⊛

Now-a-days, IUPAC (International Union of Pure and Applied Chemistry) approves names of elements. Many of the symbols are the first one or two letters of the element's name in English. The first letter of a symbol is always written as a capital letter and the second letter as a small.

TRIVIA
The largest tsunami ever recorded occurred in Lituya Bay, Alaska in 1958.

Modern Symbol of Elements:

Element	Symbol	Atomic No.	Mass No.
Hydrogen	H	1	1
Helium	He	2	4
Lithium	Li	3	7
Beryllium	Be	4	9
Boron	B	5	11
Carbon	C	6	12
Nitrogen	N	7	14
Oxygen	O	8	16
Fluorine	F	9	19
Neon	Ne	10	20
Sodium	Na	11	23
Magnesium	Mg	12	24
Aluminium	Al	13	27
Silicon	Si	14	28
Phosphorus	P	15	31
Sulphur	S	16	32
Chlorine	Cl	17	35
Argon	Ar	18	38
Potassium (Kelium)	K	19	39
Calcium	Ca	20	40
Iron (ferrum)	Fe	26	56
Copper (Cuprum)	Cu	29	64
Silver (Argentum)	Ag	47	108
Lead (plumbum)	Pb	82	207

Atomic Mass: Atomic mass is defined as the quantity mass equal to one twelfth of the mass of an atom of carbon-12 [Atomic mass unit = $\frac{1}{12}$ the mass of a carbon-12 atom, $1\mu = \frac{1}{12}$ the mass of a carbon-12 atom]

Relative atomic mass: It is defined as the number of times an element of an atom is heavier than one twelfth of an atom of carbon-12.

Relative atomic mass = $\dfrac{\text{mass of one atom the element}}{\frac{1}{12} \text{ mass of one atom of C-12}}$

Atoms and Molecules

Gram atomic mass: The atomic mass of an element expressed in grams is called the gram atomic mass of that element. It is denoted as a.m.u or u.

$$1u = 1.6605 \times 10^{-24} \text{ g}$$

Atomic masses of some common elements

Element	Symbol	Atomic mass
1. Hydrogen	H	1u
2. Carbon	C	12u
3. Nitrogen	N	14u
4. Oxygen	O	16u
5. Sodium	Na	23u
6. Magnesium	Mg	24u
7. Aluminium	Al	27u
8. Phosphorus	P	31u
9. Sulphur	S	32u
10. Chlorine	Cl	35.5u
11. Potassium	K	39u
12. Calcium	Ca	40u
13. Iron	Fe	56u
14. Copper	Cu	63.5u

How do atoms exist: The atoms of only a few elements called noble gases (He, Ne, Ar, and Kr) are chemically inactive and exist in the free state (as single atoms). Atoms of most of the elements are chemically very reactive and do not exist in the free state (as single atom) usually atoms exist in two form: (i) ions and (ii) molecules.

These molecules or ions aggregate in large numbers to form the matter that we can see, feel or touch.

Molecules

'A **molecule** is the smallest particle of a substance (element or compound) which has the properties of that substance and can exist in the free state.'

Molecules can be formed either by the combination of atoms of the 'same element', called molecules of elements or of different elements, called molecules of compounds

Molecules of Elements

The molecule of an element contains two or more similar atoms chemically combined together.

For example: H_2, Br_2, Cl_2, O_2

The number of atoms present in one molecule of an element is called its atomicity.

For example:

Atomicity of O_2 is 2 and that of CO_2 is 3.

The molecules having only one kind of atoms are called monoatomic molecules such as He, Ne, Ar.

The molecules containing two atoms are called diatomic molecules, such as O_2, H_2, Cl_2.

The molecules containing three atoms are called triatomic molecules such as CO_2, O_3, H_2O, NO_2.

The molecules containing four atoms are called tetra atomic molecules such as H_2O_2, NH_3, P_4.

The molecules containing five atoms are called pentatomic molecules, such as HNO_3, CH_4.

Molecules of Compounds

The molecules of a compound contains two or more different types of atoms chemically combined together.

For example: Hydrogen Chloride is a compound. The molecule of hydrogen Chloride (HCl) contains two different types of atoms: hydrogen atom (H) and Chlorine atom (Cl), water is a compound. A molecule of water (H_2O) is made up of two different types of atoms : hydrogen atoms (H) and oxygen atom (O).

Ions and Valency

An ion is formed by gaining or losing electrons. If an element loses electrons it forms positive ions called **cations** if an element gains electron, then it forms negative ions called **anions**.

Valency is defined as the number of electrons lost or gained to attain the stable electronic configuration of an atom.

Names and symbols of some ions

Valency	Name of Cation	Symbol	Name of Anions	Symbol
1.	**Monovalent**		**Monovalent**	
	Hydrogen	H^+	Chloride	Cl^-
	Sodium	Na^+	Bromide	Br^-
	Potassium	K^+	Iodide	I^-
	Silver	Ag^+	Hydride	H^-
	Cuprous	Cu^+	Fluoride	F^-
	Ammonium	NH_4^+	Hydroxide	OH^-
			Nitrate	NO_3^-
			Nitrite	NO_2^-
			Acetate	CH_3COO^-
2.	**Divalent Cations**		**Divalent Anions**	
	Calcium	Ca^{2+}	Oxide	O^{2-}
	Barium	Ba^{2+}	Sulphide	S^{2-}
	Cupric	Cu^{2+}	Carbonate	CO_3^{2-}
	Cadmium	Cd^{2+}	Sulphate	SO_4^{2-}
	Magnesium	Mg^{2+}	Sulphite	SO_3^{2-}
	Ferrous	Fe^{2+}		
3.	**Trivalent Cations**		**Trivalent Anions**	
	Aluminium	Al^{3+}	Phosphate	PO_4^{3-}
	Ferric	Fe^{3+}	Borate	BO_3^{3-}
	Chromic	Cr^{3+}	Nitrite	N^{3-}

Chemical Formulae

'A chemical formula represents the composition of a molecule of the substance in terms of the symbols of the elements present in the molecule.' A chemical formula is also known as **molecular formula**.

While writing the chemical formula, following rules are implemented:

(i) The valencies or charges on the ion must be balanced.

(ii) When a compound consists of a metal and a non-metal, the name or symbol of the metal is written first. For example, calcium oxide (CaO), sodium chloride (NaCl), copper oxide (CuO).

(iii) In compound formed with polyatomic ions, the ion is enclosed in a bracket before writing the number to indicate the ratio. In case the number of polyatomic ion is one, the bracket is not required. For example, NaOH. While writing the chemical formulae for compounds, We write the constituent elements and their valencies as shown.

Examples:

(i) Formula for hydrogen sulphide
 Symbol   H   S
 Valence   1   2
 Formula: H_2S

(ii) Formula for aluminium oxide
 Symbol   Al   O
 Charge   3+   2-
 Formula: Al_2O_3

(iii) Formula of magnesium hydroxide
 Symbol   Mg   OH
 Charge   2+   1-
 Formula: Mg $(OH)_2$

Atoms and Molecules

Molecular Mass

The molecular mass of a substance is defined as the sum of atomic masses of all the atoms present in the substance.

For example:

The molecular mass of H_2SO_4

= Mass of 2H + Mass of S + Mass of 4O
   atoms   atom   atoms

= 2 × 1 + 32 + 4 × 16

= 2 + 32 + 64 = 98 u

Gram Molecular Mass

The molecular mass of the substance expressed in grams is called the **gram molecular mass**.

Mole Concept

A mole is a unit for expressing the smallest unit of matter such as proton, electron, atoms, ions, etc. The number of atoms present in one gram atom of an element is equal to the 6.023×10^{23}. Thus one mole of a substance is equal to 6.023×10^{23} atoms. This is also called the **Avogadro's constant** or **Avogadro's number**. Therefore mole is 'the amount of substance which contains some number of particles as the number of carbons atoms present in 12 g of C–12 isotopes of carbon.'

Thus, 1 mole = gram atomic mass of atom

= 6.022×10^{23} atoms of the substance

For example:

1. How many moles are 9.033×10^{24} atoms of helium [He]?

Sol.

We know that,

6.022×10^{23} atoms of helium = 1 mole

So, 9.033×10^{24} atoms of helium =

$\dfrac{1}{6.022 \times 10^{23}} \times 9.033 \times 10^{23} = 15$ moles

Thus 9.033×10^{24} atoms of helium are 15 moles of atoms.

2. Calculate the number of iron atoms in a piece of iron weighing 2.8 g (atomic mass of iron = 56 u)

Sol.

1 mole of iron = gram atomic mass of iron

= 56 grams

∵ 56 g of iron contains = 6.022×10^{23} atoms

∴ 2.8 g of iron contains = $\dfrac{6.022 \times 10^{23}}{56} \times 2.8$

$= \dfrac{6.022 \times 10^{22}}{2}$

$= 3.011 \times 10^{22}$ atoms

Thus, a piece of iron metal having a mass of 2.8 grams contain 3.011×10^{22} atoms of iron.

3. What is the number of molecules in 0.25 moles of oxygen?

Sol.

We know that,

1 mole of oxygen contains

= 6.022×10^{23} molecules

0.25 mole of oxygen contains

= $6.022 \times 10^{23} \times 0.25$

= 1.505×10^{23} molecules

Thus, 0.25 mole of oxygen contains 1.505×10^{23} molecules.

Formula Unit Mass

The formula unit mass of a substance is the sum of atomic masses of all atoms in a formula unit of a compound. The only difference is that we use the word formula unit for those substances whose constituent particles are ions.

For example:

(i) Sodium chloride (NaCl) = 1 × 23 + 35.5

= 58.5u

(ii) Calcium chloride ($CaCl_2$)

= Atomic mass of Ca + (2 × atomic mass of Cl)

= 40 + 2 × 35.5 = 40 + 71

= 111u

MUST REMEMBER

- The ratio between the volume of the reactant gases and the products can be expressed in simple whole numbers.
- The atoms are very small in size and cannot be seen by naked eyes.
- The atomic mass of an element expressed in grams is called the gram atomic mass of that element.
- An ion is formed by gaining or losing electrons. If an element loses electrons it forms positive ions called cations if an element gains electron, then it forms negative ions called anions.
- A chemical formula represents the composition of a molecule of the substance in terms of the symbols of the elements present in the molecule.
- The molecular mass of a substance is defined as the sum of atomic masses of all the atoms present in the substance.
- The molecular mass of the substance expressed in grams is called the gram molecular mass.
- The formula unit mass of a substance is the sum of atomic masses of all atoms in a formula unit of a compound.

MULTIPLE CHOICE QUESTIONS

1. Certain mass of carbon burns with a given mass of oxygen to form certain mass of carbon dioxide, which law of chemical combinations is used in this process of formation of compound?
   (a) Law of conservation of mass
   (b) Law of constant proportion
   (c) Law of multiple proportion
   (d) Gay Lussac's law

2. The atomic theory of matter was proposed by _____.
   (a) Lavoisier (b) Proust
   (c) John Dalton (d) John Kennedy

3. Which postulates of Dalton's atomic theory gives laws of conservation of mass?
   (a) Atom can neither be created nor be destroyed
   (b) Atoms of same elements are similar
   (c) Atoms of different elements are different
   (d) Atom combine in fixed ratio to form compound

4. The atoms of which of the following pairs of elements are most likely to exist in free state?
   (a) Hydrogen and helium
   (b) Helium and neon
   (c) Argon and carbon
   (d) Neon and nitrogen

5. Which of the following elements has the same molecular mass as its atomic mass?
   (a) Nitrogen (b) Oxygen
   (c) Neon (d) Chlorine

6. In water, hydrogen and oxygen are present in the ratio of _____.
   (a) 1 : 2 (b) 1 : 8
   (c) 2 : 12 (d) 2 : 3

7. What is the mass of 0.2 mole of lead nitrate? (N = 14, O = 16, Pb = 207)
   (a) 33.1 g (b) 3.31 g
   (c) 66.2 g (d) 6.62 g

8. Find the total percentage of oxygen in magnesium nitrate crystal i.e., $Mg(NO_3)_2 \cdot 6H_2O$ (Atomic weight: H = 1, N = 14, O = 16, Mg = 24)
   (a) 60% (b) 65%
   (c) 70% (d) 75%

9. Kalium is the Latin name of _____.
   (a) Krypton (b) Potassium
   (c) Calcium (d) Phosphorus

10. The atomic number of an element X is 13. What will be the number of electrons in its ion X^{3+}?
    (a) 11 (b) 16
    (c) 15 (d) 10

11. The anion of an element has _____.
    (a) Less electrons than the normal atom
    (b) More electrons than the normal atom
    (c) More protons than the normal atom
    (d) Same number of electrons as normal atom

12. The smallest particle of a substance that is capable of independent existence is _____.
    (a) Electron (b) Proton
    (c) Atom (d) Molecule

13. If the number of electrons in an ion Z^{3-} is 10, the atomic number of element Z will be _____.
    (a) 7 (b) 5
    (c) 10 (d) 8

14. How many litres of ammonia are present in 3.4 kg of it? (N = 14, H = 1)?
    (a) 22.4 litres (b) 44.8 litres
    (c) 4480 litres (d) 2240 litres

15. Two elements X and Y have valencies of 5 and 3, & 3 and 2, respectively. The elements X and Y are most likely to be _____ respectively.
    (a) Sulphur and iron
    (b) Nitrogen and iron
    (c) Phosphorus and nitrogen
    (d) Copper and sulphur

16. The cation of an element has _____.
    (a) Less electrons than a neutral atom
    (b) Less protons than a neutral atom
    (c) More electrons than a neutral atom
    (d) The same number of electrons as its neutral atom

17. A particle P has 18 electrons, 20 neutrons and 19 protons. This particle must be _____.
    (a) A molecule
    (b) A cation
    (c) An anion
    (d) A binary compound

18. Molecular compounds are usually formed by combination between _____.
    (a) Two different metals
    (b) Two different non-metals
    (c) Two gaseous elements
    (d) A metal and a non-metal

19. The formula of a compound is X_3Y. The valencies of elements X and Y will be, _____ respectively.
    (a) 1 and 3
    (b) 3 and 1
    (c) 2 and 3
    (d) 3 and 2

20. What will be the mass of 1 mole of $FeSO_4 \cdot 7H_2O$?
    (a) 585 g
    (b) 278 g
    (c) 287 g
    (d) 270 g

21. What will be the formula mass of $CaCl_2$ (Ca = 40, Cl = 3.5)?
    (a) 99 amu
    (b) 100 amu
    (c) 111 amu
    (d) 122 amu

22. The mass of a single atom of an element Z is 2.65×10^{-23} g. What is its gram atomic mass?
    (a) 1.569 g
    (b) 15.69 g
    (c) 156.9 g
    (d) 15.69 mg

23. In $_8O^{16}$, the number 16 stands for _____.
    (a) Atomic number
    (b) Atomic mass
    (c) Atomic mass scale
    (d) Number of electrons

24. All samples of carbon dioxide contain carbon and oxygen in the mass ratio of 3 : 8. This is in agreement with the law of _____.
    (a) Conservation of mass
    (b) Constant proportion
    (c) Multiple proportion
    (d) Reciprocal proportion

25. The best standard for atomic mass is _____.
    (a) O – 16
    (b) S – 32
    (c) C – 12
    (d) H – 1

26. Modern atomic symbol was proposed by _____.
    (a) Berzelius
    (b) Dalton
    (c) Bohr
    (d) A. Lavosier

27. How many moles are present in 12.044×10^{22} molecules of sulphur dioxide?
    (a) 0.1 mole
    (b) 0.2 mole
    (c) 0.3 mole
    (d) 0.4 mole

28. A compound has the following percentage composition (H=2.04%, S=32.65%, O=65.31%). Relative molecular mass of compound = 98. What will be its molecular formula (H = 1, S = 32, O = 16)?
    (a) HSO_4
    (b) $H(SP_4)_2$
    (c) $H_2(SO_4)_3$
    (d) H_2SO_4

29. The symbol of a metal element which is used in making thermometers is _____.
    (a) Mg
    (b) Sg
    (c) Hg
    (d) Ag

30. What will be the atoms in 0.2 mole of sodium (Na)?
    (a) 12.044×10^{22} atoms
    (b) 6.022×10^{23} atoms
    (c) 12.044×10^{23} atoms
    (d) 1.2044×10^{22} atoms

31. The mass of a single atom of an element X is 2.65×10^{-23} g. What is its atomic mass?
    (a) 16u
    (b) 32u
    (c) 48u
    (d) 64u

32. The molar mass of HNO_3 will be _____.
    (a) 31 g
    (b) 63 g
    (c) 36 g
    (d) 64 g

Atoms and Molecules

33. The reaction between aluminium carbide and water takes place according to the following equation _____.
$Al_4C_3 + 12H_2O \rightarrow 3CH_4 + 4Al(OH)_3$
The volume of CH_4 released from 14.4 g of Al_4C_3 by excess water at S.T.P. will be _____.
    (a) 3.36 litres   (b) 67.2 litres
    (c) 6.72 litres   (d) 33.6 litres

34. A compound of sodium, sulphur and oxygen has the following percentage composition. Na = 29.11%, S = 4051%, O = 30.38%. What will be its emprical formula?
    (a) NaSO   (b) Na_2SO
    (c) NaS_2O_3 (d) $Na_2S_2O_3$

35. Which of the following is a correct statement:
    (a) Na_2S is sodium sulphide, Na_2SO_3 is sodium sulphite, Na_2SO_4 is sodium sulphate
    (b) Na_2S is sodium sulphite, Na_2SO_3 is sodium sulphide, Na_2SO_4 is sodium sulphate
    (c) Na_2S is sodium sulphide, Na_2SO_3 is sodium sulphate, Na_2SO_4 is sodium sulphite
    (d) Na_2S is sodium sulphite, Na_2SO_3 is sodium sulphite, Na_2SO_4 is sodium sulphide

HOTS

1. Which of the following is/are true?
    (i) The chemical formula of a molecular compound is determined by atomic number of each element.
    (ii) An atom is the smallest particle of elements.
    (iii) Molecules are the smallest particle of the substance, element or compound which can exist in free state under ordinary condition.
    (a) Only (i)
    (b) (i) and (ii)
    (c) (ii) and (iii)
    (d) (i), (ii) and (iii)

2. The weight of 0.885 moles of $Mg(NO_3)_2$ is _____.
    (a) 131 g   (b) 13.1 g
    (c) 85.5 g   (d) 1.31 g

3. Eutrophication is the process in which dissolved oxygen in water is reduced due to excessive growth of algae. This is the result of _____.
    (a) Change in temperature of water
    (b) Extra loading of nutrients in water body
    (c) Stratification of aquatic habitat
    (d) Bioaccumulation in algae

4. Find the number of iron atoms in a piece of iron weighing 2.8 g (Atomic mass of iron = 56).
    (a) 3.011×10^{22} atoms
    (b) 3.11×10^{23} atoms
    (c) 3.10×10^{23} atoms
    (d) 30.1×10^{21} atoms

5. Bohr's model can explain _____.
    (a) Spectrum of hydrogen molecule
    (b) Spectrum of hydrogen atom
    (c) Spectrum of any atom or ion having one electron only
    (d) Solar spectrum

SUBJECTIVE QUESTIONS

1. Define valency and give the valency for the following elements:

   Magnesium, Aluminium, Chlorine and Copper.

Ans.

Valency: The combining capacity of an element is called its valency. Valency of the following elements:

Magnesium – 2

Aluminium – 3

Chlorine – 1

Copper – 2

2. What is formula unit mass? How is it different from molecular mass?

Ans.

The formula unit mass of a substance is a sum of the atomic masses of all atoms in a formula unit of a compound. The constituent particles of formula unit mass are ions and the constituent particles of molecular mass are atoms.

3. Find the number of moles in the following:
   (i) 50 g of H_2O
   (ii) 7 g of Na

Ans.

(i) Molar mass of H_2O = 18 g
   Given mass of H_2O = 50 g
   ∴ No. of moles in 50 g of H_2O = 58/18 = 2.78 moles.

(ii) Molar mass of Na = 23 g
   Given mass of Na = 7 g
   ∴ No. of moles in 50 g of H_2O = 7/23 = 0.304 moles.

4. Find the number of atoms in the following:
   (i) 0.5 mole of C atom
   (ii) 2 mole of N atom

Ans.

(i) 0.5 mole of C atom:
   Number of atoms in 1 mole of C atom = 6.022×10^{23} atoms

   Number of atoms in 0.5 mole of C atom = $6.022 \times 10^{23} \times 0.5$
   $= 3.011 \times 10^{23}$ atoms

(ii) 2 mole of N atom:
   Number of atoms in 1 mole of N atom = 6.022×10^{23} atoms
   Number of atoms in 2 mole of N atom = $6.022 \times 2 \times 10^{23}$
   $= 1.2044 \times 10^{24}$ atoms

5. Find the mass of the following:
   (i) 6.022×10^{23} number of O_2 molecules
   (ii) 1.5 mole of CO_2 molecule

Ans.

(i) 6.022×10^{23} number of O_2 molecules:
   Mass of 1 mole of O_2 molecule = 6.022×10^{23} molecules = 32 g

(ii) 1.5 mole of CO_2 molecule:
   Mass of 1 mole of CO_2 molecule = 6.022×10^{23} molecules = 44 g
   Mass of 1.5 mole CO_2 molecule = 44×1.5 = 66 g

6. What are the rules for writing the symbol of an element?

Ans.

IUPAC → International Union of Pure and Applied Chemistry approves name of elements.

Symbols are the first one or two letters of the element's name in English. The first letter of a symbol is always written as a capital letter (upper case) and the second letter as a small letter (lower case).

e.g., Hydrogen → H Helium → He

Some symbols are taken from the names of elements in Latin, German or Greek.

e.g., Symbol of iron is Fe, its Latin name is Ferrum.

Symbol of sodium is Na, its Latin name is Natrium.

Atoms and Molecules

7. Explain relative atomic mass and relative molecular mass.

Ans.
Relative atomic mass: It can be defined as the number of times one atom of given element is heavier than 1/12 th of the mass of an atom of carbon-12. Relative Molecular Mass: It is defined as the number of times one molecule of a substance or given element is heavier than 1/12 th of the mass of one atom of carbon-12.

8. The formula of Carbon Dioxide is CO_2. What information do you get from this formula?

Ans.
(i) CO_2 represents carbon dioxide.
(ii) CO_2 is one molecule of carbon dioxide.
(iii) CO_2 is one mole of carbon dioxide i.e., it contains 6.022×10^{23} molecules of carbon dioxide.
(iv) CO_2 contains 1 atom of carbon and two atoms of oxygen.
(v) CO_2 represents 44 g of molar mass.

9. State 3 points of difference between an atom and an ion.

Ans.

Atom	Ion
An atom has no charge.	An ion has either positive or negative charge.
Number of electrons = number of protons	Number of electrons ≠ number of protons
Atom is reactive	Ion is stable

10. The ratio by mass for hydrogen and oxygen in water is given as 1:8 respectively. Calculate the ratio by number of atoms for a water molecule.

Ans.
The ratio by number of atoms for a water molecule are:

Element	Ratio by mass	Atomic mass	Mass ratio/ Atomic mass	Simplest ratio
H	1	1	1/1 = 1	2
O	8	16	8/16 = 1/2	1

Thus, the ratio by number of atoms for water is H : O = 2 : 1.

11. Calculate
(a) the mass of one atom of oxygen
(b) the mass of one molecule of oxygen
(c) the mass of one mole of oxygen gas
(d) the mass of one ion of oxygen
(e) the number of atoms in 1 mole of oxygen molecule

Ans.
(a) Mass of one atom of oxygen
1 mole of oxygen atom = 16 gm = 6.022×10^{23} atoms.
∴ Mass of one atom of oxygen = $16/6.022 \times 10^{23} = 2.65 \times 10^{23}$

(b) Mass of one molecule of oxygen
1 molecule of oxygen = O_2
$= 2 \times 16$
$= 32$ u

(c) Mass of one oxygen gas
1 molecule of oxygen gas is $O_2 = 32$ u

(d) Mass of one ion of oxygen
One mole of oxygen =
6.022×10^{23} atoms = 16 g
Mass of one ion of oxygen =
$16/6.022 \times 10^{23} = 2.65 \times 10^{23}$

(e) Number of atoms in one mole of oxygen molecule 1 mole of oxygen molecule i.e.
$O_2 = 6.022 \times 10^{23}$ molecules
1 molecule of O_2 = 2 atoms
∴ Number of atoms in 1 mole of oxygen molecule = $6.022 \times 10^{23} \times 2$ atoms
$= 1.2044 \times 10^{24}$ atoms

Structure of Atom 9

Learning Objectives : In this chapter, students will learn about:
- ✓ the structure of atom
- ✓ the contribution of Thomson, Rutherford and Bohr
- ✓ isotopes and isobars
- ✓ practical applications of isotopes

CHAPTER SUMMARY

Atoms and molecules are the building blocks of matter. Atoms are made up of three subatomic particles: electrons, protons and neutrons. Protons and neutrons are present in a small nucleus at the centre of the atom, whereas electrons are outside the nucleus. Electrons have negative charge, proton has positive charge whereas neutron has no charge, it is neutral.

Charged Particles in Matter

If we rub a comb in dry hair, this comb attracts small pieces of paper, and if we rub a glass rod with a piece of silk cloth and bring it near an inflated balloon, then the glass rod attracts the balloon.

An electrically charged object can attract an uncharged object. This means, on rubbing with dry hair, a comb gets an electric charge. Now the question arises: Where does this electric charge come from? The answer is: from within the atoms present in the comb and glass rod. These simple experiments show that some charged particles are present in the atoms of matter. So the atom is divisible.

Discovery of Electron

It was discovered by **J.J. Thomson in 1897**. In his experiment he took a discharge tube at very low pressure and passed electric current of high voltage through it.

Streams of minute particles were given out by the cathode (negative electrode). These streams of particles are called Cathode rays because they emerge from cathode. The mass and charge of the cathode ray particles does not depend on the nature of gas taken in the discharge tube.

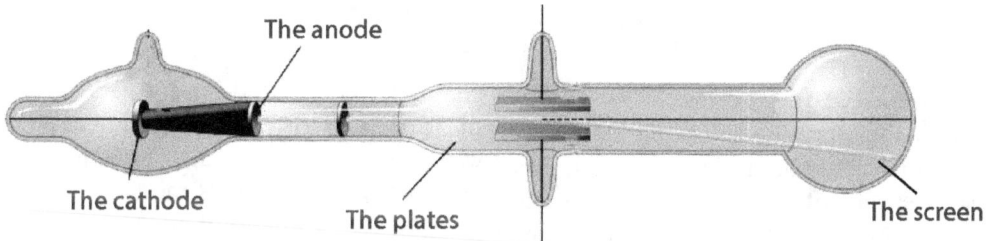

Fig. 9.1

The gas taken in the discharge tube consists of atoms, and all the atoms contain electrons. When high electrical voltage is applied, the electrical energy pushes out some of the electrons from the atoms of the gas. These fast moving electrons form cathode rays. Thus the formation of cathode rays shows that one of the subatomic particles present in all the atoms is the negatively charged 'electron'.

It was **R.A Millikan** who first measured the charge on an electron in 1909 by his famous oil drop experiment. The magnitude of charge on the electron is 1.6×10^{-19} Coulomb. The relative charge of the electron is –1. The mass of the electron is found to be 9.1×10^{-31} kg. The relative mass of an electron is approximately equal to $\frac{1}{1840}$ of the mass of the hydrogen atom.

Discovery of Proton
The proton was discovered by **E. Goldstein** in **1886**. In this experiment he took a discharge tube and applied high voltage into it. When he applied high voltage under low pressure, he observed a faint red glow on the wall behind the cathode. Those rays were also called **canal rays**.

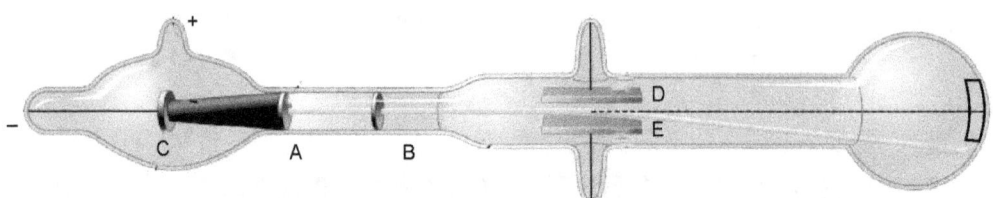

Fig. 9.2

When these rays were allowed to pass through the charge plates placed above and below the discharge tube found that these rays were deflected towards the negative plate. He concludes that these rays must possess positive charge and hence were called protons. The charge on protons was found to be 1.6×10^{-19} coulomb and the relative charge was +1. The mass of proton was found to be 1.673×10^{-24} g. The relative mass of proton was found to be 1 amu.

Discovery of Neutron
It was discovered by **James Chadwick in 1932**. When he bombarded lighter elements with alpha particles and observed the emission of a highly penetrating radiation. According to him this radiation consisted of neutral particles having 1 amu relative mass.

The nuclear reaction carried out during the discovery of neutrons is expressed as below:

$$^4Be_9 + {}^2He_4 \rightarrow {}^6Be_{12} + {}^0n_1$$

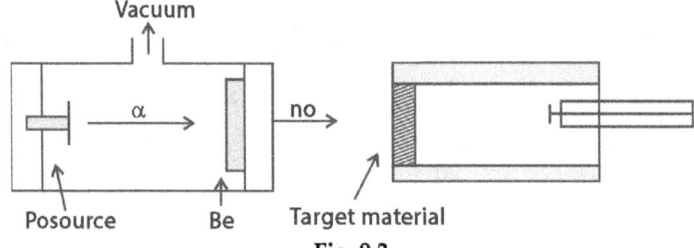

Fig. 9.3

Structure of Atom
Dalton's atomic theory suggested that atom was indivisible–which could not be broken down into smaller particles. But after discovery of subatomic particles such as electron, proton and neutron, this theory failed. For explaining this, many scientists proposed various atomic models.

Thomson's model of an atom
When J.J. Thomson proposed his model of the atom in 1903, then only electrons and protons were known to be present in the atom. According to his model, an atom consists of a positively charged sphere and electrons are embedded in it. The positive and negative charges are equal in magnitude, that is why an atom is electrically neutral. This model was also known as **watermelon model of an atom**.

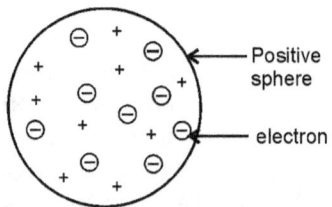

Fig. 9.4. *Thomson's Model of an Atom*

Although Thomson's model was electrically neutral, other scientists could not explain the properties of atoms using this model and hence was not accepted.

Drawbacks of Thomson's model:
(i) Since the weight of an electron is about a thousandth part of a hydrogen atom, it would mean that a single atom, especially of the heavier elements, would contain many thousand electrons. But J. J. Thomson himself found that the number of electrons in an atom cannot be greatly different from the atomic weight.
(ii) According to this model, hydrogen can give rise to only one spectral line, contrary to the observed fact of several lines.
(iii) This model could not explain the large angle scattering of alpha particle by thin metal foils.

TRIVIA

A Marburg virus outbreak struck the Democratic Republic of Congo for 2 years. With a 20-80 survival rate, the Marburg virus is the strongest known virus to date.

Rutherford's Experiment–Discovery of Nucleus
After the discovery of electrons, protons and neutrons, experiments were then carried out to find out how electrons, protons and neutrons were arranged in an atom. It was Rutherford's alpha particle scattering experiment which led to the discovery of a small positively charged nucleus in the atom containing all the protons and neutrons.

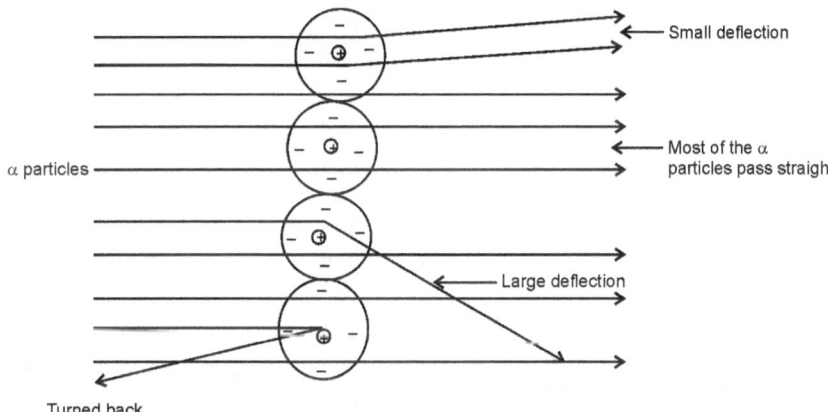

Fig. 9.5

Scattering of α particle by a gold foil:
In his experiment Rutherford bombarded a thin gold foil with the fast moving alpha particles. He took a gold foil about 1000 atoms thick and double charged helium ions.

Observation: In his experiment Rutherford noted the following observations:
(i) Most of the α-particles passed straight through the gold foil.
(ii) Few of the α-particles were deflected through a small angle as they passed through the gold foil.
(iii) Very few α-particles bounced back in the same direction in which they came.

Conclusion: On the basis of his experiment and observations he made the following conclusions:
(i) There is large empty space in the atom.
(ii) The nucleus of the atom is positively charged.
(iii) The nucleus of the atom is densely packed.

Rutherford nuclear model of an atom
This model had the following features:
(i) There is an oppositely charged centre in an atom called the nucleus. Nearly all the mass of an atom resides in the nucleus.
(ii) The electrons revolve around the nucleus in well-defined orbits.
(iii) The size of the nucleus is very small as compared to the size of the atom.

Structure of Atom

Drawback of Rutherford's model of the atom: The orbital revolution of the electron is not expected to be stable. Any particle in a circular orbit would undergo acceleration. During acceleration, charged particles would radiate energy. Thus revolving electrons would lose energy and finally fall into nucleus. If it was so, the atom would be highly unstable and hence matter would not exist in the form that we know. But this does not happen and we know that atoms are quite stable.

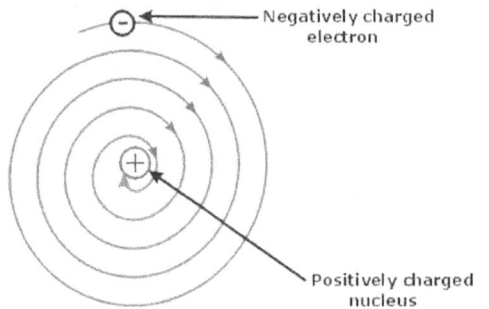

Fig. 9.6. *Diagram Showing How an Electron Losing Energy Could Fall into the Mucleus*

Bohr's Model of Atom

In order to overcome the objection raised against Rutherford's model of the atom. **Neils Bohr** put forward his model of an atom. According to this model.

An atom consists of a nucleus which contains neutrons and protons. The electrons revolve around the nucleus in fixed orbits and do not radiate energy. Energy is radiated or absorbed by an atom only when an electron moves from one shell to another. When an electron jumps from lower to higher energy level, it absorbs energy and when it jumps from higher to lower it radiates energy. The energy is always radiated or absorbed in the form of packets called **photons**. The orbit or the shell in which electrons revolve is called the energy level.

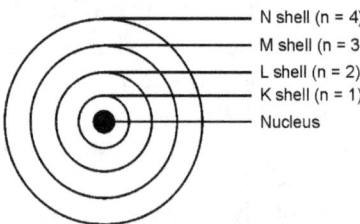

Fig. 9.7. *Energy Levels in an Atom*

These orbits or shells are represented by the letters K, L, M, N. The maximum number of electrons in first shell called K shell can be 2, in second shell L-shell can be 8, in third shell M shell can be 18 and so on. This distribution of electron is called the **electronic configuration**.

Distribution of Electrons in Different Orbits (Shells)

'The arrangement of electrons in the various shells (or energy levels) of an atom of the element is known as electronic configuration of the element.'

The distribution of electrons into different orbits of an atom was suggested by **Bohr and Bury**. According to Bohr–Bury scheme.

(i) The maximum number of electrons which can be accommodated in any energy level of the atom is given by $2n^2$ (where n is the number of that energy level.)
First orbit or K-shell will be = 2×1^2
Second orbit or L-shell will be = $2 \times 2^2 = 8$
Third orbit or M-shell will be = $2 \times 3^2 = 18$
Fourth orbit or N-shell will be = $2 \times 4^2 = 32$ and so on.

(ii) The outermost shell of an atom cannot accommodate more than 8 electrons, even if it has the capacity to accommodate more electrons.

(iii) Electrons in an atom do not occupy a new shell unless all the inner shells are completely filled with electrons.

Valency

The electrons present in the outermost shell of an atom are known as **valence electrons** (or valency electrons) because they decide the valency (combining capacity) of the atom.

Only the valence electrons of an atom take part in chemical reactions because they have more energy than all the inner electrons of the atom. An outermost shell which has eight electrons is said to possess an octet. Atoms would thus, react, so as to achieve octet in the outermost shell. This was done by sharing, gaining or losing electrons.

Hydrogen/lithium/sodium atoms contain one electron each in their outermost shell, therefore each of them can lose one electron. So, they are said to have valency of one, but if the number of electrons in the outermost shell of an atom is close to its full capacity, then valency is determined in a different way.

For example, The fluorine atom has 7 electrons in the outermost shell, and its valency could be 7. But it is easier for fluorine to gain one electron instead of losing seven electrons. Hence, its valency is determined by subtracting seven electrons from the octet, Therefore, the valency of fluorine will be 1.

Valency of Some Elements

Element	Symbol	Atomic number	Number of Protons	Number of Neutrons	Number of Electrons	Distribution of Electrons				Valency
						K	L	M	M	
Hydrogen	H	1	1	–	1	1	–	–	–	1
Helium	He	2	2	2	2	2	–	–	–	0
Lithium	Li	3	3	4	3	2	1	–	–	1
Beryllium	Be	4	4	5	4	2	2	–	–	2
Boron	B	5	5	6	5	2	3	–	–	3
Carbon	C	6	6	6	6	2	4	–	–	4
Nitrogen	N	7	7	7	7	2	5	–	–	3
Oxygen	O	8	8	8	8	2	6	–	–	2
Fluorine	F	9	9	10	9	2	7	–	–	1
Neon	Ne	10	10	10	10	2	8	–	–	0
Sodium	Na	11	11	12	11	2	8	1	–	1
Magnesium	Mg	12	12	12	12	2	8	2	–	2
Aluminium	Al	13	13	14	13	2	8	3	–	3
Silicon	Si	14	14	14	14	2	8	4	–	4
Phosphorus	P	15	15	16	15	2	8	5	–	3,5
Sulphur	S	16	16	16	16	2	8	6	–	2
Chlorine	Cl	17	17	18	17	2	8	7	–	1
Argon	Ar	18	18	22	18	2	8	8	–	0

Atomic Number

"The number of protons in one atom of an element is known as atomic number of that element." i.e.,

Atomic number of an element = Number of protons in one atom of element

It is denoted by 'Z'

For example: One atom of sodium element has 11 protons in it. So the atomic number of sodium is 11.

All the atoms of the same element have the same number of protons in their nuclei, and hence they have the same atomic number.

Note: In a normal atom (or neutral atom), the number of protons is equal to the number of electrons in it.

Mass Number

An atom consists of protons, neutrons and electrons. Since the mass of electrons is negligible, the real mass of an atom is determined by the protons and neutrons only.

Therefore, the total number of protons and neutrons present in one atom of an element is known as its mass number i.e.

(Mass number = No. protons + No. of neutrons)

Structure of Atom

For example: Atom of sodium element contains 11 protons and 12 neutrons, so the mass number of sodium is 11 + 23 = 23

Mass number is denoted by 'A'

$$A = Z + n$$

Where, n is the number of neutrons
A = mass number, Z = atomic number.

The atomic number, mass number and symbol of the element are to be written as given below

For example: Nitrogen is written as $_{7}^{14}N$

Isotopes

Isotopes are atoms of the same element having the same atomic number but different mass number. The occurrence isotopes is due to the difference in the number of neutrons in an atom.

For example, Hydrogen atom has three atomic species i.e., three isotopes namely protium ($_{1}^{1}H$), deuterium ($_{1}^{2}H$) or (D) and tritium ($_{1}^{3}H$ or T). The atomic number of each one is 1, but the mass numbers are 1, 2 and 3, respectively. Other examples of isotopes are: (i) Carbon $_{6}^{12}C$ and $_{6}^{14}C$ (ii) Chlorine $_{17}^{35}Cl$ and $_{17}^{37}Cl$ (iii) Uranium $_{235}^{92}U$ and $_{236}^{92}U$ etc.

Applications of isotopes

Some applications of isotopes are:

(i) Radioactive isotopes like (Carbon –14, Arsenic –74, Sodium –24, Iodine –131, Cobalt –60 and Uranium –235) are used as fuel in nuclear reactors of nuclear power plants for generating electricity.
(ii) An isotope of cobalt is used in treatment of cancer.
(iii) An isotope of iodine is used in treatment of goiter.
(iv) It is used in radiography.
(v) It is used in mineral analysis.
(vi) It is used in archaeological survey to determine the age of fossils.
(vii) It is used to preserve foods.

Isobars

'Atoms having different atomic number but same mass numbers are called isobars.'

For example: $_{18}^{40}Ar$ and $_{20}^{40}Ca$

MUST REMEMBER

- Electrons have negative charge, proton has positive charge whereas neutron has no charge, it is neutral.
- An electrically charged object can attract an uncharged object.
- The mass and charge of the cathode ray particles does not depend on the nature of gas taken in the discharge tube.
- When he applied high voltage under low pressure, he observed a faint red glow on the wall behind the cathode. Those rays were also called canal rays.
- It was Rutherford's alpha particle scattering experiment which led to the discovery of a small positively charged nucleus in the atom containing all the protons and neutrons.
- When an electron jumps from lower to higher energy level, it absorbs energy and when it jumps from higher to lower it radiates energy. The energy is always radiated or absorbed in the form of packets called photons.
- The arrangement of electrons in the various shells (or energy levels) of an atom of the element is known as electronic configuration of the element.
- Hydrogen/lithium/sodium atoms contain one electron each in their outermost shell, therefore each of them can lose one electron.

MULTIPLE CHOICE QUESTIONS

1. The first model of an atom was given by _____.
   (a) Eugen Goldstein
   (b) J.J. Thomson
   (c) Neils Bohr
   (d) Ernest Rutherford

2. What are cathode rays?
   (a) Positively charged
   (b) Negatively charged
   (c) Neutral
   (d) All of these

3. Which of the following statements is always correct?
   (a) an atom has equal number of electrons, protons and neutrons
   (b) an atom has equal number of neutrons
   (c) an atom has equal number of electrons and neutrons
   (d) an atom has equal number of electrons and protons

4. Rutherford's alpha particle scattering experiment led to the discovery of _____.
   (a) Electrons
   (b) Protons
   (c) Neutrons
   (d) Nucleus

5. Goldstein's experiments which involved passing high voltage electricity through gases at very low pressure resulted in the discovery of _____.
   (a) Nucleus
   (b) Electron
   (c) Proton
   (d) Neutron

6. In which year neutron was discovered?
   (a) 1886
   (b) 1897
   (c) 1932
   (d) 1909

7. Which of the following is the correct electronic configuration of sodium?
   (a) 1, 2, 8
   (b) 8, 2, 1
   (c) 2, 1, 8
   (d) 2, 8, 1

8. The particle not present in an ordinary hydrogen atom is _____.
   (a) Electron
   (b) Proton
   (c) Neutron
   (d) Neils Bohr

9. The number of electrons in the atom of an element X is 15 and the number of neutron is 16. Which of the following is the correct representation of an atom of this element?
   (a) $^{15}_{16}X$
   (b) $^{16}_{15}X$
   (c) $^{31}_{15}X$
   (d) $^{31}_{16}X$

10. The e/m for the proton is found to be _____.
    (a) 6.54×10^3
    (b) 9.58×10^4
    (c) 8.8×10^3
    (d) 5.89×10^4

11. The mass number of two atoms X and Y is the same (40 each) but their atomic number are different (being 20 an 18, respectively). X and Y are examples of _____.
    (a) Isotopes
    (b) Isobars
    (c) Solid and liquid
    (d) Chemically similar atoms

12. The atomic number of an element X is 8 and that of element Y is 4. Both these elements can exhibit a valency of _____.
    (a) 1
    (b) 2
    (c) 3
    (d) 4

13. The number of valence electrons in a sulphide ion, S^{2-} is _____.
    (a) 8
    (b) 9
    (c) 10
    (d) 16

14. For an element Z = 9. The valency of this element will be _____.
    (a) 1
    (b) 2
    (c) 3
    (d) 4

15. Drawback of Rutherford model of atom was _____.
    (a) Neutron was not known
    (b) No explanation for the neutral nature of atom
    (c) No explanation of isotopes
    (d) Could not explain the stability of atoms

Structure of Atom

16. The four atomic species can be represented as follows. Out of these, the two species which can be termed isobars are?
    (i) $^{201}_{60}X$ (ii) $^{200}_{60}X$
    (iii) $^{200}_{58}X$ (iv) $^{203}_{60}X$
    (a) (i) and (ii) (b) (ii) and (iii)
    (c) (iii) and (iv) (d) (i) and (iv)

17. The atomic numbers of four elements A, B, C, and D are 12, 13, 15 and 3, respectively. The element which cannot form a cation is _____.
    (a) D (b) C
    (c) B (d) A

18. Elements having valency one are _____.
    (a) Always metals
    (b) Always non-metals
    (c) Always metalloids
    (d) Either metals or non-metals

19. The maximum number of electrons that can be accommodated in N shell of an atom is _____.
    (a) 2 (b) 8
    (c) 18 (d) 32

20. Isotopes of cobalt is used for treatment of which one of the following?
    (a) TB (b) Cancer
    (c) Goiter (d) Diabetes

21. The number of neutron in an atom having atomic number 11 and mass number 23 is _____.
    (a) 10 (b) 11
    (c) 12 (d) 13

22. The ion an element has 3 positive charges. The mass number of atom of this element is 27 and the number of neutrons is 14. What is the number of electrons in the ion?
    (a) 10 (b) 13
    (c) 16 (d) 14

23. The correct electronic configuration of chloride ion is _____.
    (a) 2, 8 (b) 2, 8, 4
    (c) 2, 8, 8 (d) 2, 8, 7

24. Which of the following represents the correct electron distribution in magnesium ion?
    (a) 2, 8 (b) 2, 8, 1
    (c) 2, 8, 2 (d) 2, 8, 3

25. The isotopes of an element contain _____.
    (a) Same number of neutrons but different number of protons
    (b) Different number of neutrons but some number of protons
    (c) Same number of neutrons but different number of electrons
    (d) Different number of protons as well as different number of neutrons

26. Almost the entire mass of an atom is concentrated in the _____.
    (a) Proton (b) Electron
    (c) Neutron (d) Nucleus

27. The K, L and M shells of an atom are full, its atomic number is _____.
    (a) 10 (b) 12
    (c) 18 (d) 20

28. Which of the air pressure is appropriate for the production of cathode rays in the discharge tube?
    (a) 1 mm Hg
    (b) 0.001 mm Hg
    (c) 1 cm Hg
    (d) 0.001 cm Hg

29. The other name of ^1_1H is _____.
    (a) Protium (b) Deuterium
    (c) Tritium (d) Proton

30. The fixed circular paths around the nucleus are called _____.
    (a) Orbitals (b) Orbits
    (c) Mesons (d) Nucleous

31. Cathode rays are deflected towards _____.
    (a) Positive electrode
    (b) Negative electrode
    (c) Both electrode
    (d) None of electrodes

32. The proton is heavier than an electron by _____.
    (a) 100 times (b) 1000 times
    (c) 1840 times (d) 1850 times
33. There are four elements P, Q, R and S having atomic numbers of 4, 18, 10 and 16, respectively. The element which can exhibit covalency as well as electrovalency will be _____.
    (a) S (b) R
    (c) Q (d) P
34. Which of the following elements does not exhibit electrovalency?
    (a) Calcium (b) Cadmium
    (c) Carbon (d) Chromium
35. Four elements W, X, Y and Z contain 8, 11, 9 and 17 protons per atom respectively. The element which cannot form an anion is most likely to be _____
    (a) X (b) Y
    (c) W (d) Z

HOTS

1. $_7N^{15}$ and $_8O^{16}$ are pair of _____
   (a) Isotopes
   (b) Isobars
   (c) Isotones
   (d) None of these
2. Which of the following statement about the electron is incorrect?
   (a) It is a negatively charged particles
   (b) The mass of the electron is equal to the mass of the neutron
   (c) It is a basic constituent of all atom
   (d) It is a constituent of cathode rays
3. In an alpha scattering experiment, few alpha particles rebounded because
   (a) Most of the space in the atom is occupied
   (b) Positive charge of the atoms very little space
   (c) The mass of the atom is concentrated in the centre
   (d) All the positive charge and mass of the atom is concentrated in small volume
4. Which of the following statements is incorrect about the structure of an atom?
   i. The whole mass of an atom is concentrated in the nucleus
   ii. The atom is an indivisible particle
   iii. The atom as a whole is neutral
   iv. All the atoms are stable in their basic state
   Choose the right option among the following:
   (a) and (iii)
   (b) only (ii)
   (c) (ii) and (iv)
   (d) none of these
5. Which of the following is an incorrect statement in reference with observation in Rutherford's α-particle scattering experiment?
   (a) Some of the α-particles rebound after hitting the gold foil
   (b) Some of the particles deflected from their path
   (c) Some of the particles not pass through the gold foil
   (d) Most of the particles pass straight through the gold foil

Structure of Atom

SUBJECTIVE QUESTIONS

1. $^{24}_{12}Mg$ and $^{26}_{12}Mg$ are symbols of two isotopes of magnesium. Compare the atoms of these isotopes with respect to the following: (i) the composition of their nuclei (ii) their electronic configurations (iii) give the reason why the two isotopes of magnesium have different mass numbers (iv) explain why the two atoms have the same chemical reactions.

   Ans.

   $^{24}_{12}Mg$ and $^{26}_{12}Mg$

   (i) Protons = 12   Protons = 12
       Neutrons = 24 – 12 = 12   Neutrons
       = 26 – 12 = 14

   (ii) The electronic configuration of both atoms is the same i.e.,
       2, 8, 2 since they both have 12 electrons.

   (iii) Mass number is the number of protons + neutrons. Because the atoms have same number of protons but different number of neutrons. Hence their mass numbers are different.

   (iv) When chemical reactions take place, only electrons are involved in chemical reactions and the protons and neutrons are not involved. Since both the atoms have same number of electrons, the chemical reactions will be the same for both atoms.

2. What is an octate? Why would atoms want to complete their octate?

   Ans.

   When the outermost shell of an atom i.e., L, M or N are completely filled with 8 electrons in the shell, it is said an octate. Atoms would want to complete their octate because they want to become stable.

3. Find the valency of $^{14}_{7}N$ and $^{35}_{17}Cl$.

   Ans.

   The atomic number of nitrogen = 7, No. of protons = 7, No. of electrons = 7

   Electronic configuration = K L M = 2 5 –
   Valency = 3

   Because either it will gain three electrons or share 3 electrons to complete its octate.

   The atomic number of chlorine = 17, p = 17, e = 17

   Electronic configuration = K L M = 2 8 7
   Valency = 1

   Because it will gain 1 electron to complete its octate.

4. What are nucleons? What is the name given to those atoms which have same number of nucleons in it?

   Ans.

   Protons and neutrons present in the nucleus are called nucleons Isobaric elements have same number of nucleons in it.

Element	Protons	Neutrons	(Protons + Neutrons)
Argon	18	22	40
Calcium	20	20	40
Potassium	19	21	40

5. Give difference between isotopes, and isobars.

   Ans.

Isotopes	Isobars
Are atoms of same element.	Are atoms of different element
Have same atomic number	Have different atomic number
Have different mass number	Have same mass number
Number of protons and electrons are same in these atoms.	Number of protons and electrons are not same in these atoms.

Cell–The Fundamental Unit of Life   10

Learning Objectives : In this chapter, students will learn about:
- ✓ the structure of cell
- ✓ the components of cell
- ✓ cell organelles and their functions
- ✓ different types of cells

CHAPTER SUMMARY

There are different kinds of living organisms found on the earth's surface. It varies from unicellular to multicellular organisms. These organisms are of bacteria, protozoa, fungi, virus, plant and animals. The bodies of all organisms are made up of smallest unit called the **cell**. The cell has same central position in biology as an atom in the physical sciences. The cell is the basic structural and functional unit of life.

Robert Hooke in 1665 discovered the cells. He examined a thin slice of cork under a self-designed crude micro-scope and observed that the cork resembled the structure of a honey comb. Cork is a substance which is obtained from the bark of a tree. The latter consisted of many tiny compartments. Hooke called them **cellulae** (singular cellula), cellula is a latin word which means 'a little room'.

Cell: Structural and Functional Unit of Life

All living organisms are made up of cells. Thus, cell is the structural unit of life. Each living cell has the capacity to perform certain basic functions. Each cell has a distinct structure and function due to the organization of its membrane and cytoplasmic organelles in a specific way. Each kind of cell organelle performs a special function, such as making new materials in the cell (e.g., chloroplast, ribosomes), clearing up the waste materials from the cells (e.g., lysosomes), energy production (e.g., mitochondria), movement (microtubules containing spindle, cilia, flagella), etc. A cell is able to live and perform all its functions because of these organelles. These organelles together constitute the basic unit of structure and function called the cell.

What is a cell made up of?

All cells have following three major functional regions:
i. Cell membrane or plasma membrane and cell wall.
ii. Nucleus
iii. Cytoplasm

Plasma Membrane

It is a thin layer of membrane which forms the outermost layer of the cell. It is present in microorganisms, plants and animals. It is made up of phospholipids, proteins, cholesterol and polysaccharides.

Functions: Plasma membrane permits the entry and exit of some materials in the cells. Therefore the plasma membrane is called a **selective permeable membrane**. The movement of material takes place by **diffusion** and **osmosis**. Some substances like carbon dioxide (CO_2), Oxygen (O_2), water etc. move by the process of diffusion. 'Diffusion is a process in which molecules move from the region of higher concentration to the region of lower concentration.'

The spontaneous movement of water molecules through a selectively permeable membrane is called **osmosis**. Thus, 'Osmosis is the passage of water from a region of higher water concentration through a semipermeable membrane to a region of lower water concentration.' It is purely a mechanical diffusion process by which cells absorb water without spending any amount of energy.

If we put plant cell or animal cell into a solution of salt or sugar. The following three things can happen:

(i) If the medium surrounding the cell has a higher water concentration than the cell, the cell will gain the water by the process of osmosis. The cell is likely to swell up. Such solutions are called **hypotonic solution**.

(ii) If the medium surrounding the cell has same concentration as the cell, then there will no movement of water across the membrane. Such a solution is called an **isotonic solution**. The cell will stay the same size.

(iii) If the medium has lower concentration of water than the cell, the cell will lose water and water will move out of the cell by the process of osmosis. Therefore the cell will shrink. Such a solution is called a **hypertonic solution**.

TRIVIA

Tomatoes have more genes than humans. The tomato contains 31,760 genes – that is 7,000 more genes than a human.

Endocytosis: The flexibility of the cell membrane also enables the cell to engulf in food and other material from its external environment. Such process is known as endocytosis. i.e. **endocytosis** is the ingestion of material by the cells through the plasma membrane. Amoeba acquires its food through such process.

Cell Wall

It is the outer most layer of plant cell which is rigid in nature. It is non living and freely permeable and is secreted by the cell itself for the protection of its plasma membrane and cytoplasm. It provides rigidity and shape to the cell. It is made up of fibrous polysaccharide called cellulose. It consists of thin cellulose fibres called microfibrils glued together.

It permits the plant cell to become turgid. It provides mechanical strength to the plant which is increased by addition of **lignin** in tissues such as xylem. It has a narrow pores through which fine particles are able to pass.

Plasmolysis: When a living plant cell loses water through osmosis, there is a shrinkage or contraction of the protoplasm away from the cell wall. This phenomenon is called **plasmolysis**.

Thus, if a living plant cell is immersed in a concentrated sugar solution, the concentration of water molecules inside the cell will be higher than outside. As a result, water will move by osmosis from the higher water potential inside the cell to the lower water potential outside. The cell contents will shrink away from the cell wall and it will be plasmolysed.

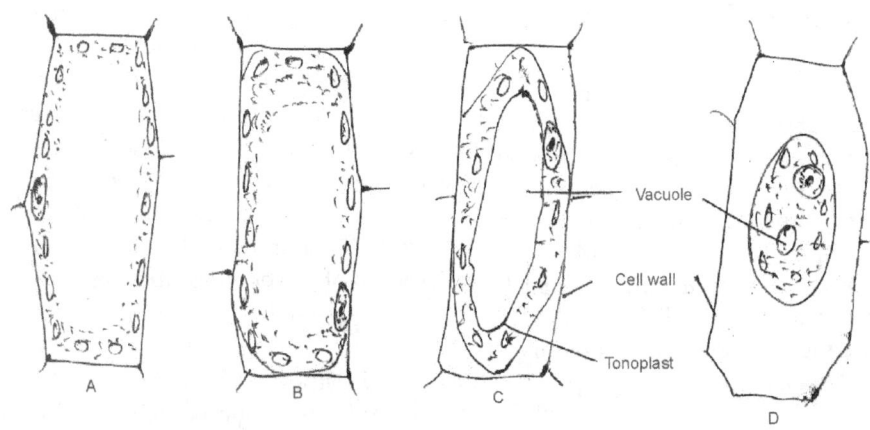

Fig. 10.1. *Plasmolysis A – Normal Plant Cell B → D Successive Stages in Shrinkage of Cell Content*

Nucleus

It is the central part of the cell which is bound by a double membrane called the **nuclear membrane**. Nuclear membrane separates nucleus from cytoplasm. The nucleus contains **nucleolus and chromatin material**. The nucleolus is not bound by any membrane and is rich in protein and RNA molecules where ribosomes are formed. Ribosome helps in protein synthesis in the cytoplasm. On the other hand, the chromatin material is a thin thread like structure that exists as chromosomes.

Chromosomes are composed of **DNA** and **protein**. DNA stores all the information necessary for the cell to function, grow and reproduce. Functional segments of DNA are called **genes**. During cell division it is condensed into two or more thick ribbon like structures. The chromosomes consist of two arms that extent out from a specialised region of DNA called **centromere**. Depending on the position of centromere chromosomes are of four types as **metacentric, submetacentric, acrocentric** and **telocentric chromosomes**.

Functions of nucleus:

(i) The nucleus regulates the cell cycle.
(ii) It controls all metabolic activities of the cell. If the nucleus is removed from a cell, the protoplasm ultimately dries up and dies.
(iii) It is concerned with the transmission of hereditary traits from the parent to offspring.

Cytoplasm

The region between the nucleus and plasma membrane filled with the fluid is called **cytoplasm**. It consists of several cell organelles. The fluid material present in the cytoplasm is called **cytosol**. Cytosol contains protein fibres called **cytoskeleton**.

Functions of cytoplasm:

(i) Cytosol (cytoplasm) acts as a store of vital chemicals such as amino acids, glucose, vitamins, ions etc.
(ii) It is the site of certain metabolic activities such as glycolysis, synthesis of fatty acids, nucleotides, and some amino acids.
(iii) Living cytoplasm is always in a state of movement.

Cell Organelles

Every cell has a membrane around it to keep its own contents separate from the external environment. Large and complex cells, need a lot of chemical activities to support their complicated structure and function. To keep these activities of different kinds separate from each other, these cells use membrane-bound little structures (or organelles) within themselves. Some important examples of cell organelles are: Endoplasmic reticulum, Golgi apparatus, Lysosomes, Mitochondria, Plastids and Vacuoles.

Endoplasmic Reticulum (ER)

ER is a network of membrane bound tubules and sheets filled with lumen fluid. It is connected with outer membrane of nucleus and plasma membrane. It occurs in three forms: cisternae, vesicles and tubules. Basically it is of two types **rough endoplasmic reticulum (RER)** and **smooth endoplasmic reticulum (SER)**. RER contains ribosomes on its surface which help in protein synthesis and SER do not contains ribosomes. The SER helps in the manufacture of fat molecules, or lipids. Some of these proteins and lipids help in building the cell membrane. This process is known as **membrane biogenesis**.

Functions of ER:

(i) It forms supporting skeletal frame work of the cell.
(ii) ER provides a pathway for the distribution of cell range from one cell to the other.
(iii) RER is concerned with the transport of proteins which are synthesized by ribosomes on their surface.
(iv) Certain enzymes present in SER synthesize fats (lipids), steroids and cholesterol.
(v) SER plays a crucial role in detoxifying many poisons and drugs.

Golgi Apparatus

The Golgi apparatus was first described by **Camillo Golgi**. Golgi body consists of a set of membrane bound, fluid-filled vesicles, vacuoles and flattened **Cisternae** (closed sacs). Cisternae are usually stacked together in parallel rows. These membranes often have connections with the membranes of ER and therefore constitute another portion of a complex cellular membrane system. Gogli apparatus is absent in bacteria, blue-green algae, mature sperms and red blood cells of mammals and other animals.

Functions of Golgi Apparatus: The main function a of Golgi body is storing, packaging of various cellular material and dispatching it from one cell to another. It is also involved in the synthesis of cell wall, plasma membrane and lysosomes.

Lysosomes

Lysosomes are membrane bound sacs filled with digestive enzymes. These enzymes are made by RER. Enzymes helps in destroying the foreign material such as bacteria that enters into the cell and cause infection. It removes all the worn out cells from the body. During breakdown of cell structure, lysosomes burst and release out the enzymes, which eat up their own cells and hence lysosomes are also known as the '**suicide bags**' of a cell.

Mitochondria

It is a small rod shaped structure found in the cell, which is bound by a double membrane covering instead of just one. Outer membrane is porus. The inner layer is deeply folded creating a large surface area for ATP generating chemical reactions. These folds are called cristae and are studded (dotted) with small round bodies known as F_1 particles or oxysomes.

ATP is known as energy currency of the cell. The body uses energy stored in the form of ATP for making new chemical compounds and for mechanical work. Mitochondria has its own DNA and ribosomes due to which it can make its own protein molecules. Hence Mitochondria are called semi autonomous.

The inner part of mitochondria is filled with fluid matrix. Mitochondria are absent in bacteria and the red blood cells of mammals.

Functions of Mitochondria

Mitochondrion is the site of cellular respiration and use atmospheric oxygen to oxidise carbohydrate and fat present in the cell into carbon dioxide and water vapour. Upon oxidation, it releases energy in the form of ATP, which is used by the cell during cellular process. Since the mitochondria synthesize, energy rich compounds (ATP), they are known as '**Power house**' of the cell.

Plastids

Plastids occur in most plant cells and are absent in animal cells. Like the mitochondria, the plastids also have their own DNA and ribosomes. They are self replicating organelles like the mitochondria, i.e., they have the power to divide. Plastids are of following three types:

(i) **Chromoplasts:** Coloured plastids (except green colour)
(ii) **Chloroplasts:** Green coloured plastids.
(iii) **Leucoplasts:** The colourless plastids.

The chloroplast contains green colour pigment called **chlorophyll**, which helps in photosynthesis in plants. Each chloroplast is bound by double membrane which divides it into two distinct region Grana and Stroma. Grana is the site of light reaction and stroma is the site of dark reaction.

The main function of plastid is to trap solar energy and use it in manufacturing food for the plants. The chromoplast imparts various colours to flowers to attract insects for pollination. Leucoplasts store food in the form of **carbohydrate, fats** and **protein**.

Vacuoles

Vacuoles are membrane bound structures which are filled with solid or liquid contents that help in storage of water glycogen and proteins. Vacuoles are normally large and distinct in plant cells and small and temporary in animal cells. The central vacuole of some plant cells may occupy 50-90% of the cell volume.

The membrane of the vacuoles is called **tonoplast** and fluid inside it is called **cell sap**.

Functions of vacuoles:

(i) Vacuoles help to maintain the osmotic pressure in the cell and provide turgidity and rigidity to the cell.
(ii) They store toxic metabolic by products or end products of plant cells.
(iii) In single-celled organisms like Amoeba and paramecium, the food vacuole contains the food items that the animal has consumed.

In some unicellular organisms specialized vacuoles also play important roles in expelling excess watar and some wastes from the cell.

Difference Between Plant and Animal Cells

No.	Animal Cell	Plant Cell
1.	Animal cells are generally small in size	Plant cells are larger than animal cells.
2.	Cell wall is absent.	The plasma membrane of plant cell is surrounded by a rigid cell wall of cellulose.
3.	Except the protozoan Euglena, no animal cell possesses plastids.	Plastids are present.
4.	Vacuoles in animal cells are many, small and temporary.	Most mature plant cells have a permanent and large central vacuole.
5.	Animal cells have a single highly complex and prominent Golgi apparatus.	Plant cells have many simpler units of Golgi apparatus, called dictyosomes.
6.	Animal cells have centrosome and centrioles.	Plant cells lack centrosome and centioles.

Prokaryotic and Eukaryotic Cells

All living organisms present on earth can be classified into following two types:

Non-cellular Organisms or Acellular Organisms

They do not contain any cells in their body organisation e.g., viruses. Viruses lack membrane and hence do not show characteristics of life until they enter a living body (i.e., prokaryotic cell or eukaryotic cell) to use its cell machinery to reproduce.

Cellular Organisms

They contain either one or many cells in their bodies *e.g.*, bacteria, plants and animals.

Cellular organisms are again divided into following two main types:

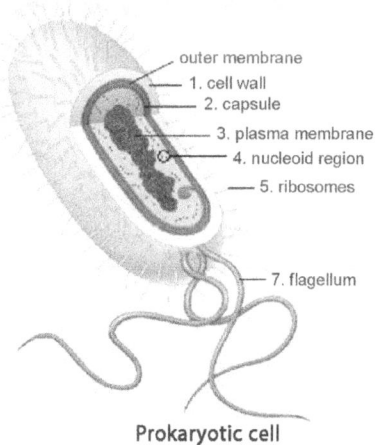 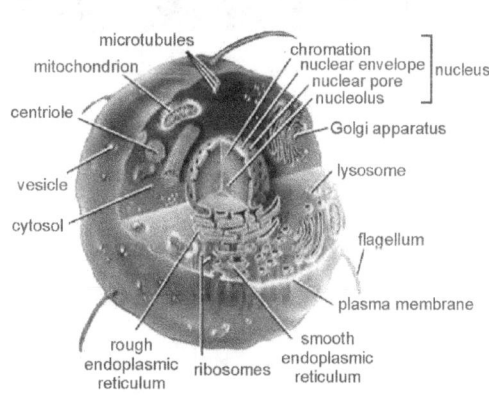

Prokaryotic cell   Eukaryotic cell

Fig. 10.2

(i) **Prokaryotes:** The nuclear region of the prokaryotic cell may be poorly defined due to the absence of a nuclear membrane. Such an undefined nuclear region containing only nucleic acids is called a **nucleoid**. In a prokaryotic cell other membrane bound organelles, such as mitochondria, are also absent. Ribosomes, however, are present in prokaryotic cells. Such organisms, whose cells lack a nuclear membrane, are called **prokaryotes**. The prokaryotes include archaebacteria, bacteria and cynobacteria. (blue green algae)

(ii) **Eukaryotes:** These have advanced and complete cells. Such cells are found in unicellular and multicelllular plants and animals and contain plasma membrane, nucleus, DNA and cytoplasm with ribosomes and cellular organelles such as mitochondria.

MUST REMEMBER

- Plasma membrane permits the entry and exit of some materials in the cells.
- Osmosis is the passage of water from a region of higher water concentration through a semipermeable membrane to a region of lower water concentration.
- Endocytosis is the ingestion of material by the cells through the plasma membrane.
- The region between the nucleus and plasma membrane filled with the fluid is called cytoplasm.
- Cytosol contains protein fibres called cytoskeleton.
- Lysosomes are membrane bound sacs filled with digestive enzymes.
- Mitochondria are absent in bacteria and the red blood cells of mammals.
- The chloroplast contains green colour pigment called chlorophyll, which helps in photosynthesis in plants.
- The main function of plastid is to trap solar energy and use it in manufacturing food for the plants.
- Vacuoles are membrane bound structures which are filled with solid or liquid contents that help in storage of water glycogen and proteins.
- The membrane of the vacuoles is called tonoplast and fluid inside it is called cell sap.

MULTIPLE CHOICE QUESTIONS

1. The term 'cell' was given by _____.
   (a) Robert Brown
   (b) Flemming
   (c) Robert Hooke
   (d) Leeuwen hoek

2. Who proposed the cell theory?
   (a) Watson and Crick
   (b) Schleiden and Schwann
   (c) Darwin and Wallace
   (d) Mendel and Morgan

3. Which one of the following is prokaryotic?
   (a) Blue green algae
   (b) Fungus
   (c) Fly
   (d) Plasmodium

4. Which of the following has an irregular or variable shape?
   (a) Amoeba   (b) Euglena
   (c) Acetabularia   (d) Paramecium

5. Nucleolus is a site of _____.
   (a) RNA synthesis
   (b) Enzyme synthesis
   (c) Ribosome
   (d) Protein synthesis

6. Genetic material of a eukaryotic cell is contained in _____.
   (a) Nucleus   (b) Nucleoid
   (c) Nucleolus   (d) Nucleoplasm

7. Which one of the following is called the power house of the cell?
   (a) Ribosomes   (b) Plastids
   (c) Mitochondria (d) Vacuoles

8. A plant cell placed in hypotonic solution will _____.
   (a) Shrink   (b) Swell
   (c) See no change   (d) Face Exosmosis

9. Which one of the following is called the suicide bag of the cell?
   (a) Ribosomes   (b) Lysosomes
   (c) Centrioles   (d) Mitochondria

10. The longest cell in the human body is _____.
    (a) Muscle cell   (b) Nerve cell
    (c) Kidney cell   (d) Liver cell

11. The idea 'omins cellula a cellula' which means that all living cells arise from pre-existing cells, was given by _____.
    (a) Parkinje
    (b) Schleiden
    (c) Rudolf Virchow
    (d) Robert brown

12. Middle lamella is formed of _____.
    (a) Calcium pectate
    (b) Cellulose
    (c) Lignin
    (d) Hemicelluloses

13. A cell placed in hypotonic solution bursts up: It is _____.
    (a) Plant cell   (b) Fungal cell
    (c) Bacterial cell (d) Animal cell

14. Which material is present in bulk in plasma membrane say 75%?
    (a) Phospholipids
    (b) Polysaccharides
    (c) Cholesterol
    (d) Protein

15. Bulk transport occurs through _____.
    (a) Exoctosis   (b) Endocytosis
    (c) Endo osmosis (d) Both (a) and (b)

16. Cytoplasm is _____.
    (a) Unit mass of protoplasm
    (b) Protoplasm excluding plasma membrane
    (c) Protoplasm excluding plasma membrane and cell organelles
    (d) Protoplasm excluding plasma membrane and nucleus

17. Protein storing plastid is _____.
    (a) Aleuroplast   (b) Elaioplast
    (c) Omyloplast   (d) Both (b) and (c)

18. Site of photosynthesis is _____.
    (a) Chromoplast (b) Leucoplast
    (c) Chloroplast (d) Omyloplast

Cell-The Fundamental Unit of Life

19. Rough ER contains _____.
    (a) Detoxification centres
    (b) Ribosomes
    (c) Lysosomes
    (d) Carbohydrate synthesizing machinery
20. The kitchen of a cell is _____.
    (a) Endoplasmic reticulum
    (b) Golgi apparatus
    (c) Chloroplast
    (d) Mitochondria
21. The undefined nuclear region of prokaryotes is also known as _____.
    (a) Nucleus   (b) Nucleoid
    (c) Nucleolus   (d) Nucleic acid
22. Lysosomes arise from _____.
    (a) Nucleus
    (b) Mitochondria
    (c) Golgi apparatus
    (d) Endoplasmic reticulum
23. The only cell organelle seen in prokaryotic cell is _____.
    (a) Mitochondria
    (b) Plastids
    (c) Ribosomes
    (d) Lysosomes
24. Chromosomes are made up of _____.
    (a) RNA   (b) DNA
    (c) Protein   (d) Both (b) and (c)
25. Find out the false statement.
    (a) Golgi apparatus is involved with the formation of lysosomes
    (b) Mitochondria is said to be the power house of the cell as ATP is generated in them
    (c) Cytoplasm is called as protoplasm
    (d) Nucleus, mitochondria and plastid have DNA, hence they are able to make their own structural proteins
26. Cell wall of which one of these is not made up cellulose?
    (a) Mango tree   (b) Hydrilla
    (c) Bacteria   (d) Cactus
27. Which one of the following is absent in plant cell?
    (a) Mitochondria   (b) Centrioles
    (c) Ribosomes   (d) Nucleus
28. Organelle without a cell membrane is _____.
    (a) Chloroplast   (b) Nucleus
    (c) Ribosome   (d) Mitochondrion
29. Which of the following is incorrect pair?
    (a) Lysosome – Secretory granules
    (b) Mitochondria – Power house of the cell
    (c) Chloroplast – Kitchen of the cell
    (d) Nucleus – Brain of the cell
30. The proteins and lipids, essential for building the cell membrane, are manufactured by _____.
    (a) Peroxisomes
    (b) Mitochondria
    (c) Golgi apparatus
    (d) Endoplasmic reticulum
31. Plasmolysis occurs due to _____.
    (a) Exomosis   (b) Endosmosis
    (c) Ssmosis   (d) Absorption
32. Plasmolysis in a plant cell is defined as _____.
    (a) Shrinkage of nucleoplasm
    (b) Shrinkage of cytoplasm is hypertonic medium
    (c) Break down (lysis) of plasma membrane in hypotonic medium
    (d) None of these
33. Amoeba acquires its food through a process termed as _____.
    (a) Exocytosis
    (b) Endocytosis
    (c) Plasmolysis
    (d) Exocytosis and endocytosis both
34. Unicellular organisms take in oxygen and pass out carbon dioxide through _____.
    (a) Active transport
    (b) Endosmosis
    (c) Exosmosis
    (d) Diffusion

35. Root hairs of plants absorb water from soil through _____.
    (a) Osmosis (b) Imbibition
    (c) Diffusion (d) All of these
36. Which cell organelle plays a crucial role in detoxifying many poisons and drugs in a cell?
    (a) Lysosomes
    (b) Smooth endoplasmic reticulum
    (c) Vacuoles
    (d) Golgi apparatus
37. Main difference between animal cell and plant cell is _____.
    (a) Growth (b) Respiration
    (c) Nutrition (d) Movement
38. Select odd one out.
    (a) Membranes are made of organic molecules such as proteins and lipids
    (b) The movement of water across a semipermeable membrane is affected by the amount of substances dissolved in it
    (c) Molecules soluble in organic solvents can easily pass through the membrane
    (d) Plasma membrane contains chitin sugar in plants
39. The infoldings in mitochondria are known as _____.
    (a) Cristae (b) Matrix
    (c) Stroma (d) Cisternal
40. Which of the following is covered by a single membrane?
    (a) Plastid (b) Nucleus
    (c) Mitochondria (d) Vacuole
41. Chlorophyll is present in _____.
    (a) Cristae (b) Thylakoid
    (c) Stroma (d) Matrix
42. Photosynthetic pigments are located in _____.
    (a) Grana
    (b) Stroma
    (c) Outer membrane of chloroplast
    (d) Inner membrane of chloroplast
43. Colourless plastids are known as _____.
    (a) Leucoplast (b) Chromoplast
    (c) Chloroplast (d) None of these
44. Solute concentration is higher in the external solution _____.
    (a) Hypotonic (b) Hypertonic
    (c) Isotonic (d) None of these
45. Which of these is not related to endoplasmic reticulum?
    (a) It transport materials between various regions in cytoplasm.
    (b) It behaves as transport channel for proteins between nucleus and cytoplasm.
    (c) It can be the site of energy generation.
    (d) It can be the site for some biochemical activities of the cell.

HOTS

1. Which of the following structures is usually present only in animal cells?
   (a) Cell wall   (b) Centrioles
   (c) Nucleus   (d) Vacuoles

2. Ribosomes are made of how many sub-units?
   (a) 0   (b) 2
   (c) 3   (d) 4

3. Haploid cells in angiosperms can be obtained by culturing _____.
   (a) young leaves   (b) Root tips
   (c) endosperms   (d) pollen grains

4. Human cheek cells stained in methylene blue and mounted in glycerine were observed with the help of a compound microscope. The components of the cell which were seen are:
   (a) cell wall, cytoplasm, nucleus
   (b) plasma membrane, cytoplasm, nucleus, mitochondria
   (c) plasma membrane, cytoplasm, nucleus
   (d) plasma membrane, cytoplasm, nucleus, mitochondria, lysosomes, Golgi bodies.

5. Which of the following is not a function of the vacuole in plants?
   (a) They store toxic metabolic wastes
   (b) They help with the process of cell division
   (c) They help to maintain turgidity
   (d) They provide structural support

6. A cell will swell up if
   (a) the concentration of water molecules in the cell is higher than the concentration of water molecules in surrounding medium
   (b) the concentration of water molecules in surrounding medium is higher than water molecules concentration in the cell
   (c) the concentration of water molecules is same in the cell and in the surrounding medium
   (d) concentration of water molecules does not matter

7. Match the following columns.

	Column I		Column II
A.	Hypotonic solution	1.	Cell will shrink
B.	Hypertonic	2.	Cell will swell up solution
C.	Isotonic solution	3.	Cell will stay the same

   Codes
   (a) A-3, B-2, C-1   (b) A-1, B-2, C-3
   (c) A-3, B-1, C-2   (d) A-2, B-1, C-3

8. Select the odd one out.
   (a) The movement of water across a semi-permeable membrane is affected by the amount of substances dissolved in it
   (b) Membranes are made of organic molecules like proteins and lipids
   (c) The cell membrane separates the content of the cell from its external environment
   (d) The cell membrane allows the movement of all material across it

9. Functional segments of DNA are called _____. In a cell which is not dividing, the DNA is present as _____ material. Choose the correct option for A and B respectively are
   (a) chromosomes, gene
   (b) gene, chromatin
   (c) chromatin, gene
   (d) chromosomes, chromatin

10. Match the following columns

	Column I		Column II
A.	Cellulose	1.	Cytoplasm
B.	Chromosomes	2.	Functional segment of DNA
C.	Cell organelles	3.	Plant cell wall
D.	Genes	4.	Nucleus

    (a) A-4, B-3, C-2, D-1
    (b) A-3, B-4, C-1, D-2
    (c) A-4, B-3, C-1, D-2
    (d) A-3, B-4, C-2, D-1

SUBJECTIVE QUESTIONS

1. What is endocytosis?

Ans. The cell membranes flexibility allows the cell engulf in food and other material from its external environment. This process is known as endocytosis. E.g., Amoeba acquires its food through such processes.

2. What is the function of vacuoles?

Ans. Vacuoles are storage sacs for solid or liquid content. In plant cells it provides turgidity and rigidity to the cell. In single-celled organisms vacuoles store food, e.g., Amoeba.

3. Why are lysosomes called suicidal bags?

Ans. Lysosomes contain digestive enzymes in it and helps in the cleaning of cell by digesting any foreign materials entering the cell, such as bacteria, food and old cell organelles.

When the lysosomes burst, the digestive enzyme digest its own cell. Hence it is called as suicidal bag.

4. What is the function of nucleus in a cell?

Ans. The nucleus plays a very important role in the reproduction of cells. It also helps the single cell to divide and form two new daughter cells.

It plays an important role in determining how the cell will develop and what form it will exhibit at maturity, by directing the chemical activities of the cell.

5. State the difference between smooth endoplasmic reticulum and rough endoplasmic reticulum.

Ans.

Smooth Endoplasmic Reticulum	Rough Endoplasmic Reticulum
It looks smooth.	It looks rough.
SER helps in the manufacture of fat molecules or lipids.	Ribosomes are attached to RER which synthesise proteins.

Tissues

11

Learning Objectives : In this chapter, students will learn about:
- ✓ the importance of tissue
- ✓ different plant tissues
- ✓ different animal tissues
- ✓ plant and animal tissues
- ✓ the protective tissues

CHAPTER SUMMARY

All living organisms are made of cells. A unicellur organism (e.g., Amoeba, Paramecium) has a single cell in its body, which performs all basic functions *i.e.*, movement of a cell, intake of food, respiration, intracellular digestion, excretion etc. However, in multicellular organisms there are millions of cells. Most of these cells are specialised to carry out only a few functions efficiently. These functions are taken up by different groups of cells. For example, In human beings, muscle cells contract and relax to cause movement, nerve cells carry messages, blood flows to transport oxygen, food, hormones and waste material and so on. In plants, vascular tissues conduct food and water from one part of the plant to other parts. So, multicellular organisms show **division of labour**. This means that a particular function is carried out by a cluster of cells at a definite place in the body. This cluster of cells is called a **tissue**.

"A group of cells similar in structure that work together to perform a particular function forms a **tissue**. All cells of a tissue have common origin."

Notes:
1. The study of tissues is called **histology**.
2. Term tissue was coined by Bichat.
3. Term histology was coined by Mayer.
4. Marcello Malpighi is considered as founder of histology.

Difference between Plants and Animals: There are noticeable differences between the two. Plants are autotrophic. They prepare their own food by photosynthesis. Moreover, plants are stationary or fixed organisms, they do not have to move from place to place in the search of their food. Since they do not consume or need much energy, most of the plant tissues are supportive which provide them with structural strength.

Animals on the other hand are heterotrophic organisms. They have to move in search of food, and shelter, so they need more energy as compared to plants.

Further, there are some tissues in plants which divide throughout life. They divide for the growth and reproduction of the plants. Such ever dividing tissues are localised in certain regions of the plant body. Thus, based on the dividing capacity of the tissues, various plant tissues can be classified as meristematic and permanent tissues. In animals nerve cells do not divide.

Plant Tissues

Plant tissues are of two types, meristematic and permanent tissues.

Meristematic Tissues

The meristematic tissues are the continuously dividing tissues, which are found in the growing region of the plant. It helps in growth and development of the plant. According to their position in the plant, they are of three types, such as **apical meristem, intercalary meristem and lateral meristem**. The apical meristem is found in the root tips or the shoot tips of the plant. It helps in longitudinal growth of the plant.

The lateral meristem is found in the bark and in vascular bundles of the dicot roots and stems of the plant, whereas the intercalary meristem is found at the base of the leaves or internodes. The main function of the meristematic tissues is to form new cells and helps in the growth of the plant. The apical meristem helps in longitudinal growth, lateral meristem helps in diametrical growth and intercalary meristems increase the length of the organ of the plant.

> **TRIVIA**
>
> The average person has 5 litres of blood. Once a person loses 40% of their blood, they will die without immediate transfusion.

Permanent Tissues

These tissues develop from meristematic tissues. Actually these are the meristematic tissue which have lost the power of division. This process of taking up a permanent shape, size and a function is called **differentiation**. They are further subdivided into two groups as simple permanent tissues and complex permanent tissues.

(i) **Simple permanent tissues:** These tissues are composed of cells which are structurally and functionally similar. Thus, these tissues are all made of one type of cells. These tissues are of three types: Parenchyma, Collenchyma and sclerenchyma.

   (a) **Parenchyma tissue:** These cells are living and still possess the power of division. They are found in different shapes such as round, oval, elongated etc. It has thin cell wall and small nucleus. It is found in stem, roots, leaves and fruits of the plant. It helps in filling the space between the other tissues and provides turgidity and rigidity to the plants. It also stores and assimilates food for the plants.

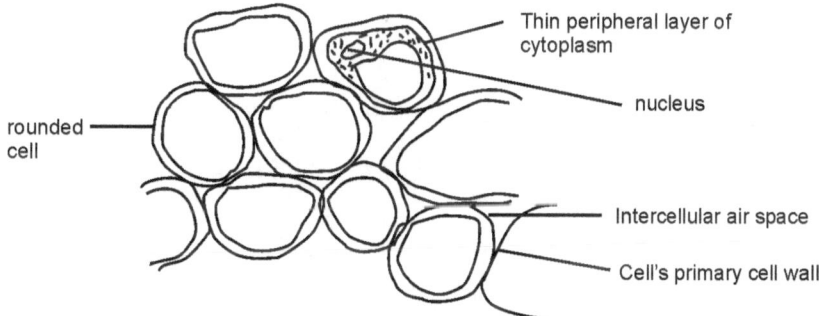

Fig. 11.1. *Parenchyma Tissue*

(b) **Collenchyma:** It is similar to that of parenchyma, except for deposition of extra cellulose at the corner of the cells. The intracellular space is generally absent and contain few chloroplast. They are located below epidermis and ribs of dicot leaves. The main function of the collenchyma tissue is to provide mechanical strength and elasticity to the plants. It also provides flexibility to the stems, which helps in bending of stems.

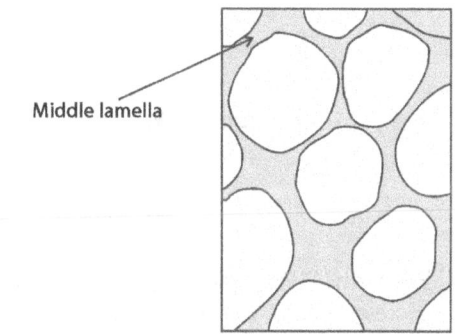

Fig. 11.2. *Collenchyma*

Tissues

(c) Sclerenchyma: These are basically dead cells and their walls are made up of thick deposition of **lignin**. It is made up of two types of cells such as **fibers** and **sclereids**. Fibers consist of long narrow, thick and lignified cells and sclereids are irregular shaped dead cells founded in cortex, pith etc. of the plants. They are also found in stems, roots, hard coverings of seeds and nuts and stems. For example, husk of coconuts is made up of sclerenchyma. The main function of sclerenchyma is to provide mechanical strength and helps to withstand various strains in plants.

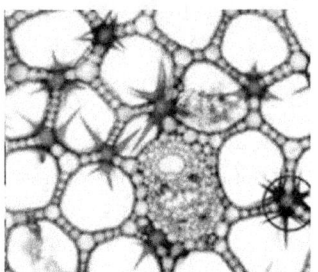

Fig. 10.3. *Sclerenchyma Tissue*

(ii) Complex permanent tissues: Complex permanent tissues are made up of more than one type of cell, having common origin. The complex permanent tissues are of two types such as, xylem and phloem tissue.

(a) Xylem: It is a conducting tissue which consists of tracheids, vessels, xylem parenchyma and xylem fibres. All the xylem elements, except for xylem parenchyma, are dead cells and bound by thick lignified wall. Vessels are long tube like structures, formed by a row of cells placed end to end. Tracheids are elongated cells, which conduct water from one cell to another via pits. Xylem parenchyma stores food and helps in lateral conduction of water. The main function of xylem is to carry water and mineral salts upwards from the roots to the different part of shoots. Since walls of tracheids, vessels and sclerenchyma of xylem are lignified, they give mechanical strength to the plant body.

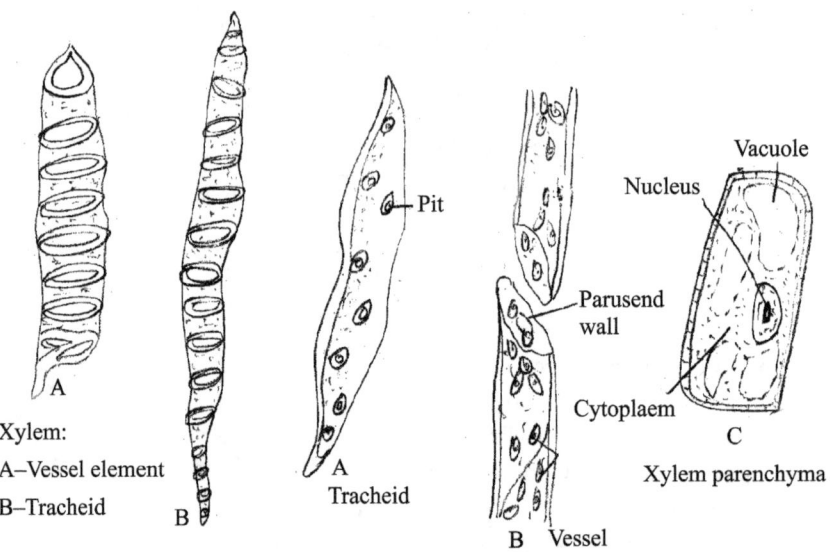

Fig. 11.4. *Different Xylam Elements*

(b) Phloem: It is made up of four types of elements: sieve tubes, companion cells, phloem fibres and the phloem parenchyma. Except for phloem fibres all are living cells. Sieve tubes are long cylindrical tube like structures composed of elongated thin walled cells. The walls of sieve tubes are perforated. The other cell is companion cell that is associated with the sieve tube containing dense and active cytoplasm.

The main function of phloem is to transport food from leaves to other parts of the plant. Phloem is unlike xylem in that, materials can move in both directions in it.

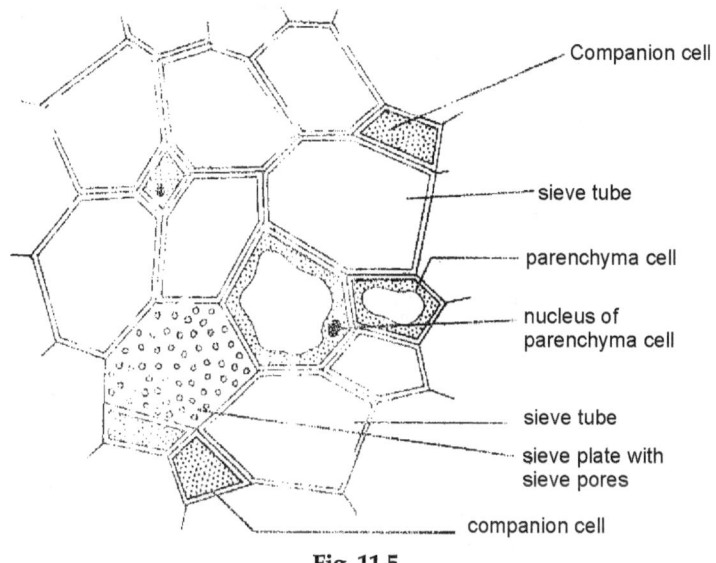

Fig. 11.5

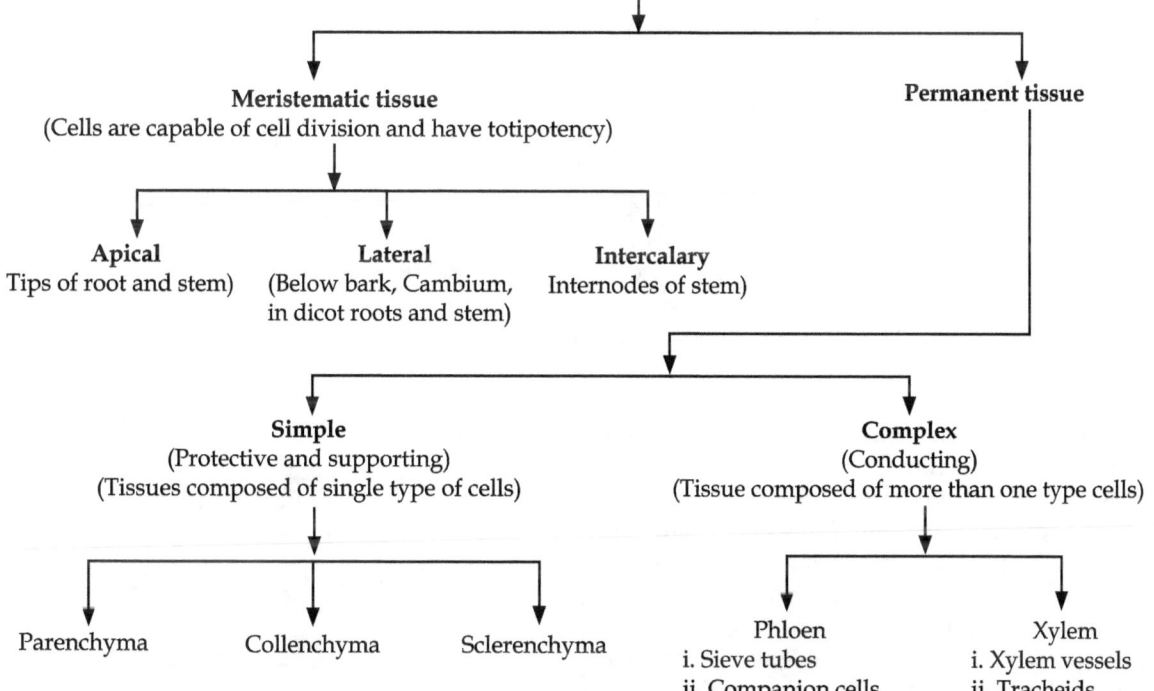

Protective Tissues

Protective tissues include epidermis and cork (or phellem).

Epidermis

The epidermis is usually present in the outermost layer of the plant body such as leaves, flowers, stem and roots. Epidermis is one cell thick and is covered with cuticle. **Cuticle** is a water proof layer of a waxy substance called **cutin** which is secreted by the epidermal cells. This aids in protection against loss of water, mechanical injury and invasion by parasitic fungi. Since, it has a protective role to play, cells of epidermal tissue form a continuous layer without inter-cellular spaces. Most epidermal cells are relatively flat. Often their outer and side walls are thicker than the inner wall.

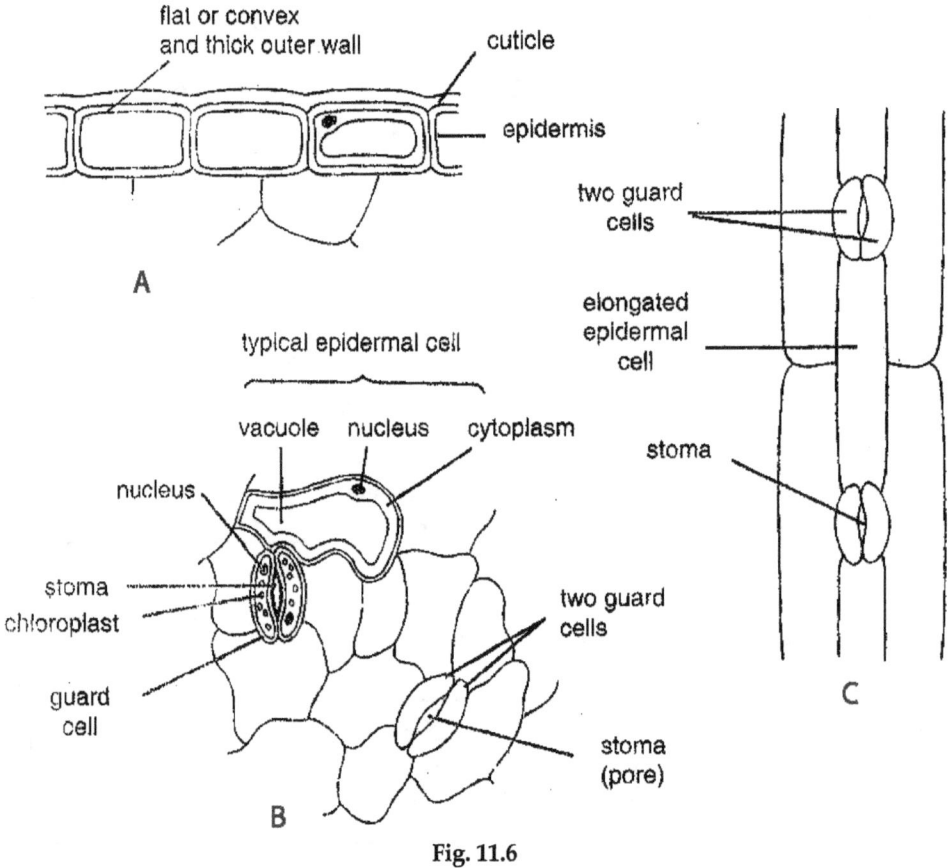

Fig. 11.6

Cork

As plants grow older, the outer protective tissue undergoes certain changes. A strip of secondary meristem called **phellogen** or **cork cambium** replaces epidermis of stem. Cells on the out side are cut off from this layer. This forms the several layer thick cork on the bark of the tree. Cells of cork are dead and compactly arranged without intercellular spaces. They also have a chemical called **suberin** in their walls that makes them impervious to gases and water.

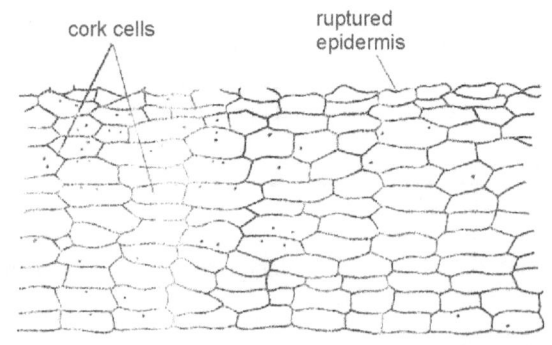

Fig. 11.7. *Transverse or Cross Section of a Cork Piece*

Stomata

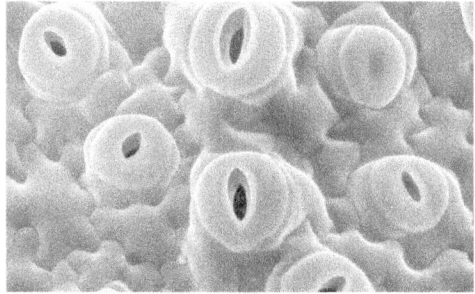

Fig. 11.8. *Stomata*

Epidermis of a leaf is not continuous at some places due to the presence of small pores, called stomata. Stomata are enclosed by two kidney-shaped cells called guard cells. Guard cells are the only epidermal cells which contain chloroplasts, the rest being colourless.

The stomata allows gaseous exchange to occur during photosynthesis and respiration. During transpiration too, water vapour also escapes through stomata.

Animal Tissues

On the basis of the function performed by the tissues in the animal body these tissues are classified as:

Different types of animal tissues.

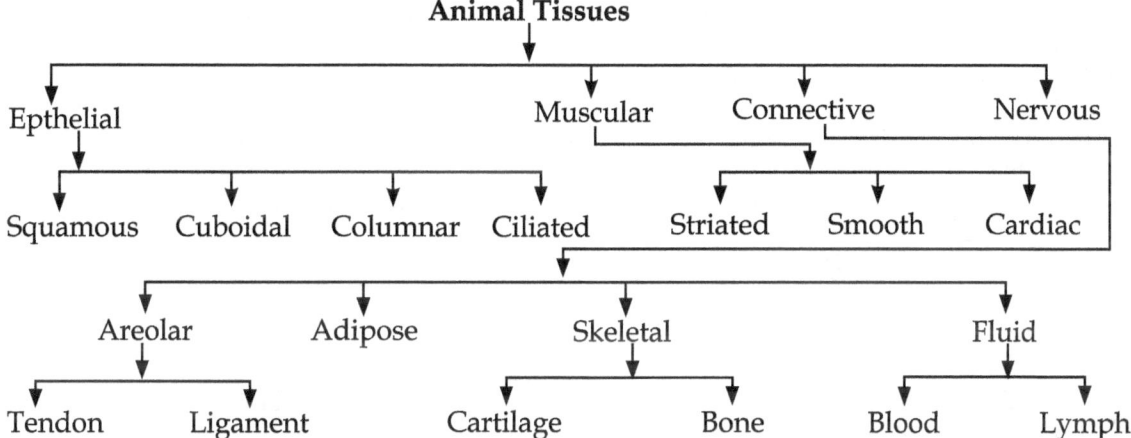

Epithelial Tissue

Epithelial tissue is the simplest tissue. It is the protective tissue of the animal body (as epidermis of plants). The cells of this tissue are tightly packed and they form a continuous sheet. Cells of epithelium contain very little or no intercellular matrix. It is found in the **inner lining of buccal cavity, blood vessel, alveoli (of lungs) and kidney tubules**.

Epithelial cells lie on a delicate non-cellular basement membrane, which contains a special form of matrix protein, called **collagen**.

Functions:

(i) It helps in absorption of water and nutrients.
(ii) It helps in elimination of waste products.
(iii) These cells protect the body from viral or bacterial infection.
(iv) Some epithelial tissues perform secretory function. They secrete a variety of substances such as sweat, saliva (mucus) enzymes. etc.

Types of epithelial tissue: Depending upon the shape and function of the cells, the epithelial tissues are classified as follows:–

(i) Squamous epithelium
(ii) Cuboidal epithelium
(iii) Columnar epithelium
(iv) Glandular epithelium
(v) Ciliated epithelium

Squamous epithelium: Simple squamous epithelial cells are extremely thin and flat and form a delicate lining. It is found in the **inner lining of mouth cavities, oesophagus, nose, blood vessels and covering of tongue**. It protects the underlying parts of the body from the injuries and germs.

Epithelial cells of skin are arranged in many layers to prevent wear and tear. Since they are arranged in a pattern of layers, the epithelium is called **stratified squamous epithelium**.

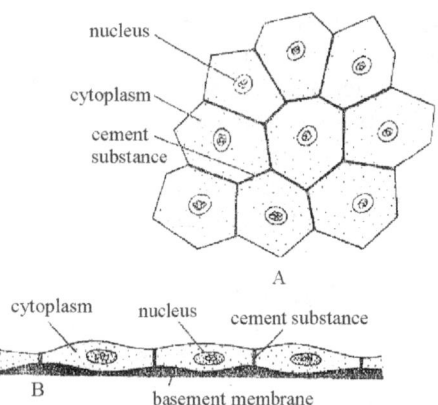

Fig. 11.9. *Squamous Epithelium*

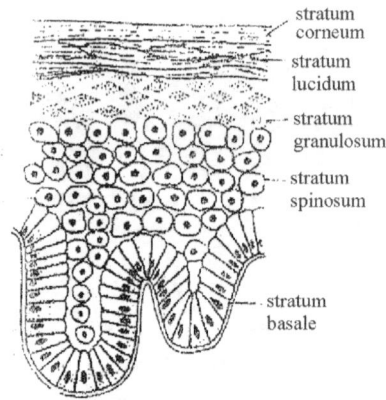

Fig. 11.10. *Epidermis of Mammalian Skin*

Cuboidal epithelium: It consists of cube like cells and hence it is called cuboidal epithelium. It is found in kidney tubules, salivary glands, sweat glands, testes and ovaries. It helps in absorption, excretion and secretion. It also provides mechanical strength to the cells.

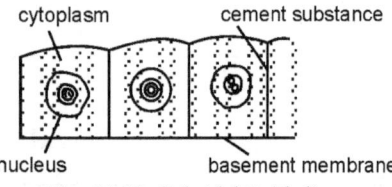

Fig. 11.11. *Cuboidal Epithelium*

Columnar epithelium: It consists of cells which are taller and pillar like. The nucleus is towards the base of the tissue. It is found in the linings of **stomach**, **small intestine**, and **colon** forming the mucous membrane. It also forms the inner lining of **gall bladder** and oviducts. Its main function is to facilitate the movements and absorption of materials and their secretion.

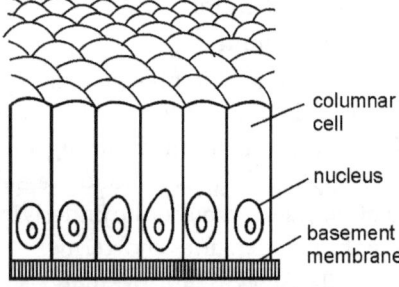

Fig. 11.12. *Columnar Epithelium*

Glandular epithelium: The columnar epithelium is often modified to form glands which secrete chemicals.

Ciliated epithelium: The columnar epithelial tissue also has **cilia**, which are hair-like projections on the outer surfaces of epithelial cells. It is found in **sperm ducts** and **wind pipe**, **bronchi**, **kidney tubules** and **oviducts**. It helps in the movement of solid particles from one part of the cell to the another.

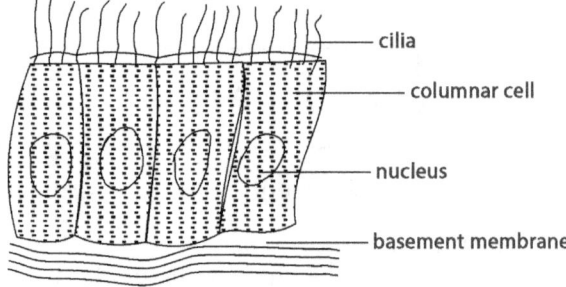

Fig. 11.13. *Ciliated Columnar Epithelium*

Muscular Tissue

They are elongated and larger in size also called **muscular fibres**. This tissue is responsible for movement in our body. Muscles contain special proteins called **contractile proteins** which contract and relax to cause movement.

On the basis of their location, structure and function, there are three types of muscle fibres:–
(i) voluntary muscles, (ii) involuntary muscles (iii) cardiac muscles

(i) **Voluntary muscles:** These muscles show alternate light and dark bands or striations, when stained appropariately. As a result they are called **striated muscles**. These muscles are mostly attached to bones and help in body movement these muscles are also called **skeletal muscles**. Since these muscles work according to our will, they are called **voluntary muscles**.

Voluntary muscles are long, elongated and unbranched. Also they are multinucleated and nuclei are in pheripheral position. They are found in muscles of limbs, body wall, face, neck, tongue, pharynx, diaphragum and upper part of oesophagus.

(ii) **Involuntary muscles:** These cells are long with pointed ends (spindle shaped) and uninucleated having delicate contractile threads called **myofibrils** that run longitudinally through the cell. Since they do not possess any bands, they are called **smooth muscles**. They are found in the walls of tubular organ except heart. They are found in the wall of alimentry canal and in the ducts of glands and blood vessels. The organ like stomach, iris, ureter, intestine etc. possess these types of muscles. These muscles do not work according to our will and hence are called **involuntary muscles**.

They help in movements of blood of food in alimentary canal, also help in rhythmic movement of stomach and intestine.

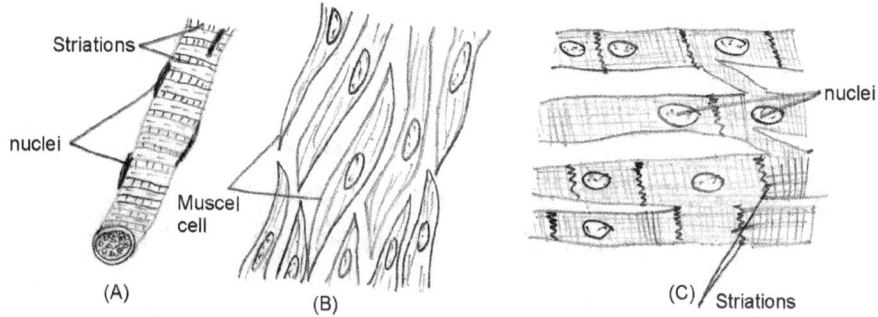

Fig. 11.14. *Types of Muscle Fibres: (A) Striated Muscle; (B) Smooth Muscle; (C) Cardiac Muscle*

(iii) **Cardiac muscles:** These muscles show the characteristics of both voluntary and involuntary muscles. Heart muscle cells are cylindrical branched and uninucleate. There is a large amount of intercellular space which is filled with loose connective tissue which contains blood capillaries. They have alternate light and dark bands and also contain densely stained cross bands. They are found in heart. Their main function is to carry out contraction and relaxation of heart which helps in pumping of blood into the body throughout life.

Connective Tissue

The connective tissue is a specialised tissue which helps in connecting the bones to muscles and binds tissues to give support to the different parts of the body. The cells of connective tissue are living separated from each other (i.e. loosely spaced) and low in number. Homogeneous, gel-like intercellular substance called medium or **matrix** forms the main bulk of the connective tissue.

Thus, space between cells is filled with a non-living matrix which may be solid as in bone and cartilage and fluid as in the blood. It is the nature of matrix which decides the function of the connective tissue.

Types of Connective Tissue

There are different types of connective tissue:
(i) Areolar (or loose) connective tissue (ii) Dense regular connective tissue (iii) Adipose tissue (iv) Skeletel tissue (v) Fluid connective tissue

(i) **Areolar tissue:** It is a loose connective tissue consisting of matrix. Its matrix consists of two kinds of fibres: **white collagen fibres** and **yellow elastic fibres**. The matrix also contains fibroblasts which can engulf bacteria and protect us from infection. It joins skin to muscles, fills space inside organs and is found around muscles, blood vessels and nerves.

It helps in diffusion of oxygen and nutrients from small blood vessels, in repair of tissues of injuried parts of the body and fixes skins to underlying muscles. It also helps in fighting foreign toxins which enter our body.

Tissues

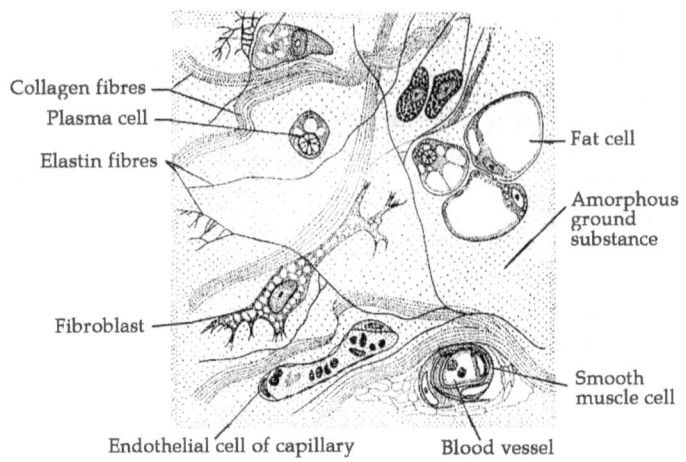

Fig. 11.15. *Areolar Connetive Tissue*

(ii) **Dense regular connective tissue:** It is a fibrous connective tissue, which is the main components of **tendons** and **ligaments**. Tendons are chord like strong, inelastic structures that join skeletal muscles to the bones. It is also a white fibrous tissue which has great strength and limited flexibility. It consists of parallel bundles of collagen fibres containing fibroblasts.

The other one is ligament. Ligament connects bones to bones. A ligament is highly elastic and has great strength but contains very little matrix. Fibroblast is compressed in between regular rows of fibres.

Ligaments strengthen the joints and permit normal movement but prevent over flexing or over extension.

Note: Sprain is caused by excessive pulling (stretching) of ligaments.

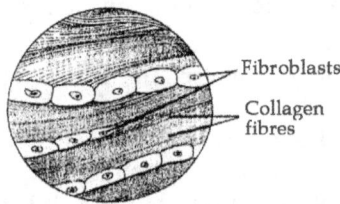

Fig. 11.16. *Dense Regular Connective Tissue*

(iii) **Adipose tissue:** It is basically an aggregation of fat cells called **adipocytes**. Each fat cell is rounded or oval in shape and are arranged into lobules separated by partitions of **collagen** and **elastin** fibres. These partitions carry blood vessels of lobules.

The adipose tissue is abundant below the skin, between the internal organs (e.g., round the kidneys) and in yellow bone marrow.

It serves as a fat reservoir and provides shape to the limbs and the body. It also forms shock absorbing cushions for some of the delicate organs like kidney, eye ball etc. it acts as an insulator and also reduces the heat loss from the body and regulates body temperature.

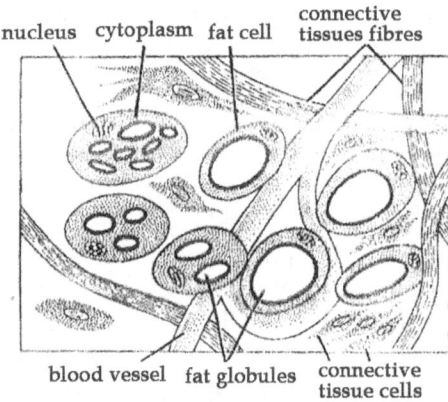

Fig. 11.18. *Adipose Tissue*

(iv) **Skeletel tissue:** The skeletal or supporting tissue includes cartilage and bone which form the endoskeleton of a vertebrate body. The cartilage is a specialised tissue which is compact and less vascular. The matrix of cartilage has a delicate network of collagen fibres and living cells. It is found in **ear pinna, nosetip, epiglottis, ends of bones and ribs and rings of trachea**. It provides support and flexibility to the body parts.

The other skeletal tissue is bone which is a very strong and non-flexible tissue. It is porous, highly vascular, mineralised, hard and rigid. It is made up of protein and minerals that are responsible for the hardness of the bone. It forms the endoskeleton of the body and provides support and shape to the body. It protects the delicate organs like **brain, lungs, heart, liver** etc.

(v) **Fluid connective tissue:** Fluid connective tissue links the different parts of the body and maintains a continuity in the body. It includes **blood and lymph**.

Blood – has a liquid matrix called plasma, in which red blood cell or corpuscles (RBCs) or erythrocytes, white blood cells (WBCs) or leucocytes and platelets are suspended. RBC and WBC are living, while blood plasma and platelets are non-living.

Plasma forms 55% of the total volume of blood. The organic substances which are present in blood plasma are soluble proteins such as albumin, globulins, fibrinogen, glucose, aminoacids, lipids, vitamins, enzymes, hormones, and waste materials such as urea and uric acid.

RBC contain iron-containing red respiratory pigment, the haemoglobin, it contains erythrocytes which play a vital role in the transport of oxygen.

WBC are of two main kinds: Phagocytes and immunocytes. **Phagocytes** are capable of phagocytosis and they carry out the function of body defence by engulfing bacteria and other foreign substances. Phagocytes include neutrophils, basophiles and eosinophils. The **immunocytes** produces antibodies and maintain the immune system of the body. This includes lymphocytes, which have a nearly spherical nucleus and little cytoplasm with no granules. Some lymphocytes later on transform into **plasma** cells.

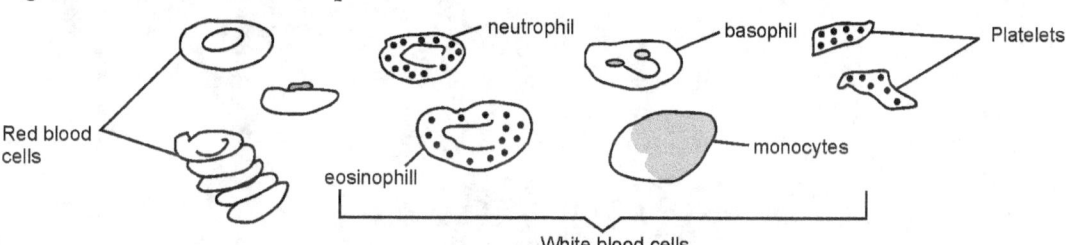

Fig. 11.19. *Various Types of Blood Cells*

Blood platelets are minute, enucleated, fragile fragments of giant bone marrow cells, called *megakaryocytes*.

Functions:
(i) Blood transports nutrients, hormones and vitamins to the cells and also removes the waste material from the blood.
(ii) RBCs carry oxygen to the tissues for the oxidation of food.
(iii) WBCs fight disease by engulfing and destroying foreign bodies.
(iv) Blood platelets disintegrate at the site of injury and help in the clotting of blood.

Lymph: It is a colourless fluid. Since it is a part of blood its composition is similar to that of blood except that red blood corpuscles and some blood protein are found in blood, while white blood corpuscles are found in lymph.

Functions:
(i) It transports nutrients and removes carbon dioxide and other nitrogenous waste from the body.
(ii) It also forms the immune system of the body.

Nervous Tissue

Nervous tissue is a specialised tissue that transmits messages from one part of our body to the other part. Brain, spinal cord and nerves are all composed of nervous tissue. Nervous tissue contains highly specialised unit cells called **nerve cells** or **neurons**. Neurons have the ability to receive stimuli from within or outside the body and conduct impulses (signals) to different parts of the body. Each neuron is divided into three parts as **cyton, dendron** and **axon**. The cyton contains nucleus and cytoplasm.

Tissues

The Dendron arises from cyton and further branches into dendrites. The axons are single long cylindrical cells which form branches with a swollen structure called a **knob**. The dendrites receive impulse and the axon takes the impulse away from the cell body.

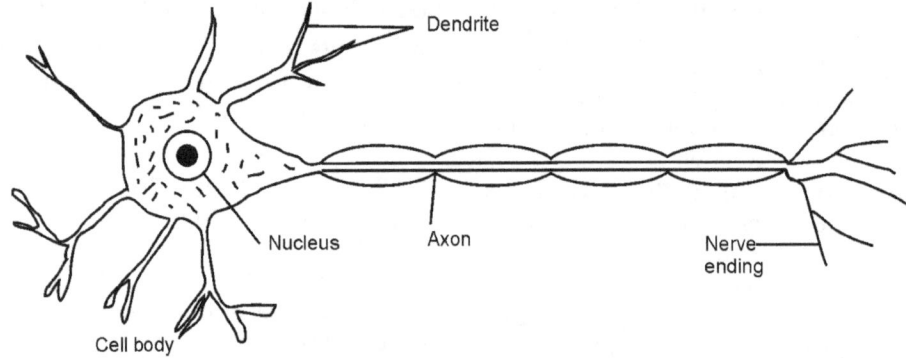

Fig. 11.20. *Neuron-unit of Nervous Tissue*

- Plants are autotrophic. They prepare their own food by photosynthesis.
- Animals are heterotrophic organisms. They have to move in search of food, and shelter, so they need more energy as compared to plants.
- The main function of sclerenchyma is to provide mechanical strength and helps to withstand various strains in plants.
- Xylem parenchyma stores food and helps in lateral conduction of water. The main function of xylem is to carry water and mineral salts upwards from the roots to the different part of shoots.
- Sieve tubes are long cylindrical tube like structures composed of elongated thin walled cells.
- The main function of phloem is to transport food from leaves to other parts of the plant.
- Epidermis is one cell thick and is covered with cuticle. Cuticle is a water proof layer of a waxy substance called cutin which is secreted by epidermal cells.
- Stomata are enclosed by two kidney-shaped cells called guard cells. Guard cells are the only epidermal cells which contain chloroplasts, the rest being colourless.
- Epithelial cells lie on a delicate non-cellular basement membrane, which contains a special form of matrix protein, called collagen.
- Muscles contain special proteins called contractile proteins which contract and relax to cause movement.
- The connective tissue is a specialised tissue which helps in connecting the bones to muscles and binds tissues to give support to the different parts of the body.
- Ligaments strengthen the joints and permit normal movement but prevent over flexing or over extension.
- Fluid connective tissue links the different parts of the body and maintains a continuity in the body.
- Nervous tissue is a specialised tissue that transmits messages from one part of our body to the other part.

MULTIPLE CHOICE QUESTIONS

1. Presence of tissues in a multicellular organisms ensures _____.
   (a) Body strength
   (b) Division of labour
   (c) Higher reproductive potential
   (d) Faster development

2. A group of cells alike in form, function and origin are called _____.
   (a) Organ   (b) Organelle
   (c) Tissue   (d) None of these

3. Parenchyma : simple :: Phloem: _____
   (a) Simple   (b) Complex
   (c) Xylem   (d) Collenchyma

4. Which are the four types of animal tissue?
   (a) Epithelial, connective, muscular, cardiac
   (b) Epithelial, squamous, muscular, connective
   (c) Connective, muscular, epithilial, nervous
   (d) Cuboidal, ciliated, glandular, columnar

5. The nuclei of meristematic cells are _____.
   (a) Small   (b) Large
   (c) Medium   (d) None of these

6. The cell wall of meristematic cell is made of _____.
   (a) Protein   (b) Peptidoglycan
   (c) Cellulose   (d) Aminoacid

7. _____ tissue forms new cells in plants.
   (a) Simple   (b) Permanent
   (c) Meristematic (d) None of these

8. Parenchyma which contains chlorophyll is called _____.
   (a) Chlorenchyma
   (b) Collenchyma
   (c) Selerenchyma
   (d) None of these

9. Tissue that is absent in monocots is _____.
   (a) Collencyma
   (b) Aerenchyma
   (c) Sclerenchyma
   (d) Chlorenchyma

10. Grit of pear is formed of _____.
    (a) Tracheids
    (b) Companion cells
    (c) Sclereids
    (d) Sclerenchyma fibres

11. Transpiration of exchange of gases are functions of _____.
    (a) Xylem
    (b) Stomata
    (c) Both (a) and (b)
    (d) Neither (a) nor (b)

12. Cuboidal: epithelial: : Cardiac _____
    (a) Epithelial   (b) Nervous
    (c) Muscular   (d) Connective

13. Tendons and ligaments are _____.
    (a) Loose connective tissue
    (b) Dense connective tissue
    (c) Muscular tissue
    (d) Vascular tissue

14. Most aboundant animal tissue is _____.
    (a) Blood   (b) Epithelium
    (c) Muscular   (d) Connective

15. Striated muscle is also called _____.
    (a) Smooth muscle
    (b) Cardiac muscle
    (c) Skeletal muscle
    (d) Involuntary muscle

16. Which of the following components of xylem is living?
    (a) Vessels
    (b) Tracheids
    (c) Xylem parenchyma
    (d) Xylem sclerenchyma

17. Collenchyma mainly forms _____.
    (a) Epidermis   (b) Hypodermis
    (c) Phloem   (d) Inner cortex

18. The term tissue was given by _____.
    (a) Bichat   (b) Mayer
    (c) Robert Hooke (d) Leeuwenhoek

Tissues

19. A cell body which contains a nucleus and cytoplasm is _____.
    (a) Tendon (b) Ligament
    (c) Neuron (d) Blood
20. Largest blood cells are _____.
    (a) Monocytes
    (b) Basophils
    (c) Neutrophils
    (d) Lymphocytes
21. Ligament connects a bone with _____.
    (a) Muscle (b) Bone
    (c) Skin   (d) Both (a) and (b)
22. Tendon connects _____.
    (a) A bone with another bone
    (b) A muscle with a muscle
    (c) A muscle with a bone
    (d) A nerve with a muscle
23. Plant length is increased by _____.
    (a) Periblem
    (b) Apical meristems
    (c) Lateral meristems
    (d) Parenchyma
24. Which of the following tissues is composed of mainly dead cells?
    (a) Xylem   (b) Phloem
    (c) Epidermis   (d) Endodermis
25. The cell division is restricted to _____.
    (a) Secretory cells
    (b) Permanent cells
    (c) Meristematic cells
    (d) All of these
26. Xylem is made of _____.
    (a) Tracheids   (b) Vessels
    (c) Both of these (d) None of these
27. Active division takes place in the cells of _____.
    (a) Xylem   (b) Phloem
    (c) Cambium (d) Sclerenchyma
28. _____ tissue prevent loss of water in plants.
    (a) Protective (b) Xylem
    (c) Phloem   (d) All of these
29. Ciliated epithelium is found in _____.
    (a) Trachea (b) Uterus
    (c) Tongue   (d) Oesophagus
30. Which type of tissue forms glands?
    (a) Epithelial (b) Nervous
    (c) Muscle   (d) Connective
31. Fluid part of blood after removal of corpuscles is _____.
    (a) Serum   (b) Plasma
    (c) Vaccine (d) Lumph
32. Sprain is caused by excessive pulling of _____.
    (a) Ligaments (b) Muscles
    (c) Nerves   (d) Tendons
33. Match the following.
    A. Blood and lymph   i. Epithelial tissue
    B. Bone and cartilage   ii. Areolar connective tissue
    C. Tendon and ligament iii. Skeletal connective tissue
    D. Ciliated and cuboidal iv. Fluid connective tissue
    (a) A - ii, B - iv, C - i, D - iii
    (b) A - iv, B - iii, C - ii, D - i
    (c) A - iii, B - iv, C - ii, D - i
    (d) A - ii, B - i, C - iv, D - iii
34. Cork cells are made imperious to water and gases by the presence of _____.
    (a) Lignin   (b) Lipids
    (c) Suberin (d) Cellulose
35. Flexibility in plants is due to _____.
    (a) Collenchyma   (b) Parenchyma
    (c) Sclerenchyma (d) Chlorenchyma
36. Smooth muscles occur in _____.
    (a) Uterus (b) Artery
    (c) Vein   (d) All of these
37. Fats are stored in human body as _____.
    (a) Adipose tissue
    (b) Bones
    (c) Cartilage
    (d) Cuboidal epithelium

38. Select the incorrect sentence.
    (a) Two bones are connected with ligament
    (b) Tendons are non-fibrous tissue and fragile
    (c) Cartilage is a form of connective tissue
    (d) Blood has matrix containing proteins, salts and harmones

39. Bone matrix is rich in _____.
    (a) Calcium and phosphorus
    (b) Fluoride and calcium
    (c) Calcium and potassium
    (d) Phosphorus and potassium

40. Which cell does not have perforated cell wall?
    (a) Vessels
    (b) Tracheids
    (c) Companion cells
    (d) Sieve tubes

41. If the tip of sugarcane is removed from the field, even then it keeps on growing in length. It is due to the presence of _____.
    (a) Apical meristem
    (b) Lateral meristem
    (c) Intercalary meristem
    (d) Cambium

42. Husk of coconut is made of _____.
    (a) Parenchyma
    (b) Collenchyma
    (c) Chlorenchyma
    (d) Sclerenchymatous tissue

43. Haversion canals are present in _____.
    (a) Tendon   (b) Ligament
    (c) Bone   (d) Cartilage

44. Blubber of whale and hump of camel are _____.
    (a) Tendon
    (b) Adipose tissue
    (c) Areolar tissue
    (d) Muscular tissue

45. Phloem in the plants perform the function of _____.
    (a) Conduction of food
    (b) Conduction of water
    (c) Providing support
    (d) Photosynthesis

HOTS

1. Which type of epithelial tissue lines the inner surface of the trachea?
   (a) Columnar   (b) Squamous
   (c) Cuboidal   (d) Hyaline cartilage

2. Collenchyma differs from sclerenchyma in _____.
   (a) having suberin cell walls and protoplasm.
   (b) having pectin cell walls and protoplasm.
   (c) having lignin cell walls and protoplasm.
   (d) having no protoplasm or pectin cell walls.

3. The cells that cannot be cultured as they have lost their centrioles are _____.
   (a) chondrocytes   (b) osteocytes
   (c) neurons   (d) mast cells

4. Nissl's granules are present in _____.
   (a) mast cells
   (b) bone cells
   (c) cartilage cells
   (d) nerve cells

5. Which of the following is the correct sequence of transportation of food in plants?
   (a) Mesophyll cells → Tracheids → Vessels → Plant parts
   (b) Mesophyll cells → Xylem vessels → Sieve tubes → Plant parts
   (c) Epidermal cells → Mesophyll cells → Sieve tube → Plant parts
   (d) Mesophyll cells → Sieve tubes → Plant parts

SUBJECTIVE QUESTIONS

1. Define (i) Hypertonic solution (ii) Hypotonic solution (iii) Isotonic solution.

   Ans.
   (i) **Hypertonic solution:** This solution has higher osmotic concentration and less solvent concentration as compared to another solution.

   (ii) **Hypotonic solution:** The solution that possesses lower osmotic concentration and higher solvent concentration as compared to another solution.

   (iii) **Isotonic solution:** The solution that has the same concentration, osmotic as well as solvent as that of another solution.

2. What will happen if:
   (a) Bone is dipped in hydrochloric acid (HCl).
   (b) Bone is dried.
   (c) Ligament gets over stretched.
   (d) Heparin is absent in blood.
   (e) Striated muscles contract rapidly for longer duration.

   Ans.
   (a) When a bone is dipped in HCl, its mineral matter dissolves. Only organic matter is left.
   (b) When a bone is dried, its organic matter gets destroyed. Only mineral matter is left.
   (c) Overstretching of ligament results in sprain.
   (d) Absence of heparin in blood result in coagulation of blood inside the blood vessels.
   (e) When striated muscles contract rapidly for longer duration, they get fatigued due to accumulation of lactic acid in them.

3. (a) Define the following: tendon, ligament and cartilage.
   (b) What is neuron?

   Ans.
   (a) (i) Tendons are cord-like, strong inelastic structures that join skeletal muscles to bones.
   (ii) Ligaments are elastic structures which connect bones to bones.
   (iii) Cartilage is a tough, flexible connective tissue found in all vertebrates consisting of cartilage cells (chondrocyte) in a matrix of collagen fibres and a rubbery protein gel (containing molecules such as chondrin).

   (b) Neuron is one of the unit cell that constitutes nervous tissues that has the property of transmitting and receiving nervous impulses. It has a nucleus containing cell body or soma dendrites and axon.

4. Give one point of difference between notochord and nerve cord.

   Ans.
   Notochord is a transient mesodermal rod in the most dorsal portion of the chordate embryo. In other words, notochord is an ensheathed flexible rod of turgid cells located along the back of chordate embryos and some primitive chordates ventral to nerve cord. It provides place for the attachment of muscles. Notochord has given rise to jointed axial skeleton of vertebral column. Nerve cord is a collection of nerve fibres that runs throughout the length of an animal. It is hollow and dorsal in chordates where it gets modified into central nervous system of brain and spinal cord. Nerve cord is solid and ventral in non chordates.

5. Give four differences between bone and cartilage.

   Ans.

Bone	Cartilage
Hard and non-flexible	Flexible not very hard
Porous	Non-Porous
Blood vessels present	Blood vessels absent
Matrix made up of protein and mineral salts.	Matrix made up of proteins.

Diversity in Living Organisms

Learning Objectives: In this chapter, students will learn about:
- ✓ the importance of diversity
- ✓ the importance of evolution
- ✓ binomial nomenclature
- ✓ classification of different organisms
- ✓ classification of five kingdom

CHAPTER SUMMARY

There is a large variety of living organisms in this world and each organism is unique in its own way. This uniqueness of each organism is called **diversity**. There are a vast number of living organisms in this biosphere and they have great diversity in shape, size and form. It is practically not possible to study each and every organism separately at individual level. It is therefore, advisable to study the diversity of organisms by classifing them in an orderly manner.

The living organisms vary in size from a few micrometers (*e.g.*, microscopic bacteria) to more than 30 metres in length (*e.g.*, blue whale) and more than 100 metres in height (*e.g.*, red wood trees of California)

The living organisms vary in longevity from a few days (*e.g.*, mosquitoes) to several thousand years (*e.g.*, pine trees)

The living organisms range from colourless or transparent to brightly coloured birds and flowers.

Basis of Classification

'The method of arranging organisms into groups or sets on the basis of similarities and differences is called **classification**.' The more basic characteristic for classifying organisms is the kind of cells they are made of. It is erroneous to classify organisms on the basis of the place where they live (such as aquatic, terrestrial, aerial etc.) because many different kinds of organisms may live in the same habitat but they do not belong to the same group. For example, sponges, corals, whales, octopuses, starfishes, fishes (sharks), etc. live in sea but they differ from each other.

The primary characteristic used for making the broadest division of organisms is that whether the organisms are prokaryotic or eukaryotic.

Plants and animals are both eukaryotic organisms. Both are classified into different groups on the basis of their mode of nutrition as well as their body designs. Plants are autotrophic and perform photosynthesis whereas animals are heterotrophic and get food from other organisms. Plant cells have cell wall (of cellulose) whereas animal cells do not have any cell wall.

Importance of Classification

The science of classification is known as taxonomy. It is an important branch of biological science. Classification of living organisms has the following advantages:

(i) Classification makes the study of a wide variety of organisms easy.

(ii) Classification projects before us a picture of all life forms at a glance.

(iii) Classification is essential to understand the interrelationships among different groups of organisms.

(iv) Classification forms a base for the development of other biological sciences. For example, biogeography which is the study of geographical distribution of plants and animals is totally dependent on the information supplied by classification.

Classification and Evolution

Living things are identified and categorised on the basis of their body design in relation to their form and function. Some characteristics are likely to make more wide-ranging changes in body design than the others. There is a role of time (for evolution) in this as well. In other words, characteristics that came into existence earlier are likely to be more fundamental than characteristics that have come into existence later.

So, the classification of life forms is closely related to their evolution. Most life forms that we see today have arisen by an accumulation of changes in their body design that allow the organisms possessing them to survive better. It is called evolution. Charles Darwin (1809–1882) first described this idea of evolution in his book 'The origin or species' published in 1839.

If the idea of evolution is connected to classification, it becomes apparent that some groups or organisms with ancient body designs, have not changed much. There are other groups of organisms that have evolved their current body designs, relatively recently. Those in the first group (i.e., with ancient body designs) are commonly referred to as **"primitive"** or **"lower"** organisms, while those in second group (i.e., with recent body designs) are called **'advanced'** or 'higher' organisms.

In other words, it can be said that first formed (ancient, older) organisms are simpler, while younger organisms (later formed, modern) are more complex, i.e., complexity in design of simpler forms has increased over evolutionary time, so that they have ultimately become more complex.

Hierarchy of Classification–Groups

The main aim of a taxonomic study is to assign organisms an appropriate place within the systematic framework of classification. This framework is called **taxonomic hierarchy** by which the taxonomic groups are arranged in a definite order, from higher to lower categories.

A category is called **taxon**. The taxa or taxon or categories used in the classification are – kingdom

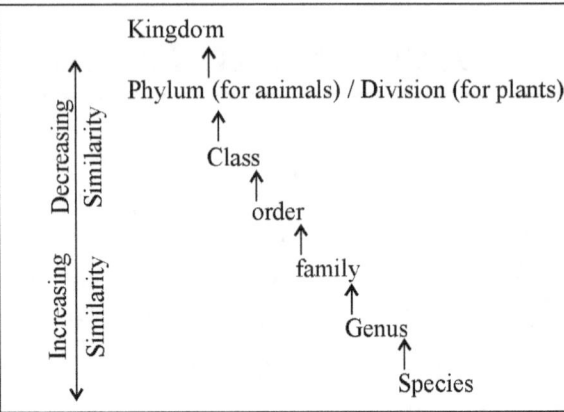

Fig. 12.1. *Hierarchy of Taxonomic Categories*

So, the basic unit classification is **species**. Both in animal and plant kingdoms, the lowest category is a species and highest is a kingdom. As we go upwards from the species towards the kingdom, the number of similar characters decreases.

Robert Whittaker in 1959, proposed five kingdoms classification which included five kingdoms namely Monera, Protista, fungi, plantae, and animalia. These groups are formed on the basis of their cell structure, mode and source of nutrition and body organisation.

Carl woese further classified monera into Archae bacteria (or Archoca) and Eubacteria (or Bacteria).

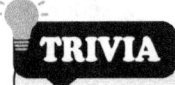 **TRIVIA**

Gasoline can contain between 150 and 1,000 different chemical compounds.

Characteristics of Five Kingdoms

The important characteristics of the five kingdoms of Whittaker are as follows:

Monera

There are basically unicellular organisms which do not have well defined nucleus nor have any cell organelles. Some of them have cell wall while some do not. The mode of nutrition of organisms are either autotrophic or heterotrophic in nature. This group includes bacteria, blue-green algae or cynobacteria, mycoplasma halophiles, cocci, bacilli and spirilla.

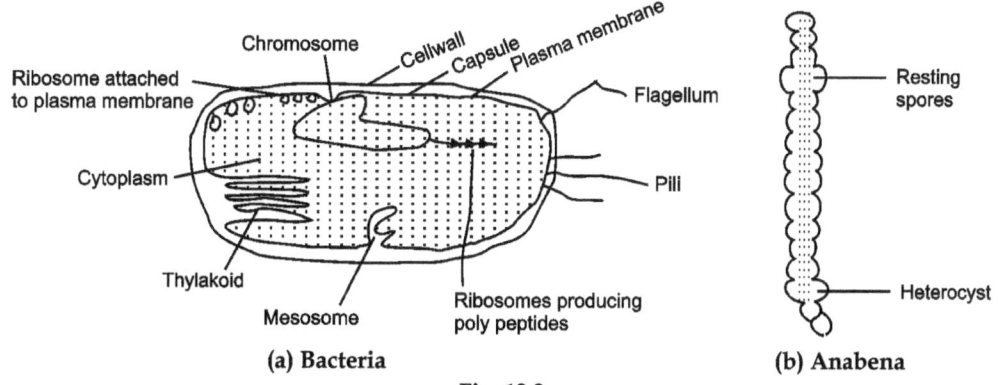

Fig. 12.2

Protista

This kingdom includes many kinds of unicellular eukaryotic organisms which use appendages such as cilia and flagella for movement from one place to another. They are either autotrophic or heterotrophic. Most of them are aquatic in nature having irregular body design. Cytoplasm is divided into two parts, outer and inner parts. They reproduce either sexually or asexually. Organisms like algae, diatoms and protozoans come in this category.

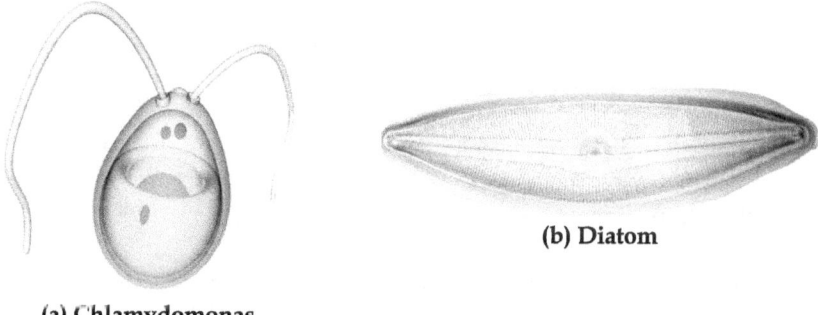

Fig. 12.3

Fungi

These are heterotrophic eukaryotic organisms. Some fungi, such as Puccinia, Albugo, ustilago, etc. are parasites and draw food from the living cells of their host plants. Some fungi, such as Mucor, Rhizopus, Penicillium and Agaricus are decompsers, saprophytes or saprobionts, deriving their nourishment from the dead remains of plants and animals.

They may be unicellular (yeast) or filamentous (most fungi). The body of a multicellular and filamentous fungus is called a mycelium and is composed of several thread-like structures, termed **hyphae**.

Fungi have a cell wall containing a mixture of chitin and cellulose, chitin is a tough complex sugar. The reserve food is glycogen.

Examples: Bread mold (**Rhizopus, Mucor**), yeast (**Sacharomyces**), pink bread mold (**Neurospora**), Green mold (**Penicillium**), Cup fungus, peziza, morel, guchi or sponge fungus or gill fungus (**Morchella**), Mushroom or gill fungus (**Agaricus**), Rust (**Puccinia**), smut (**Ustilgo**) and **Aspergillus**.

Lichens: Some fungal species live in permanent mutually dependent relationships with blue-green algae (or cyanobacteria). Such relationships are called symbiotic. These symbiotic life forms are called **lichens**. The algal component of the lichen is known as **phycobiont** and the fungal component as **mycobiont**.

Diversity in Living Organisms

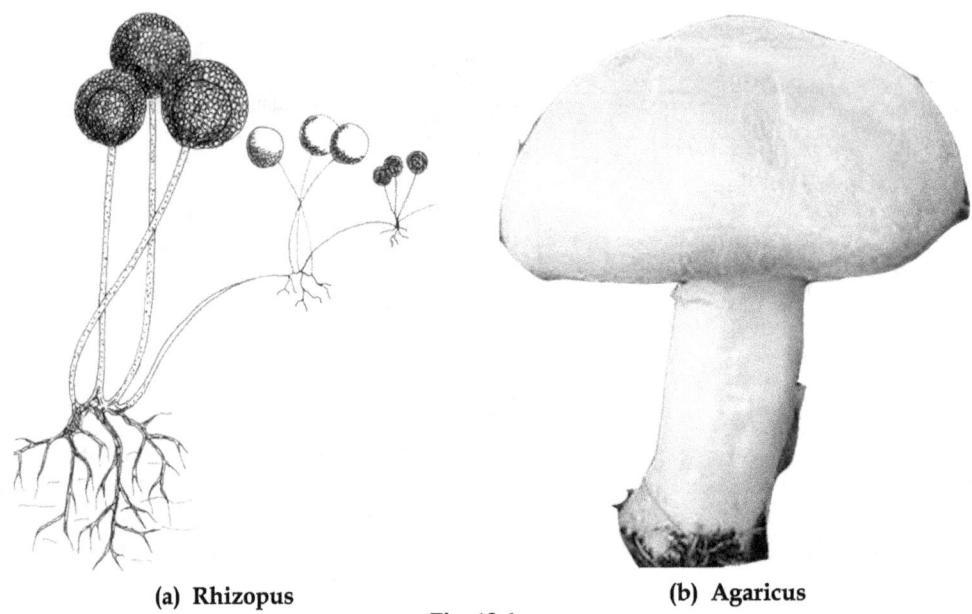

(a) Rhizopus (b) Agaricus

Fig. 12.4

Plantae

Plantae includes multicellular eukaryotes with cell walls. They are autotrophs and use chlorophyll for photosynthesis. Cellulose – containing cell wall occurs around the cell. Reserve food of plant is starch and lipids (oil/fat). In all plants cells double membrane covered cell organelles, called plastids are presat. Growth in plants is generally indefinite due to presence of growing points.

Animalia

This kingdom includes all organisms which are multicellular eukaryotes without cell walls. They are hterotrophs. Animals have organisation of cellular, tissue, organs and organ system level. Animals generally possess a definite shape, size and symmetry. Growth of animals is limited and stops after reaching maturity.

Classification of Plantae Kingdom

Kingdom plantae is further divided into various divisions based on various criteria.

(i) The first level of classification among plants depend on whether the plant body has well differentiated, distinct components.

(ii) The next level of classification is based on whether the differentiated plant body has special tissues (vascular tissues – the xylem and phloem) for transport of water and other substances within the plant body.

(iii) Further classification of plants involve criteria, such as, ability to bear seeds and whether the seeds are enclosed within fruits.

The plants are further sub-classified into three subgroups such as Thallophyta, Bryophyta, Pteridophyta.

Thallophyta

This group includes the most primitive plants which do not have well differentiated body design. The body cannot be differentiated into **stem**, **roots** and **leaves** and is in the form of undivided body, called thallus.

The plants in this group are commonly called algae. These plants are aquatic in nature and are found in both fresh and marine water. They contain the pigment called **chlorophyll** which helps them in photosynthesis and hence they are autotrophic in nature. They have cell wall around their cell and do not have any conducting tissue. They generally reproduce by spore formation.

Ulothrix   Cladophora   Ulva

Fig. 12.5. *Thallophyta – Algae*

Bryophyta

These are multicellular plants found in the damp places and are called **amphibians of the plant kingdom**. Their body can be differentiated into stem and leaf and does not possess any specialised tissue, such as xylem and phloem for conduction of water and minerals from one part to another.

For example: Riccia, moss (funaria), marchantia and barbula.

Riccia   Funaria

Fig. 12.6. *Common Bryophytes*

Pteridophyta

This group includes the plants whose bodies can be differentiated into **roots**, **stem** and **leaves**. It contains the specialised tissue for conduction of water and mineral, from one part of the plant to other parts.

For example: Marsilea, ferns and horse-tails.

The thallophytes, the bryophytes and the pteridophytes have naked embryos that are called **spores**. The reproductive organs of plants in all these three groups are very inconspicuous and they are therefore called "**cryptogammae**" or "those with hidden reproductive organ."

Marsilea   Selaginella

Fig. 12.7. *Pteridophytes*

Diversity in Living Organisms

On the other hand, plants with well differentiated reproductive tissues that ultimately make seeds are called **phanerogams**.

Seeds are the result of the reproductive process. They consist of the embryo along with stored food, which serves for the initial growth of the embryo based on whether the seeds are naked or enclosed in fruits, giving us two groups: Gymnosperms and angiosperms.

Gymnosperms: They are most primitive and simple seed plants. The seeds produced by these plants are naked and are not enclosed within fruits. Gymnosperms are usually perennial, evergreen and woody plants. Sporophylls are aggregated to form cones. There are separate male and female cones. Xylem lacks vessels and phloem lacks companion cells. Gymnospermae includes the following two groups: Cycas, Ginkgo.

Cycas

Ginkgo

Fig. 12.8. *Gymnosperms*

Angiosperms: The angiospermes include the covered seeds which are developed inside an organ and i.e., modified to become fruits. These are also called **flowering plants**. The seeds have structures called **cotyledons**. The angiosperms are divided into two groups on the basis of cotyledons present in the seeds as **monocotyledons** and dicotyledons. The plants having single cotyledons in the seeds are called **monocotyledons** or **monocots** such as maize, wheat, rice, sugarcane, barley etc.

The other one is the plant having two cotyledons in the seeds and are called **dicotyledons.**

For example: Pea, rose, sunflower, apple, grams.

Monocotyledon

Dicotyledon

Fig. 12.9. *Angiosperms*

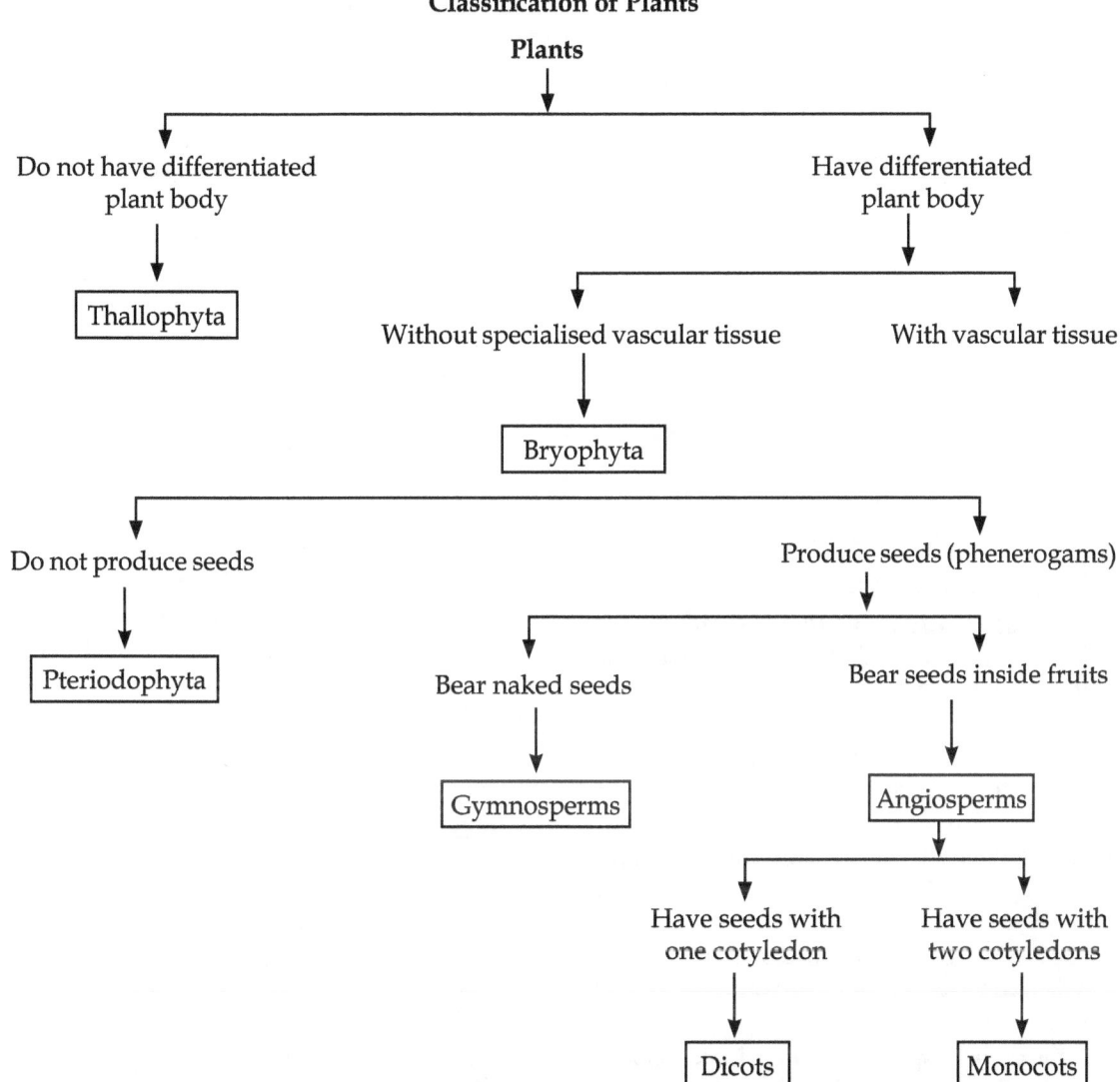

Classification of Animalia Kingdom

These organisms are multicellular and heterotrophic. Most of them can move from one place to another and lack cell wall in their cell. They are further classified on the basis of a body design and cell structure. Some of phyla of the animal kingdom are discussed below:

Porifera

(i) These organisms have small holes on their bodies and are non-motile in nature.
(ii) They have hard outcovering on their body.
(iii) Commonly called sponges and are mainly found in marine habitats.
(iv) They are multicellular and diploblastic, which have radial symmetry.
(v) These small holes on their body forms the canal system in the body and helps in circulating water, oxygen and food.
(vi) They do not have any well developed organs like mouth, body cavity and anus.

For example: Cliona (boring sponge), spongilla, Euspongia (bath sponge).

Diversity in Living Organisms

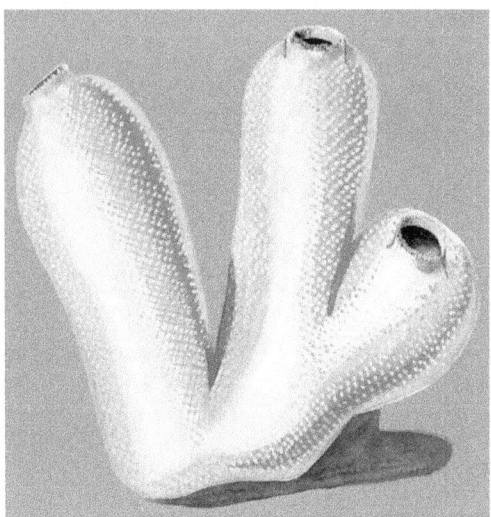

Fig. 12.10. *Sycon*

Coelenterata or Cnidaria
(Gr. Koilos–hollow, enteron–gut)
(i) These are multicellular and diploblastic animals having more organised tissue structure.
(ii) Their body shows radial symmetry and are mostly founded in marine water, except few such as Hydra.
(iii) They have only cells of nervous system and can reproduce by both sexual and asexual methods.
(iv) They possess central gastrovascular cavity which consists of mouth surrounded by short and slender tentacles.
(v) Some of these species live in colonies (corals), while others have a solitary life– span (Hydra) and Jelly fish.

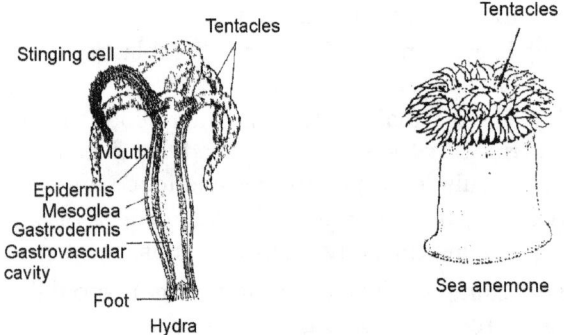

Fig. 12.11. *Coelenterata*

Platyhelminthes
(Gr. platys–flat, helmins–worm)
(i) Bilaterally symmetrical (i.e., the left and right halves of the body have the same design) and dorsoventrally flattended animals, which is why these animals are called **flatworms**.
(ii) Body is thin, soft leaf-like or ribbon-like.
(iii) There are three layers of cells from which differentiated tissues can be made; that is why they called triploblastic.
(iv) Digestive cavity has (when present) a single opening mouth (anus is absent)
(v) Suckers and hooks are usually present.
(vi) Circulatory and respiratory systems and skeleton are absent.
(vii) Flame cells are present for excretion.
(viii) They are also hermaphrodites i.e., both the sexes, male and female are present in the same individuals.

For example: Planaria are free living and liverflukes are parasitic in nature.

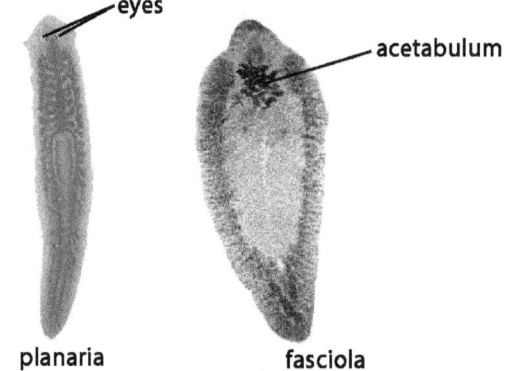

Fig. 12.12. *Platyhel Minthes*

Nematoda
(i) Their bodies show bilateral symmetry and are triploblastic.
(ii) Their bodies have tissues and have true body cavity, but no real organs.
(iii) The body is covered with tough resistant cuticle that provides their bodies some sorts of shape and structure.
(iv) Males and females exist in different individuals.

(v) These are very familiar as parasitic worms causing diseases, such as the worms causing elephantiasis (filarial warms) or the worms in the intestines (round worm or pin worms)

For example: Ascaris, wuchereria.

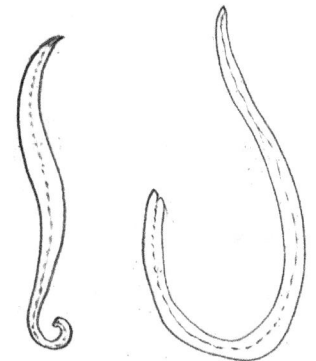

Male Ascaris   Female Ascaris

Fig. 12.13. *Nematodes*

Annelida
(L. annelus–aring, segmented Worms)

(i) These organisms show bilateral symmetry and are triploblastic.
(ii) They also have true body cavity, this allows true organs to be packaged in the body structure. There is, thus, extensive organ differentiation. This differentiation occurs in a segmental fashion, with the segments lined up one after the other from head to tail.
(iii) The body is covered with thin cuticles and have lateral appendages for locomotion.
(iv) They have nephridia for removal of waste and nervous system consists of dorsal brain and a ventral nerve chord having ganglia and lateral nerve in each segment of the body.

(v) These animals are found in a variety of habitats – fresh water, marine water as well as land.

For example: Earthworm, leeches, Nereis, Hirudinaria

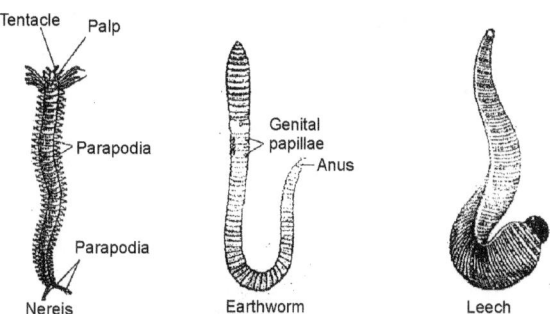

Fig. 12.14. *Annelide*

Arthropoda: (Gr. Arthros – jointed; podos – foot, jointed – legged animals)

(i) This is the largest phylum of the animal kingdom.
(ii) The body of the organism is bilaterally symmetrical and are triplobastic.
(iii) The body is divided into two parts: head and thorax.
(iv) The head part consists of brain, and sense organs.
(v) There is an open circulatory system and hence the blood does not flow in well defined blood vessels.
(vi) The male and female sexes are usually different and show internal fertilization.
(vii) The coelomic cavity is blood-filled.
(viii) They are free living or parasitic in nature.
(ix) Excretion through coelomducts, malphigian tubules or green or coxal glands.

Example: Housely, spider, butterfly cockroach.

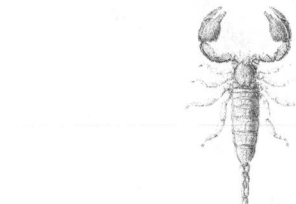      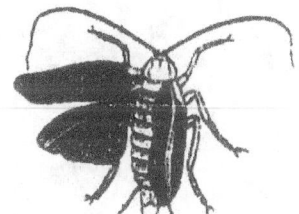

Palamnaeus (Scorpion)   Butter fly   Pariplaneta (Cockroach)

Fig. 12.15. *Arthropodes*

Mollusca (L molluscus – soft)

(i) Body is soft, bilaterally symmetrical, with little segmentation and without appendages.
(ii) Body cavity is haemocoel. True coelom is reduced.
(iii) Circulatory system is open except in cephalopods.
(iv) Respiration through gills (called ctenidia), mantle or lung of the mantle.
(v) Excretion by a pair of metanephridia or kidneys.
(vi) Sexes are usually saparate and are mostly aquatic in nature.
(vii) Sensory organs of touch, smell taste, equilibrium and vision (in some).
(viii) There is a foot that is used for moving around.

For example: Octopus, Unio, Pila, Chiton.

Note: Osmoregulatory organs known as **nephridia** occur in many invertebrates. When they are closed at the inner end they are called **protonephridia**, but when they open into a coelomic space at their inner end, they are called **metanepridia**.

Pila

Unio

Fig. 12.16. *Mollusca*

Echinodermata (Gr. Echinos – spiny or hedge or hedge hog; derma – skin, spiny skinned animals)

(i) Simple animals may be star-like, spherical or elongate.
(ii) Body triploblastic, coelomate, unsegmented and radially symmetrical (larva bilaterally symmetrical)
(iii) Body lacks head, but has oral and aboral surface. Oral surface of body has five radial areas called **ambulacra**.
(iv) They have hard outer covering made up of calcium carbonate.
(v) Body cavity is modified into a unique **water vascular system** which moves respiratory and locomotary organs, the **tube feet** or **podia**.
(vi) Digestive system is usually complete. Anus is absent in ophiuroids.
(vii) Excretory organs absent.
(viii) Reproduction sexual, asexual or by regeneration. Sexes are separate.
(ix) Exclusively marine, free living and gregarious (live in groups animals).

For example: Star firsh, Antedon, Urchins, Ophioderma etc.

Antedon
(feather star)

Holothuria
(sea cucumber)

Asterias
(star fish)

Fig. 12.17. *Echinodermates*

Protochordata
(i) They are bag-like, sessile, soft bodied, non-metameric animals.
(ii) Adult have cellulose covering over their bodies.
(iii) These animals are bilaterally symmetrical triploblastic and have a coelom.
(iv) They have notochord in their bodies having dorsal tubular nerve chord.
(v) The notochord is a long rod like support structure that runs along the back of the animal separating the nervous tissue from the gut.
(vi) It provides a place for muscles to attach for case of movement.
(viii) Gill slits form the respiratory system and connects the pharynx with outside.
(viii) No nephridia single glomerulus connected to blood vessels has a excretory function.
(ix) Protochordates are marine animals.

For examples: Balanoglossus, Herdmania and Amphioxus.

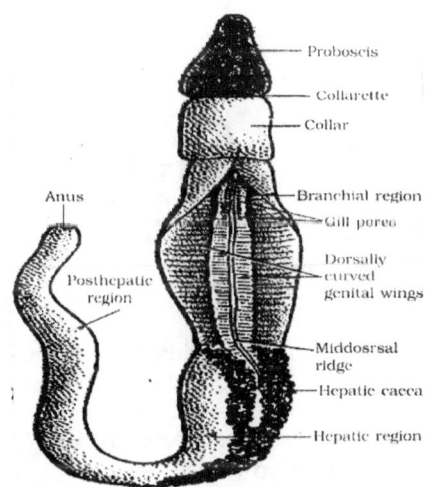

Fig. 12.18. *A protochordata: Blanoglorrus*

Vertebrata
(i) These animals have a true vertebral column and internal skeleton.
(ii) These are bilaterally symmetrical, triploblastic, coelomic and segmented.
(iii) They have complex differentiation in body tissues and organs.

All chordates possess the following features:
(a) Have a notochord
(b) Have a dorsal nerve cord
(c) Are triploblastic
(d) Have paired gill pouches
(e) Are coelomate

Vertebrates are grouped into five classes: Pisces, amphibia, reptilia, aves and mammalia.

Pisces
(i) These are fishes and are exclusively aquatic animals. Their skin is covered with scales.
(ii) They obtained oxygen dissolved in water using gills.
(iii) They have streamlined body and muscular tails which are used for movement.
(iv) They are cold blooded animals and heart is two chambered.
(v) They reproduce by laying eggs
(vi) The skeleton is entirely made up of cartilage valves.
(vii) The digestive system is with J-shaped stomach and intestine with spiral valves.
(viii) They have well developed sense of smell, vibration reception, and electro reception.
(ix) Their size varies from few mm to several meters.

For example: Tuna, rohu, lion fish, sting ray.

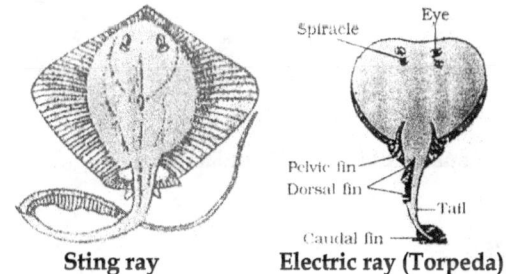

Sting ray   Electric ray (Torpeda)

Fig. 12.19. *Pisces*

Amphibia
(i) The amphibians are the groups of animals having chordates which live on land as well as in water.
(ii) They have three chambered heart and respire through gills or lungs.
(iii) Excrete either ammonia (tadpole larva) or urea.

Diversity in Living Organisms

(iv) They have mucus glands in the skin and are cold blooded animals.
(v) They reproduce by laying eggs i.e., oviparous and fertilization is external in case of frogs and toads, but internal in salamanders and apoda.
(vi) These animals differ from the fish in the lack of scales.

For example: frog, toads and salamanders, hyla, necturus.

Reptilia
(i) These animals are cold-blooded, have scales on their skin.
(ii) Teeth are present in all reptiles except in tortoises and turtles.
(iii) Respiration is through lungs only, gills are not present.
(iv) Heart is three chambered heart, but few of them like crocodiles have four chambered heart.
(v) Fertilization takes place internally.
(vi) They have two pairs of limbs with five digits.
(vii) Most of them are oviparous and lay their eggs with tough coverings and do not need to lay their eggs in water but few are viviparous like turtles, crocodiles, lizard and snakes.

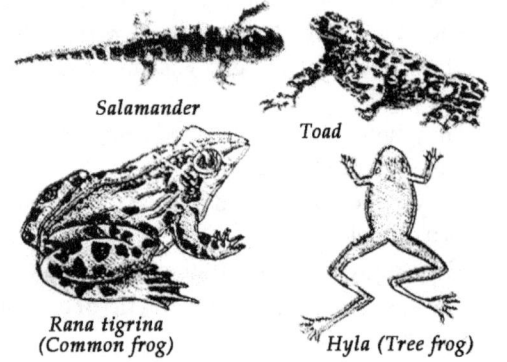

Fig. 12.20. *Amphibia*

For examples: Snakes, turtles crocodiles, chamaeleon, lizards.

House wall lizard (Hemidactylus)

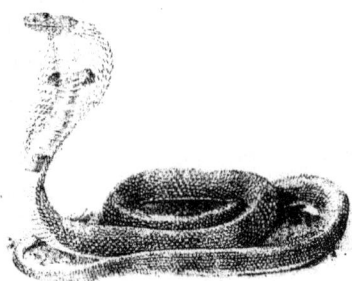
King Cobra

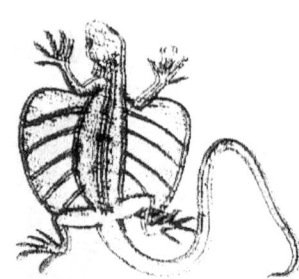
Flying lizard (Draco)

Fig. 12.21. *Reptilia*

Aves
(i) These are warm-blooded animals.
(ii) Horny scales persist on the feet but feathers cover most of the body. Cutaneous glands are absent
(iii) Two forelimbs are modified into wings which help them in flight.
(iv) Bones have air cavity and hence are light which helps them to fly.
(v) They have four chambered heart with two auricles and two ventricles.
(vi) They breathe through lungs.
(vii) They are oviparous and reproduce by laying eggs. Fertilization is internal.
(viii) Body is divided into head, neck, trunk and tail.
(ix) Their size ranges from the smallest bird being the humming bird to largest bird being the ostrich.

For example: pigeon, sparrow, ostrich, crow etc.

Male Tufted Duck (Aythya fuligula)　　　Pigeon　　　Crow

Fig. 12.22. *Aves (Birds)*

Mammalia
(i) These are warm-blooded animals.
(ii) Body is divided into head, neck, trunk and tail. Movable eyelids are present.
(iii) Females have milk producing mammary glands for the production of milk to nourish their young ones.
(iv) Their skin has hair as well as sweat and oil glands.
(v) They have external ear which helps them to hear sounds from the surroundings.
(vi) Heart is four-chambered.
(vii) Respiration is through lungs and fertilization is internal, penis is always present in males.
(viii) Most mammals produce live young ones. However, a few of them like platypus and echidna lay eggs and some like kangaroos give birth to very poorly developed young ones.
(ix) They have two pairs of pentadactyl limbs which are variously adapted for walking and running.

Example: Cat, Dog, Human, Macaca (monkey), Pteropus manis (ant eater), Panthera Tigris (tiger)

Fig. 12.23. *Mammalia*

Nomenclature

It would be difficult for people speaking or writing in different languages to know when they are talking about the same organism. This problem was resolved by agreeing upon a scientific name for organism. The system of scientific naming or nomenclature was introduced by **Carolus Linnaeus** in eighteenth century Linnaeus is considered to be the **Father of Taxonomy** as he developed the binomial system of nomenclature i.e., each organism is given two names, the first name is called genus and the second name is called species. The genus represents the community to which the organism belongs and the second name represents specific organism to which it belongs.

Certain conventions are followed while writing the scientific names:
(i) The name of the genus begins with a capital letter.
(ii) The name of the species begins with a small letter.
(iii) When printed, the scientific name is given in italics.

Diversity in Living Organisms

(iv) When written by hand, the genus name and the species name have to be underlined separately. The scientific name of some of the common organisms are given below:

S. No.	Common Name	Scientific Name
1.	Lion	*Panther Leo*
2.	Tiger	*Pinthra Tigress*
3.	Dog	*Canis Lupus*
4.	Cat	*Felis Catus*
5.	Rat	*Tattus Norvegicus*
6.	Mango	*Mangifera Indica*
7.	Neem	*Azadirochta Indica*
8.	Potato	*Solanum Tuberosum*
9.	Lotus	*Nelumbo Nucifera*
10.	Honey bee	*Apis mellifera*
11.	Ant	*Formicidae*
12.	Peacock	*Pavo Cristatus*
13.	Wheat	*Triticum Aestivum*

Do you know

1. In Lichens, there exists a "master and slave symbiotic relationship" between alge and fungi. This is called **helotism**.
2. Sphagnum (peat moss) had been used to replace absorbent cotton for dressing wound in second world war, so it is called **cotton moss**.

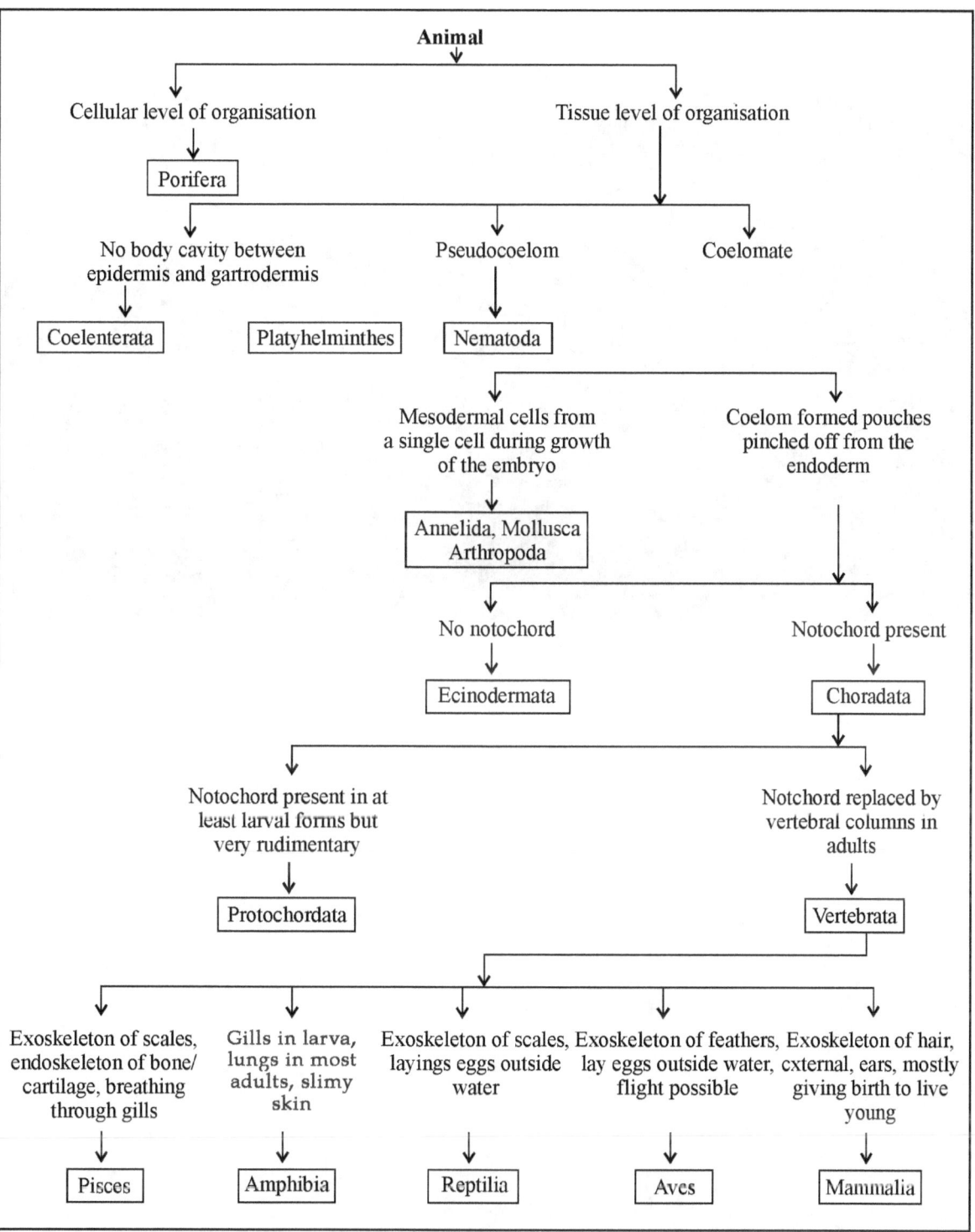

Diversity in Living Organisms

MUST REMEMBER

- Plants are autotrophic and perform photosynthesis whereas animals are heterotrophic and get food from other organisms.
- The science of classification is known as taxonomy.
- The main aim of a taxonomic study is to assign organisms an appropriate place within the systematic framework of classification.
- Fungi have a cell wall containing a mixture of chitin and cellulose, chitin is a tough complex sugar.
- The algal component of the lichen is known as phycobiont and the fungal component as mycobiont.
- The thallophytes, the bryophytes and the pteridophytes have naked embryos that are called spores.
- Sporophylls are aggregated to form cones.
- The angiospermes include the covered seeds which are developed inside an organ and i.e., modified to become fruits.
- Osmoregulatory organs known as nephridia occur in many invertebrates.

MULTIPLE CHOICE QUESTIONS

1. Which taxonomic term may be substituted for any rank in the classification?
   (a) Class (b) Taxon
   (c) Genus (d) Species

2. Algae belong to _____.
   (a) Thallophytes
   (b) Bryophytes
   (c) Pteridophyte
   (d) All of these

3. The most primitive and simple plants whose body cannot be differentiated into stem, roots and leaves are called _____.
   (a) Bacteria (b) Fungus
   (c) Mushroom (d) Algae

4. Who is known as the father of taxonomy?
   (a) Walter G. Rosen
   (b) Ernst Mayer
   (c) Linnaeus
   (d) Charles Darwin

5. What is scientific name of wheat?
   (a) Salanum tuberosum
   (b) Triticum aestirnum
   (c) Mangi ferra
   (d) Felis catus

6. Who gave the five kingdom of classification?
   (a) Walter G. Rosen
   (b) Linnaeus
   (c) Whittaker
   (d) Charles Darwin

7. Who has divided Prokaryota (Monera) into Archea and Eubactria?
   (a) Woese (b) Copeland
   (c) Whittaker (d) Haeckel

8. Hotspots of biodiversity means _____.
   (a) Area of the Earth that contain many endemic species
   (b) Species diversity at particular areas
   (c) Species in particular niche/area
   (d) Species serves as proxy for entire communities in particular areas.

9. The science of naming organism is called _____.
   (a) Taxonomy (b) Classification
   (c) Nomenclature (d) Identification

10. The system of nomenclature evolved by Linnaeus is _____.
    (a) Mononomial (b) Binomial
    (c) Polynomial (d) Vernacular

11. The basic unit of classification is _____.
    (a) Species (b) Genus
    (c) Variety (d) Family

12. Genetic material of prokaryoates is called _____.
    (a) Nucleolus (b) Mesosome
    (c) Nucleoid (d) Plasmid

13. Amoeba belongs to kingdom _____.
    (a) Monera (b) Protista
    (c) Fungi (d) Animalia

14. The eukaryotic kingdom protista was created by _____.
    (a) Woese
    (b) Whittaker
    (c) Margulis and Schwartr
    (d) Heckel

15. Who proposed the concept of evolution?
    (a) Aristotle (b) Darwin
    (c) Theophratus (d) Linnaeus

16. The science of classification is called _____.
    (a) Biology (b) Taxonomy
    (c) Domography (d) None of these

17. Phylogeny is the study of _____.
    (a) Evolution of species
    (b) Development of an individual
    (c) Embryonic development of an argan
    (d) Ecological adaptation of an organisms

18. Class is a category between _____.
    (a) Family and genes
    (b) Order and family
    (c) Kingdom and phylum
    (d) Phylum and order

19. Fungi resemble animals in having _____.
    (a) Mycelium   (b) Chitin
    (c) Glycogen   (d) Both (b) and (c)
20. A plant body not differentiated into root, stem and leaves is termed as _____.
    (a) Herb   (b) Thallus
    (c) Hyphae   (d) Mycelium
21. A group of similar freely inter-breeding organisms constitutes a _____.
    (a) Class   (b) Family
    (c) Species   (d) Genera
22. Chlorophyll containing, autotrophic thallophytes are called _____.
    (a) Lichens   (b) Algae
    (c) Fungi   (d) Bryophytes
23. The ability of nitrogen fixation is found in _____.
    (a) Monerans only
    (b) Protistans only
    (c) Both monerans and protisyans
    (d) Fungi only
24. A group of related genera, with still less number of similarities as compared to the genus and species, constitutes _____.
    (a) Class   (b) Order
    (c) Family   (d) Division
25. The algal partner of a lichen is called _____.
    (a) Phycobiont
    (b) Mycobiont
    (c) Both (a) and (b)
    (d) None of these
26. The body of _____ has chitinous cell wall and is made up of hyphae and mycelium.
    (a) Funaria   (b) Riccia
    (c) Rhizopus   (d) Spirogyra
27. Naked seeds are present in _____.
    (a) Lemon   (b) Mango
    (c) Mustard   (d) Pinus
28. The compound plants composed of algae and fungi are called _____.
    (a) Algae   (b) Lichens
    (c) Bryophytes   (d) Pteridophytes
29. Which of the following group of plants is called vascular cryptogams?
    (a) Angiospermae
    (b) Bryophyta
    (c) Pteridophyta
    (d) Thallophyta
30. Homo : generic name :: sapiens : _____
    (a) Species name
    (b) Organism name
    (c) Human name
    (d) Division name
31. Reproductive structure of flowers is _____.
    (a) Pteridophytes
    (b) Gymnosperms
    (c) Angiosperms
    (d) Both (a) and (b)
32. The phylum of sedentary animals is _____.
    (a) Porifera
    (b) Mollusca
    (c) Echinodermata
    (d) Both (b) and (c)
33. Radial symmetry is found in _____.
    (a) Protozoa   (b) Coelenterate
    (c) Flatworms   (d) Arthropoda
34. Cnidaria is characterised by _____.
    (a) Tissue level of organisation
    (b) Coelenteron
    (c) Nematoblasts
    (d) All of these
35. Tapeworm is a member of phylum _____.
    (a) Annelida   (b) Porifera
    (c) Nematoda   (d) Platyhelminthes
36. An example of phylum echinodermata is _____.
    (a) Starfish   (b) Prawan
    (c) Octopus   (d) Apis
37. Protochordates consist of _____ and _____.
    (a) Urochordata and vertebrata
    (b) Urochordata and cephalochordata
    (c) Cephalochordate and vertebrata
    (d) None of these

38. Subphylum urochordata includes _____.
    (a) Terristrial animals
    (b) Marine animals
    (c) Amphibians
    (d) All of these
39. Choanocytes are unique to _____.
    (a) Porifera
    (b) Protozoa
    (c) Mollusca
    (d) Echinodermata
40. Echinoderms have _____.
    (a) Canal system
    (b) Water wascular system
    (c) Jet propulsion
    (d) Book lungs
41. Match the column A with column B.

S. No.	Group	Name of Animal
i.	Porifera	(a) Hydra
i.	Coelenterata	(b) Ascaris
iii.	Annelida	(c) Euplectela
iv.	Nematoda	(d) Leech

    (a) i – a, ii – c, iii – d, iv –b
    (b) i – c, ii – a, iii – d, iv – b
    (c) i – b, ii – c, iii – d, iv – a
    (d) i – a, ii – d, iii – c, iv – b
42. 'Venus flower basket' is the dried skeleton of _____.
    (a) Euspongia   (b) Spongilla
    (c) Euplectella   (d) Leueosolenia
43. The book "Systema Nature" was written by _____.
    (a) Haeckel   (b) Linnacus
    (c) Whittaker (d) Robert Brown
44. The book "Origin of Species" is written by _____.
    (a) Darwin   (b) Haeckel
    (c) Linnaeus   (d) Whittaker
45. What is scientific name of the national bird of India?
    (a) Psittocula cupatra
    (b) Passer domesticus
    (c) Pavo cristatus
    (d) Corvus splendens
46. Birds differ from bats in absence of _____.
    (a) Homeothermy
    (b) Diaphragm
    (c) Four chambered heart
    (d) Trachcae
47. Elephantitis is caused by _____.
    (a) Wuchereria   (b) Pinworm
    (c) Planarians   (d) Liver fluke
48. Pteridphytes do not have _____.
    (a) Root   (b) Stem
    (c) Flowers (d) Leaves
49. Find out the false statement.
    (a) Fishes, amphibians and reptiles are oviparous
    (b) All of the mammals are viviparous
    (c) Aves are warm blooded, egg laying and have four chambered heart
    (d) Aves have feather covered body, fore limbs are modified as wings
50. Which one is the most striking (or common) character of chordates?
    (a) Presence of coelom
    (b) Presence of notochord
    (c) Presence of gill pouches
    (d) Presence of triploblastic condition

Diversity in Living Organisms

HOTS

1. Symbiosis between fungi and algae leads to the formation of _____.
   (a) algae   (b) lichens
   (c) fungi   (d) yeast

2. The kingdom Protista consists of _____.
   (a) multicellular organisms whose chromosomes are not enclosed in a nuclear membrane.
   (b) unicellular organisms whose chromosomes are not enclosed in a nuclear membrane.
   (c) multicellular organisms whose chromosomes are enclosed in a nuclear membrane.
   (d) unicellular organisms whose chromosomes are enclosed in a nuclear membrane.

3. Suppose you accidently find an old preserved permanent slide without a label. In order to identify it, you place the slide under microscope and observe the following features:
   (i) Unicellular
   (ii) Well defined nucleus
   (iii) Biflagellate - one long flagellum, lying longitudinally and the other short flagellum.
   What would you identify it as? Also name the kingdom it belongs to.
   (a) Diatom ; Fungi
   (b) Trypanosoma ; Protozoa
   (c) Paramecium ; Protozoa
   (d) Euglena ; Protista

4. Match column I with column II and select the correct option from the codes given below.

Column I	Column II
(A) Thallophyta	(i) Marsilea
(B) Bryophyta	(ii) Pinus
(C) Pteridophyta	(iii) Ulothrix
(D) Gymnospermae	(iv) Ficus
(E) Angiospermae	(v) Funaria

   (a) (A)-(iii), (B)-(ii), (C)-(i), (D)-(iv), (E)-(v)
   (b) (A)-(i), (B)-(ii), (C)-(iii), (D)-(iv), (E)-(v)
   (c) (A)-(i), (B)-(v), (C)-(iii), (D)-(ii), (E)-(iv)
   (d) (A)-(iii), (B)-(v), (C)-(i), (D)-(ii), (E)-(iv)

5. Match column I with column II and select the correct option from the given codes.

Column I	Column II
(A) Pore bearing animals	(i) Arthropoda
(B) Cnidoblasts	(ii) Coelenterata
(C) Metameric segmentation	(iii) Porifera
(D) Jointed legs	(iv) Echinodermata
(E) Soft bodied animals	(v) Mollusca
(F) Spiny skinned animal	(vi) Annelida

   (a) (A)-(iv), (B)-(v), (C)-(i), (D)-(vi), (E)-(iii), (F)-(ii)
   (b) (A)-(vi), (B)-(i), (C)-(iv), (D)-(ii), (E)-(v), (F)-(iii)
   (c) (A)-(iii), (B)-(ii), (C)-(vi), (D)-(i), (E)-(v), (F)-(iv)
   (d) (A)-(i), (B)-(ii), (C)-(iv), (D)-(vi), (E)-(v), (F)-(iii)

SUBJECTIVE QUESTIONS

1. (a) Why are protozoa are regarded as early animals?
   (b) Differentiate the nature of skin in four classes of tetrapoda.

Ans.
   (a) Protozoa are regarded as early or primitive animals because: (i) they exhibit a cellular level of organisation, (ii) the tissues, organs and organ systems have not developed in them, (iii) they are microscopic and exhibit a primitive models of reproduction.
   (b) The nature of skin in four classes of tetrapoda are:
      (i) Class Amphibia – Thin, moist, glandular and respiratory skin.
      (ii) Class Reptilia – Dry and non-glandular skin with horny scales or scutes.
      (iii) Class Aves – Dry and non-glandular skin with feathers.
      (iv) Class Mammalia – Glandular skin with hairs.

2. Give the characteristics of Monera.

Ans.
   (a) Organisms are unicellular, do not have a defined nucleus.
   (b) Organisms may have cell wall or may not have cell wall.
   (c) Mode of nutrition is either autotrophic or heterotrophic.

3. Give the characteristics of Protista.

Ans.
   (a) Organisms are unicellular and eukaryotic.
   (b) Use appendages for locomotion like cilia, flagella, etc.
   (c) Nutrition is either autotrophic or heterotrophic.
   (d) E.g.: algae, protozoa.

4. Give the characteristic features of Echinodermata.

Ans.
   (a) Spikes present on skin.
   (b) Free living, marine animals.
   (c) Triploblastic and have a coelomic cavity.
   (d) Have a peculiar water driven tube system used for moving around.
   (e) Have hard calcium carbonate structure that is used as a skeleton.

   Example: Starfish.

5. Give the characteristics of mammals.

Ans.
   (a) Mammals are warm-blooded animals.
   (b) Four-chambered heart.
   (c) Mammary glands for production of milk to nourish their younger one.
   (d) Skin has hairs, sweat glands and oil glands.
   (e) Most of them produce their young ones (viviparous).

Why do We Fall Ill   13

Learning Objectives : In this chapter, students will learn about:
- ✓ health and its significance
- ✓ the factors affecting health
- ✓ disease-causing factors
- ✓ infectious and non-infectious diseases

CHAPTER SUMMARY

Health is one of the most important aspects of human life. Health and diseases are interconnected with each other. Cells are the fundamental units of living organisms. They are made of a variety of chemical substances such as proteins, carbohydrates, fats or lipids and so on. There are various specialized activities in our bodies and all the activities are interconnected with each other. Whenever there is malfunctioning of any organ of the body; it affects the entire system of the body and our body starts functioning abnormally. This situation is called a **disease**. Thus, diseases can be defined as the **abnormal functioning** of the body.

Significance of Health

Health is described as the state of complete physical, mental and social well being. Thus, being healthy means that one feels good physically, has a positive outlook and is able to keep with the social and mental pressure without much difficulty. Being healthy is for more than just being free from diseases.

For maintaining a healthy life cycle, a person needs to have a balanced and varied diet, needs to exercise, live regularly in a proper shelter and get enough sleep. Maintaining a good hygiene also reduces the chance of developing an infection.

A disease usually indicates malfunction in the body. A doctor is able to diagnose disease by identifying the symptoms. Symptoms of a disease may be physical, mental or both.

Both personal and community issues matter for health:

To prevent diseases we need to keep our environment and our surroundings clean and hygienic. Since we live in a society, individual health is important to keep our society healthy. We must take care of the garbages, which should not be left open on the streets and in the open areas. We should have closed water of the drain. The drainage system should have no blockage in it to keep the dirty water flowing and there should not be stagnation of water.

To keep ourselves healthy we must take balanced diet. It keeps us mentally sharp and alert to fight any sort of problems.

We need to be happy in order to be truly healthy, and if we mistreat each other and are afraid of each other, we cannot be happy or healthy. Thus, we see that there is an overlap of personal and community issues for health.

The conditions essential for good health are:
(i) Better sanitation.
(ii) Availability of clean drinking water.
(iii) Availability of adequate, nutritious food.
(iv) Social equality and harmony.

Distinction between 'healthy' and 'disease free' state:

Disease, literally means being uncomfortable. We talk of disease when we can find a specific and particular cause for discomfort. This does not mean that we have to know the absolute final cause: we can say that someone is suffering from diarrhoea without knowing exactly what has caused the loose motions.

We can now easily see that it is possible to be in poor health without actually suffering from a particular disease. Good health for a dancer may mean being able to stretch his body into difficult but graceful positions. On the other hand, good health for a musician may mean having enough breathing capacity in his/her lungs to control the notes from his/her flute. To have the opportunity to realise the unique potential in all of us is also necessary for real health.

So, we can be in poor health without there being a simple cause in the form of an identifiable disease. This is the reason why, when we think about health, we think about societies and communities. On the other hand, when we think about disease, we think about individual sufferers.

Disease and its Causes

How do we know that there is a disease? When there is a disease, either the functioning or the appearance of one or more systems of the body will change for worse. These changes give rise to symptoms and signs of disease.

The following symptoms indicate disease and urge us to go to see doctor:

(i) having headache, shivering and body temperature.
(ii) having diarrhoea (loose-motions) and
(iii) having a wound with pus.

Signs of disease are what physicians look for on the basis of the symptoms. Signs will give a little more definite indication of the presence of a particular disease. Physicians will also get laboratory tests done to investigate the disease further.

Acute and Chronic Diseases

The diseases which get cured in short time is called **acute diseases**. The diseases like common cold, influenza, are acute diseases. The acute diseases do not cause any major effect on the health of the affected person. Affected persons do not lose weight, do not become short of breath, and do not feel tired all the time.

The diseases which last for long time and are almost incurable are called **chronic diseases**. For example: Tuberculosis of lungs, AIDS, cancer, Leprosy etc. The chronic diseases affect the health drastically. The person becomes weak and loses weight. It also reduces our ability to learn and understand the matters and reduces the memory power.

Causes of Disease

There can be various factors which act as cause of disease.

Intrinsic Factors

The disease causing factors which exist within the human body are called **intrinsic factors**. The important intrinsic factors are:

(i) Malfunctioning or improper functioning of various body parts such as heart, kidney, liver etc.
(ii) Genetic disorders
(iii) Hormonal imbalances
(iv) Malfunctioning of immune system of body, for example allergy.

The diseases caused by intrinsic sources are called **organic** or **metabolic diseases**. Some common diseases are:

(i) Cardiac failure (ii) Kidney failure
(iii) Osteoporosis (iv) Myopia
(v) Cataract (vi) Sickle cell anaemia
(vii) Haemophilia (viii) Dwarfism
(ix) Gigantism (x) Cretinism
(xi) Diabetes (xii) Allergies (asthma)
(xiii) Arthritis (xiv) Cancer

Extrinsic Factors

The factors which enter into our bodies from outside and cause the diseases are called **extrinsic factors**. The extrinsic factors which cause diseases are microorganisms, environmental factors, alcohol, drugs and unbalanced diet. Some of the diseases which are caused by extrinsic factors are Beri-Beri, Pellagra, Scurvy, AIDS, Cholera, Leprosy, Dengue, Hepatitis etc.

Infectious and Non-infectious Causes

Some diseases caused by microbes or microorganisms are called infectious diseases.

This is because the microbes can spread in the community, and the diseases they cause will spread with them.

On the other hand, there are also diseases that are not caused by infections agents. Their causes vary, but they are not external causes like microbes that can spread in the community. Instead, these are mostly internal, non-infections causes.

For example: Some cancers are caused by genetic abnormalities. High blood pressure can be caused by excessive weight and lack of exercise.

Note: Two Australians **Robin Warren and Barry Marshall** made a discovery that a bacterium *Helicobacter pylori*, was responsible for peptic ulcers. They saw these small curved bacteria in the lower part of the stomach in many patients. They noticed that signs of inflammation were always present around these bacteria and this disease can be cured by a short period of treatment with antibiotics.

Infectious Diseases

Infectious Agents

The microorganisms which carry pathogens that cause disease are called infectious agents. Some of the infection agents are virus, bacteria, fungi, protozoans etc. Some common diseases caused by virus are common cold, influenza, dengue, AIDS etc. The disease caused by bacteria are cholera, TB, anthrax, typhoid, etc. These pathogens cause the diseases either by damaging the tissue or by toxin secretion. The virus is considered to be the border line between living and non living organisms. When they are inside the human cell they act like living and when they are outside they behave like non-living. The diseases caused by bacteria can be cured by taking antibiotics, whereas the disease caused by virus can be cured by taking antiviral agents called **interferon**. The antibodies act inside the cell, where as interferons act outside the cells. Interferons act very quickly against the viruses. But the action is temporary.

Diseases caused by different microorganisms

S. No.	Microorganism	Diseases
1.	Bacteria	Cholera, Typhoid, TB, Anthrax, Tetanus, Food poisoning, Meningitis, diphtheria etc.
2.	Virus	AIDS, common cold, Influenza, measles, Hepatitis-B, chicken pox, mumps
3.	Fungi	Skin disease, Ring worm.
4.	Protozoans	Malaria, Dysentry, Sleeping sickness, kala azar
5.	Worms	Elephantiasis, Intestinal infections

Note:

Acquired diseases: The diseases which develop after birth are called acquired diseases. They are further classified in two types – communicable and non-communicable diseases. The diseases which spread from one person to another are called **communicable diseases**. These diseases are caused by microorganisms such as fungi, bacteria, protozoans and viruses. The **non-communicable diseases** are those which do not spread from one person to another. The non communicable diseases are of four types as organic diseases, deficiency diseases, allergies and cancer.

Means of Spread

Infectious diseases spread from one infected person to other normal persons by various methods.

(i) **Air-borne diseases:** For example, common cold, pneumonia and tuberculosis. Such disease causing microbes are spread through out the air. The transmission of these microbes occurs through the little droplets coughed out by an infected person who sneezes or coughs. A person in the vicinity of such a person can inhale these disease causing microbes and may become infected.

(ii) **Water-borne diseases:** These diseases occur when a fecal sample from someone suffering from an infectious gut disease, such as **cholera** or **amoebiasis**, gets mixed with the drinking water used by people living nearby. The cholera-infected bacteria can enter new hosts through the water they drink and can cause disease in them.

(iii) **Sexually transmitted diseases:** The disease like AIDS, syphilis etc. are sexually transmitted diseases. They get transmitted when the infected person has sexual intercourse with the healthy person. Such disease are not spread by casual physical contact. Casual physical contacts include hand shakes or hugs or sports, like wrestling or by any of the other ways in which we touch each other socially.

Other than sexual contact, the AIDS virus can also spread through blood to blood contact with infected person or from an infected mother to her baby during pregnancy or through breast feeding.

(iv) **Spread of disease through vectors:** Many animals which live with us may carry disease. These animals carry the infecting agents from a sick person to another potential host. These animals are thus the intermediators and are called vectors. The commonest vectors are mosquitoes. In many species of mosquitoes, the females need highly nutritious food in the form of blood in order to be able to lay mature eggs. Mosquitoes feed on many warm-blooded animals, including us. In this way, they can transfer diseases from person to person.

Organ-Specific and Tissue Specific Manifestations

There are various means by which disease causing microorganism enters into our body. Different microbes affect to different parts of our body. If they enter from air via nose they are likely to go to lungs, which is seen in case of bacteria that cause TB. If they enter through mouth, they lie in the inner lining of guts and can cause typhoid or if they go to liver they can cause jaundice. Malaria causing microbes enter into our body by biting of mosquitoes.

The signs and symptoms of a disease will thus depend on the tissue or organ which the microbe targets. If the lungs are the target then symptoms will be cough and breathlessness. If the liver is targeted there will be jaundice. If the brain is the target we will observe headaches, vomiting, fits or unconsciousness.

On the other hand tissue specific disease depends on the fact that the immune system of the body becomes active and recruits many cells to the affected tissue to destroy the disease causing microbes, which is called **inflammation**. As a part of this process, there are local effects such as **swelling, pains** and most general effect is **fever**. In case of HIV infection, the virus goes to the immune system and damages its function. Thus, many of the effects of HIV-AIDS are because the body can no longer fight off the many minor, infections that we face every day. Instead, every small cold can become pneumonia. Similarly, a minor gut infection can produce major diarrhoea with blood loss. Ultimately, it is these other infections that kill people suffering from HIV-AIDS.

The severity of the disease depends on the number of microbes in the body. If the number of microbes is less, then the disease is minor and if the number of microbes is in large number, then the disease can be major and can be life taking. It is the immune system of the body that determines the number of microbes in the body. The body with strong immune system will have lesser number of microbes and hence is less prone to the disease.

Principle of Treatment

There are two principles of treatment i.e., either by reducing the effect of disease or by killing the cause of the disease. In the first type, the treatment provided will reduce the symptoms by giving the medicines. However symptoms related treatments are not sufficient to cure the disease. To cure the disease we have to kill the microbes by identifying them and giving the proper drugs. Since each microbes can be killed by a specific drug, it is essential to isolate and specifically target them. Each groups of organisms will have some essential bio-chemical life process, which are different from others. We have to find the drugs that will block the metabolic pathway of microbes, without affecting our own.

TRIVIA

Brain freeze is scientifically known as "Sphenopalatine ganglioneuralgia."

Principles of Prevention of Disease

Following three limitations are normally confronted while treating an infectious disease:

(i) Once someone gets a disease, his or her body functions get damaged and may never recover completely.

(ii) Treatment of a disease takes time. This means if someone is suffering from a disease, he is likely to be bed-ridden for sometime, even if he is given proper treatment.

(iii) The person suffering from an infectious disease can serve as the medium for further spread of infection to other people.

Hence prevention of diseases is better than their cure.

General ways of prevention of infectious disease

Public hygiene is one basic key to the prevention of infectious diseases. In this method, following practices are adopted:

(i) To avoid exposure to air borne microbes, adopt living conditions that are not overcrowded.

(ii) To prevent exposure to water-borne microbes, safe drinking water should be provided.

(iii) To avoid vector-borne infections, we can provide clean environment as it would not allow mosquito breeding.

Specific ways of prevention of infectious diseases

If someone is suffering from a cold and cough in the class, it is likely that the children sitting around will be exposed to the infection. But not all of them will acquire the infection. This may be due to a strong immune system.

Immune system and immunisation

Children usually escape cold and cough infection because of their immune system. These cells become active every time disease-causing microbes enter the body. Normally, immune cells manage to kill off the infection long before it assumes major proportions. If the spread of the infecting microbes are controlled, the symptoms and effects of a disease will be minor. In other words, exposure to infection or an infectious microbes, does not necessarily imply that symptoms are not noticeable, So, one way of looking at severe infectious disease is that it represents a failure of the immune system. The functioning of the immune system, like any other system in the body, will not be good enough if proper and sufficient nourishment and food is not available.

Vaccination: You had smallpox once, there was no chance of suffering from it again. So, having the disease once was a means of preventing subsequent attacks of the same disease.

This happens because, when the immune system first sees an infectious microbe. It responds against it and then remembers it specifically. So the next time when that particular microbe or its close relatives enter the body, the immune system responds with even greater vigour. This eliminates the infection even more quickly than the first time around. **This is the basis of the principle of immunisation**.

In this way, we 'fool' the immune system into developing a memory of a particular infection, by injecting something that mimics the microbe we want to vaccinate against, into the body. This does not cause the disease but helps prevent any subsequent exposure to the infecting microbe from turning into an actual disease. There are vaccines against (1) Tetanus (2) Diphtheria (3) Whooping cough (4) Measles (5) Polio (6) Hepatitis-B (7) Cholera (8) Tuberculosis (9) Plague (10) Mumps etc.

Note: Edward Jenner induced vaccination against **smallpox**.

Vaccine	Disease	Age Group	Safety Level
1. DPT - Hib	Diphtheria (coryne bacterium diptheriae), Tetanus, pertussis (whooping cough) and Haemophilus influenzae type B.	To all infants of $1\frac{1}{2}$, $2\frac{1}{2}$ and $3\frac{1}{2}$ month age.	90% – 99%
2. Hepatitis - B	Hepatitis (serum hepatitis)	All infant, children and even adult.	Not yet confirmed.
3. Polio	Poliomyelitis	All infants up to 5 years of age, minimum of three doses at one month interval.	Nearly 100%
4. BCG	Tuberculosis	All children between 10 and 14 years	Nearly 70%

Important Vaccines for Infants and Children

MUST REMEMBER

- Maintaining a good hygiene also reduces the chance of developing an infection.
- A disease usually indicates malfunction in the body.
- The diseases which get cured in short time is called acute diseases.
- The disease causing factors which exist within the human body are called intrinsic factors.
- Some diseases caused by microbes or microorganisms are called infectious diseases. This is because the microbes can spread in the community, and the diseases they cause will spread with them.
- The microorganisms which carry pathogens that cause disease are called infectious agents.

Why do We Fall Ill

MULTIPLE CHOICE QUESTIONS

1. Infectious diseases spread through _____.
   (a) Water (b) Sexual
   (c) Vectors (d) All of these

2. Common cold is _____.
   (a) A genetic disorder
   (b) An acute disease
   (c) A chronic disease
   (d) A congenital disease

3. Pain in abdomen is _____.
   (a) Symptom (b) Effect
   (c) Sign (d) Cause

4. Which one of diseases is not infectious?
   (a) Leprosy (b) Leukemia
   (c) Measles (d) Typhoid

5. Which of the following is non-communicable disease?
   (a) Malaria (b) Diarrhoea
   (c) Allergy (d) Tuberculosis

6. A protozoan disease is _____.
   (a) Kala-azar
   (b) Malaria
   (c) Sleeping sickness
   (d) All of these

7. Which one of the following is the intrinsic factor of disease?
   (a) Tobacco
   (b) Alcohol
   (c) Environment
   (d) Hormonal imbalance

8. The insect vectors which cause yellow fever is _____.
   (a) Aedes
   (b) Culex
   (c) Anopheles mosquitoes
   (d) House fly

9. What is other name of rabies?
   (a) Ophidiophobia
   (b) Hydrophobia
   (c) Herpetophobia
   (d) Chemophobia

10. A communicable disease is caused by _____.
    (a) Allergy
    (b) Pathogen
    (c) Hormonal balance
    (d) Metabolic disorder

11. Ascariasis spreads through _____.
    (a) Formites
    (b) Droplets
    (c) Contaminated food and water
    (d) Vectors

12. The anti-viral proteins are known as _____.
    (a) Antibodies (b) Interferons
    (c) Antibiotics (d) Virus protein

13. Acne are caused by _____.
    (a) Staphylococcus (b) Leishmania
    (c) Trypanosoma (d) H_1N_1 virus

14. A disease transmitted through sexual contact is _____.
    (a) HIV (b) Syphylis
    (c) Gonorrhoea (d) All of these

15. Clean drinking water is related to _____.
    (a) Public hygiene
    (b) Personal hygiene
    (c) Social status
    (d) Economic status

16. Match the diseases with their agent.

S. No.	Disease		Agents
i.	T.B.	A.	Vibro cholerae
ii.	Ring worm	B.	Wuchereria Histalytica
iii.	Cholera	C.	Fungi
iv.	Elephantitis	D.	Mycobacterium Tuberculosis

   (a) i - A, ii - C, iii - A, iv - D
   (b) i - D, ii - B, iii - A, iv - C
   (c) i - D, ii - C, iii - A, iv - B
   (d) i - C, ii - D, iii - A, iv - B

17. Jaundice is a disease of ———.
    (a) Pancreas (b) Liver
    (c) Kidney (d) Duodenum
18. AIDS is caused due to ———.
    (a) Reduction to number of helper T-cells
    (b) Auto immunity
    (c) Non-production
    (d) Reduction to number of killer T-cells
19. AIDS virus has ———.
    (a) Single strand DNA
    (b) Single strand RNA
    (c) Double strand DNA
    (d) Double strand RNA
20. TB is cured by ———.
    (a) Encitol (b) Ubiquinone
    (c) Streptomycin (d) Griseofuluin
21. Goitre is caused due to deficiency of ———.
    (a) Fluorine (b) Iodine
    (c) Vitamin C (d) Vitamin D
22. A chronic disease is ———.
    (a) Hypertension (b) Kala-azar
    (c) Typhoid (d) Diarrehoea
23. Droplet method of transmission of disease is found in ———.
    (a) Syphilis (b) AIDS
    (c) Common cold (d) Hepatitis
24. In chronic disease a patient suffers from ———.
    (a) Tiredness
    (b) Short breath
    (c) Poor appetite
    (d) All of these
25. Ascaris lumbricoides is common roundworm of ———.
    (a) Bile duct
    (b) Small intestine
    (c) Large intestine
    (d) Liver
26. Which one of the following diseases is not transmitted by mosquito?
    (a) Dengue (b) Brain fever
    (c) Malaria (d) Typhoid
27. Vectors can be defined as ———.
    (a) Microorganisms which cause many diseases
    (b) Animals carry the infecting agents from sick person to another healthy person.
    (c) Infected person
    (d) Diseased plants
28. Human disease caused by a bacterium is ———.
    (a) Polio (b) Dengue
    (c) Tuberculosis (d) Measles
29. Which one of the following has a long term effect on the health of an individual?
    (a) Stress
    (b) Common cold
    (c) Chicken pox
    (d) Chewing tobacco
30. Choose the wrong statement.
    (a) Acne is caused by staphylococci
    (b) Peptic ulcers are caused by eating acidic food
    (c) High blood pressure is caused by excessive weight and lack of exercise
    (d) Cancers can be caused by genetic abnormalities
31. Which one of the following diseases is not caused by bacteria?
    (a) Typoid (b) Anthrax
    (c) Malaria (d) Tuberculosis
32. Which one of the following diseases in not a viral disease?
    (a) Dengue (b) Typhoid
    (c) AIDS (d) Influenza
33. If you live in an overcrowded and poorly ventilated house, it is possible that you may suffer from ———.
    (a) Cancer
    (b) AIDS
    (c) Air borne diseases
    (d) Cholera
34. Which of the following is a mismatch?
    (a) Malaria – protozoan infection
    (b) AIDS – bacterial infection
    (c) Leprosy – bacterial infection
    (d) Elephantiasis – nematode infection

Why do We Fall Ill

35. Hemophilia is a _____.
    (a) Chronic disease
    (b) Deficiency disease
    (c) Congenital disease
    (d) Acute disease
36. Congenital diseases are those which _____.
    (a) Are spread from man to man
    (b) Are present from time of birth
    (c) Are deficiency diseases
    (d) Occur during life time
37. Which one of the following causes kala-azar?
    (a) Bacteria   (b) Ascaris
    (c) Leishmania   (d) Trypanosoma
38. _____ is the commonest carrier of pathogens.
    (a) Housefly   (b) Helminth
    (c) Mosquito   (d) None of these
39. Which of the following is a bacterial disease?
    (a) Tetanus   (b) Malaria
    (c) Poliomyelitis (d) Hepatitis B
40. Female Anopheles mosquito is a carrier of a pathogen that causes _____.
    (a) Dengue   (b) Filariasis
    (c) Yellow fever   (d) Malaria
41. We should not allow mosquitoes to breed in our surroundings because they _____.
    (a) Bite and cause skin diseases
    (b) Are vectors for many disease
    (c) Multiply very fast and cause pollution
    (d) Are not important insects
42. Which one of the following is incorrect about tuberculosis?
    (a) Patient's sputum contains blood
    (b) It commonly affects lungs
    (c) Bacteria release tuberculin toxin
    (d) It is caused by salmonella
43. Which one of the following is not important for individual health?
    (a) Social equality and harmony
    (b) Living in a large and well furnished house
    (c) Living in a clean space
    (d) Good economic condition
44. What do we call the uncontrolled growth of tissue in any parts of body?
    (a) Cancer
    (b) Metabolic disorder
    (c) Degenerative disease
    (d) Deficiency disease
45. Who first discovered the disease TB?
    (a) M. Thomas
    (b) J. Martin
    (c) Louis pastures
    (d) Robert Koach
46. The vaccine for TB is _____.
    (a) BCG   (b) IVP
    (c) TAB   (d) Hepatitis B_1
47. Fever, delirium, slow pulse, abdominal tenderness and rose coloured rash indicate the disease _____.
    (a) Tetanus   (b) Typhoid
    (c) Measles   (d) Chicken pox
48. Making anti-viral drugs is more difficult than making anti-bacterial medicines because _____.
    (a) Viruses have very few biochemical mechanisms of their own
    (b) Viruses have a protein coat
    (c) Virus make use of host-machinery
    (d) Viruses are on the border line of living and non living
49. SARS and Swine flue are caused by _____.
    (a) Virus and bacterium
    (b) Virus and protozoan
    (c) Virus and helminth
    (d) Virus
50. You are aware of Polio Eradication Programme in your city. Children are vaccinated because _____.
    (a) Prevents the entry of polio causing organism
    (b) It creates immunity in the body against polio causing organism
    (c) Vaccination kills the polio-causing microorganisms
    (d) All of these

HOTS

1. The coelom in arthropods is reduced and is known as 'haemocoel' because _____.
   (a) blood flows in the coelom.
   (b) coelom is filled with haemoglobin.
   (c) blood flows in the blood vessels present in the coelom.
   (d) coelomic fluid flows in the blood vessel.
2. Which of these statements listed below is true about common cold?
   (a) Common cold is not contagious.
   (b) Common cold virus can leave the body through the mucus of the infected people.
   (c) Common cold usually takes two months to clear up.
   (d) All of these
3. Anthrax is a _____ disease.
   (a) congenital   (b) genetic
   (c) infectious   (d) dangerous
4. The bacterium responsible for peptic ulcers is _____.
   (a) staphylococcus aureus
   (b) Helicobacter pylori
   (c) Streptococcus pneumonia
   (d) Nisseria
5. The diseases caused by defects that are present right from the birth are known as _____ diseases.
   (a) hereditary   (b) hormonal
   (c) genetic   (d) congenital

SUBJECTIVE QUESTIONS

1. (a) Why it is difficult to develop vaccines for some diseases?
   (b) While going abroad, why is it essential to get vaccinated against certain diseases?
   (c) Name such a vaccine which saves the life of bodies from three diseases.

Ans.
(a) It is difficult to develop vaccines against the diseases caused by viruses. Viruses are very specific to hosts. They live and multiply only in the living cells. They cannot be cultured on artificial medium. It is because of these factors that vaccines are difficult to be prepared in such cases.

However, living cells of human's body which are exposed to action of a virus, secrete a heat stable basic antiviral glycoprotein of low molecular weight, called interferon.

(b) A person may be carrier of some disease. Such a person may take that particular disease to a foreign country. Therefore, all visitors to a foreign country are vaccinated against the disease which is not prevalent in that country.

(c) D.P.T. is a vaccine which is three-in-one. Babies should be immunised within the first six weeks of birth.

D.P.T: D = Diphtheria, P = Pertuassis (whooping cough), T = Tetanus.

2. State two main causes of disease.

Ans.
Two main causes of disease are immediate cause and contributory cause. Immediate cause: This is due to the organisms that enter our body and cause disease. Example, virus, protozoa, bacteria.

Contributory cause: These are the secondary factors which lead these organisms to enter our body. Example, dirty water, unclean surrounding, contaminated food etc.

3. Define vaccine and name two vaccines.

Ans.
Vaccine is a chemical/drug given in advance to a body to give immunity against certain diseases.

Vaccines given to children are:
(a) BCG – for tuberculosis prevention
(b) Polio drops – for polio prevention

Why do We Fall Ill

4. Bacteria is a cell, antibiotics can kill these bacteria (cell), Human body is also made of cells how does it affect our body?

Ans. Antibiotics block the biochemical pathway of bacteria by which it makes a protective cell wall around it. Antibiotic does not allow the bacteria to make this cell wall because of which they die. Human body cell don't make any cell wall so antibiotics cannot have any such effect on our body.

5. How does cholera becomes an epidemic in a locality?

Ans. Cholera is an infectious disease that spreads due to unsafe water. It can spread in a locality; if a person suffering from cholera lives in the locality and the excreta of this person, get mixed with the drinking water used by people living nearby. The cholera-causing microbe enters the new hosts through the water they drink and cause disease in them.

Natural Resources   14

Learning Objectives : In this chapter, students will learn about:
- ✓ environment
- ✓ causes and prevention of air pollution
- ✓ biogeochemical cycles
- ✓ the importance of air
- ✓ the importance of water
- ✓ the importance of ozone layer

CHAPTER SUMMARY

Everything that surrounds us is collectively termed as the environment. Environment acts as a life support system for us, since it is from the environment that we get food to eat, water to drink, air to breathe and all other requirements of our day-to-day life.

Natural Resources

The resources which are provided to us by the nature are called **natural resources**. Earth is the only planet where life exists. The natural resources of the earth are land, water and air. The outer crust of the earth is called the **lithosphere**. Water covers 75% of the earth surface and these comprise the **hydrosphere**. Air form the blanket over the surface of earth called **atmosphere**. All the components atmosphere, lithosphere and hydrosphere together constitute **biosphere**. Organisms in relation to their physical environment form the ecosystem. There are two components of ecosystem **biotic** and **abiotic components**. The biotic components include living organisms like plants and animals, whereas abiotic components include air, water and land.

Air: Breath of Life

On earth, we human beings along with all other biota are surrounded by air. Air is a mixture of gases such as nitrogen, oxygen, carbon dioxide and water vapour.

On the planets Venus and Mars, Carbon Dioxide forms the major component constituting up to 95-97% of the atmosphere. No life is known to exist there. On the contrary, air forms the blanket around the earth having mixture of many gases. Earth has life on it.

Oxygen is required by all living beings (eukaryotic cells and many prokaryotic cells) for respiration and for burning (combustion) of materials. Air contains about 20% oxygen and its percentage in air is balanced by the process of photosynthesis.

Despite this, the percentage of carbon dioxide in our atmosphere is a mere fraction of a percent because carbon dioxide in two ways: (i) Green plants convert carbon dioxide into glucose in the presence of sunlight and (ii) many marine animals use carbonates dissolved in sea water to make their shells.

Role of Air in Climate Control

Air is an inexhaustible natural resource. In a world without air, there would be no plant or animal life, no winds, no fires and no protection against harmful solar radiations. This is because the atmosphere covers the earth like a blanket. Atmosphere also maintains the variation of temperature and pressure. It does not allow the drastic variation of temperature during day and night. For instance, Moon which is about the same distance from the Sun that the Earth is, lacks atmosphere. As a consequence, on the surface of the moon, the temperature ranges from –190°C to 110°C. Thus, moon's temperature rises during the sunlight period (day) to about 110°C, and cools to –190°C during dark period (night).

Wind The Movement of Air:

A cool evening breeze after a hot day or rain after a few days of hot weather bring us considerable relief. Some questions may strike our mind: What drives the movement of air? What decides whether this movement of air will be in the form of a gentle breeze, a strong wind or a terrible storm? What brings the rain?

All these phenomena are the result of changes that take place in our atmosphere due to the heating of air and the formation of water vapours.

The movement of wind is due to the difference of pressure in the lower layer and upper layer of the atmosphere, on land and water bodies, when solar radiation falls on the earth, some is absorbed. But most of it is reflected back into the atmosphere by the land and water bodies. The reflected radiation heats up the lower layer of the atmosphere, as a result **convection current** sets up in the air. But since the land gets heated faster than the water bodies, the air over the land also gets heated and create a region of low pressure on land. Thus, wind moves to the region of lower pressure over land from the region of high pressure on the water bodies and creates winds. During day time the wind blows from sea to land and during night the process is reversed, as the wind blows from land to sea.

This temperature difference across the earth generates the development of major wind belt over the earth's surface, which forms the climatic zone of the world.

Factors Influencing Movement of Air

(i) Uneven heating of land at different parts of Earth.
(ii) Vaporisation and condensation of water vapours.
(iii) Rotation of earth.
(iv) Differences in heating and cooling of land and water bodies.
(v) Presence of high mountain ranges in the path of winds.
(vi) Difference in topography over which the wind passes.

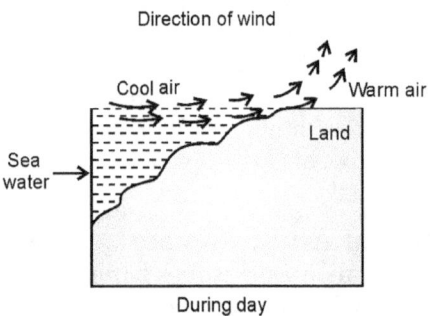

Fig. 14.1

Rain

When the water bodies heat up during the day, the upper layer of water bodies changes into vapour and goes up in the atmosphere with the air. As this air reaches the upper layer of the atmosphere it expands and cools. On cooling, the water vapours get condensed in the form of tiny droplets of water. An enormous collection of tiny droplets of water appears in the form of clouds. When the collection of water vapour becomes heavier and bigger, it falls down in the form of rain.

When the temperature of air is very low, precipitation then may occur in the form of snow, sheet or hail.

The rainfall pattern is decided by the prevailing wind pattern. In the country like India, the rain is mostly brought by the south-west or north-east monsoons. The south-west monsoons blows from sea to land during the month of **April** and **May**. Local rains in coastal regions are caused due to sea breezes and rains in the **great topographic relief** are caused by mountains and valley breezes.

Air Pollution

Contamination of air of poisonous gases released by various means and many other chemicals is called **air pollution**. The main reason for air pollution is the rapid industrialization and urbanization. Air pollution is the addition of air pollutants such as particulate matter, gases and vapours into the atmosphere. It has adverse effects on humans, animals, vegetation and human assets. Particulate air pollutants are also called **suspended particulate matter** or SPM because they remain suspended in air for a good period of time.

The combustion of fossil fuels like coal and petroleum increases the amount of suspended particles in air. These suspended particles could be unburnt carbon particles or substances called **hydrocarbons**. Presence of high level of all these pollutants causes visibility to be lowered, especially in cold weather when water also condenses out of air. This is known as **smog** and is a visible indication of air pollution.

Water: A Wonderful Liquid

Oceans, rivers, streams, lakes, ponds, pools, polar ice caps, water vapour. collectively form the hydrosphere. Hydrosphere comprises of water which is an inexhaustible natural resource. About 75% of the earth's surface is covered with water, but the concentration of fresh water i.e., potable water is very less and is nearly 2.5%. The movement of substance from one part of the body to the another part cannot take place in the form of solid molecules, it flows in the form of liquid, dissolved in water, that is why potable water is considered so essential.

Terrestrial life forms require fresh water for this because their bodies cannot tolerate or get rid of the high amounts of dissolved salts in saline water. Thus, water sources need to be easily accessible for animals and plants to survive on land.

The availability of water is not the only factor that decides the number of individuals, of each species that are able to survive. There are many other factors like temperature and nature of soil which also matter.

Water Pollution

An undesirable change in the physical, biological or chemical qualities of water (due to addition of foreign organic, inorganic, biological or radioactive substances) that adversely affects the aquatic life and makes the water unfit for use, is called **water pollution**. The water pollution is of three types; inland water pollution, underground water pollution, and marine water pollution.

Minerals Rich in the Soil

Soil is an important resource that decides the diversity of life in an area. The outermost layer of our earth is called the **crust**. Over long periods of time, thousands and millions of years, the rocks at or near the surface of the earth are broken down by various physical, chemical and some biological processes. The end product of this breaking down is the fine particles of soil. Soil is a mixture of small particles of rocks and humus (i.e., organic matter obtained from decaying of living organisms or their wastes). Temperature variations due to radiations of the sun, rain water, winds and living organisms influence the formation of soil from the rocks involving two processes: weathering and pedogenesis.

Breaking down of bigger rocks into small, fine soil particles is called **weathering**. Under the influence of solar radiations, rocks heat up and expand. At night, these rocks cool down and contract. Since all the parts of rocks do not expand and contract at the same rate, cracks appear in the rocks and ultimately the large rocks breakdown into smaller pieces. Flow of water through or over the rocks make the cracks bigger. On freezing the water expands in rocks crevices and breaks the rocks. Similarly, strong winds continue to rub against hard rocks and erode them. Growth of lichens, mosses and other plants also influence the formation of soil by eroding the rocks over which they are growing.

Pedogenesis involves the decomposition of organic materials by bacteria and fungi and humification and mineralization of decomposed organic matter. Earthworms also play an important role in soil formation.

TRIVIA

If you get exposed to nuclear substances, the best course of action is to remove all of your clothes. This will remove 90% of the radioactive substance you were exposed to.

Biogeochemical Cycles

There is continuous transfer of energy between various components of the biosphere. Both living and non-living components of the biosphere constantly interact with each other for this purpose. The nutrient elements derived from the earth by the living organisms, for their growth and metabolism are called **biogeochemicals**.

These biogeochemicals are constantly recycled and used again and again. The different biogeochemical cycles are: **water cycle, Nitrogen cycle, Carbon cycle** and **Oxygen cycle**.

Water Cycle: (Hydrological Cycle)

Water is considered to be one of the most important liquids for the survival of life process on the earth's surface. The heat of the Sun evaporates water from the water bodies and subsequent condensation of this water vapour leads to rain.

The whole process in which water evaporates and falls on the land as rain and later flows back into the sea via rivers is known as **water cycle**.

All of the water that falls on the land does not immediately flow back into the sea. Some of it keeps into the soil and becomes part of the underground reservoir of fresh water. Some of this underground water finds its way to the surface through springs, or we bring it to the surface for our use through wells or tubewells. Water is also used by terrestrial animals and plants for various life-processes.

Water is also capable of dissolving a large number of substances. As water flows through or over rocks containing soluble minerals. Some of them get dissolved in water. Thus rivers carry many nutrients from the land to the sea, and these are used by the marine organisms.

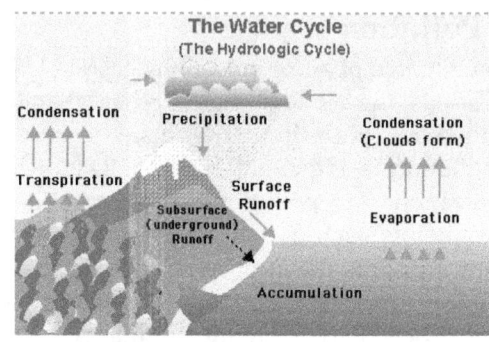

Fig. 14.2. *Water Cycle*

Nitrogen Cycle

Nitrogen is another important chemical on the earth and is present in all the living organisms, in the form of protein, amino acids, and nucleic acids. It exists in the molecular form (N_2). But atmospheric nitrogen, the most abundant component of air (78%) is chemically inert and cannot be used in its pure form by the majority of organisms. First it needs to be converted into nitrates (NO_3^-) for the use by plants.

The conversion can be done either by industrial nitrogen fixation (i.e., manufacturing of ammonium salts and urea or chemical fertilizers) or by some nitrogen fixing bacteria such as **Azotobacter** (occurs freely in soil) and **Rhizobium** (occurs in root nodules of leguminous plants as pea, gram, bean etc.) which convert the atmospheric nitrogen into water soluble **nitrates**. The process of biofixation of nitrogen is called **nitrogen fixation**.

During lightning, the temperature and pressure created in the air convert nitrogen into oxides of nitrogen. These oxides dissolve in water to give nitric and nitrous acids and fall on land along with rain. These are then utilized by various life forms.

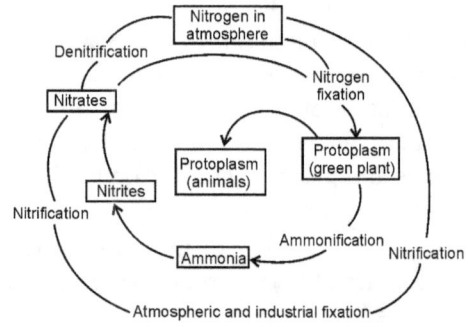

Fig. 14.3. *Nitrogen Cycle*

When animals consume the plants, they break down the nitrogenous compound. When the animals or the plants die, some bacteria carry out ammonification and produce ammonium ions (NH_4^+). This process of formation of ammonia is called **ammonification**. Some of the microorganisms convert this ammonia into nitrates, again reduced back into the atmosphere. This process is known as **denitrification**. A different type of bacteria converts the nitrates and nitrites into elemental nitrogen.

Thus, there is a nitrogen cycle in nature in which nitrogen passes from its elemental form in the atmosphere into simple molecules in the soil and water, which get converted to more complex molecules in living beings and back again to the simple nitrogen molecules in the atmosphere.

Carbon Cycle

Carbon is one of the important constituents of all organic compounds and are found in almost all living organisms, in the form of carbohydrates, fats and nucleic acids. In atmosphere it is present in 0.03%. Plants use atmospheric carbon for the process of photosynthesis, in the form of its oxides and releases oxygen into the atmosphere. This oxygen is used by the animals for the process of respiration, which in turn release carbondioxide back into the atmosphere.

The other way round in which carbon cycle is formed is that, all the living organisms are constituted of major parts of carbon. When these animals and plants die, their bodies are decomposed by the microorganisms into simpler forms and releases carbon to the atmosphere, either in the form of carbon or the oxides of carbon, like carbon dioxide or carbon monoxides.

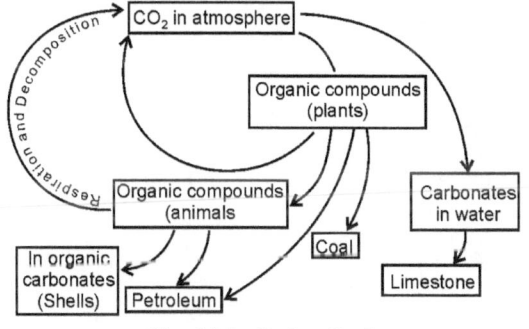

Fig. 14.4. *Carbon Cycle*

Greenhouse effect: Heat is trapped by glass, and hence the temperature inside a glass enclosure will be much higher than the surroundings. This phenomenon was used to create an enclosure where tropical plants could be kept warm during the winters in colder climates. Such enclosures are called greenhouses.

Some gases prevent the escape of heat from the earth. An increase in the percentage of such gases in the atmosphere would cause the average temperature to increase world wide and this is called the **green house effect**. Gases such as carbon dioxide (CO_2), methane (CH_4), Ozone (O_3), nitrogen oxide (N_2O) and Chlorofluorocarbons (CFCs) are called greenhouse gases (GHGs). Carbon dioxide is one of the greenhouse gases. As increase in the carbondioxide content in the atmosphere would cause more heat to be retained by the atmosphere and lead to global warming.

Oxygen Cycle

Oxygen is one of the constituents of water and forms about 21% of the air in the atmosphere. It also occurs in combined form in the Earth's crust as well as in the air in the form of carbon dioxide. In the crust, it is found as the oxides of most metals and silicon, and also as carbonate, sulphate, nitrate and other minerals. It is also on essential component of most biological molecules like carbohydrates, proteins, nucleic acids and fats (or lipids).

Oxygen from the atmosphere is used up in three processes, namely combustion, respiration and in the formation of oxides of nitrogen. Oxygen enters the living world through respiration, it oxidises the food materials and produces energy and carbon dioxide:

$$C_6H_{12}O_6 + 6O_2 \longrightarrow 6CO_2 + 6H_2O + \text{Energy}$$
(Glucose)

This carbon dioxide is used by the plants for the process photosynthesis to prepare their own food and there after release oxygen back into the atmosphere thus, completing the biochemical cycle.

$$6CO_2 + 6H_2O + \text{Light energy} \rightarrow C_6H_{12}O_6 + 6O_2$$
(Carbon Dioxide) (Water) (Glucose) (Oxygen)

Some forms of life, especially bacteria, are poisoned by elemental oxygen. In fact, even the process of nitrogen-fixing by bacteria does not take place in the presence of oxygen.

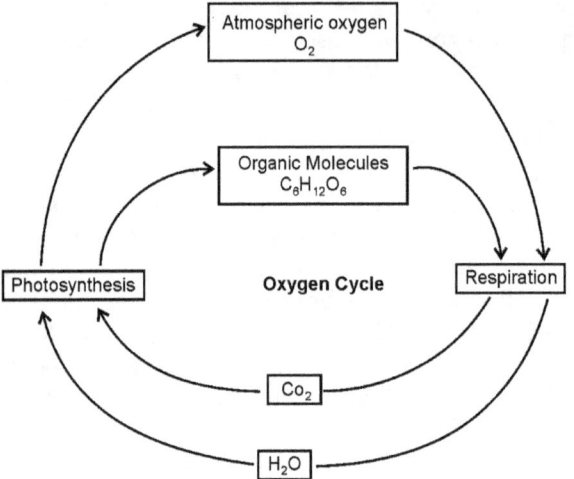

Fig. 14.5. *Oxygen – Cycle in Nature*

Ozone Layer

Elemental oxygen is normally found in the form of a diatomic molecule. However in the upper layer of the atmosphere, a molecule containing three atoms of oxygen is found. i.e., O_3 and this called ozone. Ozone is poisonous. It absorbs harmful radiations from the Sun. This prevents those harmful radiations from reaching the surface of the Earth where they may damage many forms of life.

Recently it has been found that ozone layer was getting depleted. Various man-made compounds like CFCs (Carbon compounds having fluorine and chlorine which are very stable and not degraded by any biological process) were found to persist in the atmosphere. This resulted in a depletion of the ozone layer and recently the scientists have discovered a hole in the ozone layer above Antartica.

MUST REMEMBER

- The resources which are provided to us by the nature are called natural resources.
- The outer crust of the earth is called the lithosphere.
- Air form the blanket over the surface of earth called atmosphere.
- When the water bodies heat up during the day, the upper layer of water bodies changes into vapour and goes up in the atmosphere with the air.
- When the temperature of air is very low, precipitation then may occur in the form of snow, sheet or hail.
- The combustion of fossil fuels like coal and petroleum increases the amount of suspended particles in air.
- About 75% of the earth's surface is covered with water, but the concentration of fresh water i.e., potable water is very less and is nearly 2.5%.
- Temperature variations due to radiations of the sun, rain water, winds and living organisms influence the formation of soil from the rocks involving two processes: weathering and pedogenesis.
- Pedogenesis involves the decomposition of organic materials by bacteria and fungi and humification and mineralization of decomposed organic matter.
- The whole process in which water evaporates and falls on the land as rain and later flows back into the sea via rivers is known as water cycle.
- The process of biofixation of nitrogen is called nitrogen fixation.
- Some gases prevent the escape of heat from the earth. An increase in the percentage of such gases in the atmosphere would cause the average temperature to increase world wide and this is called the green house effect.
- Oxygen from the atmosphere is used up in three processes, namely combustion, respiration and in the formation of oxides of nitrogen.

MULTIPLE CHOICE QUESTIONS

1. The term used to identify the living components of the environment is _____.
   (a) Topographic (b) Ecosystem
   (c) Biotic (d) Abiotic

2. Air is a mixture of _____.
   (a) Nitrogen, oxygen, carbon monoxide, water vapours
   (b) Nitrogen, oxygen, carbon dioxide, water vapours
   (c) Nitrogen, carbon dioxide, oxygen, carbon monoioxide
   (d) Nitrogen, oxygen, methane, carbon dioxide

3. Which one is inexhaustible resource?
   (a) Soil (b) Solar radiation
   (c) Fossil fuels (d) Minerals

4. What is the range of temperature of the surface of moon?
   (a) –180°C to 100°C
   (b) –170°C to 100°C
   (c) –170°C to 120°C
   (d) –190°C to 110°C

5. The species of certain plants and animals which are present within certain region or area is called _____.
   (a) Phytoplankton
   (b) Biota
   (c) Kingdom
   (d) Zooplankton

6. Cloud formation takes place in which part of atmosphere _____.
   (a) Troposphere
   (b) Ozonosphere
   (c) Stratosphere
   (d) Thermosphere

7. Major component of the atmosphere on the Venus and Mars planets is _____.
   (a) Carbondioxide
   (b) Water vapours
   (c) Oxygen
   (d) Nitrogen

8. Biosphere occurs _____.
   (a) In atmosphere and hydrosphere
   (b) In lithosphere
   (c) In lithosphere and hydrosphere
   (d) At place of interatction of lithosphere, hydrosphere, hydrosphere and atmosphere.

9. All the elements of life support system are _____.
   (a) Inter connected
   (b) Inter related
   (c) Inter dependent
   (d) All of these

10. Percentage of total water found as fresh water is _____.
    (a) 32% (b) 2.5%
    (c) 16% (d) 46%

11. In a natural ecosystem, decomposers include _____.
    (a) Parasitic algae
    (b) Bacteria and fungi
    (c) Macroscopic animals
    (d) All of these

12. SPM includes _____.
    (a) Dust (b) Flyash
    (c) Soot and smoke (d) All of these

13. Photochemical smog is formed by _____.
    (a) CO (b) SO_2
    (c) NO_2 (d) CO_2

14. Which of the following soils is the best for plant growth?
    (a) Sandy soil (b) Loamy soil
    (c) Gravel (d) Clay

15. In the atmosphere, the layer above the troposphere is _____.
    (a) Exosphere (b) Mesosphere
    (c) Stratosphere (d) Thermosphere

16. _____ is the major raw material for biogas.
    (a) Cow dung (b) Mud
    (c) Grass (d) Plant leaves

17. Biogas generation is mainly based on the principle of ―――――.
    (a) Degradation (b) Purification
    (c) Fermentation (d) Both (a) and (b)
18. Sanctuaries are established to ―――――.
    (a) Entrap animals
    (b) Protect animals
    (c) Rear animals for milk
    (d) None of these
19. The death of the last individual of a species is called ―――――.
    (a) Clad
    (b) Extinction
    (c) Neither (a) nor (b)
    (d) Species diversity
20. Red Data Book provides a list of ―――――.
    (a) Disease resistant animals
    (b) Advanced plants
    (c) Rare endangered or endemic species
    (d) None of these
21. Which of the following soils is transported by air?
    (a) Alluvial (b) Glacial
    (c) Aeolian (d) Elluvial
22. Green plants in an ecosystem are called ―――――.
    (a) Producers (b) Consumers
    (c) Decomposers (d) All of these
23. Signs of eutrophication of water bodies include ―――――.
    (a) Fluorosis
    (b) Algal bloom
    (c) Reduced oxygen
    (d) Rapid decomposition of organic matter
24. Match the column A with column B.

Column A	Column B
i. Hydrilla	a. Terrestrial
ii. Rat	b. Sea adaption
iii. Horse	c. Aquatic adaption
iv. Whale	d. Hydrophyte

    (a) i – d, ii – a, iii – b, iv – c
    (b) i – b, ii – a, iii – d, iv – c
    (c) i – d, ii – a, iii – c, iv – b
    (d) i – d, ii – c, iii – a, iv – b

25. Nif genes occur in ―――――.
    (a) Aspergillus (b) Penicillium
    (c) Rhizobium (d) Streptococcus
26. In nitrogen cycle which bacteria are responsible for nitrification?
    (a) Rhizobium
    (b) Clostridium
    (c) Nitrosomonas
    (d) Nitrosomonas and nitrobacter
27. The conversion of NO_3 to N_2 is called ―――――.
    (a) Nitrification
    (b) Denitrification
    (c) Ammonifiction
    (d) Nitrogen fixation
28. Nitromonas bacteria convert ―――――.
    (a) Nitrite to nitrate
    (b) Ammonia into nitrate
    (c) Ammonia into nitrite
    (d) Nitrite into ammonia
29. The two forms of oxygen found in the atmosphere are ―――――.
    (a) Water and oxygen
    (b) Water and ozone
    (c) Water and carbon dioxide
    (d) Ozone and oxygen
30. What would happen, if all land and water present in the environment is converted to ozone?
    (a) We will be protected more
    (b) Ozone is not stable, hence it will be toxic
    (c) It will become poisonous and kill living forms
    (d) It will help harmful sun radiations to reach earth and damage many life forms
31. If there were no atmosphere around the earth, the temperature of the earth will ―――――.
    (a) Be unaffected
    (b) Increase
    (c) Go on decreasing
    (d) Increase during day and decrease during night

32. Ozone layer is getting depleted because of _____.
    (a) Excessive deforestation
    (b) Excessive use of automobiles
    (c) Excessive formation of industrial units
    (d) Excessive use of man made compounds containing both fluorine and chlorine

33. 'Ozone-hole' means _____.
    (a) Thining of the ozone layer
    (b) A large sized hole in the ozone layer
    (c) Small holes scattered in the ozone layer
    (d) Thickening of ozone in the ozone layer

34. Major source of mineral in soil is the _____.
    (a) Plants
    (b) Animals
    (c) Bacteria
    (d) Parent-rock from which soil is formed

35. One of the following factors does not lead to soil formation in nature _____.
    (a) Sun   (b) Polythene bags
    (c) Water   (d) Wind

36. Rainfall patterns depend on _____.
    (a) The underground water table
    (b) The prevailing season in an area
    (c) The number of water bodies in an area
    (d) The density pattern of human population in an area

37. Which of the following processes is not a step involved in water-cycle operating in nature?
    (a) Precipitation   (b) Transpiration
    (c) Photosynthesis   (d) None of these

38. Oxygen is returned to the atmosphere mainly by _____.
    (a) Burning of fossil fuel
    (b) Photosynthesis
    (c) Respiration
    (d) Fungi

39. Low visibility during cold weather is due to _____.
    (a) Formation of fossil fuel
    (b) Lack of adequate power supply
    (c) Unburnt carbon particles or hydrocarbons suspended in air
    (d) None of these

40. Oxygen is harmful for _____.
    (a) Ferns
    (b) Chara
    (c) Mango tree
    (d) Nitrogen-fixing bacteria

41. An increase in carbon dioxide contents in the atmosphere would not cause _____.
    (a) Increase in photosynthesis in plants
    (b) Global warming
    (c) Abundance of desert plants
    (d) More heat to be retained by the environment

42. Choose the correct sequence _____.
    (a) CO_2 in atmosphere → decomposers → organic carbon in animals → organic carbon in plants
    (b) Organic carbon in animals → decomposers → CO_2 in atmosphere → organic carbon in plants
    (c) CO_2 in atmosphere → organic carbon in plants → organic carbon in animals → inorganic carbon in soil
    (d) Inorganic carbonates in water → organic carbon in plants → organic carbon in animals → scavengers.

43. Which step is not involved in the carbon cycle?
    (a) Respiration
    (b) Transpiration
    (c) Photosynthesis
    (d) Burning of fossil fuels

44. Growth of lichens on barren rocks is followed by the growth of _____.
    (a) Moss
    (b) Algae
    (c) Ferns
    (d) Gymnosperms

45. Marked temperature changes in aquatic environment can affect _____.
    (a) Availability of nutrients
    (b) More growth of aquatic plants
    (c) Process of digestion in animals
    (d) Breeding of animals

HOTS

1. Identify the labelled parts P and R in the given cycle:

   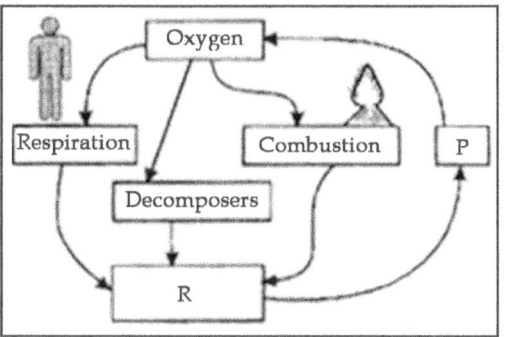

	P	R
(a)	Photosynthesis	Nitrogen
(b)	Respiration	Combustion
(c)	Excretion	Oxygen
(d)	Photosynthesis	Carbon dioxide

2. Which of the following cause greenhouse effect?
   (i) Deforestation
   (ii) Emission of gases from factories
   (iii) Melting of polar ice
   (a) Only (i) and (ii)   (b) Only (i) and (iii)
   (c) Only (ii) and (iii)   (d) (i), (ii) and (iii)

3. Which of the following processes represents P, Q and R?

   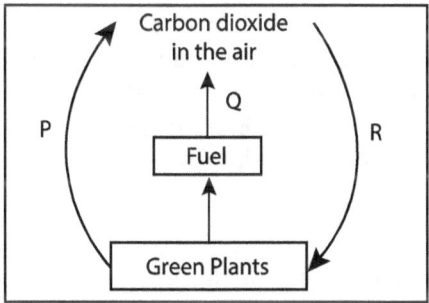

   (a) P-Respiration, Q-Photosynthesis, R-Combustion
   (b) P-Respiration, Q-Combustion, R-Photosynthesis
   (c) P-Combustion, Q-Decay, R-Respiration
   (d) P-Decay, Q-Respiration, R-Photosynthesis

4. Which of the following processes labelled with arrows are brought about by bacteria?

   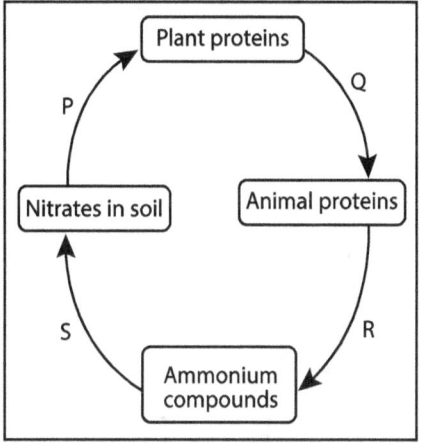

   (a) P and Q   (b) Q and R
   (c) R and S   (d) S and P

5. Which of the following processes represents X, Y and Z in the given cycle?

   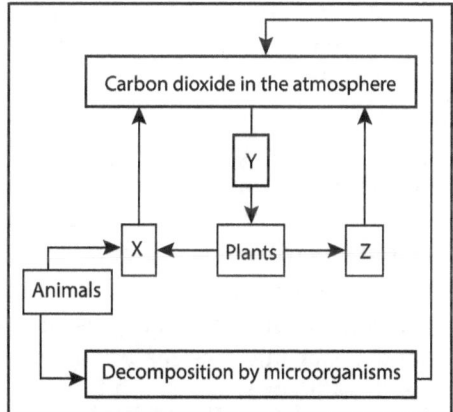

	X	Y	Z
(a)	Respiration	Photosynthesis	Decomposition
(b)	Photosynthesis	Respiration	Decomposition
(c)	Decomposition	Photosynthesis	Respiration
(d)	Decomposition	Respiration	Photosynthesis

Natural Resources

SUBJECTIVE QUESTIONS

1. (a) Fill in the blanks marked 1–5 in figure of nitrogen cycle.
   (b) What will happen if the step of ammonification does not take place?
   (c) What will happen if the step of denitrification does not take place?

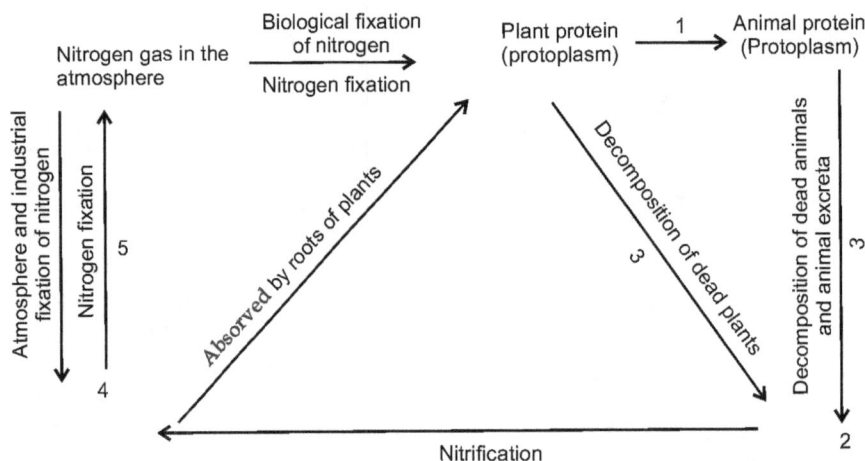

Ans.
(a) (1) Animal nutrition (2) Ammonia in soil (3) Ammonification (4) Nitrates in soil (5) Denitrification.
(b) If ammonificaiton does not take place, the conversion of complex organic compounds such as proteins and nucleic acids of decaying organisms into ammonia will not take place.
(c) If denitrification does not take place, conversion of nitrate salts present in soils and water into free molecular nitrogen will not occur.

2. What is biosphere?

Ans.
This life supporting zone of the Earth where the atmosphere, the hydrosphere and the lithosphere interact and make life possible, is known as the biosphere. It accommodates several types of living organisms which remain dependent on natural resources. The biosphere ranges between 6km, above sea level and 10 kms below sea.

3. How is our atmosphere different from the atmosphere on Venus and Mars?

Ans.
Earth's atmosphere is quite different from the atmosphere present on Venus and Mars. The atmosphere of the earth consists of Nitrogen (79%), Oxygen (20%), small fraction of carbon dioxide and other gases which make it suitable for living. The atmosphere of Venus or Mars has carbon dioxide as the major component (95-97%)
   i. It prevents the sudden increase in temperature during the daylight hours.
   ii. During the night, it slows down the escape of heat into outer space.

4. What causes winds?

Ans.
Uneven heating of the earth's surface and water surface causes winds. On heating up the air rises up creating a low pressure region. Air travels from high pressure region to low pressure region forming winds. In addition the rotation of the Earth and the presence of mountain ranges in the paths of the wind also influence to winds.

5. List any three human activities that you think would lead to air pollution.

Ans.

Three human activities leading to air pollution are:
i. Rapid urbanization and industrialization.
ii. Deforestation
iii. Burning of fuels like coal and petroleum.
iv. Burning of coal in thermal power plants.

6. What is smog?

Ans.

Smoke + Fog = Smog. The presence of unburnt hydrocarbons in air when mixed with condensed water vapours forms a thick layer called smog. It lowers the visibility during winter season and is an indication of air pollution.

7. How do fossil fuel cause air pollution?

Ans.

The fossil fuels like coal and petroleum contain traces of nitrogen and sulphur. When these fuels are burnt, nitrogen and sulphur too are burnt and this produces different oxides of nitrogen and sulphur. These oxides of nitrogen and sulphur are poisonous and can cause respiratory problems. These oxides when mix with rain water give rise to acid water due to formation of nitric and sulphuric acids.

8. What are the effects of acid rain?

Ans.

Effects of acid rain are:
- Acidification of soil reduces fertility of soil.
- Destroys aquatic life and pollutes water resources.
- Causes irritation to eyes and skins of human beings and cattle.
- Causes corrosion to buildings, bridges, statues etc.

9. What are biogeochemical cycles? Names two examples.

Ans.

Biogeochemical cycles are the cyclic pathways through which chemical substances move through biotic environment (biosphere) and abiotic environment (lithosphere, atmosphere and hydrosphere) components of the earth.

A few example of biogeochemical cycles are:
- Water Cycle
- Nitrogen Cycle
- Carbon Cycle
- Oxygen cycle

10. How are clouds formed?

Ans.

Due to various weather phenomena (e.g. uneven heating of land and water bodies on the earth surface), warm and cold convection of air currents generate. Water vapours which are also present in air due to evaporation also rise up. Since air cools down on rising, it leads to condensation of water vapours present in it. Thus vapours condense onto a tiny salt particles called condensation nuclei which form clouds.

Broadly clouds formed are of four types:
i. Nimbostratus: (Nimbus means rain). These clouds carry thick precipitation or rains.
ii. Altostratus: These clouds form a foggy, gray and dull weather look.
iii. Cirrostratus: these clouds form fluffy cotton like pattern.
iv. Cirrus: These are high-level clouds seen during fair weather.

Improvement in Food Resources   15

Learning Objectives : In this chapter, students will learn about:
- ✓ sustainable agriculture and organic farming
- ✓ different types of crops and crop seasons
- ✓ techniques used for improvement in crop yields
- ✓ importance of animal husbandry

CHAPTER SUMMARY

All the living organisms need food for their survival. We use both plants and animals for our food, but most of our food is obtained from agriculture and animal husbandry.

Sustainable Agriculture and Organic Farming

The population of our country is above one billion and is still increasing at a very fast rate. Therefore, it is necessary to increase production of both plants and animals. To meet the demands of growing Indian population, our scientists (such as Swaminathan, Kurien) adopted methods to increase food production. This resulted in a variety of 'revolutions', which helped India become self-reliant. These revolutions include: **green revolution** (high production of food grains), **blue revolution** (enhanced fish production), **white revolution** (increased milk production) and **yellow revolution** (increased oil production), **golden revolution** (increase the pulse production).

Sustainable agriculture is the adoption of various farming and production management techniques to maximize agriculture yield and **organic farming** is the practice of raising crops which have not been polluted. It involves use of manures, biofertilizers and bio-pesticides. The different methods we should follow to increase the food production are **mixed farming, inter cropping and integrated farming practices.**

Types of Crops

Cereals such as wheat, rice, maize, millets and sorghum provide us carbohydrate for energy requirement. Pulses like gram (chana), pea (matar), black gram (urad), green gram (moong), pigeon pea (arhar), lentil, (masoor), provide us with protein. And oil seeds including soyabean, ground nut, sesame, castor, mustard, linseed, and sunflower provide us with necessary fats. Vegetables, spices and fruits provide a range of vitamins and minerals in addition to small amounts of proteins, carbohydrates and fats. In addition to these food crops, fodder crops like barseem, oats or sudan grass are raised as feed for the livestock.

Crop Seasons

Different crops require different climatic conditions, temperature and photoperiod for their growth and maturity. Sunlight is required for photosynthesis – the process of manufacturing food by green plants. **Photoperiods** are duration of sunlight that influence plants in their growth, flowering of storage organs, leaf fall etc. In India, there are two main seasons of crop growth: Kharif and Rabi.

Kharif Season

Some crops grow during rainy season (from the month of June to October) are called **Kharif crops**. Summer crops, the chief kharif crops are Paddy. Soyabean, Pigeon, Pea, Maize, Cotton, Green gram and Black gram etc. Vegetables of

Kharif crops are spinach, gourd, garlic, lady finger, pumpkin and brinjal. Fruits of Kharif crops are watermelon, muskmelon, mango, litchi, plum, peach.

Rabi Season

Some crops grow during winter season (from November to April) are called **Rabi crops** or winter crops. The chief Rabi crops are wheat, barley, gram, peas, mustard, linseed. Vegetables of Rabi crops are cabbage cauliflower, radish, turnip, beans etc. Fruits of Rabi crops are apple pomegranate, orange.

Improvement in Crop Yields

Following three scientific approaches are adopted in India to obtain high yields from our agriculture farms:

(i) Crop variety improvement
(ii) Crop production improvement or management
(iii) Crop protection management

Crop Variety Improvement

The art of recognizing valuable trails and incorporating them into future generations is very important in plant breeding; Breeders search for individual plants that exhibit desirable traits. The two most desirable qualities of food plants are high yield and natural resistance to disease. Such traits occasionally arise spontaneously through a process called **mutation**, but the natural rate of mutation is too slow and unreliable to produce all the plants that breeders would like to see.

Plant breeders select plant varieties with desired characters and cross them. The developed offspring inherit the attributes of both parents. These varieties are multiplied and supplied to farmers.

Crop variety improvement is done for the following reasons:

(i) **Higher yields:** The main aim of crop variety improvement is to increase the production per unit hectare.
(ii) **Quality improvement:** Quality consideration of crop products varies from crop to crop. For example, baking quality of wheat, protein quality in pulse, oil quality in oil seed and shelf life of fruits and vegetables.

(iii) **Biotic and abiotic resistance:** Crop production can go down due to biotic (disease, insects and nematodes) and abiotic (draught, salinity, water logging, heat, cold and frost) stress under different situations. Varieties resistant to the stress can improve crop production.

(iv) **Change in maturity duration:** Shortening the duration of crop maturity increases the production and multiple crops can be produced at the same time.

(v) **Wider adaptability:** Developing the crop varieties of wider adaptability will help in stabilising the crop production under different environmental conditions and hence will be able to produce more crops of different kinds in different regions.

(vi) **Desirable agronomic traits:** Development of crops of desired agronomic traits such as, cereal plant of dwarf size will help to produce more cereals in the small area and will also intake less nutrients.

Crop Production Management

India is an agriculture based country. In this country, agriculture sector engages about 70% of its population and accounts for 40% of the Gross National Product (G.N.P.). Farming practices being followed depend upon size of land holding, education and financial conditions of the farmers. The production practices include 'no cost' production, 'low cost' production and 'high cost' production. High cost production is based on improved high yield varieties, improved farming practices, modern technology, latest agricultural machines and implements. **Crop production management** refers to controlling the various aspects of crop production, to obtain maximum and best yield. It has the following three components:

(i) Nutrient management
(ii) Irrigation
(iii) Cropping pattern

(i) **Nutrient management:** Just as human being needs nutrient for his growth and development, the plants also require nutrients for their proper growth and development. Plants get their nutrients from soil, water and air. There are sixteen nutrients required by the plants for proper growth and development. These nutrients are divided into two groups as micronutrients and macronutrients. Out of these, carbon and oxygen are supplied by air, hydrogen is supplied by water and remaining thirteen nutrients are supplied by soil.

(a) **Micronutrients:** The nutrients which are required by the plants in small quantities are called the micronutrients. There are seven micronutrients viz. chlorine, zinc, copper, iron, manganese, boron, and molybdenum.

(b) **Macronutrients:** The nutrients which are required by the plants in large quantities are called macronutrients. There are six macronutrients as nitrogen, phosphorous, potassium, calcium, sulphur and magnesium.

(ii) **Irrigation:** Water is one of the important requirements for crop production. To have good harvest we should have proper arrangement of water (known as irrigation) for the agriculture. It is not necessary that there will be proper rainfall at the time of farming. In such case we should have proper arrangement of water supply for the agriculture.

India has a wide variety of water resources and a highly varied climate. Depending on the kinds of water resources available there are different kinds of irrigation systems.

(iii) **Cropping patterns:** The different cropping patterns can be followed to increase the productivity of the crops. The different cropping patterns are mixed cropping, inter cropping and crop rotation.

Crop Protection Management

Crops are infected by large number of weeds, insect pests and disease. If these are not controlled at right time it can lead to large scale destruction of crops.

Weeds are unwanted plants in the cultivated field. For example, xanthium (gokhroo), Parthenium (gajar ghas), cyperinus rotundas (motha). They compete for food, space and light. Weeds take up nutrients and reduce the growth of the crops. Therefore, removal of weeds from cultivated fields during the early stages of crop growth is essential for a good harvest.

Generally, insect pests attack the plants in three ways (i) they cut the root, stem and leaf (ii) they suck the cell sap from various parts of the plant and (iii) they bore into stem and fruits. Diseases in plants are caused by pathogens such as bacteria, fungi and viruses: These pathogens can be present in and transmitted through the soil, water and air.

The chemicals used to kill the pests are known as **pesticides**. These pesticides include insecticides, weedicides and fungicides. Some of the common methods to control the weeds are **uprooting, hand picking, burning** and **flooding**. This can also be done with the help of using chemicals such as 2,4-dichloro phenoxyacetic acid, atrazine etc.

Some common diseases of crops are:

S. No.	Crop	Disease	Pathogen
1.	Rice	Blast	Fungus
2.	Wheat	Rust	Fungus
3.	Chick pea	Wilt	Fungus
4.	Pigeon pea	Stem rot	Fungus
5.	Mustard	White rust, downy mildew	Fungus

TRIVIA

Zealandia, also known as the New Zealand continent or Tasmantis, is an almost entirely submerged continent.

Animal Husbandry

It is the branch of science which deals with the rearing and management of animals. For commercial purpose it includes various aspects such as feeding, breeding and disease control. Animal based farming includes cattle, goat, sheep poultry and fish farming.

Cattle Farming

Cattle farming is done for two purposes, that is, for milk and transportation. Indian cattle belong to two different species, Bos indicus, cows and

Bos bubalis, buffaloes. Milk producing females are called **milch animals** (dairy animals), while the ones used for farm labour are called **draught animals**.

Lactation period (i.e., the period of milk production after the birth of a calf) affects the milk production. Milk production can be increased by increasing the lactation period. Exotic or foreign breeds (for example, Jersey, Brown Swiss) are selected for long lactation period, while local breeds (for example: Red Sindhi, Sahiwal) show excellent resistance to disease. The two can be crossbred to get animals with both the desired qualities.

For the health of animals and for production of milk, proper cleaning and shelter facilities are a must. Animals require regular brushing to remove dirt and loose hair. They should be sheltered under well-ventilated roofed sheds that protect them from rain, heat and cold. The floor of the cattle shed needs to be sloping so as to stay dry and to facilitate cleaning.

The cattle feed is also equally important. The animal feed includes two types of substance; Roughage and Concentrates. The roughage largely consists of fibres, silage, hay and legumes, while the concentrates include the mixtures of substances which are rich in vitamins, minerals and carbohydrates.

Cattle suffer from a number of diseases. The diseases, besides causing death, reduce milk production. The parasites of cattle may be both external and internal. The external parasites live on skin and mainly cause skin diseases. The internal parasites like worms, affect stomach and intestine while flukes damage the liver. Infectious diseases such as foot and mouth disease, anthrax, hemorrhagic septicemia, black quarter are cause by bacteria and viruses.

Vaccinations are given to protect animals against many major viral and bacterial diseases.

Note: Dr. Kurien is known as the **Architect of India's Modern Dairy Industry** and **the Father of white revolution**. White revolution means huge increase in milk production and it becomes possible by using new, improved breeds of cattle and buffalo, giving them better feed and care.

Poultry Farming

Rearing and management of hen for meat and eggs is called poultry farming. There are three types of poultry indigenous, exotic and cross breeds. The cross breeding programmes between Indian (indigenous, for example: Ascel, Kadaknath, bursa) and foreign (exotic, for example: White leghorn, rhode island red) breeds for variety improvement are focused on to develop new varieties for the following desirable traits:

(i) Number and quality of chicks.
(ii) Dwarf broiler parent for commercial chick production.
(iii) Summer adaptation capacity/tolerence to high temperature.
(iv) Low maintenance requirements.
(v) Reduction in the size of the egg-laying bird with ability to utilise more fibrous cheaper diets formulated using agricultural by-products.

Egg and Broiler Production: There are two basic targets of poultry farming (i) obtaining more and more eggs (ii) getting flesh

(i) Production of eggs: In chickens, egg production is the most important economic trait. A layer starts laying eggs at the age of 20 weeks. The egg production period in commercial layer is 500 days. To develop new varieties or to improve quality of chicken with respect to quantity and quality of eggs the following points are considered:

(i) Egg number
(ii) Sexual maturity
(iii) Egg weight
(iv) Body weight
(v) Feed efficiency
(vi) Egg size
(vii) Shell colour
(viii) Shell quality
(ix) Internal quality of eggs.

Note: The fertile eggs rot not rapidly than the infertile eggs, thus the production of infertile eggs is desired. Hens can lay eggs without a cock and the eggs thus obtained are infertile. Such eggs are called **vegetarian eggs**.

Improvement in Food Resources

(ii) **Production of Broilers:** Chickens are raised up to 6-7 weeks in the poultry farm. They grow to a weight of 700g to 1.5 kg in this period. They are fed with vitamin rich supplementry feed for good growth rate and better feed efficiency. Care is taken to prevent mortality and enable feathering and maintain carcass quality. They are produced as broilers and sent to market to be sold as meat.

The housing, nutritional and environmental requirements of broilers are somewhat different from those of egg layers. The ration (daily food requirement) for broilers is protein rich with adequate fat. The level of vitamins A and K is kept high in the poultry feeds.

Some of the common diseases founded in the poultry are caused by virus, such as bird flu, cholera Aspergillus etc. Vaccination can prevent the occurrence of infectious diseases and reduce loss of poultry during an outbreak of disease.

Fish Production

The rearing and management of fish on large scale for commercial purposes is called **pisciculture**. There are two ways of obtaining fish. One is from natural resources called **capture fishing**. The other way is by fish farming called **culture fishery**. Fishing can be done by capture and culture of fish in marine and freshwater ecosystems.

(i) **Marine fisheries:** The marine fisheries include fisheries of ocean and sea. Popular marine fish varieties include pomphrets, mackerel, tuna, sardines, Bombay duck, eel, hilsa, salmon, ribbon fish, flat fish or sole, reer, flying fish.

Some marine fish of high economic value are also farmed in sea water. This includes finned fishes like mullets, bhetki and pearl spats, shell fish such as prawns, mussels and oysters as well as sea weed. Oysters are also cultivated for the pearls they make.

Marine culture: The marine fishes cultured in coastal waters of India on commercial basis include mullet, bhetki, pearl spots, rardines, cell and milk fish.

(ii) **In land fisheries:** The fresh water fisheries include river, lakes, ponds and fields. The common fish founded in this region are catla, ribbon fish, mugil etc.

Fish culture is sometimes done in combination with a rice crop, so that fish are grown in the water in the paddy field, this system is known as **composite fish cultural system**. In such a system, a combination of five or six fish species is used in single fishpond. These species are selected so that they do not compete for food among them having different types of food habits. As a result, the food available in all the parts of the pond is used. The food habits of some species are as follows:

(i) The silver corp (hypophthalmichthys), (molitrix) is a surface feeder are feeds on phytoplankton.
(ii) The catla is also surface feeder and it feeds on zooplankton.
(iii) The rohu (Labeo rohila) feeds in middle zone of the pond i.e., column feeder, and feeds on decaying plants and detritus.
(iv) The grass corp (ctenopharyngodon idella) feeds on all macrovegetation and consumes the aquatic plants/weeds not used by other species in this group.
(v) The mrigal (Cirrhinus mrigala) is a bottom feeder using decoying plants and detritus.
(vi) The common corp (cyprinus carpio) is an omnivorus bottom feeder.

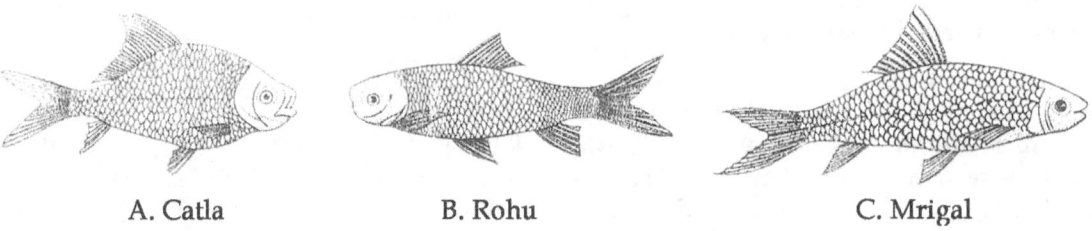

A. Catla B. Rohu C. Mrigal
Fig. 15.1. *Major Indian Corps of Fish*

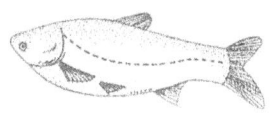 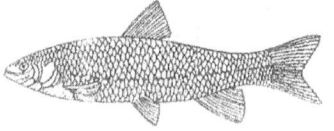 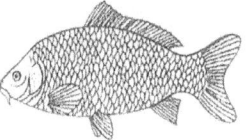

A. Silver corp   B. Grass corp   C. Common corp

Fig. 15.2. *Exotic Corps of Fish*

Thus, these species can use all the food in the pond without competing with each other. This increases fish yield from the pond.

Bee-keeping

Bee keeping or **apiculture** is the rearing, care and management of honey bees for obtaining honey, wax and other substances. Honey is known to have medicinal value. Since bee keeping needs low investments, farmers use it as an additional income generating activity.

There are two varieties of bee used for honey production such as indigenous and exotic breeds. The indigenous (Indian) breeds include Apis cerana indica, Apis dorsata, (Rock bee) and Apis florae (Little bee). The exotic breeds includes Apis mellifera (Italan bee), and Apis adamsoni, an Italian bee variety. Apis mellifera, has also been brought in to increase yield of honey. This is the variety commonly used for commercial honey production. Italian bees have high honey collection capacity. They sting some what less. They stay in a given beehive for long periods and breed very well. For commercial honey production, bee farms or apiaries are established.

The value and quality of honey depends upon the pasturage or orchards. i.e., posturage is the availability of flowers for nectar and pollen collection for the honey bee. The quality and taste of honey is determined by the kind and quantity of posturage.

MUST REMEMBER

- Sustainable agriculture is the adoption of various farming and production management techniques to maximize agriculture yield and organic farming is the practice of raising crops which have not been polluted.
- Photoperiods are duration of sunlight that influence plants in their growth, flowering of storage organs, leaf fall etc.
- High cost production is based on improved high yield varieties, improved farming practices, modern technology, latest agricultural machines and implements. Crop production management refers to controlling the various aspects of crop production, to obtain maximum and best yield.
- Crops are infected by large number of weeds, insect pests and disease.
- Some of the common diseases founded in the poultry are caused by virus, such as bird flu, cholera Aspergillus etc.
- The rearing and management of fish on large scale for commercial purposes is called pisciculture.
- Fish culture is sometimes done in combination with a rice crop, so that fish are grown in the water in the paddy field, this system is known as composite fish cultural system.
- Bee keeping or apiculture is the rearing, care and management of honey bees for obtaining honey, wax and other substances.
- The value and quality of honey depends upon the pasturage or orchards. i.e., posturage is the availability of flowers for nectar and pollen collection for the honey bee.

Improvement in Food Resources

MULTIPLE CHOICE QUESTIONS

1. Increase in oil production is _____.
   (a) White revolution
   (b) Blue revolution
   (c) Yellow revolution
   (d) Golden revolution

2. Organic farming does not include _____.
   (a) Crop rotation
   (b) Chemical fertilizers
   (c) Green manures
   (d) Compost and farmyard manures

3. The place for keeping and studying dry plants is called _____.
   (a) Museum
   (b) Vasculum
   (c) Arboreum
   (d) Herbarium

4. Which one of the following nutrients do we get from cereals?
   (a) Carbohydrates
   (b) Vitamins
   (c) Proteins
   (d) Minerals

5. Pulses are rich in _____.
   (a) Proteins
   (b) Oils
   (c) Vitamins and minerals
   (d) Carbohydrates

6. Which one is a micronutrient for the crop plants?
   (a) Potassium
   (b) Iron
   (c) Magnesium
   (d) Calcium

7. The technique used to obtain variety with high yield and other desirable characters is _____.
   (a) Hybridization
   (b) Selection
   (c) Introduction
   (d) Both (b) and (c)

8. Pusa lerma is an improved variety of _____.
   (a) Maize
   (b) Wheat
   (c) Rice
   (d) Soyabean

9. The botanical name of Dhaincha is _____.
   (a) Crotalaria
   (b) Trifolium alexandrium
   (c) Lens culinaris
   (d) Sesbania aculeata

10. The rust disease in wheat is caused by which one of the following microorganisms?
    (a) Puccinia
    (b) Smut
    (c) Pyricularis
    (d) Wachuria

11. Choose the complex fertilizer _____.
    (a) Triple super phosphate
    (b) Urea ammonium phosphate
    (c) Calcium ammonium nitrate
    (d) Potassium sulphate

12. Choose the abiotic factor _____.
    (a) Moisture content
    (b) Birds
    (c) Insects
    (d) Fungi

13. All animals are _____.
    (a) Autotrophic
    (b) Heterotrophic
    (c) Parasitic
    (d) Saprophytic

14. The chief cereal crop of India is _____.
    (a) Maize
    (b) Wheat
    (c) Sorghum
    (d) Rice

15. Which is the most important source of food and fooder?
    (a) Cereal
    (b) Fungi
    (c) Algae
    (d) Lichen

16. Nodules with nitrogen-fixing bacteria are present in _____.
    (a) Wheat
    (b) Cotton
    (c) Gram
    (d) Mustrd

17. Gundhi bug is a pest of _____.
    (a) Wheat
    (b) Rice
    (c) Maize
    (d) Sorghum

18. Which of the following is not a sustainable agriculture technique?
    (a) Crop rotation
    (b) Mixed farming
    (c) Crop selection
    (d) Slash and burn farming

19. The element which is required in largest quantity by plants is _____.
    (a) Calcium
    (b) Nitrogen
    (c) Sulphur
    (d) Phosphorus

20. Application of nitrogen manure to a plant causes _____.
    (a) Early fruiting
    (b) Early flowering
    (c) Vigorous vegetative growth
    (d) Growth retardation due to toxicity
21. The lactation period for Red Sindhi is _____.
    (a) 230 to 394 days
    (b) 184 to 354 days
    (c) 250 to 410 days
    (d) 231 to 394 days
22. Who carried out the first experiment of artificial insemination?
    (a) Whitalker   (b) John Dove
    (c) Spallanzani   (d) Charles Martin
23. Find out the wrong statement from the following:
    (a) White revolution is meant for increase in milk production
    (b) Increasing food production without compromising with environment quality is called as sustainable agriculture.
    (c) Blue revolution is meant for increase in fish production
    (d) None of these
24. What is pulse rate of buffalo/minute?
    (a) 40 – 60/minutes
    (b) 70 – 72/minutes
    (c) 40 – 45/minutes
    (d) 16 – 18/minutes
25. Which of the poultry bird lays maximum number of eggs?
    (a) HH –260   (b) B –77
    (c) IBL –80   (d) ILS –82
26. Which of the following is not a draught animal?
    (a) Sheep   (b) Horse
    (c) Elephant   (d) Camel
27. Rotation of crops is essential for _____.
    (a) Increasing quality of proteins
    (b) Increasing fertility of soil
    (c) Increasing quality of minerals
    (d) Getting different kinds of crops
28. Which part of the plant breeding is an art?
    (a) Clonal selection
    (b) Pure line selection
    (c) Technique of hybridisation
    (d) Acclimatisation
29. Match the following.

i	White leghorn	a	Meat yielding poultry
ii	Karan swiss	b	Egg laying poultry
iii	Murrah	c	Buffalo
iv	Aseel	d	Exotic breed of cow

    (a) i –c, 2 –a, iii –d, iv –b
    (b) i –b, 2 –d, iii –c, iv –a
    (c) i –c, 2 –d, iii –a, iv –b
    (d) i –d, 2 –c, iii –b, iv –a
30. Which is the oldest breeding method?
    (a) Selection   (b) Mutation
    (c) Hybridization   (d) Introduction
31. The unlikely row pattern practiced in intercropping is _____.
    (a) 1 : 1   (b) 1 : 2
    (c) 1 : 3   (d) 1 : 4
32. A popular improved variety of maize is _____.
    (a) Shakti   (b) Durga
    (c) Aasha   (d) Manak
33. Milk does not provide _____.
    (a) Iron
    (b) Vitamin A and D
    (c) Carbohydrates, proteins and fats
    (d) Minerals such as phosphorus and calcium
34. Weeds affect the crop plants by _____.
    (a) Dominating the plants to grow.
    (b) Competing for various resources of crops (plants) causing low availability of nutrients.
    (c) Killing of plants in field before they grow.
    (d) All of these
35. To solve the food problem of country, which among the following necessary?
    (a) Easy access of people to the food grain
    (b) Increased production and storage of food grains
    (c) People should have money to purchase the grains
    (d) Both (a) and (b)

Improvement in Food Resources

36. Which of the following is gaseous fumigant?
    (a) Ethylene dichloride
    (b) Methyl bromide
    (c) Aluminium phosphide
    (d) DDT
37. Which one of the following is the fastest growing carp?
    (a) Catla (b) Rohu
    (c) Mrigal (d) Singhara
38. Which of the following is natural insecticide?
    (a) Pyrethrum (b) Neem
    (c) Nicotene (d) All of these
39. The fungal disease causing maximum death of poultry bird is ———.
    (a) Rickets (b) Aspergillosis
    (c) Pullorium (d) Coryza
40. Wax glands of honey bee are present in ———.
    (a) Queen (b) Drones
    (c) Workers (d) Both (a) and (c)
41. 'Drones' in the honey bee colony are born out from ———.
    (a) Unfertilized eggs
    (b) Fertilized eggs giving heat treatment
    (c) Same as workers bee
    (d) Fertilized eggs and well nourished larval
42. Several embryos can be produced at a time in a single cow by the process of ———.
    (a) Hybridization
    (b) Embryo transfer
    (c) Random mating
    (d) Artificial insemination
43. The botanical name of lentil is ———.
    (a) Lens culinaris
    (b) Sesbania aculeate
    (c) Torifolium alexandrium
    (d) Crotolaria juncea
44. The botanical name of Egyption clover is ———.
    (a) Lens culinaris
    (b) Crotolaria juncea
    (c) Torifolium alexandrium
    (d) Sesbania aculeate
45. Which of the following is Indian cattle?
    (a) Bos indicus (b) Bos vulgaris
    (c) Bos domestica (d) Bos bubalis
46. Which one of the following species of honey bee is an Italian species?
    (a) Apis mellifera
    (b) Apis dorsata
    (c) Apis floral
    (d) Apis cerana indica
47. Preventive and control measures adopted for storage of grains include ———.
    (a) Fumigation (b) Proper disjoining
    (c) Strict cleaning (d) All of these
48. Find out the correct sentence about manure.
    (i) It increases the water holding capacity of sandy soil.
    (ii) Manure contains large quantities of organic matter and small quantities of nutrients.
    (iii) It helps in draining out of excess of water from clayey soil.
    (iv) Its excessive use pollutes environment because it is made of animal excretory waste.
    (a) (i) and (ii) (b) (ii) and (iii)
    (c) (i) and (iv) (d) (iii) and (iv)
49. Which one is an oil yielding plant among the following?
    (a) Sunflower (b) Lentil
    (c) Cauliflower (d) Hibiscus
50. Kranti, Pusa agarni and pusa bold are improved varieties of ———.
    (a) Chick pea (b) Mustard
    (c) Urad bean (d) Sunflower

HOTS

1. Select the correct match.

	Affected organism	Disease	Causal organism
(a)	Cattle	Anthrax	Bacteria
(b)	Poultry	Rinderpest	Virus
(c)	Cattle	Ranikhet	Virus
(d)	Poultry	Haemorrhagic septicaemia	Bacteria

2. Complete the given statements by selecting the correct words from the options given below.
   (a) ____(i)____ is a kind of manure which is prepared in the field itself to enrich soil with nitrogen and phosphorus.
   (b) ____(ii)____ is a draught breed of cattle.
   (c) In ____(iii)____ water escapes from revolving nozzle and falls like rain on the crops.
   (d) ____(iv)____ is the process of crossing individuals of two different species to produce hybrid.

	(i)	(ii)	(iii)	(iv)
(a)	Vermi compost	Malvi	Drip irrigation	Intravarietal hybridisation
(b)	Farm yard manure	Sahiwal	Chain pump	Intervarietal hybridisation
(c)	Compost	Gir	Moat	Intraspecific hybridisation
(d)	Green manure	Nageri	Sprinkler system	Interspecific hybridisation

3. Read the given statements.
   (i) Bee wax obtained from beehive is deposition of excretory products of honeybee.
   (ii) Fish culture is sometimes done in combination with rice crop so that fish are grown in the water accumulated in the paddy field.
   (iii) Fish feed in different zones of pond to make most efficient use of available food.
   (iv) Sahiwal and Murrah are exotic breeds used extensively in cattle farming.
   (v) Intercropping is growing two or more crops simultaneously on the same field in a definite pattern.

   Which of the given statements are incorrect?
   (a) (i), (ii) and (iii) only
   (b) (ii) and (iv) only
   (c) (i) and (iv) only
   (d) (i), (iv) and (v) only

4. Read the following statements (A–C) and select the option which correctly fills up the blanks in any two statements.
   (A) ___(i)___ nutrients are required in large quantity and called as ___(ii)___.
   (B) Kharif crops are cultivated from ___(iii)___ to ___(iv)___.
   (C) Berseem is an important ___(v)___ crop.
   (a) (i) - 17, (ii) - Micronutrients, (iii) - June, (iv) - October
   (b) (iii) - June, (iv) - October, (v) - Fodder
   (c) (i) - 17, (ii) - Macronutrients, (v) - Field
   (d) (iii) - November, (iv) - April, (v) - Rabi

5. The steps in the preparation of green manure are given below in a random order. Select the option that represents these steps in the correct sequence.
   (A) Green plants are decomposed in soil.
   (B) Quick growing green plants are cultivated.
   (C) Plants are ploughed and mixed into the soil.
   (D) After decomposition it becomes green manure.
   (a) (C)→(B)→(A)→(D)
   (b) (A)→(C)→(B)→(D)
   (c) (A)→(B)→(C)→(D)
   (d) (B)→(C)→(A)→(D)

Improvement in Food Resources

SUBJECTIVE QUESTIONS

1. (a) Discuss two ways of incorporating desirable characteristics into crop varieties.
   (b) What is inter-cropping? How are crops selected for inter-cropping?

   Ans.
   (a) Desirable characteristics can be incorporated in a crop variety by two methods:
   - (i) **Hybridization:** This is a genetical technique. This method involves crossing of the selected plants having one or more of the desirable characteristics.
   - (ii) **Genetic engineering:** Introduction of desirable characteristics with the help of techniques available in biotechnology.

   (b) **Inter cropping:** It is growing of two or more crops simultaneously in the same field but in different row of patterns.

   Crops are selected for inter-cropping on the basis of different nutrient requirement and different. Showing and reaping (harvesting) times, e.g., soyabean and maize.

2. State the difference between macro-nutrients and micro-nutrients.

   Ans.

Macro-nutrients	Micro-nutrients
These are required by crops in larger quantity.	These are required by crops in very small quantity.
Six macro-nutriets are: Nitrogen, phosphorus, potassium, calcium, magnesium and sulphus.	Seven micro-nutrients are: Iron, manganese, boron, zinc, copper, molybdenum and chlorine.

3. State the difference between manure and fertilizer.

   Ans.

Manure	Fertilizer
It consists of organic matter.	It consists of inorganic matter.
Prepared from animal excreta and plant waste.	It is prepared commercially from chemicals.
Its use causes no pollution.	It caused pollution in soil and water.

4. What decide the quantity and quality of honey production in apiary?

   Ans.
   For quality of honey: The pasturage, i.e., the kind of flowers available to the bees for nectar and pollen collection will determine the taste of the honey. For quantity of honey: Variety of bee used for the collection of honey. For example, A. mellifera is used to increase yield of honey.

5. How are crops useful to us? What do they provide?

   Ans.
   Crops provide us food for our daily body nutrient, Carbohydrate for energy requirement – Cereals such as wheat, rice, maize, Protein for body building — Pulses like gram, lentil. Fats for energy — Oil seed like mustard, sunflower. Vitamins and minerals — From vegetables, spices and fruits. Fodder crops — For livestocks.

SECTION 2
LOGICAL REASONING

Analogy

Learning Objectives : In this chapter, students will learn about:
- ✓ Analogy
- ✓ Simple Analogy
- ✓ Detecting Analogy

CHAPTER SUMMARY

Analogy is a comparison between two objects or systems of objects. Analogical reasoning is the logic that relies upon analogy.

Type 1 : Completing the Analogous Pair

In this type of question, two words are given which are related to each other in some way. Another word is also given. The candidate is required to find out the relationship between the first two words and choose the word from the given alternatives which have the same relationship to the third word as the first two have.

Example 1: Square : Diamond : : Circle : ?
   (a) smooth   (b) oval
   (c) round   (d) ball

Sol. (b)
   The second is the shape obtained by pulling the opposite ends of the first.

Example 2: Safe : Secure : : Protect : ?
   (a) conserve   (b) sure
   (c) guard   (d) lock

Sol. (c)
   The words in each pair are synonyms of each other.

Example 3: Lion : Deer : : Mongoose : ?
   (a) rat   (b) snake
   (c) Lizard   (d) squirrel

Sol. (b)
   The first kills and feeds on the second.

Type 2 : Direct/Simple Analogy

Example 4: Betel is related to chew in the same way as football is related to _____
   (a) play   (b) run
   (c) roll   (d) kick

Sol. (d)
   The first is the object and the second is the action performed on it.

Example 5: Starvation is related to nutrition in the same way as exhaustion is related to _____
   (a) energy   (b) bravery
   (c) freshness   (d) courage

Sol. (a)
   The first denotes the lack of the second.

Type 3: Detecting Analogies

In this type, candidate is required to trace out the hidden analogy or common properties among the given words.

Example 6: Barauni : Digboi : Ankleshwar.
   (a) They are famous for oil fields.
   (b) They are famous religious places.
   (c) They are tourist places of south India
   (d) They are famous for hand looms.

Sol. (a)

Example 7: Nissan : Toyota : Isuzu
   (a) These are cities in Japan.
   (b) These are tele programmes.
   (c) These are cars from Japan.
   (d) These are ports in Japan.

Sol. (c)

MULTIPLE CHOICE QUESTIONS

Directions (1 - 30): See the analogy given in the first pair of words and choose the correct option to establish the same relationship in the second pair.

1. Misogamy : Marriage : : Misogyny : ?
   (a) Husband (b) Women
   (c) Relations (d) Children
2. Coherent : Consistent : : Irate : ?
   (a) Unhappy (b) Irritated
   (c) Angry (d) Unreasonable
3. Skirmish : War : : Disease : ?
   (a) Patient (b) Medicine
   (c) Infection (d) Epidemic
4. Accomodation : Rent : : Journey : ?
   (a) Octroi (b) Fare
   (c) Freight (d) Expense
5. Elegance : Vulgarity : : Graceful : ?
   (a) Comely (b) Awkward
   (c) Dirty (d) Asperity
6. Dungeon : Confinement : : Asylum : ?
   (a) Mercy (b) Refuse
   (c) Remorse (d) Truanay
7. Darwin : Evolution : : Archimedes : ?
   (a) Lubrication (b) Friction
   (c) Liquids (d) Buoyancy.
8. College : Dean : : Museum : ?
   (a) curator (b) warden
   (c) supervisor (d) custodian
9. Election : Manifesto : : Meeting : ?
   (a) Report (b) Preface
   (c) Agenda (d) Circular
10. Hermit : Solitude : : Intruder : ?
    (a) Privacy (b) Burglar
    (c) Alm (d) Thief
11. Ruby : Red : : Sapphire : ?
    (a) Silver (b) White
    (c) Green (d) Blue
12. India : President : : State : ?
    (a) Prime minister (b) Mayor
    (c) Governor (d) Chief minister
13. Horse : Jockey : : Car : ?
    (a) Brake (b) Steering
    (c) Mechanic (d) Chauffeur
14. Canoe : Boat : : Mansion : ?
    (a) House (b) Bungalow
    (c) Hut (d) Palace
15. Smoke : Pollution : : War : ?
    (a) Treaty (b) Victory
    (c) Peace (d) Destruction
16. Conference : Chairman : : News paper : ?
    (a) Editor (b) Reporter
    (c) Printer (d) Distributor
17. Wine : Cellar : : Weapons : ?
    (a) Godown (b) Armoury
    (c) Dungeon (d) Arsenal
18. Electricity : Wire : : Water : ?
    (a) River (b) Pipe
    (c) Bottle (d) Jug
19. Wax : Wane : : Zenith : ?
    (a) Nadir (b) Fall
    (c) Bottom (d) Depth
20. Porcupine : Rodent : : Mildew : ?
    (a) Germ (b) Insect
    (c) Pathogen (d) Fungus
21. Radical : Moderate : : Revolution : ?
    (a) Peace (b) Reformation
    (c) Change (d) Chaos
22. Dilatory : Expeditious : : Direct : ?
    (a) Tortuous (b) Straight
    (c) Curved (d) Circumlocutory
23. Heart : Pericardium : : Brain : ?
    (a) Head (b) Skull
    (c) Bones (d) Cranium
24. Novelty : Oldness : : Newness : ?
    (a) Discovery (b) Culture
    (c) Model (d) Antiquity
25. Rill : Stream : : Pony : ?
    (a) Mulef (b) Donkey
    (c) Horse (d) Mare

Analogy

26. Pyrophobia : Fire : : Ochlophobia : ?
    (a) Foreigners   (b) Light
    (c) Horses   (d) Crowd
27. Shark : Fish : : Lavender : ?
    (a) Tree   (b) Shrub
    (c) Herb   (d) Climber
28. Venerate : Worship : : Extol : ?
    (a) Homage   (b) Glorify
    (c) Recommend   (d) Complement
29. Anatomy : Zoology : : Paediatrics : ?
    (a) Medicine   (b) Chemistry
    (c) Mechanics   (d) Palaeontology
30. Roster : Duty : : Inventory : ?
    (a) Produce   (b) Exports
    (c) Furnace   (d) Goods

Classification   2

Learning Objectives: In this chapter, students will learn about:
- Classification
- Types of Classification

CHAPTER SUMMARY

Classification means to analyse the items of a given group on the basis of certain common properties they possess and then mark the odd one.

In this type of questions a group of certain items are given, out of which all, except one are, similar to one another in some manner. We have to choose the odd one, which is not suitable for this given group.

There are mainly three types of classification.

Type 1 : Choosing the Odd Word
In this type students have to choose the word which is different from the other three.

Example 1:
(a) Aquarium (b) House
(c) Kennel   (d) Stable

Sol. (b)
All other words are the staying places of specific animals.

Example 2:
(a) Heart (b) Club
(c) Spade (d) Brick

Sol. (d)
Except brick, all others are suits of playing cards.

Example 3:
(a) Chalk   (b) Cardamom
(c) Rubber (d) Cinchona

Sol. (a)
All except chalk are obtained from a plant.

Example 4:
(a) Telescope   (b) Periscope
(c) Microscope (d) Stethoscope

Sol. (d)
All except stethoscope are optical instruments.

Type 2 : Choosing the Odd Numeral
In this type, four numbers are given, out of these numbers, all except one have some common properties or they follow some certain rules. We have to choose the odd numeral.

Example 5:
(a) 442 (b) 362
(c) 962 (d) 575

Sol. (d)
Here $575 = 24^2 - 1$; $442 = 21^2 + 1$
$362 = 19^2 + 1$; $962 = 31^2 + 1$
∴ odd numeral = 575

Example 6:
(a) 1234 (b) 2345
(c) 3456 (d) 7856

Sol. (d)
Except 7856, all numbers are made by consecutive digits.

Example 7:
(a) 752 (b) 853
(c) 962 (d) 945

Sol. (c)
Except 962, in all three numbers, the middle number is difference of first and last.

Example 8:
   (a) 1233   (b) 1456
   (c) 1789   (d) 4235

Sol. (d)
   In all three numbers, the sum of all digits in these numbers is a perfect square.

Type 3 : Choosing the Odd Pair of Words

In this type, four pairs of words are given. In all pairs, except one have some common relationship. We have to choose the odd pair of words.

Example 9:
   (a) Curd : Milk
   (b) Train : Engine
   (c) Atom : Electron
   (d) House : Room

Sol. (a)
   In all three pairs, the second is the part of first.

Example 10:
   (a) Capacitance : Farad
   (b) Time : Second
   (c) Force : Newton
   (d) Pressure : Barometer

Sol. (d)
   In all other pairs, the second is the unit of measuring the first one.

Example 11:
   (a) Hammer : Nail
   (b) Pen : Pencil
   (c) Shovel : Mud
   (d) Screwdriver : Screw

Sol. (b)
   In all pairs, the first is a tool which works on second.

Example 12:
   (a) Apple : Jam   (b) Orange : Squash
   (c) Tomato : Pury   (d) Lemon : Citrus

Sol. (d)
   In all pairs of words, the second is the form in which the first is preserved.

MULTIPLE CHOICE QUESTIONS

Directions (1 – 15): In each of the following questions four words have been given. Out of which three are alike in some manner, while the fourth one is different. Choose the odd one.

1. (a) Pallete (b) Trigger
   (c) Muzzle (d) Barrel
2. (a) Avalancle (b) Hurricane
   (c) Explosion (d) Earthquake
3. (a) Pepper (b) Cinnamon
   (c) Groundnut (d) Clove
4. (a) Dribble (b) Scoop
   (c) Bully (d) Bunker
5. (a) Pepsinogen (b) Plasma
   (c) Lymphocytes (d) Fibrinogen
6. (a) Premolar (b) Dentine
   (c) Incisor (d) Canine
7. (a) Record (b) Morse
   (c) Codes (d) Semaphore
8. (a) Decantation (b) Centrifugation
   (c) Condensation (d) Sublimation
9. (a) Distress (b) Calm
   (c) Dull (d) Gloomy
10. (a) Goblet (b) Goblin
    (c) Dinn (d) Gnome
11. (a) Ascetic (b) Pious
    (c) Hermit (d) Mendicant
12. (a) Direct (b) Counsel
    (c) Advise (d) Suggest
13. (a) Alveoli (b) Auricle
    (c) Pharynx (d) Bronchiole
14. (a) Koala (b) Alpaca
    (c) Walrus (d) Beaver
15. (a) Ruffian (b) Paragon
    (c) Pirate (d) Gangster

Directions (16-30): In each of the following questions, there are four numbers in which three numbers are alike in some certain manner, but one number is different. Find the odd number.

16. (a) 675 (b) 323
    (c) 440 (d) 362
17. (a) 3715 (b) 6715
    (c) 7351 (d) 9571
18. (a) 2864 (b) 6248
    (c) 8672 (d) 2648
19. (a) 1368 (b) 1764
    (c) 961 (d) 2809
20. (a) 671 (b) 495
    (c) 583 (d) 472
21. (a) 817 (b) 936
    (c) 634 (d) 752
22. (a) 8157 (b) 6148
    (c) 9123 (d) 7164
23. (a) 5243 (b) 3627
    (c) 8359 (d) 6859
24. (a) 1237 (b) 2347
    (c) 5677 (d) 3857
25. (a) 625 (b) 195
    (c) 675 (d) 445
26. (a) 555 (b) 888
    (c) 777 (d) 999
27. (a) 1643 (b) 2837
    (c) 9572 (d) 6538
28. (a) 6521 (b) 4657
    (c) 8967 (d) 2789
29. (a) 3241 (b) 7261
    (c) 8731 (d) 2792
30. (a) 67 (b) 87
    (c) 97 (d) 47

Directions (31 – 40): In the given questions four pairs of words are given, out of which the words in three pairs have a certain common relationship. Choose the pair in which the words are differently related.

31. (a) Daring : Timid
    (b) Clear : Vague
    (c) Native : Alien
    (d) Beautiful : Pretty
32. (a) Biology : Botany
    (b) Mycology : Fungi
    (c) Entomology : Insects
    (d) Ornithology : Birds

Classification

33. (a) Butcher : Chopper
    (b) Farmer : Plough
    (c) Author : Book
    (d) Jockey : Tack
34. (a) Malaria : Protozoa
    (b) Cholera : Bacteria
    (c) Rabies : Wound
    (d) Influenza : Virus
35. (a) Man : Garage (b) Horse : Stable
    (c) Cow : Shed (d) Pig : Sty
36. (a) Neck : Tie (b) Wrist : Band
    (c) Shoe : Lace (d) Waist : Belt
37. (a) Death : Disease
    (b) Water : Oxygen
    (c) Milk : Butter
    (d) Grape : Wine
38. (a) Holmes : Suspense
    (b) Donald : Comedy
    (c) Robinson : Adventure
    (d) Premchand : Novel
39. (a) Termite : Wood (b) Locust : Plant
    (c) Aphid : Paper (d) Moth : Wool
40. (a) Loom : Cloth (b) Book : Page
    (c) Car : Wheel (d) Table : Drawer

Series Completion   3

Learning Objectives : In this chapter, students will learn about:
- Series
- Types of Series

CHAPTER SUMMARY

In this type of test, a series of numbers or alphabetical letters is given in the question. The given series follows a certain rule and pattern throughout. Hence, we are required to recognize the pattern and to complete the given series or find out the wrong term in the series.

There are mainly three types of questions:

Type 1 : Number Series
In this type, the given series follow a certain pattern. We have to find that pattern and find the missing term.

Example 1: 4, 6, 12, 14, 28, 30, ?
Sol. Here

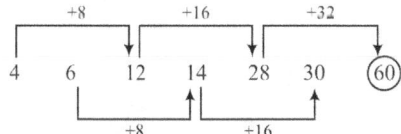

∴ Missing term = 60

Example 2: 4, 9 15, 22, 30, ?
Sol.

In this series, the pattern is:
$4 \to 4 + 5 = 9$; $9 \to 9 + 6 = 15$
$15 \to 15 + 7 = 22$; $22 \to 22 + 8 = 30$
$30 \to 30 + 9 = 39$
∴ ? = 39

Example 3: 1, 8, 27, 64, 125, 216, ?
Sol.

In this series, the pattern is 13, 23, 33, 43, 53, 63
∴ Missing term = 7^3 = 343

Example 4: 5, 8, 14, 26, 50, 98, ?
Sol.
Here $5 \times 2 - 2 = 8$; $8 \times 2 - 2 = 14$
$14 \times 2 - 2 = 26$; $26 \times 2 - 2 = 50$
$50 \times 2 - 2 = 98$; $98 \times 2 - 2 = 194$
∴ Missing term = 194

Type 2 : Alphabet Series
In this type, a series of single, pair or group of letters or numbers is given. The series follow a certain pattern. We have to find the missing term according to pattern.

Example 5: DGK, HMS, MTB, SBL?
Sol.

The pattern of the given series is:

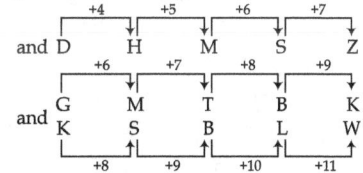

∴ Missing term = ZKW

Type 3 : Alpha Numeric Series
The given series consists of combination of letters and numerals which follows a certain pattern. We have to find that pattern and fill in the blanks with proper letters or numbers.

Example 6: Z1A, X2D, V6G, T21J ?
$Z \xrightarrow{-2} X \xrightarrow{-2} V \xrightarrow{-2} T \xrightarrow{-2} R$
$1 \times 1 + 1 = 2; 2 \times 2 + 2 = 6$
$6 \times 3 + 3 = 21; 21 \times 4 + 4 = 88$
$A \xrightarrow{+3} D \xrightarrow{+3} G \xrightarrow{+3} J \xrightarrow{+3} M$
∴ Missing term = R88M

MULTIPLE CHOICE QUESTIONS

Directions (1 – 22): There is a series of numbers which follow some definite order. Find the missing term and complete the series.

1. 3, 4, 5, 5, 12, 13, 7, 24, 25, 9, ?, 41
   (a) 40   (b) 35   (c) 24   (d) 16
2. 1, 3, 6, 10, 15, 21, ?
   (a) 26   (b) 25   (c) 28   (d) 30
3. 10, 17, 26, 37, 50, ?
   (a) 76   (b) 65   (c) 95   (d) 84
4. 80, 63, 72, 72, 64, 81, 56, ?
   (a) 96   (b) 98   (c) 89   (d) 90
5. 2, 4, 4, 8, 16, 16, 256, ?
   (a) 60   (b) 36   (c) 32   (d) 180
6. 19, 4, 14, 7, 10, 11, 7, ?
   (a) 15   (b) 16   (c) 17   (d) 23
7. 1, 5, 7, 14, 18, 20, 40, 44, 46, ?
   (a) 50   (b) 48   (c) 52   (d) 92
8. 8, 24, 16, ?, 7, 14, 6, 18, 12, 5, 5, 10
   (a) 5   (b) 7   (c) 10   (d) 14
9. 5, 12, 7, 15, 8, 18, 10, ?
   (a) 10   (b) 11   (c) 21   (d) 28
10. 2, 3, 10, 15, 26, 35, 50, 63, ?
    (a) 80   (b) 82   (c) 83   (d) 84
11. 325, 259, 204, 160, 127, 105, ?
    (a) 94   (b) 96   (c) 92   (d) 98
12. 198, 194, 185, 169, ?
    (a) 114   (b) 124   (c) 144   (d) 136
13. 0, 2, 3, 5, 8, 10, 15, 17, 24, 26, ?
    (a) 30   (b) 32   (c) 34   (d) 35
14. 8, 9, 8, 7, 10, 9, 6, 11, 10, ?
    (a) 5   (b) 7   (c) 8   (d) 11
15. 120, 99, 80, 63, 48, ?
    (a) 35   (b) 38   (c) 39   (d) 40
16. 11, 13, 17, 19, 23, 25, ?
    (a) 26   (b) 27   (c) 29   (d) 37
17. 1, 1, 4, 8, 9, 27, 16, ?
    (a) 64   (b) 81   (c) 144   (d) 256
18. 24, 60, 120, 210, ?
    (a) 300   (b) 336
    (c) 420   (d) 525
19. 10, 14, 26, 42, 70, ?
    (a) 114   (b) 116   (c) 118   (d) 120
20. 1, 3, 4, 8, 15, 27, ?
    (a) 37   (b) 44   (c) 50   (d) 55
21. 5, 2, 7, 9, 16, 25, ?
    (a) 41   (b) 45   (c) 48   (d) 52
22. 2, 12, 36, 80, 150, ?
    (a) 252   (b) 254
    (c) 256   (d) 258

Directions (23 – 34): In each of the following questions, one term in the number series is wrong. Find out the wrong term.

23. 196, 169, 144, 121, 101
    (a) 101   (b) 121
    (c) 169   (d) 196
24. 125, 126, 124, 127, 123, 129
    (a) 124   (b) 126
    (c) 123   (d) 129
25. 2, 6, 24, 96, 285, 568, 567
    (a) 6   (b) 24   (c) 285   (d) 567
26. 56, 58, 62, 70, 84, 118, 182
    (a) 58   (b) 84   (c) 62   (d) 118
27. 93, 309, 434, 498, 521, 533
    (a) 498   (b) 521
    (c) 434   (d) 309
28. 4, 27, 61, 122, 213, 340, 509
    (a) 27   (b) 122   (c) 61   (d) 509
29. 3, 2, 8, 9, 13, 22, 18, 32, 23, 42
    (a) 9   (b) 13   (c) 18   (d) 23
30. 1, 3, 10, 21, 64, 12   9, 356, 777
    (a) 129   (b) 356   (c) 777   (d) 64
31. 8, 13, 21, 32, 47, 63, 83
    (a) 47   (b) 13   (c) 32   (d) 83
32. 6, 15, 35, 77, 165, 221
    (a) 221   (b) 165   (c) 77   (d) 35
33. 380, 188, 92, 48, 20, 8, 2
    (a) 48   (b) 20   (c) 92   (d) 188
34. 24, 96, 386, 1536, 6144, 24576
    (a) 386   (b) 98
    (c) 1536   (d) 6144

Directions (35 – 40): Choose the missing term out of given alternatives.

35. ABD, DGK, HMS, MTB, SBL, ?
    (a) ZAB (b) ZKU
    (c) XKW (d) ZKW

36. PMT, OOS, NQR, MSQ, ?
    (a) LUP (b) LVP
    (c) LVR (d) LWP

37. BZA, DYC, FXE, ?, JVI.
    (a) HWG (b) HUG
    (c) UHG (d) WHG

38. AZ, GT, MN, ?, YB.
    (a) JH (b) SH
    (c) SK (d) TS

39. DF, GJ, KM, NQ, RT, ?
    (a) YZ (b) UW
    (c) UX (d) XZ

40. AYD, BVF, DRH, ?, KGL.
    (a) FMI (b) GLT
    (c) GMJ (d) HLK

Series Completion

Coding and Decoding

Learning Objectives : In this chapter, students will learn about:
- ✓ Concept of Coding and Decoding
- ✓ Types of Coding and Decoding

CHAPTER SUMMARY

In this type of test, secret messages are given in certain code which has to be decoded to understand the message. These secret messages or code are conveyed according to some set rules called 'principles'. By applying the same principles the candidate has to decode or code word messages.

Type 1 : Letter Coding

In this type, the letter in a word are replaced by certain other letters according to a certain rule to form its code. The candidate is required to detect the coding pattern.

Example 1: If HEALTH is written as GSKZDG then how will NORTH be written in that code?
- (a) OPSUI
- (b) GSQNM
- (c) FRLMP
- (d) IUOBP

Sol. (b)
Here HEALTH → HTLAEH → GSKZDG
∴ NORTH → HTRON → GSQNM

Example 2: If TEMPLE is written as GNOGV then how will CLOUD be written in that code?
- (a) FWQNE
- (b) EWPOF
- (c) EUQMG
- (d) FVPMF

Sol. (a)
Here, TEMPLE → ELPMET → GNOGV
∴ CLOUD → DUOLC → FWQNE

Type 2 : Direct Letter Coding

In this type of coding, particular letters are made codes for particular letters without there being any set pattern. This type of coding is called direct coding.

Example 3: If REPRINT is coded as FGBFXJK and CHILDREN is coded as MOXQUFGJ, then how is RECENT coded in that language?
- (a) FGMGJK
- (b) FMGJGK
- (c) FGJMKJ
- (d) GFMGJK

Sol. (a)
Here.

Letter	R	E	P	I	N	T	C	H	L	D
Code	F	G	B	X	J	K	M	O	Q	U

∴ The code for RECENT is FGMGJK.

Example 4: If STARK is written as LBFMG and MOBILE is written as TNRSPJ. How is BRISK written in that code?
- (a) RSMLJ
- (b) RMSLG
- (c) RMSGL
- (d) RNSLG

Sol. (b)
Here,

Letter	S	T	A	R	K	M	O	B	I	L	E
Code	L	B	F	M	G	T	N	R	S	P	J

∴ BRISK → RMSLG

Type 3 : Number/Symbol Coding

In this type, either numerical code values are assigned to a word or alphabetical code letters are assigned to the numbers. Students have to analyse the code as per the given question.

Example 5: If C = 3, CAT = 24, then what is code for MOUSE?

(a) 63 (b) 73
(c) 83 (d) 53

Sol. (b)
Here, A = 1; B = 2; C = 3; D = 4;
E = 3; X = 24, Y = 25, Z = 26
CAT = 3 + 1 + 20 = 24
∴ MOUSE = 13 + 15 + 21 + 19 + 5 = 73

Example 6: If PEN = 35; B = 2, then what is the code for PENCIL?

(a) 49 (b) 53
(c) 59 (d) 69

Sol. (c)
Here, B = 2, C = 3, ..., T = 20, Y = 25, Z = 26.
∴ PEN = 16 + 5 + 14 = 35
PENCIL = 16 + 5 + 14 + 3 + 9 + 12 = 59

Type 4 : Deciphering Message Word Codes

In this type, some messages are given in the coded language and the code for the particular word is asked. To analyse such codes, any two messages bearing a common word are picked up. The common word will represent that word.

Example 7: In a certain code, "Sun shines brightly is written as Jaa Laa Maa. 'Houses are brightly lit' is written as Laa Daa Saa Baa. and 'Light comes from sun' is written as Taa Naa Haa Jaa. Then what is code for sun and brightly?

Sol.
Here, Jaa |Laa| Maa → Sun shines |brightly|
|Laa| Daa Saa Baa → Houses are |brightly| lit
∴ Brightly → Laa
|Jaa| Laa Maa → |Sun| shines brightly
Taa Naa Haa |Jaa| → Light comes from |sun|
∴ Jaa → Sun

Coding and Decoding

MULTIPLE CHOICE QUESTIONS

1. In a certain code ZIP = 198, VIP = 222 then ZAP will be equal to _____.
   (a) 256 (b) 296
   (c) 246 (d) 276

2. In a certain system of coding, the word STATEMENT is written as TNEMETATS. In the same system of coding, what would be the code for the word POLITICAL?
   (a) LATILIOP (b) LCATILIOP
   (c) LACITILOP (d) LCAITIOLP

3. In a certain code 134 means 'good and tasty', 478 means 'see good pictures' 728 means 'pictures are faint. Which of the following digit stands for pictures?
   (a) 4 (b) 7
   (c) 8 (d) 2

4. In a certain code, 'it be pee' means 'roses are blue', 'sik hee' means 'red flowers' and 'pee mit hee' means flowers are vegetables. How is 'red' written in that code?
   (a) hee (b) be
   (c) sik (d) pee

5. If water is called food, food is called tree, tree is called sky, sky is called wall, then on which of the following grows a fruit?
   (a) Tree (b) Wall
   (c) Sky (d) Food

6. If room is called 'bed', bed is called 'window' window is called flower, flower is called cooler. On what would a man sleep?
   (a) Bed (b) Window
   (c) Flower (d) Cooler

7. If paper is called 'wood', wood is called straw, 'straw is called grass, 'grass is called rubber,' rubber is called cloth, then what is the furniture made up of ?
   (a) paper (b) grass
   (c) wood (d) straw

8. If DEER = 12215 and HIGH = 5645, how will you code HORSE ?
   (a) 51215162 (b) 51214172
   (c) 51216152 (d) 51215173

9. If DRIVER = 12, CAR = 6, ACCIDENT = 16 then PEDESTRIAN = is equal to _____.
   (a) 20 (b) 18
   (c) 21 (d) 23

10. In a certain code DEAF is written as 3587 and FILE is written as 7465. How is DEAL written in that code?
    (a) 3586 (b) 3587
    (c) 3578 (d) 3568

11. In a certain code STRING is written as % = * – $ + and PRAISE as ? * @ – % × how will the word GRAPES be written in that language?
    (a) + * @ ? × % (b) + @ * × ? %
    (c) + * ? @ ? % × (d) + @ × % ? *

12. In a certain code SWITCH is coded as TVJSDG, which word would be written as CQFZE?
    (a) BREAD (b) BARED
    (c) BRAED (d) BRADE

13. In a certain code STOVE is written as FNBLK, then how will VOTES be written in the same code?
    (a) LNBKF (b) LKNBF
    (c) LBNKF (d) FLKBN

14. If MOBILITY is coded as 46293927 then EXAMINATION is coded as _____.
    (a) 56149512965 (b) 57159413955
    (c) 67250623076 (d) 45069516542

15. If ENGLAND is coded as 1234526, FRANCE is written as 785291, then what is the code for GREECE?
    (a) 381191 (b) 381171
    (c) 812271 (d) 382171

16. If 2 = 5, 4 = 18, 6 = 39 then what is value of 10?
    (a) 100 (b) 105
    (c) 81 (d) 45

17. If orange is called butter, butter is called soap, soap is called ink, ink is called honey, honey is called orange, then which of the following is used for washing clothes?
    (a) Soap (b) ink
    (c) orange (d) butter

18. If eye is called hand, hand is called mouth, mouth is called ear, ear is called nose and nose is called tongue then which of following is used for finding a smell?
    (a) Nose　　　　　(b) Tongue
    (c) Ear　　　　　　(d) Mouth

19. If E = 5, H = 8, J = 10, T = 20, then what is the code for POWER?
    (a) 165231518　　(b) 162352318
    (c) 161523518　　(d) 162315518

20. In a code A = 26, C = 24, T = 7, X = 3 then what is the code for MANGO?
    (a) 1426122013　(b) 1426132012
    (c) 26141312 20　(d) 1413262012

21. If J = 1, L = 3, Z = 8, T = 2, then what is the code for TOUR?
    (a) 2639　　　　　(b) 2369
    (c) 2693　　　　　(d) 2638

22. If T = 2, S = 8, W = 1, N = 3, then what is the code for MOST?
    (a) 2428　　　　　(b) 2482
    (c) 2842　　　　　(d) 2248

23. If E = 5, I = 9, Y = 25, U = 21, then what is the code for TRAIN?
    (a) 20181914　　(b) 20189114
    (c) 20918114　　(d) 20191814

24. If 13 = 4; 16 = 7; 23 = 5; 30 = 3, then what is the code for 2578?
    (a) 11231626　　(b) 11162326
    (c) 11162623　　(d) 16112326

25. In certain code ON = 29; RAT = 39, then what is the code for COW?
    (a) 69　　　　　　(b) 49
    (c) 41　　　　　　(d) 48

26. In certain code 123 is coded as 14, 234 as 29 then what is the code for 531?
    (a) 32　(b) 34　(c) 35　(d) 37

27. In a code language AT is coded as 401; CAT is coded as 410. What is the code for MAT?
    (a) 470　　　　　(b) 490
    (c) 570　　　　　(d) 590

28. In a certain code 'Ram and Shyam' is written as La ba Na. Sita and Geeta is written as Ma Ja Na. What is code for 'and' in that language?
    (a) Ja　　　　　　(b) Na
    (c) La　　　　　　(d) Ba

29. If Cat is called Dog, Dog is called Snake, Snake is called Lion, Lion is called Deer. Then which is called king of the forest?
    (a) Lion　　　　　(b) Snake
    (c) Deer　　　　　(d) Dog

30. If SIMPLE is coded as AGTNOX, SAND is coded as AURW, then what is the code for MIDDLE?
    (a) TGWWOX　　(b) TWGGOX
    (c) TGOOWX　　(d) TGOWWX

Number, Ranking and Time Sequence Test 5

Learning Objectives : In this chapter, students will learn about:
- Number Test
- Time Sequence Test

CHAPTER SUMMARY

Ranking is a relation between a set of items such that for any two items, the first is either ranked higher than, lower than, or equal to the second.

Number Test

In this test a series of numbers is given. We have to find out how many times a number satisfying the condition specified in the given question occurs.

Example 1: In the given series how many 8's are there, each of which is exactly divisible by its immediately preceding as well as succeeding numbers.

2 8 3 8 2 4 8 2 4 8 6 6 8 2 8 2 4 8 3 8 2 8 6

(a) One (b) Two
(c) Three (d) Four

Sol. (b)
There are two such sets of 3 numbers namely 482 and 282.

Example 2: In the following series of numbers find out how many times 1, 3 and 7 have appeared together, 7 being in the middle and 1 and 3 on either side of 7?

2 9 7 3 1 7 3 7 7 1 3 3 1 7 3 8 5 7 1 3 7 7 1 7 3 9 0 6

(a) 3 (b) 2
(c) 5 (d) More than 5

Sol. (a)
1, 3, and 7 appears 3 times as per given condition.

Ranking Test

Generally the number of persons are arranged in either ascending or descending order of their performance in a certain activity.

Consider there are n persons who qualify in a certain event. A particular man Rakesh whose rank from TOP is 14th and from bottom is 26th.

Then the number of persons = n = 14 + 26 – 1
= 40 – 1 = 39

Example 3: Shanti ranked 9th from the top and 37th from the bottom in a class. How many students are in the class?

(a) 36 (b) 46
(c) 45 (d) 47

Sol. (c)
Number of students in the class = 9 + 37 – 1
= 46 – 1 = 45

Example 4: In a row of 21 girls when Manisha was shifted by four places towards the right she became 12th from the left. What was her earlier position from the right end of the row?

(a) 9th (b) 10th
(c) 11th (d) 14th

Sol. (d)

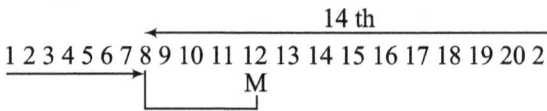

Example 5: Mohan is 14th from the right end in a row of 40 boys. What is his position from left?
(a) 26th (b) 27th
(c) 25th (d) none of these

Sol. (b)
Number of boys towards left of Mohan
= 40 − 14 = 26
Mohan is (26 + 1) = 27th from left.

Time Sequence Test

These problems are based on years, months, days, hours, minutes and seconds. In these problems, 12 calender months. Leap year, century also included.

Example 6: Manoj went to the movie nine days ago. He goes to the movies only on Thursday. What day of the week is today?
(a) Monday (b) Saturday
(c) Thursday (d) Friday

Sol. (b)
Nine days ago, it was Thursday. So, today is Saturday.

Example 7: If the first day of the year was Friday then which will be the last day of that year if that year was not a leap year.
(a) Monday (b) Tuesday
(c) Sunday (d) Friday

Sol. (b)
If the given year is not a leap year then the last day is same as the first day of that year. So last day will be Friday.

Example 8: A bus for Lucknow leaves every 30 minutes from a bus stand. An enduring clerk told a passenger that the bus had already left 10 minutes ago and the next bus will leave at 9:35 a.m. at what time did the inquiry clerk give this information to the passenger?
(a) 9:10 am (b) 9:15 am
(c) 8:55 am (d) 9:05 am

Sol. (b)
The next bus leaves at 9:35 am. It means that previous bus had left at 9:05 am. But it happened 10 minutes ago, the clerk gave information to the passenger.

So, the enquiry clerk gave this information at 9:05 + 10 = 9:15 am.

MULTIPLE CHOICE QUESTIONS

1. Raju is 5th from the left and Pankaj is 12th from the right end in a row of students. If Pankaj shifts three places towards Raju, his position is 10th from the left. How many students are there in the row?
   (a) 24
   (b) 28
   (c) 26
   (d) 27

2. If the day after tomorrow is Saturday. What day was three days before yesterday?
   (a) Monday
   (b) Sunday
   (c) Friday
   (d) Tuesday

3. In a particular year 1st November is Wednesday. What day was 1st October in that year?
   (a) Tuesday
   (b) Sunday
   (c) Friday
   (d) Monday

4. How many days will be there from 26th January 2008 to 15th may 2008 if both days are included?
   (a) 114
   (b) 113
   (c) 117
   (d) 111

5. Some students stand in a row. Manish's position is 19th from both the ends. How many students are there in that row?
   (a) 37
   (b) 41
   (c) 39
   (d) 42

6. Ganesh is 7 ranks ahead of Suman in a class of 39. If Suman's rank is 17th from the last. What is Ganesh's rank from the start?
   (a) 18th
   (b) 16th
   (c) 19th
   (d) 21th

7. Navin ranks 18th in a class of 49 students. What is his rank from the last?
   (a) 30
   (b) 32
   (c) 31
   (d) 21

8. Rohit is 15th from the front in a column students. There are thrice as many behind him as there are in front. How many students are there between Rohit and the 7th students from the end of column?
   (a) 32
   (b) 33
   (c) 35
   (d) 34

9. The position of how many digits in the number 321465987 will remain same when the digits are arranged in ascending order?
   (a) Two
   (b) Four
   (c) Three
   (d) Five

10. What will be the difference between the sum of odd digits and the sum of even digits in the number 9286571?
    (a) 4
    (b) 6
    (c) 2
    (d) 5

11. The position of the 1st and 5th digits in the number 83256479 are interchanged. Similarly the position of 2nd and 6th digits are interchanged. Which of the following is the third to the right of the 7th digit from the right end after rearrangement?
    (a) 7
    (b) 8
    (c) 9
    (d) 6

12. How many times even numerals are used if you write all the numbers from 291 to 299?
    (a) 10
    (b) 11
    (c) 12
    (d) 13

13. How many numbers amongst the number 9 to 81 are there which are divisible by 9 but not by 3?
    (a) 5
    (b) 7
    (c) 9
    (d) none

14. Himanshu is 14th from the right end in a row of 40 boys. What is the his position from the left end?
    (a) 25th
    (b) 26th
    (c) 27th
    (d) 24th

15. If Aman finds that he is 12th from the right in a line of boys and 4th from the left. How many boys should be added to the line such that there are 28 boys in the line?
    (a) 12
    (b) 13
    (c) 14
    (d) 16

16. Manju is 8th rank ahead of Minu who ranks 26th in a class of 42. What is the Manju's rank from the last?
    (a) 24th
    (b) 25th
    (c) 21th
    (d) 23rd

17. If the 25th of August in a year is Thursday, the number of Mondays in that month is _____.
    (a) 4 (b) 5
    (c) 6 (d) none of these

18. If the day before yesterday was Saturday, what day will fall on the day after tomorrow?
    (a) Wednesday (b) Tuesday
    (c) Friday (d) None of these

19. Which two months in a year have the same calendar?
    (a) April, July
    (b) June, October
    (c) January, November
    (d) March, November

20. In a row of boys, Sanjay is 5th from the left and Ranjan is 6th from the right. When they exchange their position, then Sanjay becomes 13th from the left. What will be Ranjan's position from the right?
    (a) 11th (b) 12th
    (c) 14th (d) 16th

21. Aman is 6th from the left end and Bimal is 10th from the right end in a row of boys. If there are 8 boys between Aman and Bimal. How many boys are there in the row?
    (a) 22 (b) 24
    (c) 25 (d) 27

22. How many times between 4 am and 5 am the minute and hour hand of a clock will be at right angle?
    (a) 1 (b) 2
    (c) 3 (d) 4

23. The last day of a century cannot be _____.
    (a) Tuesday (b) Monday
    (c) Friday (d) Sunday

24. When the time by the watch is 20 minutes past 7. What is the angle between the hands of the watch?
    (a) 90° (b) 80°
    (c) 100° (d) 70°

25. The number of odd days in a leap year is _____.
    (a) 1 (b) 2
    (c) 3 (d) 4

26. Smt Indira Gandhi died on 31st October 1984. What was the day of the week?
    (a) Sunday (b) Monday
    (c) Wednesday (d) Friday

27. Shanti is at 27th position from the top in a class of 43 students. What is her rank from the other side?
    (a) 15th (b) 16th
    (c) 17th (d) 21th

28. Nilesh's position is 11th from the top and thirty one from the bottom in a class. How many students are there in the class?
    (a) 40 (b) 41
    (c) 42 (d) 43

29. If a test score goes up 15% from x to 69. What was the previous test score?
    (a) 52 (b) 60
    (c) 65 (d) 68

30. How many even numbers are there in the given sequence of number which are immediately followed by an odd number as well as immediately preceded by an even number?
    8 6 7 6 8 9 3 2 7 5 3 4 2 2 3 5 5 2 2 8 1 1 9
    (a) 1 (b) 3
    (c) 4 (d) 6

Number, Ranking and Time Sequence Test

Alphabet Test

Learning Objectives: In this chapter, students will learn about:
- Concept of Alphabet Test
- Types of Alphabet Test

CHAPTER SUMMARY

In this test you are given letters in alphabet from A to Z. The position of a letter is given in the form of a puzzle. The candidate is required to find this letter. Sometimes a random letter series is given and the candidate is required to find out how many times a letter satisfying the conditions specified in question, occurs.

Type 1 : Alphabetical Order of Words

In this type, words are arranged in alphabetical order. It means that in this arrangement words are in the same manner as they appear in English dictionary. In this arrangement, first we consider the first letter of each word, then arrange the words in the order in which the letters appear in English alphabet.

Example 1: Arrange the given words according to English dictionary.

Client, Prison, Cattle, Daisy, Chain

Sol.

The words are arranged according to English dictionary as cattle, chain, client, Daisy, Prison.

Example 2: Arrange the given words according to English dictionary.

Eagle, Wisdom, Pattern, Polite, Sustain

Sol.

The words are arranged according to English dictionary as Eagle, Pattern, Polite, Sustain, Wisdom.

Example 3: Arrange the words according to dictionary?

Snake, Sanction, Surname, Sink, Suggest

Sol.

The words are arranged according to English dictionary as, Sanction, Sink, Snake, Suggest, Surname.

Type 2 : Rule Detection

In this type, four groups of letters are given which follow the same pattern. We have to find the pattern.

Example 4: Find out which of the letter series follow the rule that number of letters skipped in between adjacent letters of the series goes on increasing successively by one?

(a) DINSXC   (b) FHKOTZ
(c) EHKNQT   (d) AEIMQU

Sol. (b)

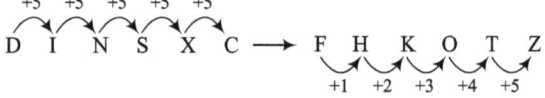

In this question, option (b) follows the given rule.

Example 5: Find out which of the letter series follow the rule that number of letters skipped in between adjacent letters in the series is equal?

(a) SUXADF   (b) RVZDFG
(c) RVZDHL   (d) HKNGSW

Sol. (c)

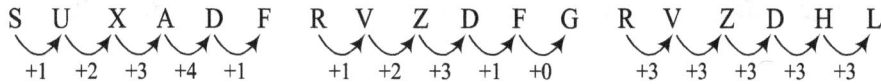

Hence (c) is correct answer.

Type 3 : Letter - Word Problem

In this type, students have to find such pairs of letters in the given word which has as many letters between them in the word as in the English alphabet.

Example 6: If the letters of the word POWERFUL are arranged as they appear in the English alphabet, the position of how many letters will remain unchanged after the new arrangement.

   (a) One   (b) Two
   (c) Three   (d) None

Sol. (a)

P O W E R F |U| L
E F L O P R |U| W

Position of U remains unchanged.

Example 7: Find out in the word PICKLE, how many such pairs of letters are there in the word as many letters in English alphabet?

   (a) Two   (b) Three
   (c) Four   (d) Five

Sol. (d)

Letters in the Word	Letter in English Alphabet
K L	K L
I C K	I J K
I C K L	I J K L
P I C K L	P O N M L

| I C K L E | | I H G F E |

Type 4 : Alphabetical Quibble

In this test, generally a letter series is given, be it the English alphabet from A to Z or a randomized sequence of letters. Students have to trace the letters satisfying certain conditions as regards their position in the given sequence.

Example 8: In English alphabet which letter is 5th to the right of 18th letter from your right?

   (a) N   (b) M
   (c) D   (d) C

Sol. (a)

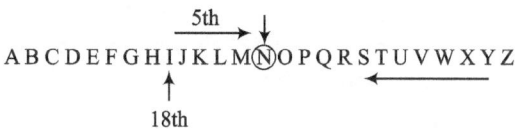

Hence N is correct answer.

Example 9: Which of the following is the 12th letter to the left of 17h letter from the left end?

   (a) G   (b) F
   (c) E   (d) H

Sol. (c)

Hence E is correct answer.

MULTIPLE CHOICE QUESTIONS

1. If the English alphabet is written in reverse order then what will be the 4th letter to the right of 13th letter from the left?
   (a) G (b) J
   (c) L (d) K

2. If in the English alphabet, starting from 5th letter from the left, if 12 letters are written in reverse order then which letter will be 7th to the left of 14th letter from the right?
   (a) L (b) O
   (c) M (d) N

3. If 1st and 26th, 2nd and 25th, 3rd and 24th and so on, letters of English alphabet are paired then which of the following pairs is correct?
   (a) CW (b) IP
   (c) GR (d) EV

4. If the order of English alphabet is reversed which will be the 8th letter to the right of O?
   (a) W (b) V (c) G (d) E

5. In the given arrangement, which letter is 10th to the right of the letter which is exactly the middle letter between F and D?
   F J M P O W R N B E Y C K A V L D G X U H Q I S Z T
   (a) X (b) U (c) H (d) G

6. If the order of English alphabet is reversed then which letter would be exactly in the middle?
   (a) K (b) L
   (c) N (d) None of these

7. If the last 10 letters of English alphabet and written in reverse order. Which of the following will be 6th to the right of 13th from the left end?
   (a) W (b) X (c) Y (d) V

8. If only first half of English alphabet is reversed, how many letters will be there between K and R?
   (a) 10 (b) 12
   (c) 14 (d) 16

9. Select the combination of numbers so that the letters arranged accordingly will form a meaning word.
   P N O A C L M I
   1 2 3 4 5 6 7 8
   (a) 5, 3, 7, 1, 6, 4, 8, 2
   (b) 4, 7, 5, 2, 6, 8, 1, 2
   (c) 7, 1, 8, 5, 6, 2, 4, 3
   (d) 2, 7, 8, 6, 4, 3, 1, 5

10. Unscramble the letters in the words given and find the odd one out.
    (a) UPJM (b) UNR
    (c) PEESL (d) ALWK

11. Unscramble the letters in the words given and find the odd one out.
    (a) TERAH (b) NVESU
    (c) NOMO (d) MSRA

12. Unscramble the letters in the words given and find the odd one out.
    (a) RDAK (b) NREGE
    (c) DER (d) ENOGAR

13. If T = 20; NET = 39 then NUT = ?
    (a) 56 (b) 53 (c) 55 (d) 50

14. Which letter in the word CYBERMETICS occupies the same position as it does in the English alphabet?
    (a) E (b) I (c) T (d) C

Directions (15–20): In each of the following questions find out how many such pairs of letters are there in the given word each of which has as many letters between them in the word as in English alphabet?

15. BRIGHTER
    (a) One (b) Two
    (c) Three (d) Four

16. PRESENCE
    (a) One (b) Two
    (c) Three (d) Four

17. PRODUCTION
    (a) One (b) Two
    (c) Three (d) Four

18. INSTRUCTION
    (a) One   (b) Two
    (c) Three   (d) Four
19. CORPORATE
    (a) One   (b) Two
    (c) Three   (d) Four
20. PRISON
    (a) One   (b) Two
    (c) Three   (d) Four

Directions (21 – 23): Arrange the given words in the alphabetical order and find the word that comes last.

21. (a) Achieve   (b) Actuate
    (c) Abandon   (d) Accurate
22. (a) Translate   (b) Transport
    (c) Transmit   (d) Transfer
23. (a) Proud   (b) Promise
    (c) Prayer   (d) Proposal
24. How many meaningful words can be formed with the first, third, 7th and 9th letters of the word SEPARATION using each letter only once in each word?
    (a) One   (b) Two
    (c) Three   (d) None of these
25. Choose one word which cannot be formed from the letters of the word CONSULTATION?
    (a) SALUTE
    (b) STATION
    (c) NATION
    (d) CONSTANT
26. If the given words are arranged as in dictionary, then which word comes at 3rd position?
    (a) Schedule   (b) Scorpion
    (c) Scissors   (d) Science

Direction (27 – 30): In each of the following questions, find out which of the letter series follow the given rule.

27. Number of letters skipped in between adjacent letter decrease in order.
    (a) AGMRV   (b) NSXCH
    (c) HNSWA   (d) SYDHK
28. Number of letter skipped in between adjacent letter in series decreases by three.
    (a) HVDKP
    (b) DMSXA
    (c) HUELO
    (d) HUELP
29. Number of letter skipped between adjacent letter in a series increase by one.
    (a) CEHLQW
    (b) CIOUBK
    (c) HLPTXN
    (d) CHMRWB
30. Number of letters skipped in between the adjacent letters in the series are multiples of 3.
    (a) DHLPU   (b) GKOTZ
    (c) LORUX   (d) AELPZ

Directions (31 – 34): In these questions jumbled letters of a meaningful word are given. Rearrange these letters and select the word which is almost opposite in meaning to the rearranged word.

31. TRAYD
    (a) Quack   (b) Quiet
    (c) Dirty   (d) Quick
32. UPCBAELL
    (a) Repair   (b) Renew
    (c) Excusable   (d) Docile
33. LPRMOEB
    (a) Answer   (b) Solution
    (c) Reply   (d) Repeat
34. NGDILEU
    (a) Forego   (b) Neglect
    (c) Avoid   (d) Abstain

Directions (35 – 37): Unscramble the letters of the words given and find the odd one.

35. (a) WHLEA   (b) WROC
    (c) ALEEG   (d) SORWARP
36. (a) IGRN   (b) TSIKR
    (c) ABGELN   (d) ECLNKAEC
37. (a) EAPPL   (b) EANOGR
    (c) ABAANN   (d) HARCI

Directions (38 – 40): Letters of the words in these questions have been jumbled up. Each letter has been numbered and each word is followed by four options. Choose the option which gives the correct order of letters as indicated by the numbers to form words.

38. A M D E N R
    1 2 3 4 5 6
    (a) 1, 6, 2, 4, 5, 3
    (b) 2, 1, 5, 3, 4, 6
    (c) 6, 4, 2, 1, 5, 3
    (d) 3, 4, 5, 2, 1, 6

39. E M I H T R
    1 2 3 4 5 6
    (a) 1, 2, 3, 4, 5, 6
    (b) 9, 1, 2, 3, 5, 4
    (c) 4, 1, 6, 2, 3, 5
    (d) 5, 1, 6, 4, 3, 2

40. E L B M A G
    1 2 3 4 5 6
    (a) 3, 1, 6, 4, 5, 2
    (b) 4, 5, 6, 3, 1, 2
    (c) 6, 5, 4, 3, 2, 1
    (d) 2, 1, 6, 3, 5, 4

Blood Relations Test

Learning Objectives : In this chapter, students will learn about:
- ✓ Concept of Blood relation Test
- ✓ Types of Blood relation Test

CHAPTER SUMMARY

Blood relation test involves analysis of information an blood relationship among members of a family. Candidates are supposed to be familiar with the knowledge of different relationships in a family.

Type 1

In this test blood relations of more than two persons are mentioned. The candidate is required to analyse the given information and answer the given questions.

Example 1: There are six children namely J, K, L, M, N, O playing football. J and N are brothers. O is sister of N. L is the only son of J's uncle. K and M are the daughters of the brother of C's father. Then how many male members are there?

(a) Three (b) Four
(c) Five (d) Two

Sol. (a)

J and N are brothers, so they are male. L is only son. Hence, male. O is sister of N. K and M are daughers. So, there are 3 male members.

Example 2: P is Q's sister. R is Q's mother. S is R's father. T is S's mother. Then how is P related to S?

(a) Grandmother (b) Grandfather
(c) Daughter (d) Granddaughter

Sol. (d)

P is Q's sister.
R is Q's mother, hence P is daughter of R.
S is father of R. So, P is granddaughter of S.

Example 3: Mahesh is uncle of Rajni, who is daughter of Mukesh. Mukesh is daughter-in-law of Pintu. How is Mahesh related to Pintu?

(a) Son (b) Brother
(c) Son-in-law (d) Father-in-law

Sol. (a)

Rajni is daughter of Mukesh.

Mukesh is daughter in law of Pintu. So, Pintu is grandfather of Rajni.

Mahesh is uncle of Rajni, means Mahesh is brother of Rajni's father. Hence, Mahesh is son of Pintu.

Type 2 : Deciphering Jumbled up Descriptions

In this type, a description of certain relationships is given, the candidate has to analyse the whole chain or link of relations and decipher the direct relationship between the persons concerned.

Example 4: Pointing to a lady in the photograph, Sheela said, Her son's father is the son-in-law of my mother. How is Sheela related to the lady?

(a) Sister (b) Mother
(c) Aunt (d) Cousin

Sol. (a)

Lady's son's father is Lady's husband. Lady's husband is son-in-law of Sheela's mother. So, lady is the sister of Sheela.

Blood Relations Test

Example 5: Pointing to a lady Amit said, The son of her only brother is the brother of my wife. How is the lady related to Amit?
- (a) Mother-in-law
- (b) Sister of father-in-law
- (c) Grandmother
- (d) Mother's sister

Sol. (b)
Son of lady's brother is the brother in law of Amit. So, lady's brother is man's father-in-law.

Example 6: Geeta introduced Navin as the son of daughter of the father of her uncle. Navin is Geeta's _____.
- (a) Son
- (b) Uncle
- (c) Brother
- (d) Nephew

Sol. (c)

Daughter of uncle's father → Uncle's sister
↓
Brother ← Aunt's son ← Aunt

Type 3 : Coded Relations

In this type, the relationships are represented by certain codes or symbols. We have to analyse the given code and determine the relationship between a set of persons.

Example 7: A + B means A is father of B.
A × B means A is brother of B.
A − B means A is mother of B.
Then which of the given alternative is true about R − P + Q ?
- (a) P is son of R
- (b) R is mother of Q
- (c) Q is father of P
- (d) Q is son of P

Sol. (a)
R − P + Q stands for R is mother of P, who is father of Q.
Now, it is clear that P is a male and the son of R.

Example 8: If P + Q means P is father of Q. P − Q means P is wife of Q. P × Q means P is the brother of Q. P ÷ Q means P is the daughter of Q.
Then if A − C + B, then which of the following is true?
- (a) A is mother of B
- (b) B is daughter of A
- (c) A is aunt of B
- (d) A is sister of B

Sol. (a)
A − C + B means A is wife of C who is father of B.
∴ A is mother of B.

MULTIPLE CHOICE QUESTIONS

1. Pointing towards Meena, Rajan said, "I am the only son of her mother's son." How is Meena related to Rajan?
   (a) Mother (b) Aunt
   (c) Niece (d) Cousin

2. Introducing Rekha, Sarita said, "she is the only daughter of my father's only daughter." How is Sarita related to Rekha?
   (a) Mother (b) Niece
   (c) Cousin (d) Aunt

3. Pointing to Kanchan, Sulekha said, "He is the son of my father's only son." How is Kanchan mother related to Sulekha?
   (a) Sister (b) Aunt
   (c) Daughter (d) Sister-in-law

4. Mohan told Rajesh, "Yesterday I defeated the only brother of the daughter of my grandmother." Whom did Mohan defeat?
   (a) Son (b) Brother
   (c) Father (d) Cousin

5. Pointing to a man in a photograph, a woman said, "His brother's father is the only son of my grandfather." How is the woman related to the man in the photograph?
   (a) Sister (b) Aunt
   (c) Daughter (d) Mother

6. When Ankush saw Manoj, he recalled, "He is the son of the father of my daughter's mother." Who is Manoj to Ankush?
   (a) Brother (b) Uncle
   (c) Brother-in-law (d) Cousin

7. Introducing a man, woman said, "His wife is the only daughter of my father." How is the man related to the woman?
   (a) Husband (b) Brother
   (c) Father-in-law (d) Maternal uncle

8. Rani introduced Mahesh as the son of the daughter of the father of her uncle. Who is Mahesh to Rani?
   (a) Brother (b) Nephew
   (c) Son (d) Uncle

9. Showing the man receiving the prize, Sanjay said, "He is the brother of my uncle's daughter." Who is the man to Sanjay?
   (a) Cousin (b) Son
   (c) Uncle (d) Nephew

10. If Nitu says, "Ankita's father Roshan is the only son of my father-in-law Shyam." Then how is Shalu, who is sister of Ankita related to Shyam?
    (a) Granddaughter
    (b) Wife
    (c) Daughter
    (d) Niece

11. Pointing to a woman, Naren said, "She is the daughter of the only child of my grandmother." How is the woman related to Naren?
    (a) Sister (b) Cousin
    (c) Niece (d) None of these

12. Pointing to a lady Mamta said, "She is the sister of my father of my mother's son." Who is the lady to Mamta?
    (a) Aunt (b) Niece
    (c) Sister (d) Mother

13. There are 6 children playing cricket, namely P, Q, R, S, T, U. P & T are brothers. U is the sister of T. R is only son of P's uncle. Q & S are the daughters of the brother of C's father. Then how many male players are there?
    (a) Two (b) Three
    (c) Four (d) One

14. Satish Sharma has 3 children – Rina, Ayush and Satyam. Satyam married Majula the eldest daughter of Mr. R.K. Tiwari. Tiwari married his youngest daughter to the eldest son of Mr. & Mrs. Mishra, and they had two children Anil and Sumit. Mr. Tiwari have two more children Rajit and Kalpna both elder to Sherya. Shashi and Akash are sons of Satyam & Majula. Rakhi is the daughter of Anil. What is the surname of Rakhi?
    (a) Tiwari (b) Mishra
    (c) Sharma (d) None of these

Blood Relations Test

15. Mohini is Raju's sister. Suman is Raju's mother. Rohit is Suman's father. Sanjana is Rohit's mother. Then how is Mohini related to Rohit.
    (a) Daughter
    (b) Grandmother
    (c) Granddaughter
    (d) Grandfather

16. Z is the son of V. Y is the son of W. Z is married to X. X is W's daughter. How is Y related to Z?
    (a) Father in law
    (b) Brother
    (c) Brother in law
    (d) None of these

17. I is the father of K. But K is not his son. M is the daughter of K. N is the spouse of I. J is brother of K. L is the son of J. O is the spouse of J. P is the father of O then who is son of N?
    (a) J   (b) K   (c) L   (d) M

18. M and N are married couples. P & Q are brothers. P is brother of M. how is Q related to N?
    (a) Brother
    (b) Cousin
    (c) Brother in law
    (d) none of these

19. A is uncle of B, who is daughter of C and C is daughter in law of E. How is A related to E?
    (a) Nephew   (b) Brother
    (c) Son   (d) Brother in law

20. Z is the son in law of X is the brother in law of W who is the brother of Y. How is W related to X?
    (a) Son   (b) Nephew
    (c) Father   (d) Brother

21. If X + Y means X is the father of Y. X × Y means X is brother of Y. X − Y means X is mother of Y, then which of the following is true about R − P + Q?
    (a) P is the son of R
    (b) Q is the son of P
    (c) Q is the father of P
    (d) R is the mother of Q

22. P + Q means P is the daughter of Q.
    P − Q means P is the husband of Q.
    P × Q means P is the brother of Q, then which of the following is true for A × B + C.
    (a) A is cousin of C   (b) A is the son of C
    (c) A is brother of C   (d) A is father of C

23. If A × B means A is the father of B.
    'A − B' means A is the sister of B.
    'A + B' means A is the mother of B.
    A ÷ B means A is the brother of B, then which of the following represents R is niece of M?
    (a) M − J + R − N   (b) M ÷ K × T − R
    (c) R − M × T ÷ W   (d) M − R × W ÷ T

24. 'A + B' means 'A is daughter of B'; 'A − B' means A is husband of B'; 'A × B' means A is brother of B. then if P + Q × R, then which of the following is true?
    (a) P is sister of R
    (b) P is cousin of R
    (c) P is daughter of R
    (d) P is niece of R

25. 'P + Q' means P is the mother of Q. 'P − Q' mans 'P is brother of Q'; 'P × Q' means 'P is sister of Q'. 'P ÷ Q' means P is father of Q. then if J + K ÷ L − M, then J is M's _____.
    (a) Sister   (b) Father
    (c) Brother   (d) Grandmother

26. 'A + B' means 'A is the son of B'; 'A − B' means 'A is the wife of B'; 'A × B' means 'A is the brother of B'; 'A ÷ B' means 'A is mother of B'. 'A = B' means 'A is sister of B', then what does L = N + M mean?
    (a) L is daughter of M
    (b) L is aunt of M
    (c) L is sister of M
    (d) L is niece of M

27. 'P + Q' means 'P is daughter of Q'.
    'P − Q' means 'P is wife of Q. 'P × Q' means 'P is the son of Q'. If A × B − C, then which of the following is true?
    (a) A is daughter of B
    (b) C is father of A
    (c) C is wife of B
    (d) B is father of A

Direction (28 – 30): 'P + Q' means 'P is father of Q'. 'P - Q' means 'P is wife of Q'. 'P × Q' means 'P is the brother of Q'. 'P ÷ Q' means 'P is daughter of Q', then.

28. If A – C × B, then which of the following is true?
   (a) B is son of A
   (b) B is husband of A
   (c) A is sister in law of B
   (d) A is sister of B

29. If A ÷ C + D + B, then which of the following is true?
   (a) A is aunt of B
   (b) A is mother of B
   (c) A is daughter of B
   (d) B is aunt of A

30. If A × C ÷ B, then which of the following is correct?
   (a) A is father of B
   (b) A is uncle of B
   (c) A is brother of B
   (d) A is son of B

Mathematical Operations   8

Learning Objectives : In this chapter, students will learn about:
- Concept of Mathematical Operations
- Types of Mathematical Operations

CHAPTER SUMMARY

In the mathematical operations test, questions based on simple mathematical operations. Usual mathematical operations i.e. minus, plus, multiplication, division, less than, greater than etc. are denoted by common symbols. Candidates are required to substitute the given signs with the new signs and solve the questions accordingly.

There are three types of problems based on mathematical operations.

Type 1 : Problem Solving by Substitution

In these problems, BODMAS rule is applied.
Here, B → Bracket; O → Of; D → Division.
M → Multiplication; A → Addition;
S → Substitution.

In these problems, for various mathematical symbols some substitutions are provided. We have to solve the problems according to real signs and rule.

Example 1: If L stands for +, M stands for −, N stands for ×, P stands for ÷, then what is the value of 17N12L25P5M13?

Sol.
We have 17N12L 25P5M13
$= 17 \times 12 + 25 \div 5 - 13$
$= 17 \times 12 + 5 - 13$
$= 204 + 5 - 13$
$= 209 - 13 = 196$

Example 2: If + means ×, × means −, ÷ means +, and − means ÷, then what is the value of
$87 \div 25 \times 19 + 15 - 3$?

Sol.
Here $87 \div 25 \times 19 + 15 - 3$
$= 87 + 25 - 19 \times 5$
$= 87 + 25 - 95$
$= 87 - 70 = 17$

Example 3: If × means −, + means ÷, − means ×, and ÷ means +, then what is the value of
$77 + 11 - 18 \times 37 \div 53$?

Sol.
Given, $77 + 11 - 18 \times 37 \div 53$
$= 77 \div 11 \times 18 - 37 + 53$
$= 7 \times 18 - 37 + 53$
$= 126 - 37 + 53$
$= 89 + 53 = 142$

Type 2 : Interchange of Numbers and Signs

In these types of problems the symbols and numerals are interchanged.

Example 4: If signs − & ÷ and numbers 4 & 8 are interchanged, then which of the following is correct?
(a) $6 - 8 \div 4 = -1$
(b) $8 - 6 \div 4 = 1$
(c) $4 \div 8 - 2 = 6$
(d) $4 - 8 \div 6 = 2$

Sol.
Considering option **(c)**
$4 \div 8 - 2 = 8 - 4 \div 2 = 8 - 2 = 6$
Hence option (c) is correct.

Example 5: Select the correct set of symbols for the given equation 5 0 3 5 = 20.
(a) ×, ×, × (b) −, +, ×
(c) ×, +, × (d) +, −, ×

Sol.
Let us take (b)
$5 − 0 + 3 × 5 = 5 + 3 × 5 = 5 + 15 = 20$
Hence (b) is correct.

Example 6: The expression or either side of (=) will have the same value if two terms on either side or same side are interchanged. Find the correct option.
$7 × 2 − 3 + 8 ÷ 4 = 5 + 6 × 2 − 24 ÷ 3$
(a) 2, 6 (b) 6, 5
(c) 3, 24 (d) 7, 6

Sol.
Considering **(d)** 7, 6
Here, $7 × 2 − 3 + 8 ÷ 4 = 5 + 6 × 2 − 24 ÷ 3$
$\Rightarrow \quad 14 − 3 + 2 = 5 + 12 − 8$
$\Rightarrow \quad 13 = 9$
and $6 × 2 − 3 + 8 ÷ 4 = 5 + 7 × 2 − 24 ÷ 3$
$\Rightarrow \quad 12 − 3 + 2 = 5 + 14 − 8$
$\Rightarrow \quad 11 = 11$
Hence (d) is correct option.

Type 3 : Deriving the Appropriate Conclusions

Example 7: If $A + B > C + D$ and $B + C > A + D$, then which of the given options is correct?
(a) $D > B$ (b) $A > D$
(c) $B > D$ (d) $C > D$

Sol. (c)
Given $A + B > C + D$ ...(i)
and $B + C > A + D$ ...(ii)
Adding (i) and (ii)
$A + B + B + C > C + D + A + D$
$\Rightarrow A + 2B + C > A + C + 2D$
$\Rightarrow 2B > 2D$
$\Rightarrow B > D$

Example 8: It is given, + denotes 'greater than' '−' denotes 'less than'. × denotes 'not greater than' '÷' denotes 'not less than'. Which of the given statements is correct?
$a × b ÷ c$ implies
(a) $a − b + c$ (b) $c × b ÷ a$
(c) $a − b − c$ (d) $b ÷ a ÷ c$

Sol. (b)
We have $a × b ÷ c$
$\Rightarrow a \quad b \quad c$
$\Rightarrow c × b ÷ a$ which is true.

MULTIPLE CHOICE QUESTIONS

1. If P means addition, Q means multiplication, R means division, S means subtraction, then what is the value of 4P10Q6R3S8?
   (a) 34 (b) 24
   (c) 16 (d) 8

2. If A denotes multiplication, B denotes addition, C denotes division and D denotes subtraction, then what is the value of 14A6B8C2D12?
   (a) 76 (b) 86
   (c) 82 (d) 72

3. If J stands for subtraction, K stands for multiplication, L stands for division and M stands for addition, then find the value of 27J15K2M18L3.
   (a) 30 (b) 3
   (c) 13 (d) 18

4. If × denotes –, ÷ denotes +, + denotes ÷ and – denotes ×, which one of the following equations is correct?
   (a) 15 – 5 ÷ 5 × 20 + 10 = 6
   (b) 8 ÷ 10 – 3 + 5 × 6 = 8
   (c) 6 × 2 + 3 ÷ 12 – 3 = 15
   (d) 3 ÷ 7 – 5 × 10 + 3 = 10

5. If + means ÷, ÷ means –, – means ×, × means + then 12 + 6 ÷ 3 – 2 × 8 = ?
   (a) 2 (b) 4 (c) 6 (d) 8

6. If P means ×, R means +, T means ÷, S means –, then what is the value of 8P4R28T7S15?
   (a) 32 (b) 21
   (c) 49 (d) 39

7. If A means addition, M means division, S means multiplication, R means subtraction then what is the value of 15A78M13S2R17?
   (a) 1 (b) 10
   (c) 12 (d) 14

8. If numbers 3 and 6 are interchanged and signs – and × are interchanged, then which of the following is correct?
   (a) 3 × 6 – 4 = 33 (b) 6 × 3 – 4 = 15
   (c) 3 – 6 × 8 = 10 (d) 6 – 3 × 2 = 9

9. If signs + & × are interchanged and numbers 4 & 5 are interchanged, then which of the following is correct?
   (a) 5 × 4 + 20 = 40
   (b) 5 × 4 + 20 = 104
   (c) 5 × 4 + 20 = 85
   (d) 5 × 4 + 20 = 95

10. If A stands for +, B stands for –, C stands for ×, then what is the value of (10C4)A (4C4)B6?
    (a) 50 (b) 56
    (c) 66 (d) 60

11. If A + E = B + C, A + B = C + D, B + C > D + E, A + D > B + E, A + E > C + D, then which of the following is correct?
    (a) C > A > E > B > D
    (b) D > B > E > A > C
    (c) A > E > C > D > B
    (d) A > C > B > E > D

12. If A + B = 2C & C + D = 2A, then which of the following is correct?
    (a) A + C = 2D (b) A + C = 2B
    (c) A + D = B + C (d) A + C = B + D

13. If A + B = C + D and A + D > B + C, then which of the following is definitely wrong?
    (a) B > D (b) C > D
    (c) A > C (d) A > B

14. If L stands for +, M stands for –, N stands for × and P stands for ÷, then what is the value of 37N10L65P13M16?
    (a) 359 (b) 539
    (c) 356 (d) 536

15. If A stands for ÷, B stands for ×, C stands for +, D stands for –, then what is the value of 95C361A19B7D15?
    (a) 937 (b) 160
    (c) 213 (d) none of these

16. If P stands for addition, L for division, M for subtraction and Z for multiplication, then what is the value of 182P117L13M7Z16?
    (a) 256 (b) 79
    (c) 97 (d) none of these

17. If '−' stands for division, '+' for multiplication, '÷' for subtraction and × for addition, then which of the following is correct?
    (a) 6 ÷ 20 × 12. + 7 − 1 = 70
    (b) 6 − 20 ÷ 12. × 7 + 1 = 57
    (c) 6 + 20 − 12. ÷ 7 − 1 = 38
    (d) 6 + 20 − 12. ÷ 7 × 1 = 62

18. If × stands for addition, '−' for division, ÷ for subtraction & '+' for multiplication then which of the following statements is correct?
    (a) 4 × 5 × 9 + 3 ÷ 4 = 11
    (b) 4 ÷ 5 + 9 − 3 + 4 = 18
    (c) 4 − 5 ÷ 9 × 3 − 4 = 17
    (d) 4 × 5 + 9 − 3 ÷ 4 = 15

19. If 'x' stands for addition, '+' for division '<' for subtraction, '>' for multiplication, '−' for equal to '÷' for 'greater than'. '=' for less than, then which of the following is correct?
    (a) 3 × 2 < 4 ÷ 16 − 2 + 4
    (b) 5 × 3 < 7 ÷ 8 + 4 × 1
    (c) 3 × 4 > 2 − 9 + 3 < 3
    (d) 5 > 2 + 2 = 10 < 4 × 8

20. If '<' stands for minus, '−' stands for equal to '>' stands for multiplication, '÷' stands for greater than, '×' for addition, '+' stands for division, '=' stands for less than, then which of the following statements is correct?
    (a) 5 < 2 × 1 + 3 > 4 × 1
    (b) 5 + 2 × 1 = 3 + 4 > 1
    (c) 5 > 2 < 1 − 3 × 4 × 1
    (d) 5 > 2 × 1 − 3 > 4 < 1

Direction (21 − 25): If > denotes +, + denotes ÷, − denotes =, × denotes > and = denotes <, < denotes − and ↑ denotes ×, then choose the correct statement in each of the following problems :

21. (a) 14 > 18 + 9 = 16 + 4 < 1
    (b) 12 > 9 + 3 < 6 × 25 + 5 > 6
    (c) 4 > 3 ↑ 8 < 1 − 6 + 2 > 24
    (d) 3 < 6 ↑ 4 > 25 = 8 + 4 > 1

22. (a) 35 > 3 < 2 = 4 > 8 ↑ 7
    (b) 34 > 6 + 2 = 6 < 5 ↑ 2
    (c) 29 < 18 + 6 = 36 + 6 ↑ 4
    (d) 18 > 12 + 4 × 7 > 8 ↑ 2

23. (a) 12 > 12 < 12 + 12 = 25
    (b) 12 ↑ 12 > 12 + 12 = 12 ↑ 12 > 3
    (c) 12 < 12 + 12 = 8
    (d) 12 + 12 > 12 = 9

24. (a) 14 + 7 > 3 = 6 − 3 > 2
    (b) 14 < 6 + 2 = 9 > 4
    (c) 4 > 6 + 2 × 32 + 4 < 1
    (d) 9 + 3 > 8 = 4 + 2 < 1

25. (a) 12 > 5 > 6 − 49 + 7 > 16
    (b) 28 + 4 ↑ 2 = 6 ↑ 4 + 2
    (c) 16 > 7 < 5 + 5 = 3 ↑ 2
    (d) 9 < 3 < 2 > 1 × 8 ↑ 2

Directions (26 − 30): In these questions the different alphabets stand for various arithmetical and logical symbols. We have to choose the correct alternative according to given letter symbols.

Letters	C	H	N	P	W	Y	X
Symbols	+	−	×	÷	<	>	=

26. (a) 5 W 4 N 3 C 5 N 3 H 11
    (b) 8 W 2 N 3 N 4 P 4 N 2
    (c) 10 X 2 C 2 N 4 C 1 H 2
    (d) 24 X 4 C 2 P 1 N 4 N 2

27. (a) 32 X 8 P 2 N 3 P 1 N 2
    (b) 16 W 8 N 3 C 1 N 2 H 2
    (c) 16 X 3 N 3 N 2 H 8 P 4
    (d) 2 W 1 N 1 P 1 C 1 N 1

28. (a) 5 P 5 N 5 C 5 W 5 N 2
    (b) 6 P 3 C 4 N 3 Y 7 N 3
    (c) 3 C 3 C 10 P 2 X 10 N 2
    (d) 3 C 4 P 4 H 2 W 7 P 1

29. (a) 16 P 4 N 3 H 5 X 31 H 24
    (b) 4 P 4 N 8 H 5 X 16 H 7
    (c) 3 N 1 C 17 Y 7 N 1 C 6
    (d) 12 P 4 N 5 C 8 Y 6 N 2 P 2 C 7

30. (a) 17 C 5 P 5 N 7 H 3 Y 5 C 12 P 3 N 2
    (b) 7 C 8 P 8 N 7 H 2 X 2 C 12 P 3 N 2
    (c) 14 C 13 P 13 N 6 H 5 W 2 C 12 P 3 N 2
    (d) 14 C 3 P 3 N 6 H 2 Y 3 C 8 P 2 N 2

Mathematical Operations

Arithmetical Reasoning   9

Learning Objectives : In this chapter, students will learn about:
- ✓ Concept of Arithmetic Reasoning
- ✓ Types of Problems

CHAPTER SUMMARY

In this test preliminary concepts of arithmetical operations such as addition, subtraction, multiplication and division, percentages, ratio and proportion are applied.

The problems based on arithmetical reasoning are following:

Type 1 : Problem Based on Ages

Example 1: Ten years ago a man was four times as old as his son. Ten years hence a man's age will be twice the age of his son. What is the difference between their present ages?

    (a) 30 years   (b) 20 years
    (c) 40 years   (d) 50 years

Sol. (a)

If the son's present age is x years.
And father's present age is y years.
Thus, according to question
$$y - 10 = 4(x - 10)$$
$$\Rightarrow 4x - y = 30 \quad \ldots(i)$$
and $y + 10 = 2(x + 10)$
$$\Rightarrow y + 10 = 2x + 20$$
$$\Rightarrow 2x - y = -10 \quad \ldots(ii)$$
From (i) and (ii), we get
$$\begin{array}{r} 4x - y = 30 \\ 2x - y = -10 \\ -\;\;+\;\;\;\;\;+\;\;\;\; \\ \hline 2x = 40 \end{array} \Rightarrow x = 20$$

Now putting the value of x in (i), we get $4(20) - y = 30 \Rightarrow y = 80 - 30 = 50$
Hence, difference $= y - x = 50 - 20 = 30$ years.

Example 2: 25 years ago A was thrice as old as B and 10 years later A shall be twice as old as B. What is the sum of their present ages?
    (a) 50   (b) 60
    (c) 70   (d) 80

Sol. (c)

Five years ago, B's age = x
Five years ago, A's age = $3x$
10 years later, B's age = $x + 5 + 10$
10 years later, A's age = $3x + 5 + 10$
$$3x + 15 = 2(x + 15)$$
$$3x + 15 = 2x + 30$$
$$x = 15$$
B's present age = $x + 5 = 15 + 5 = 20$ years
A's present age = $3x + 5 = 45 + 5 = 50$ years
Sum of their ages = $20 + 50 = 70$ years

Example 3: If twice the son's age is added to the mother's age, the sum is 70. But if twice the mother's age is added to son's age, the sum will be 95. What is difference between their ages?

Sol.

Let son's age be x.
$$2x + \text{mother's age} = 70 \quad \ldots(i)$$
$$2x + 2 \times 2 \text{ mother's age} = 95 \times 2 \quad \ldots(ii)$$
$$\begin{array}{r} -\;\;\;\;\;\;\;-\;-\;\;\;\; \\ \hline +3 \text{ mother's age} = +120 \end{array}$$
Mother's age = 40 years
$$\therefore \quad \text{Son's age} = \frac{70-40}{2} = 15 \text{ years.}$$
Hence, difference = $40 - 15 = 25$ years.

Type 2 : Problem Based on Calculations

Example 4: What is the smallest number which when divided by 12, 15, 20 or 54, then in each condition, remainder is 4?

Sol.

L.C.M of 12, 15, 20, 54 = 540

Required number = 540 + 4 = 544

Example 5: In a two-digit number, the digit at the unit's place is 2 more than 10's digit. The product of the number and sum of digits of numbers is 144, then what is the number ?

Sol.

Let 10's digit be x.

Unit's digit = $x + 2$

Number = $10 \times x + 1(x + 2)$

$= 10x + x + 2 = 11x + 2$

$\therefore (11x + 2) \times [x + x + 2] = 144$

$\Rightarrow (11x + 2)(2x + 20) = 144$

$\Rightarrow 22x^2 + 22x + 4x + 4 = 144$

$\Rightarrow 22x^2 + 26x - 140 = 0$

$\Rightarrow 11x^2 + 13x - 70 = 0$

$\Rightarrow 11x^2 + 35x - 22x - 70 = 0$

$\Rightarrow x(11x + 35) - 2(x + 35) = 0$

$\Rightarrow (x - 2)(11x + 35) = 0$

$\Rightarrow x = 2 \quad \left(\because x \neq -\dfrac{35}{11} \text{ is not possible}\right)$

$\therefore$ Number = $11x + 2 = 11 \times 2 + 2 = 24$

Example 6: The average of five consecutive even numbers is 42. What is the difference of largest number and smallest number?

Sol.

Let the numbers are $x, x + 2, x + 4, x + 6, x + 8$.

$\therefore \dfrac{x + x + 2 + x + 4 + x + 6 + x + 8}{5} = 42$

$\Rightarrow 5x + 20 = 210$

$\Rightarrow 5x = 190$

$\Rightarrow x = 38$

Largest number = $x + 8 = 38 + 8 = 46$

Smallest number = 38

$\therefore$ Difference = 46 − 38 = 8

Example 7: If 54 kg gram is sufficient for 35 horses for 21 days, them for how many days 72 kg gram is sufficient for 28 horses.

Sol.

$\because$ 35 horses eat 54 kg gram in 21 days

$\therefore$ 1 horse eat 54 kg gram in 21 × 35

$\therefore$ 28 horses will eat 72 kg gram in

$= \dfrac{21 \times 35 \times 72}{28 \times 54}$

= 35 days

Arithmetical Reasoning

MULTIPLE CHOICE QUESTIONS

1. A certain number of horses and an equal number of men are going some where. Half of the men are on their horse's back while the remaining ones are walking along leading their horses. If the number of legs walking on the ground is 70. Find the number of horses.
   (a) 16 (b) 10
   (c) 14 (d) 12

2. Ram is three times as old as Mohan. Lokesh was twice as old as Ram four years ago. In four year's time Ram will be 31. What is the difference between present ages of Mohan and Lokesh?
   (a) 41 years (b) 36 years
   (c) 37 years (d) 40 years

3. Today is Mukesh's birthday. One year from today he will be twice as old as 12 years ago. What was the age of Mukesh 5 years ago?
   (a) 20 years (b) 25 years
   (c) 30 years (d) 15 years

4. Rajesh got twice as many sums wrong as he got right. If he attempted 84 sums in all. How many sums did he solve correctly?
   (a) 24 (b) 28
   (c) 26 (d) 32

5. Five bells begin to toll together and toll respectively at intervals 6, 5, 7, 10, 12 seconds. How many times will they toll together in one hour excluding the one at the start?
   (a) 7 times (b) 8 times
   (c) 9 times (d) 10 times

6. Punam says, "If you reverse my own age, the figure represents my husband's age. He is of course senior to me and the difference between our ages is one-eleventh of their sum." What is the age of Punam?
   (a) 45 years (b) 42 years
   (c) 23 years (d) 35 years

7. A number consists of two digits whose sum is 11. If 27 is added to the number, then the digits change their places. What is the number?
   (a) 92 (b) 83
   (c) 65 (d) 47

8. A total of 324 coins of 20 paise and 25 paise make a sum of Rs. 71. What is the number of 25 paise coin?
   (a) 200 (b) 144
   (c) 124 (d) 120

9. What is the smallest number of ducks that could swim in this formation two ducks in front of a duck, two ducks behind a duck and a duck between two ducks?
   (a) 3 (b) 5
   (c) 7 (d) 9

10. In a family, a couple has a son and a daughter. The age of the father is three times that of his daughter and the age of son is half that of his mother. The wife is 9 years younger than her husband and the brother is seven years older than his sister. What is the age of the mother?
    (a) 40 years (b) 50 years
    (c) 45 years (d) 60 years

11. The taxi charges in a city comprise of a fixed change together with the change of the distance covered. For a journey of 16 km, the charges paid are Rs. 156 and for a journey of 24 km, the charges paid are Rs. 204. What will a person have to pay for travelling a distance of 30 km?
    (a) Rs. 236 (b) Rs. 248
    (c) Rs. 240 (d) Rs. 252

12. In a group of cows and hens, the number of legs are 14 more than twice the number of heads. What is the number of cows?
    (a) 5 (b) 7
    (c) 10 (d) 12

13. In a family, each daughter has the same number of brothers as she has sisters and each son has twice as many sisters as he has brothers. How many sons are there in the family?
    (a) 2 (b) 3
    (c) 4 (d) 6

14. A few sweets have to be distributed. If I keep 2, 3, or 4 in a pack, I am left with one sweet. If I keep 5 in a pack I am left with none. What is the minimum number of sweets I have to pack and distribute?
    (a) 37 (b) 54
    (c) 25 (d) 65

15. A farmer built a fence around his square plot. He used 27 poles on each side of the square. How many poles did he need altogether?
    (a) 108 (b) 100
    (c) 104 (d) 102

16. In a city 40% of adults are illiterate while 85% of the children are literate. If the ratio of adults to that of the children is 2 : 3, what percent of the population is literated.
    (a) 25% (b) 75%
    (c) 50% (d) 80%

17. After distributing the sweets equally among 25 children, 8 sweets remain. Had the number of children been 28, 22 sweets would have been left after equal distribution. What was the total number of sweets?
    (a) 358 (b) 348
    (c) 328 (d) 338

18. A says, "If B gives me Rs. 40, he well have half as much as C, but if C gives me Rs. 40, then three of us will all have the same amount." What is the total amount of money that A, B and C have between them?
    (a) Rs. 360 (b) Rs. 380
    (c) Rs. 420 (d) Rs. 340

19. Ganesh is 3 years older to Mahesh and 3 years younger to Suresh. While Mahesh and Lokesh are twins. How many years older is Suresh to Lokesh?
    (a) 4 (b) 6
    (c) 8 (d) 12

20. Three bells ring after a regular interval of 36 seconds, 40 seconds and 48 seconds respectively. If the three bells start ringing at same time, then after how much time they will ring together?
    (a) 6 minutes (b) 12 minutes
    (c) 18 minutes (d) 24 minutes

21. Rs. 1540 is distributed among Amar, Raju and Sonu such that the amount received by Raju is $\frac{3}{11}$ th of the money received by Amar and Sonu together. What is the share of Raju?
    (a) 330 (b) 420
    (c) 880 (d) 1210

22. If a number is increased by 10% and then it is decreased by 10%, then the value of number will _____.
    (a) remain unchanged
    (b) increase by 1%
    (c) decrease by 1%
    (d) decrease by 0.1%

23. A train whose length is 130 m cross a bridge in 21 seconds. If the speed of train is 90 km/hour, then what is the length of bridge?
    (a) 285 m (b) 295 m
    (c) 395 m (d) 495 m

24. The cost price of 11 objects is ₹10 and the selling price of 10 objects is ₹11. What is the gain or loss percentage in whole transaction?
    (a) 12.5% loss (b) 12.5% profit
    (c) 21% profit (d) none of these

25. 64 persons can dig a canal in 81 days. How many persons should be required to finish the work in 9 days?
    (a) 576 (b) 476
    (c) 640 (d) 596

26. The total monthly income of 16 persons is ₹80800 and monthly income of one of the persons is greater than their average monthly income by 120%. What is the income of that person?
    (a) ₹5050 (b) ₹6660
    (c) ₹6060 (d) ₹6160

27. A number of friends decided to go on a picnic and planned to spend ₹252 on eatables. Four of then did not turn up. So the remaining ones had to contribute ₹4 each extra. What is the number of friends who attended the picnic?
    (a) 14 (b) 18
    (c) 16 (d) 22

Arithmetical Reasoning

28. On a certain festival, sweets were to be equally distributed among 200 students. But 50 students were absent, therefore each student got 4 sweets extra. What is the number of sweets available for distribution?
    (a) 2800   (b) 2000
    (c) 2400   (d) 2200

29. What is the number which when added to itself 16 times gives 153?
    (a) 8   (b) 9   (c) 7   (d) 11

30. Three friends had lunch at a restaurant. Arjun paid $\frac{2}{3}$ as much as Jay paid and Jay paid $\frac{1}{2}$ as much as Rakesh paid. What fraction of the bill did Jay pay?
    (a) $\frac{3}{11}$ (b) $\frac{5}{11}$
    (c) $\frac{2}{11}$ (d) $\frac{5}{8}$

Inserting the Missing Character 10

Learning Objectives : In this chapter, students will learn about:
✓ Concept of Inserting the missing character

CHAPTER SUMMARY

In this type of test, there may be a figure or an arrangement of a matrix, each of which has certain characters which may be numbers or letters that follow a particular pattern. According to that pattern, we have to find out the missing character:

Example 1: Find the missing number in the following question.

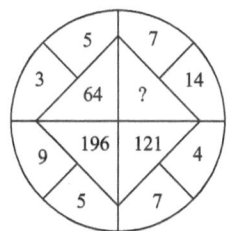

Sol.
Here $5 + 3 = 8 \to 8^2 = 64$
and $9 + 5 = 14 \to 14^2 = 196$
and $7 + 4 = 11 \to 11^2 = 121$
and $7 + 14 = 21 \to 21^2 = 441$
∴ Missing number = 441

Example 2: Find the value of question mark.

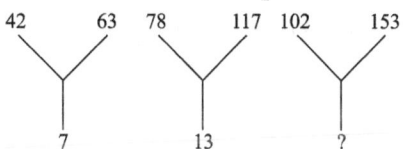

Sol.
$7 \times 6 = 42; \ 7 \times 9 = 63$
$13 \times 6 = 78; \ 13 \times 9 = 117$
$x \times 6 = 102 \implies x = \dfrac{102}{6} = 17; \ 17 \times 9 = 153$

Example 3: Find the missing number in the given pattern.

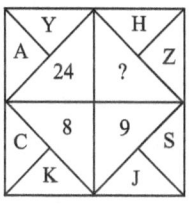

Sol.
Here
$AY = 25 - 1 = 24; \ CK = 11 - 3 = 8$
$JS = 19 - 10 = 9; \ HZ = 26 - 8 = 18$
∴ Missing number = 18

Example 4: Find the missing number in the given pattern.

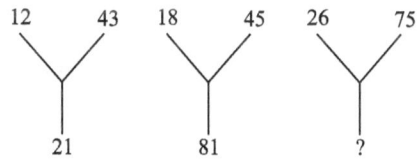

Sol.
Here $(1 + 2) \times (4 + 3) = 3 \times 7 = 21$
$(1 + 8) \times (4 + 5) = 9 \times 9 = 81$
$(2 + 6) \times (7 + 5) = 8 \times 12 = 96$
∴ Missing number = 96

Example 5: Find the missing number in the given pattern.

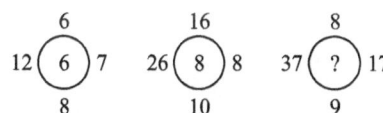

Sol.

Clearly $\frac{12 \times 7}{6+8} = \frac{84}{14} = 6$; $\frac{26 \times 8}{16+10} = 8$

$\therefore \frac{37 \times 17}{8+9} = 37$

Example 6: Find the missing number in the given pattern.

43 (14) 23   81 (12) 42   87 (?) 16
12   61   49
43   24   25

Sol.

Here we see

$[(4 + 3) \times (2 + 3)] - [(1 + 2) \times (3 + 4)]$
  $= 35 - 21 = 14$

$[(8 + 1) \times (4 + 2)] - [(6 + 1) \times (2 + 4)]$
  $= 54 - 42 = 12$

$[(8 + 7) \times (1 + 6)] - [(4 + 9) \times (2 + 5)]$
  $= 105 - 91 = 14$

Example 7: Find the missing number in the given pattern.

18	37	?
13	19	28
44	75	115

Sol.

$18 + 13 \times 2 = 18 + 26 = 44$
$37 + 19 \times 2 = 37 + 38 = 75$
$x + 28 \times 2 = 115 \implies x = 115 - 56 = 59$

Example 8: Find the missing number in the given pattern.

A	D	G
D	I	N
I	P	?

Sol.

$A \xrightarrow{+3} D \xrightarrow{+3} G$
$D \xrightarrow{+5} I \longrightarrow N$
$I \xrightarrow{+7} P \xrightarrow{+7} W$

$\therefore$ Missing term = W

Example 9: Find the missing number in the given pattern.

17   8   38   9
   88   ?
9   3   23   7

Sol.

$(17 - 9) \times (8 + 3) = 8 \times 11 = 88$
$(38 - 23) \times (9 + 7) = 15 \times 16 = 240$

Example 10: Find the missing number in the given pattern.

Sol.

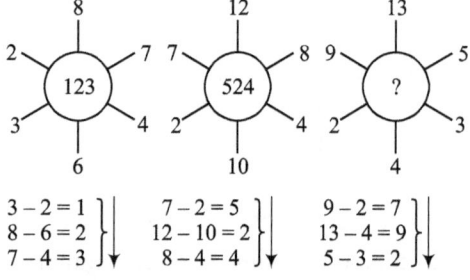

$\begin{matrix} 3-2=1 \\ 8-6=2 \\ 7-4=3 \end{matrix}$ $\begin{matrix} 7-2=5 \\ 12-10=2 \\ 8-4=4 \end{matrix}$ $\begin{matrix} 9-2=7 \\ 13-4=9 \\ 5-3=2 \end{matrix}$

$\therefore$ Missing number = 792

MULTIPLE CHOICE QUESTIONS

Directions (1 – 10) Find the value of question mark (?) in the following questions:

1.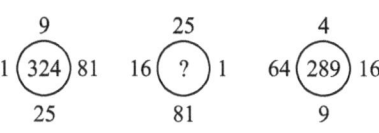
   (a) 361 (b) 381
   (c) 369 (d) 389

2.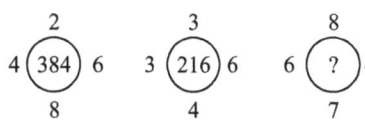
   (a) 1344 (b) 1244
   (c) 1342 (d) 1542

3.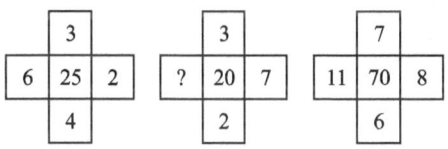
   (a) 4 (b) 6 (c) 8 (d) 5

4.
17		2	9		7	7		8
	88			?			44	
5		7	4		8	3		3

   (a) 72 (b) 75
   (c) 80 (d) 90

5.
466	534	721
354	286	569
224	496	?

   (a) 314 (b) 302
   (c) 304 (d) 294

6.
84	28	6
?	16	12
108	12	18

   (a) 96 (b) 86
   (c) 98 (d) 108

7.
18	54	4
8	?	32
34	144	68

   (a) 44 (b) 46
   (c) 42 (d) 45

8.
4	25	52
6	16	35
12	18	?

   (a) 48 (b) 42
   (c) 46 (d) 56

9.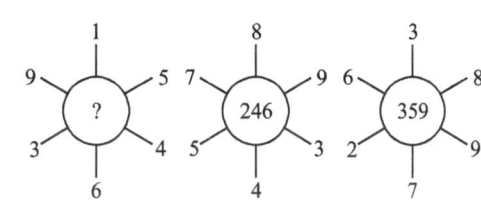
   (a) 451 (b) 651
   (c) 551 (d) 441

10.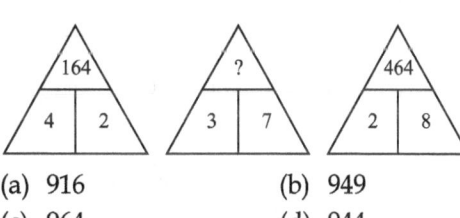
    (a) 916 (b) 949
    (c) 964 (d) 944

Directions (11–30) In each of the following questions a set of figures carrying certain characters is given. The characters in each set follow a similar pattern. What is the missing character in each case?

11.
   25   49   25
 25(4)25   36(4)9   100(?)100
   25   16   25

   (a) 4 (b) 6
   (c) 8 (d) 2

Inserting the Missing Character   233

12.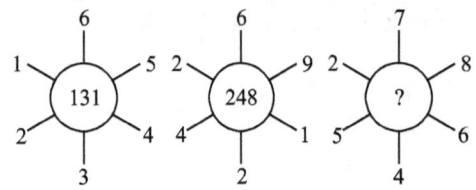
(a) 342 (b) 332
(c) 343 (d) 334

13.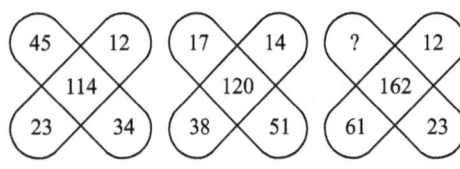
(a) 76 (b) 66
(c) 86 (d) 56

14.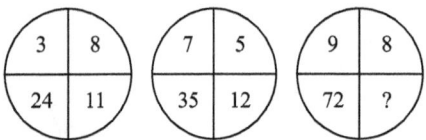
(a) 16 (b) 15
(c) 17 (d) 18

15.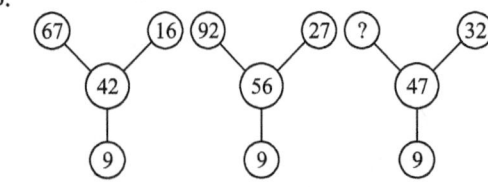
(a) 78 (b) 68
(c) 98 (d) 88

16.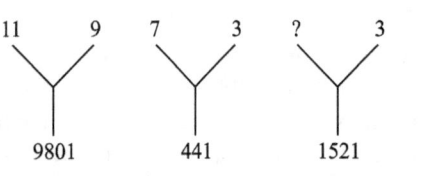
(a) 12 (b) 14 (c) 13 (d) 16

17.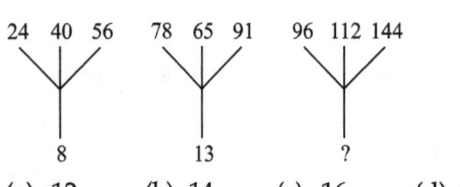
(a) 12 (b) 14 (c) 16 (d) 18

18.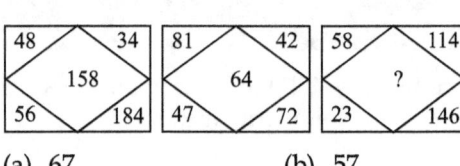
(a) 67 (b) 57
(c) 87 (d) 97

19.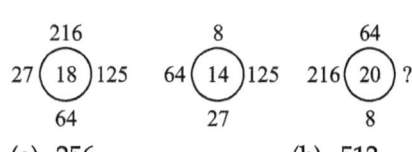
(a) 256 (b) 512
(c) 216 (d) 144

20.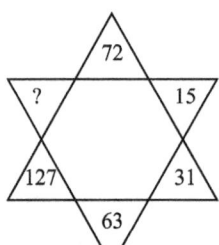
(a) 255 (b) 236
(c) 254 (d) 252

21.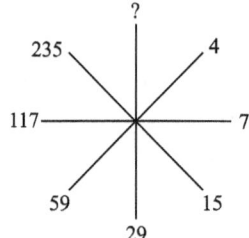
(a) 459 (b) 469
(c) 449 (d) 427

22.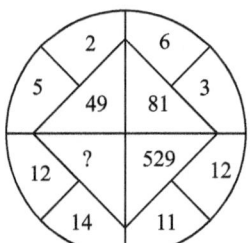
(a) 576 (b) 625
(c) 649 (d) 676

23.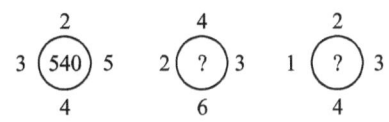
(a) 640 (b) 650
(c) 670 (d) 630

24.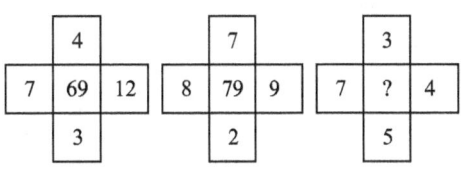
(a) 46 (b) 47
(c) 49 (d) 51

25.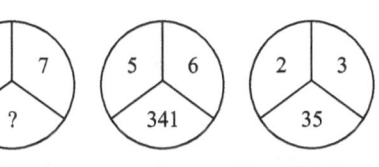
(a) 417 (b) 407
(c) 421 (d) 427

26.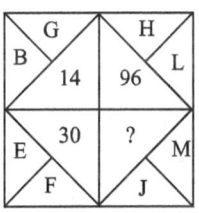
(a) 120 (b) 132
(c) 130 (d) 140

27.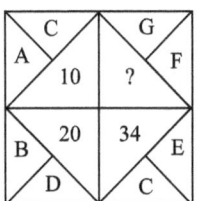
(a) 85 (b) 61 (c) 100 (d) 75

28.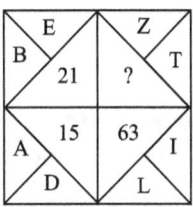
(a) 176 (b) 276
(c) 235 (d) 315

29.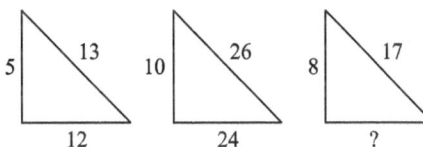
(a) 15 (b) 13 (c) 14 (d) 16

30.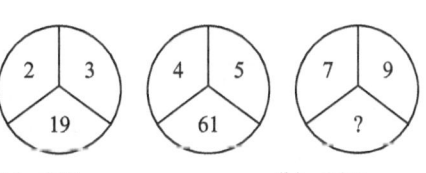
(a) 286 (b) 287
(c) 386 (d) 387

Inserting the Missing Character

Series 11

Learning Objectives : In this chapter, students will learn about:
- ✓ Problems based on continuation of figures

CHAPTER SUMMARY

This chapter deals with the problems based upon the continuation of figures. There are various types of problems on series. However, the fundamental concept for each type is the same. There is a sequence of figures depicting a change step by step. Either one of these figures is out of order and has to be omitted or figure has to be selected from a separate set of figures, which would continue the series.

This type of problems on series consists of five figures numbered A, B, C, D and E forming the set of **Problem Figures**, followed by five other figures numbered 1, 2, 3, 4 and 5 forming the set of **Answer Figures**. The five consecutive Problem Figures form a definite sequence and it is required to select one of the figures from the set of Answer Figures which will continue the same sequence.

Example 1: Find the correct answer figure to complete the series given in problem figures.

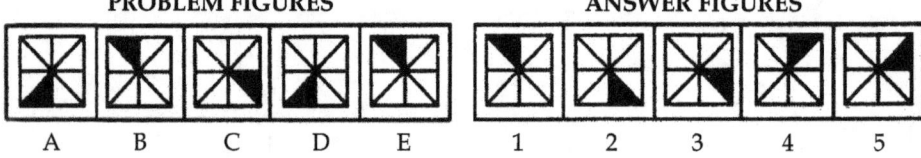

Sol.
The figure rotates 90° CW in each step and half a line segment and one complete line segment are added to the figure alternately. Clearly, fig. (1) is the answer.

Example 2: Find the correct answer figure to complete the series given in problem figures.

PROBLEM FIGURES   ANSWER FIGURES

  A   B   C   D   E   1   2   3   4   5

Sol.
The shading moves two spaces CW and three spaces CW alternately. Clearly, fig. (5) is the answer.

236 National Science Olympiad – 9

Example 3: Find the correct answer figure to complete the series given in problem figures.

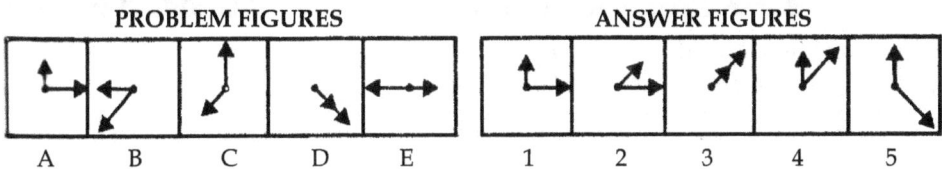

Sol.

The smaller arrow rotates through 90° ACW and 45° ACW alternately while the larger arrow rotates through 135° CW in each step. Hence, the answer is fig (4).

Example 4: Find the correct answer figure to complete the series given in problem figures.

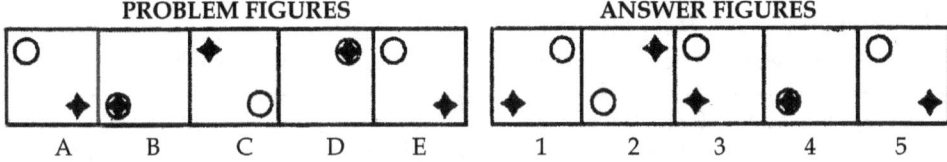

Sol.

In each step, the circle moves to adjacent corner (of the square boundary) in an ACW direction while the other element moves to the adjacent corner in a CW direction. Clearly, fig. (4) is the answer.

Example 5: Find the correct answer figure to complete the series given in problem figures.

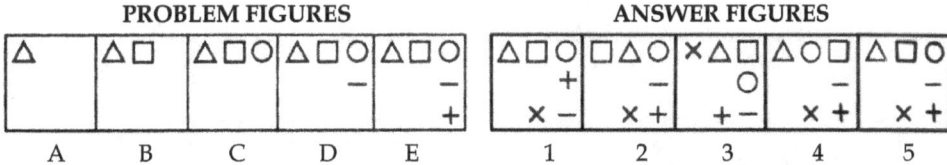

Sol.

Clearly, in each step, one new element is added to the figure at the CW end of the existing elements. Hence, fig. (5) is the answer.

Example 6: Find the correct answer figure to complete the series given in problem figures.

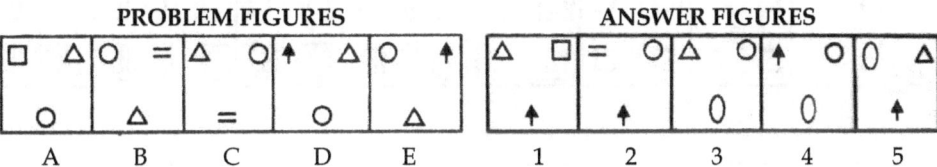

Sol.

Series

MULTIPLE CHOICE QUESTIONS

In each step, the elements move in the squence [diagram]. The circle and the triangle remain unchanged while the third element is replaced by a new element in first, third, fifth, ... steps. Clearly, fig. (3) is the answer.

Directions (1 – 30): Each of following questions consists of five figures marked A, B, C, D and E called the Problem Figures followed by five other figures marked a, b, c, d and e called the Answer Figures. Select a figure from amongst the Answer Figures which will continue the same series as established by the five Problem Figures.

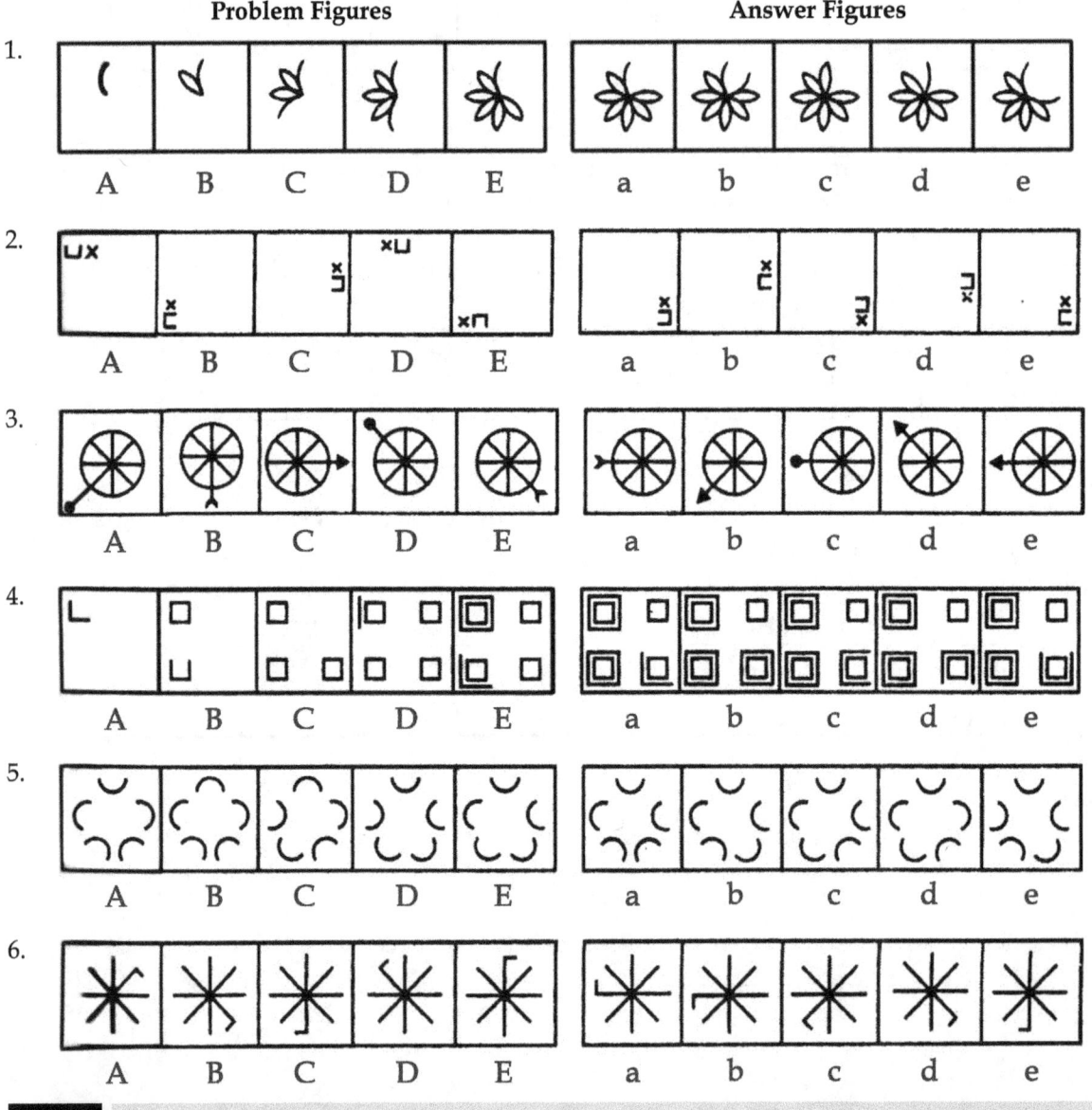

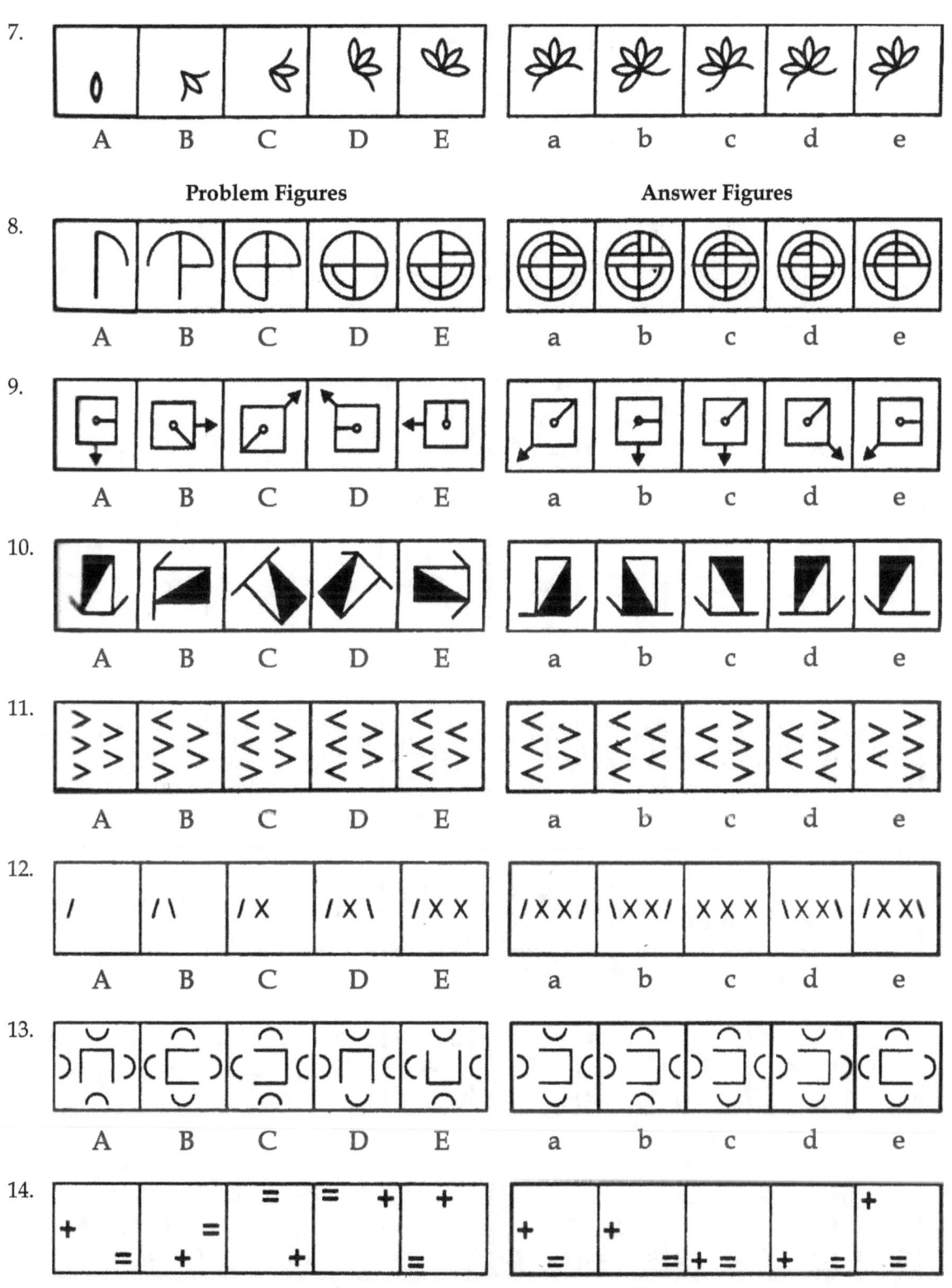

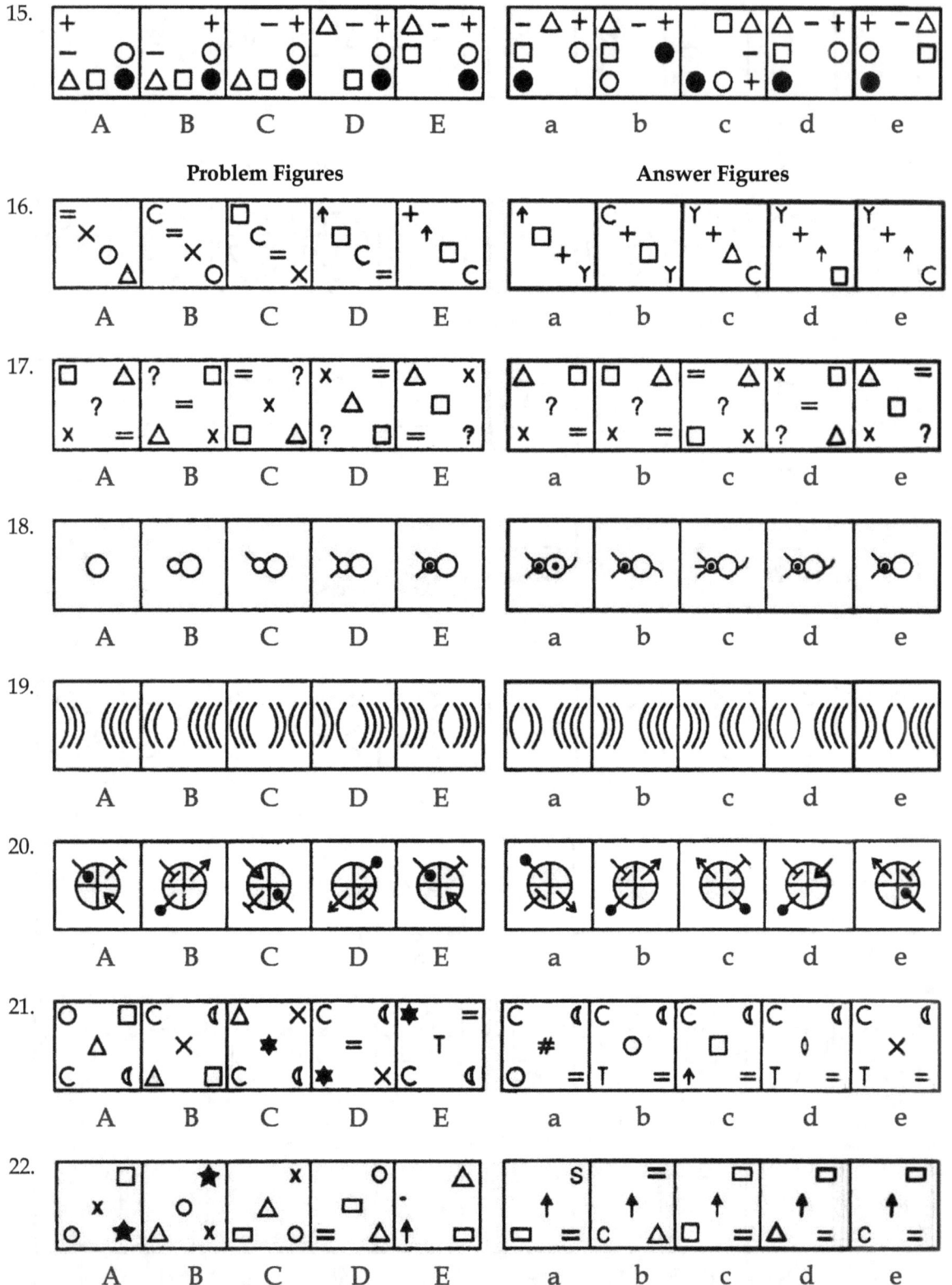

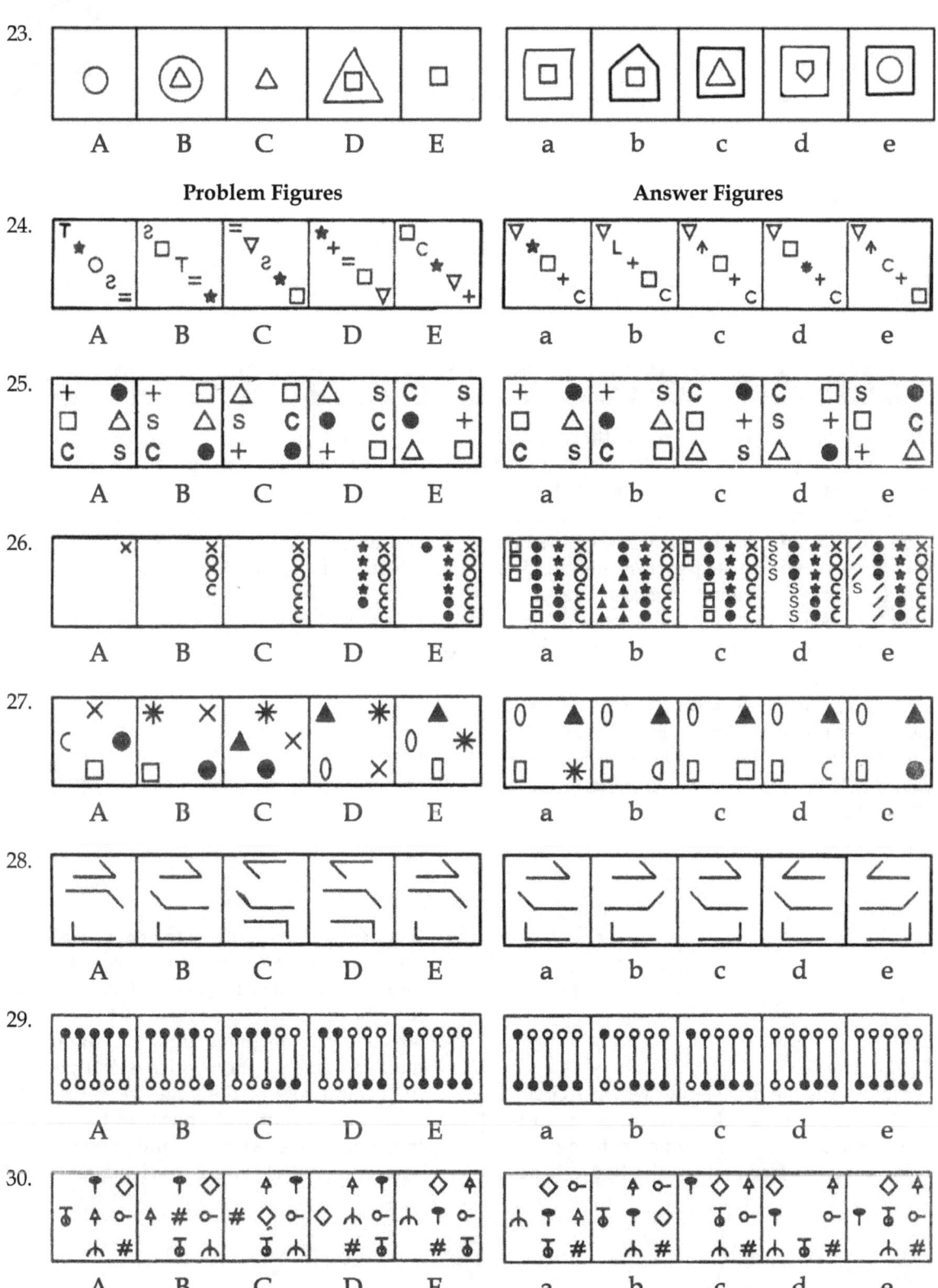

Problem Figures   Answer Figures

Series

Paper Cutting 12

Learning Objectives: In this chapter, students will learn about:
✓ Solving questions related to paper cutting

CHAPTER SUMMARY

In the questions based on paper cutting, a few figures are given showing the manner in which a piece of paper is folded and then cut from a particular section. A cut may be of varying designs. The design on the paper, after the cut, which appears when the paper is unfolded is shown by four or five answer figures. One of the answer figures correctly represents the design that the paper have after it is unfolded. This option is the correct answer.

Examples 1: The three figures marked X, Y, Z show the manner in which a paper is folded step by step and then cut. From the answer figures (a), (b), (c), (d) select the one, showing the unfolded position of the paper after the cut.

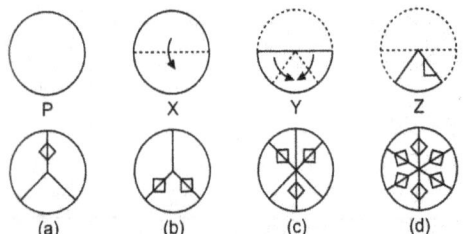

Sol. (b)

Figure X is the first step in which a circular piece of paper is folded from upper to the lower half along the diameter. In figure Y, both the extreme ends of the figure X have been folded to form a triangle and then as given in figure Z, a cut has been marked form the right side. It is clear that this cut will result into two marks, one in the lower half and one in the upper half of the paper when it will be unfolded. Answer figure (b) represents the correct design of the unfolded paper and hence, is the correct answer.

Examples 2:

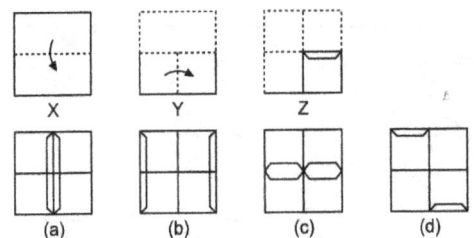

Sol. (c)

It is clear that in figure X, the paper has been folded from the upper half to lower half. In figure Y, the paper has been folded from left to right making it one-fourth of the original size. Now as in given figure Z, the cut is marked at the position which is occupied by the central row of the page. Therefore, the design of the cut will appear in the central line of the page, when it is unfolded. Hence, answer figure (c) is the correct answer.

MULTIPLE CHOICE QUESTIONS

Directions (1 – 45): In each of the following questions, a set of three figures X, Y, and Z have been given, showing a sequence in which a paper is folded and finally cut from a particular section. Below these figures a set of answer figures marked (a, b, c, d) showing the design which the paper actually acquires when it is unfolded are given. You have to select the answer figure which most closely resembles the unfolded piece of paper.

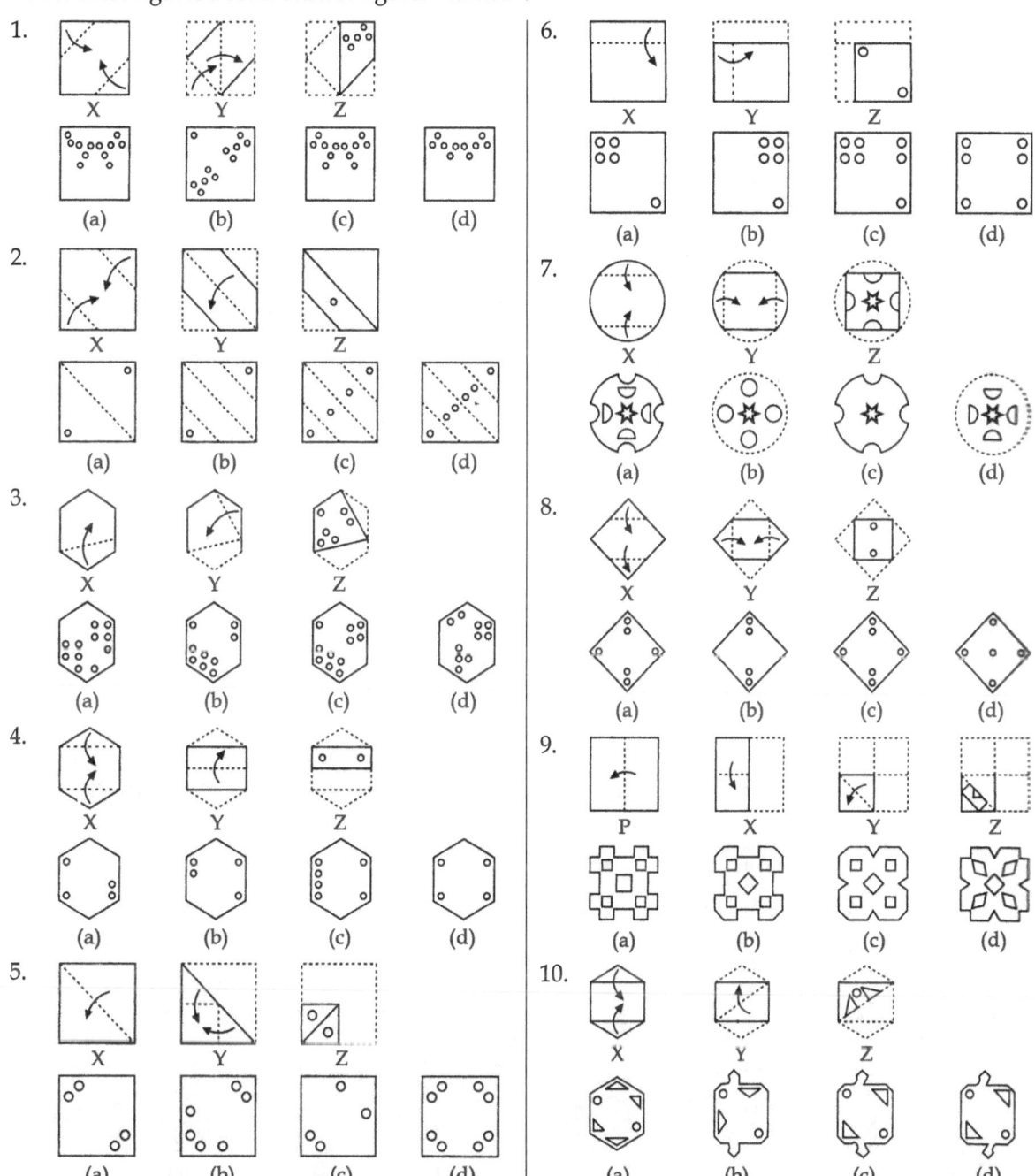

Paper Cutting

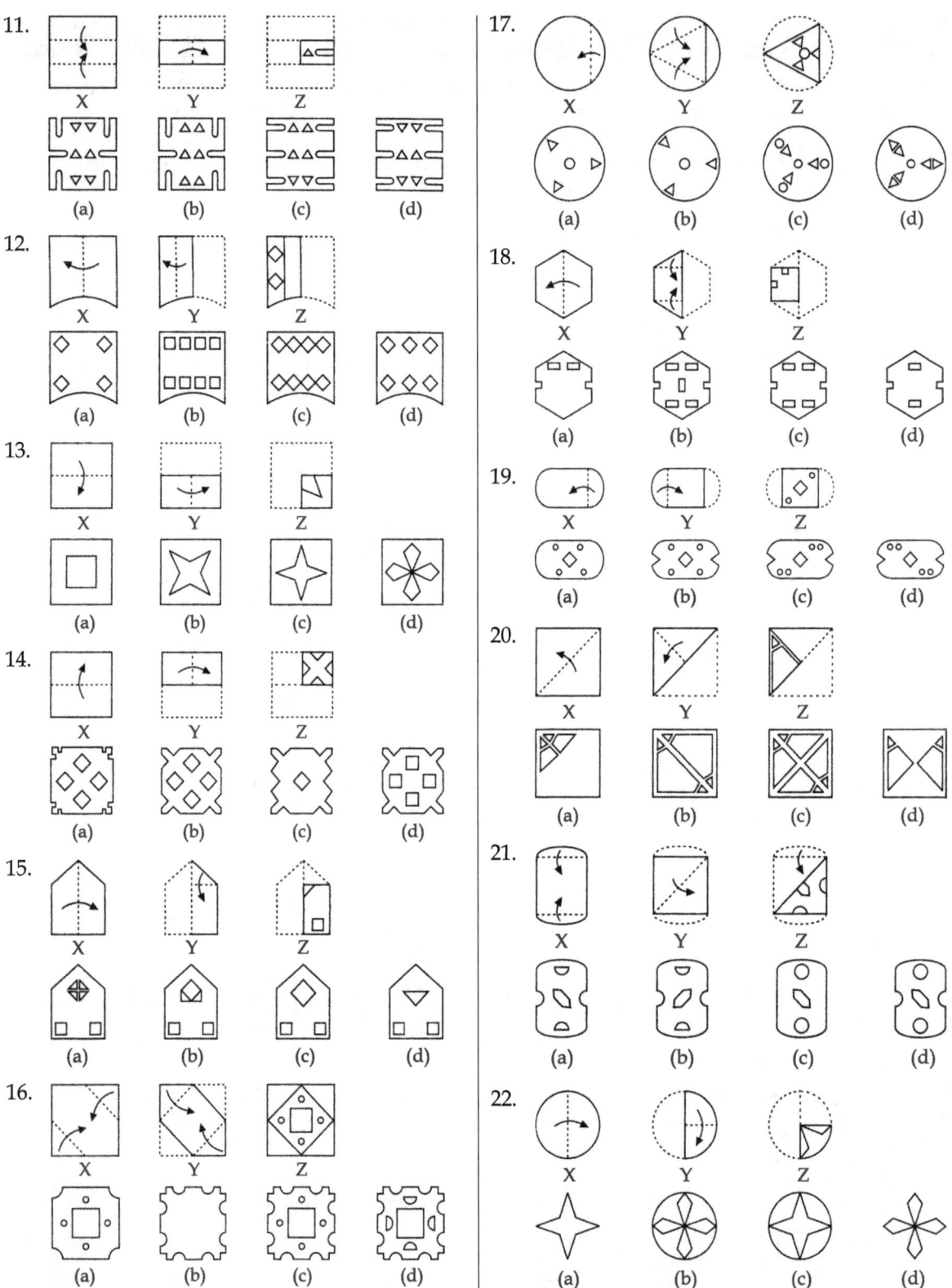

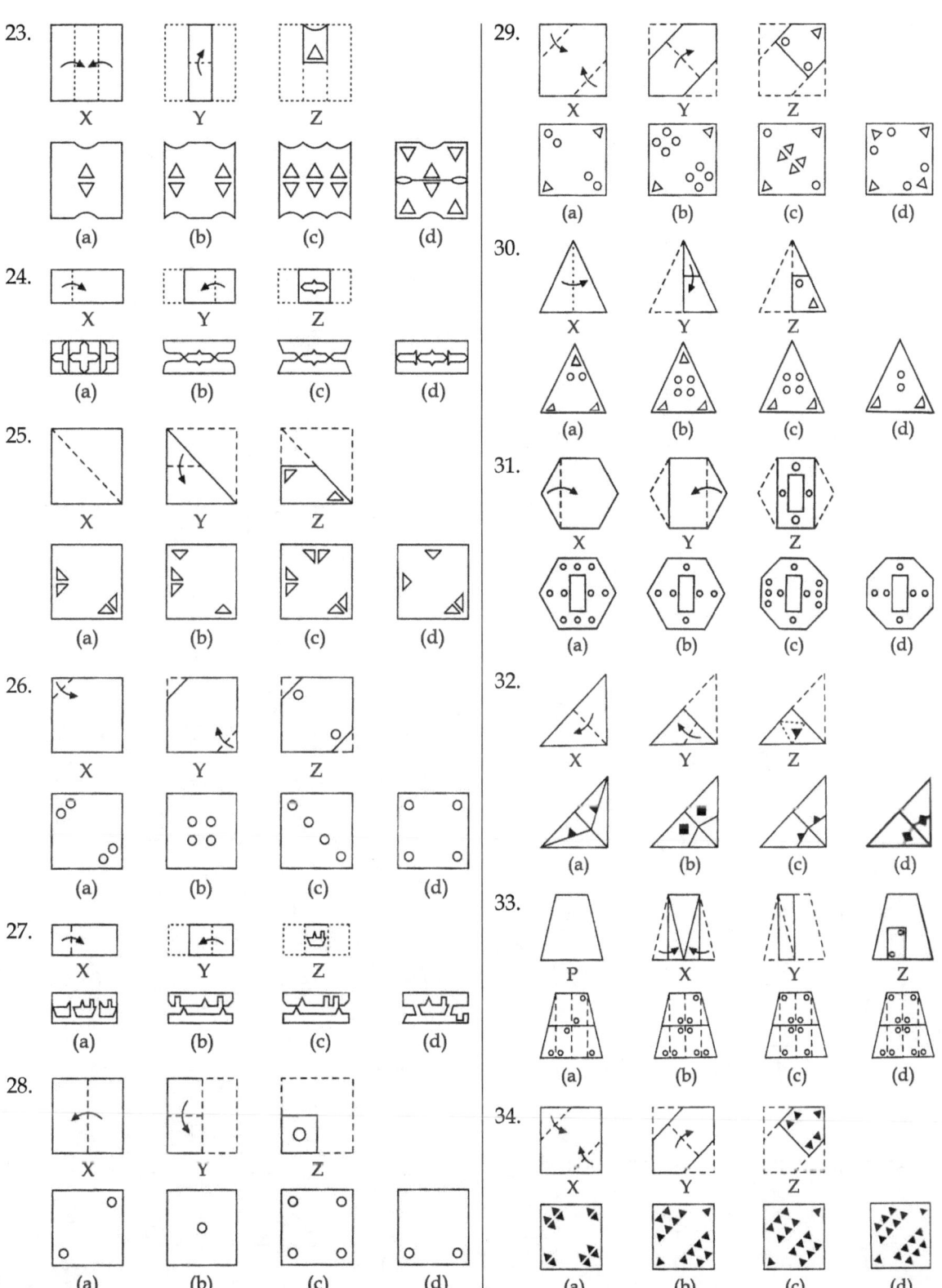

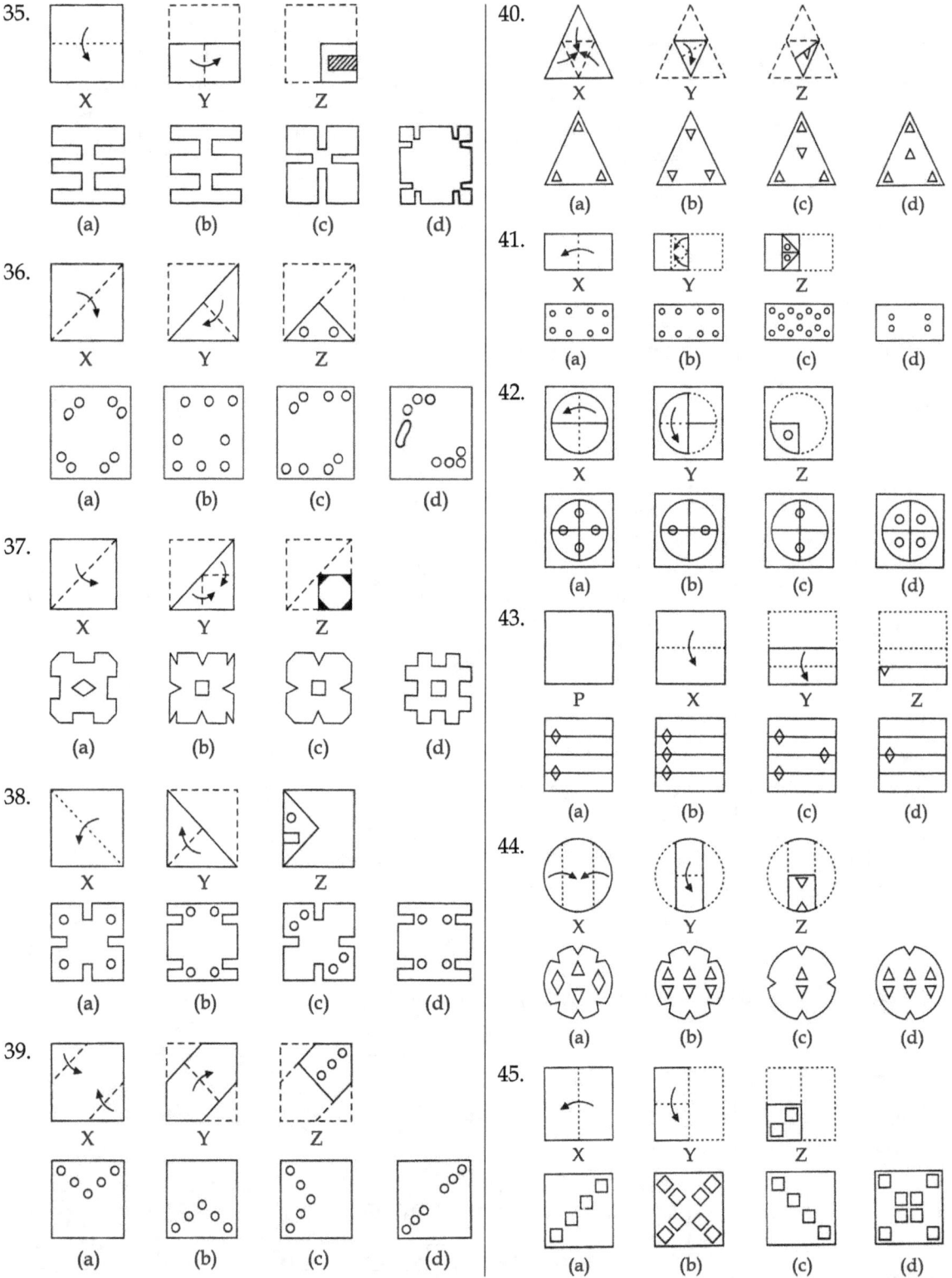

Mirror Images

Learning Objectives : In this chapter, students will learn about:
- ✓ Concept of Mirror Images

CHAPTER SUMMARY

Reflection of an object into the mirror is called its mirror-image. It is obtained by inverting an object laterally i.e., towards the sides. Example of lateral inversions of few figures and words are given below:

Objects having differnt mirror images

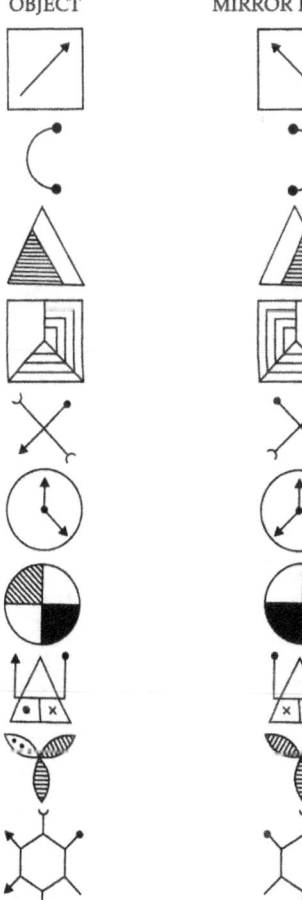

Objects having identical mirror images

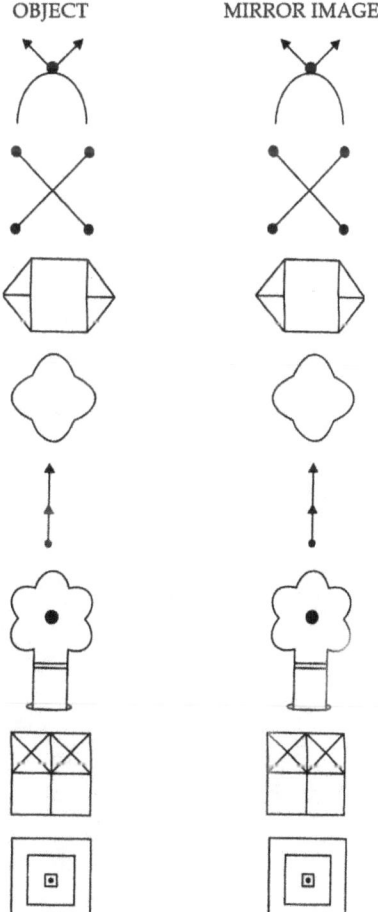

Mirror imges of certain words and numbers:

Word	Mirror Image	Number	Mirror Image	Word	Mirror Image	Number	Mirror Images
PREDICTION	NOITCIDERP	32596	69523	SARCASM	MSACRAS	5693	3965
HOSPITAL	LATIPSOH	8932	2398	LIBERAL	LAREBIL	8964	4698
DARPAN	NAPRAD	868	868	OFFENCE	ECNEFFO	7362	2637
STRIGENT	TNEGIRTS	786	687	ADVANCE	ECNAVDA	5893	3985
OPULENT	TNELUPO	10190	09101	IMAGES	SEGAMI	7839	9387

MULTIPLE CHOICE QUESTIONS

Directions (1 – 55): Select one alternative which exactly matches with the mirror image of the word given in each question.

1. NIRMALA
   (a) ALAMRIN
   (b) ALAMRIN (mirrored)
   (c) NRILAMA
   (d) INRMALA

2. VINAYAKA
   (a) INVAYAKA
   (b) AKAYANIV
   (c) AKAYANIV (mirrored)
   (d) NIVYAAKA

3. OBSTINATE
   (a) OBSTINATE (mirrored)
   (b) BOSTINATE
   (c) ETANITSBO
   (d) SOBTNIATE

4. PROCRASTINATE
   (a) ETANITSARCORP
   (b) PROCRASTINATE (mirrored)
   (c) RPORCASTNITAE
   (d) ETPROCRASTINA

5. PRECARIOUS
   (a) PRECARIOUS (mirrored)
   (b) SUOIRACERP
   (c) SUOPRECARI
   (d) SPRECARIOU

6. PERFECTION
   (a) NOITCEFERP
   (b) RPEFECTION
   (c) PERFECTION (mirrored)
   (d) ERPFECTION

7. FANTASY
   (a) FANTASY (mirrored)
   (b) FNTASAY
   (c) YSATNAF
   (d) YFANTSAY

8. INDULGENCE
   (a) ECNEGLUDNI
   (b) DNIULGENCE
   (c) ECNINDULGE
   (d) INDULGENCE (mirrored)

9. RADIANT
   (a) TNAIDAR
   (b) RADIANT (mirrored)
   (c) TRADIAN
   (d) TIANRAD

10. BENEDICTION
    (a) NOITCIDENEB
    (b) NEBEDICTION
    (c) BENEDICTION (mirrored)
    (d) NOIBENEDICT

11. VERBAL
    (a) LABREV
    (b) LRVEBA
    (c) REVBAL
    (d) VERBAL (mirrored)

12. ARIHANT
    (a) ARIHANT (mirrored)
    (b) TNAHIRA
    (c) TARIHAN
    (d) TRIHANA

13. MAHAVIR
    (a) RIVAHAM
    (b) RMAHAVI
    (c) RIVAHAM (mirrored)
    (d) HAMAVIR

14. CONSOLIDATE
    (a) ETADILOSNOC
    (b) CONSOLIDATE (mirrored)
    (c) TAECONSOLID
    (d) OCNSOLIDATE

15. FORTIFY
    (a) YFITROF
    (b) FORTIFY (mirrored)
    (c) ROFTIFY
    (d) ORFTIFY

16. STRENGTHEN
    (a) STRENGTHEN (mirrored)
    (b) NEHTGNERTS
    (c) TSRENGTHEN
    (d) NSTRENGTHE

17. RECALCITRANT
    (a) RECALCITRANT (mirrored)
    (b) NTARTICLACER
    (c) TNARTCILACER
    (d) CITRANTRECAL

18. OPPORTUNITY
    (a) YTINUTROPPO
    (b) YOPPORTUNIT
    (c) OPPORTUNITY (mirrored)
    (d) TYINUTROPPO

19. TRIUMPHS
    (a) SHPMUIRT
    (b) SPHMIURT
    (c) STRIUMPH
    (d) TRIUMPHS (mirrored)

20. POSSESSION
    (a) NIOPOSSESS
    (b) NOISSESSPO
    (c) POSSESSION (mirrored)
    (d) NPOSSEISSO

21. PHILOSOPHER
    (a) REHPOSOLIHP
    (b) PHILOSOPHER (mirrored)
    (c) PHILOREHPOS
    (d) RHEPOSOLIHP

22. INCREDIBLE
    (a) ELBIDERCNI
    (b) EBLIDERCNI
    (c) ENICREDIBL
    (d) INCREDIBLE (mirrored)

23. INCARNATION
    (a) INCARNATION (mirrored)
    (b) NINCARNATIO
    (c) NOITANRACNI
    (d) ONITANRACNI

24. EMANCIPATION
    (a) NEMANCIPATIO
    (b) NOITAPICNAME
    (c) EMANCIPATION (mirrored)
    (d) NMEANCIPATIO

Mirror Images

25. APPETITE
   (a) ETITEPPA   (b) APPETITE (reversed)
   (c) EPPAETIT   (d) ETITAPPE

26. PAMPER
   (a) PAMPER (reversed) (b) REPMAP
   (c) REPAMP   (d) RPAPME

27. CRITICISM
   (a) MSICITIRC   (b) MRCITICIS
   (c) CMSICITIR   (d) CRITICISM (reversed)

28. INSOMANIA
   (a) AINAMOSNI   (b) AININSOMA
   (c) AINAMOSNI (reversed) (d) ASOINMANI

29. SEDATIVES
   (a) SEVITADES   (b) SDAETIVES
   (c) SEVITADES (reversed) (d) SEDATIVES (reversed)

30. EXCRUCIATING
   (a) EXCRUCIATING (reversed) (b) GNITAICURCXE
   (c) GEXRCUICAITN   (d) EXCRUCIATING (reversed)

31. PANIPAT
   (a) TAPNIPA   (b) PANIPAT (reversed)
   (c) PANIPAT (reversed) (d) QANIPAT

32. EMANATE
   (a) ETANAME   (b) EMANATE (reversed)
   (c) ENAMEAT   (d) EATEMAN

33. Nu56p7uR
   (a) Ru7P65uN   (b) RNu56p7u
   (c) Nu56p7uR (reversed) (d) Nu56p7uR (reversed)

34. CAR27aug
   (a) CAR27aug (reversed) (b) CAR27aug (reversed)
   (c) guaCAR27   (d) gua72RAC

35. KALINGA261B
   (a) B162AGNILAK   (b) KALINGA261B (reversed)
   (c) KALINGA261B (reversed) (d) KALINGA261B (reversed)

36. JUDGEMENT
   (a) TNEMEGDUJ   (b) TJUDGEMEN
   (c) JUDGEMENT (reversed) (d) DJUGEMNET

37. DL3N469F
   (a) DL3469FN   (b) DL3N469F (reversed)
   (c) DL3N469F (reversed) (d) F964N3DL

38. test5auto
   (a) test5auto (reversed) (b) otua5tset
   (c) tset5uato   (d) test5auto (reversed)

39. 247593
   (a) 395742   (b) 247593 (reversed)
   (c) 392457   (d) 247593 (reversed)

40. GANDHI1869
   (a) GANDHI1869 (reversed) (b) 1968IHDNAG
   (c) GANDHI1869 (reversed) (d) 196GANDHI8

41. CHEAPER
   (a) REPAEHC   (b) CHEAPER (reversed)
   (c) CHEAPER (reversed) (d) REHCEAP

42. TARAIN1014A
   (a) TARAIN1014A (reversed) (b) A4101NIARAT
   (c) A410ARTAIN1   (d) TARAIN1014A (reversed)

43. eagle45
   (a) eagle45 (reversed) (b) 54elgaae
   (c) 54aglee   (d) eagle45 (reversed)

44. disturb
   (a) disturb (reversed) (b) disturb (reversed)
   (c) brutsid   (d) bdistur

45. qutubgarh
   (a) qutubgarh (reversed) (b) hragbutuq
   (c) putubgarh   (d) qutubgarh (reversed)

46. 1965INDOPAK
   (a) KAPODNI5691   (b) K1965INDOPA
   (c) 1965INDOPAK (reversed) (d) 1965INDOPAK (reversed)

47. kurukshetra
   (a) artehskuruk   (b) kurukshetra (reversed)
   (c) kurukshetra (reversed) (d) arkurukshet

48. BR4AQ16HI
   (a) BR4AQ16HI (reversed) (b) BR4AQ16HI (reversed)
   (c) IBR4AQ16H   (d) IH91QARRB

49. EFFECTIVE
   (a) EFFECTIVE (reversed) (b) EVIEFFECT
   (c) EVITCEFFE   (d) EFFECTIVE (reversed)

50. INFORMATIONS
   (a) SNOITAMROFNI   (b) INFORMATIONS (reversed)
   (c) SNOITAMRPFNI   (d) SINFROMAOITN

51. FIXING
   (a) GNIXIF   (b) FIXING (reversed)
   (c) FIXING (reversed) (d) GIFIXN

52. COLONIAL
   (a) COLONIAL (reversed) (b) LAINOLOC
   (c) COLALINO   (d) COLONIAL (reversed)

53. BUZZER
   (a) BUZZER (reversed) (b) RUZZEB
   (c) BUZZER (reversed) (d) REZZBU

54. LATERAL
   (a) LALATER   (b) LATERAL (reversed)
   (c) LATALER   (d) LATERAL (reversed)

55. QUALITY
   (a) YTILAUQ   (b) YUALITQ
   (c) YTILAUQ (reversed) (d) QUALITY (reversed)

Water Images   14

 **Learning Objectives :** In this chapter, students will learn about:
- ✓ Concept of Water Images

CHAPTER SUMMARY

The reflection of an object into the water is called water image of that object. It is obtained by inverting an object vertically. Examples of formation of water images of some figures are given below:

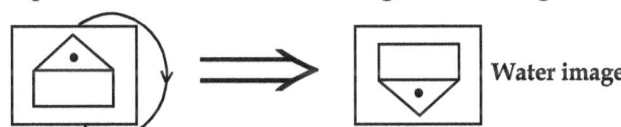 Water image

Figures having identical water images: **Figures having different water images:**

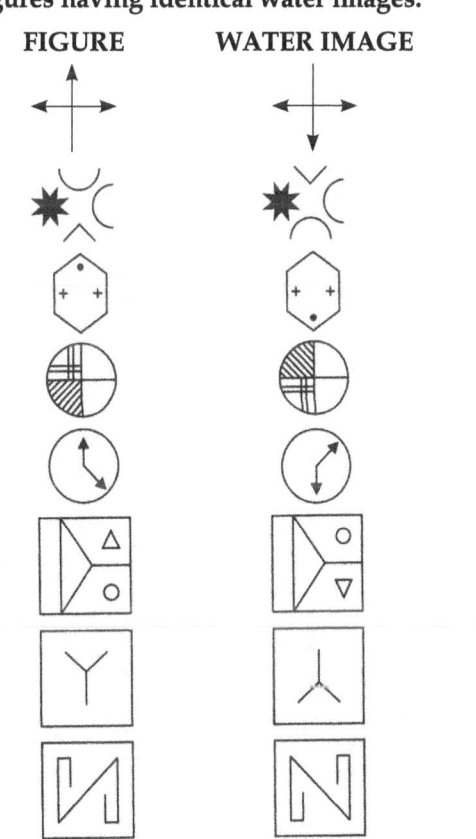   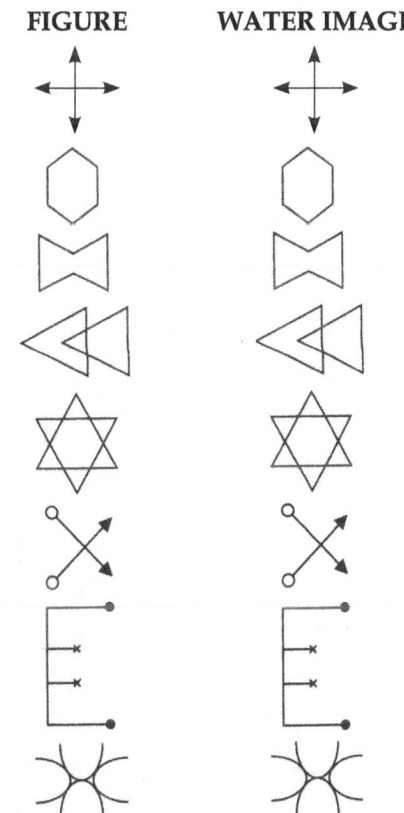

Water imgaes of a few words:

WORD	WATER IMAGE	WORD	WATER IMAGE
IMAGINE	IMAGINE (inverted)	PRACTICAL	PRACTICAL (inverted)
REGULAR	REGULAR (inverted)	OTHERS	OTHERS (inverted)
FORTUNE	FORTUNE (inverted)	LANGUISH	LANGUISH (inverted)
ELASTIC	ELASTIC (inverted)	FERVENT	FERVENT (inverted)
IDENTITY	IDENTITY (inverted)	VERTICAL	VERTICAL (inverted)
		FORMATION	FORMATION (inverted)

MULTIPLE CHOICE QUESTIONS

Directions (1 – 40): In each of the following questions, a word is followed by four alternatives (a), (b), (c), (d) showing possible water images of that word. Choose the alternative which shows the correct water-image of that word.

1. CORDIAL
   (a) LAIDROC
   (b) CORDIAL (water image)
   (c) CORDIAL (water image)
   (d) CORDIAL (water image)

2. PRECARIOUS
   (a) PRECARIOUS (water image)
   (b) PRECARIOUS (water image)
   (c) SUORECARIP
   (d) PRECARIOUS (water image)

3. SUPERFLOUS
   (a) SUPERFLOUS (water image)
   (b) SUPERFLOUS (water image)
   (c) SUPERFLOUS (water image)
   (d) SUPERFLOUS (water image)

4. POLEMIC
   (a) POLEMIC (water image)
   (b) POLEMIC (water image)
   (c) POLEMIC (water image)
   (d) POLEMIC (water image)

5. FECUND
   (a) DNUCEF
   (b) FECUND (water image)
   (c) FECUND (water image)
   (d) DNUCEF (water image)

6. RADIANT
   (a) TADIANR
   (b) TADIANR (water image)
   (c) TNAIDAR
   (d) RADIANT (water image)

7. MUNDANE
   (a) EUNDANM
   (b) EUMDANM
   (c) MUNDANE (water image)
   (d) MUNDANE (water image)

8. OBLITERATE
   (a) OBLITERATE (water image)
   (b) OBLITERATE (water image)
   (c) OBLITERATE (water image)
   (d) OBJITERATE

9. SARCASM
   (a) SARCASM (water image)
   (b) SARCASM (water image)
   (c) SARCASM
   (d) SARCASM (water image)

10. DETERRENT
    (a) DETERRENT (water image)
    (b) DETERRENT (water image)
    (c) DETERRENT (water image)
    (d) DETERRENT (water image)

11. QUESTION
    (a) QUESTION (water image)
    (b) QUESTION (water image)
    (c) QUESTION (water image)
    (d) QUESTION (water image)

12. SURFACE
    (a) SURFACE (water image)
    (b) SURFACE (water image)
    (c) SURFACE (water image)
    (d) SURFACE (water image)

13. EXPOSE
    (a) ESOPXE
    (b) EXPOSE
    (c) EXPOSE (water image)
    (d) EPOSXE

14. DISCLOSE
    (a) DISCLOSE (water image)
    (b) DISCLOSE (water image)
    (c) ESOLCSID
    (d) DISCLOSE (water image)

15. TERMINATE
    (a) TERMINATE (water image)
    (b) TERMINATE (water image)
    (c) TERMINATE (water image)
    (d) TERMINATE (water image)

16. STRAIN
    (a) NIARTS
    (b) NIARTS (water image)
    (c) NIARTS
    (d) STRAIN (water image)

17. CLOSELY
    (a) CLOSELY (water image)
    (b) CLOSELY (water image)
    (c) CLOSELY
    (d) CLOSELY (water image)

18. IMAGES
    (a) IMAGES (water image)
    (b) SEGAMI
    (c) IMAGES
    (d) IMAGES (water image)

19. DARPAN
    (a) DARPAN (water image)
    (b) DARPAN (water image)
    (c) DARPAN (water image)
    (d) DARPAN (water image)

20. BK50RP62
    (a) BK50RP62 (water image)
    (b) BK50RP62 (water image)
    (c) BK50RP62 (water image)
    (d) BK50RP62 (water image)

21. 5DOB6V2
    (a) 5DOB6V2 (water image)
    (b) 5DOB6V2 (water image)
    (c) 5DOB6V2 (water image)
    (d) 5DOB6V2 (water image)

22. bridge
    (a) bridge (water image)
    (b) bridge (water image)
    (c) bridge (water image)
    (d) bridge (water image)

23. national
    (a) national (water image)
    (b) national (water image)
    (c) national (water image)
    (d) national (water image)

24. DL2CA34OO
    (a) DL2CA34OO (water image)
    (b) DL2CA34OO (water image)
    (c) DL2CA34OO (water image)
    (d) DL2CA34OO (water image)

Water Images

25. D6Z7F4
    (a) D6Z7F4 (b) D6Z7F4
    (c) D6Z7F4 (d) D6Z7F4

26. FRUIT
    (a) FRUIT (b) FRUIT
    (c) FRUIT (d) FRUIT

27. ACOUSTIC
    (a) ACOUSTIC (b) ACOUSTIC
    (c) ACOUSTIC (d) ACOUSTIC

28. FAMILY
    (a) FAMILY (b) FAMILY
    (c) FAMILY (d) FAMILY

29. U4P15B7
    (a) U4P15B7 (b) U4P15B7
    (c) U4P15B7 (d) U4P15B7

30. PQ8AF5BZ9
    (a) PQ8AF5BZ9 (b) PQ8AF5BZ9
    (c) PQ8AF5BZ9 (d) PQ8AF5BZ9

31. 96FSH52
    (a) 96FSH52 (b) 96FSH52
    (c) 96FSH52 (d) 96FSH52

32. 50JA32DEO6
    (a) 50JA32DEO6 (b) 50JA32DEO6
    (c) 50JA32DEO6 (d) 50JA32DEO6

33. VAYU8436
    (a) VAYU8436 (b) VAYU8436
    (c) VAYU8436 (d) VAYU8436

34. UP15847
    (a) UP15847 (b) UP15847
    (c) UP15847 (d) UP15847

35. rise
    (a) rise (b) esir
    (c) rise (d) esir

36. wrote
    (a) wrote (b) wrote
    (c) wrote (d) wrote

37. NUCLEAR
    (a) NUCLEAR (b) NUCLEAR
    (c) NUCLEAR (d) NUCLEAR

38. QUARREL
    (a) QUARREL (b) QUARREL
    (c) QUARREL (d) QUARREL

39. RAJ589D8
    (a) RAJ589D8 (b) RAJ589D8
    (c) RAJ589D8 (d) RAJ589D8

40. GR98AP76ES
    (a) GR98AP76ES (b) GR98AP76ES
    (c) GR98AP76ES (d) GR98AP76ES

Cubes and Dice

15

Learning Objectives : In this chapter, students will learn about:
- Concept of Cubes and Dice

CHAPTER SUMMARY

Now a days, problems based on cubes and dice have become integral part of verbal reasoning. This test is meant to judge a candidate's ability, how does he/she solve to problems in a three-dimensional-perspective. These types of problems are usually based on a six faced cube and dice.

Example: Study the different positions of a cube as given below. Which numbers will occur on the face opposite to 4.

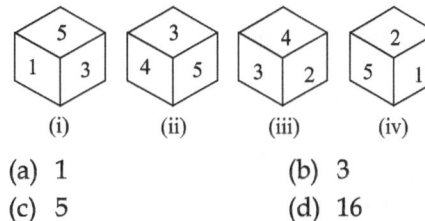

(a) 1   (b) 3
(c) 5   (d) 16

Sol.
From fig (i) 5 and 3 exist with 1.
From fig (ii) 5 and 3 exist with 4.
From (i) and (ii) 1 will be opposite of 4.

MULTIPLE CHOICE QUESTIONS

Directions (1 – 6) Find the number of cubes in the following figures.

1.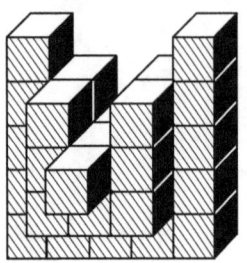
   (a) 34   (b) 32   (c) 30   (d) 25

2.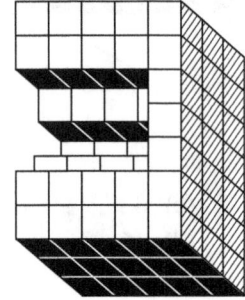
   (a) 89   (b) 88   (c) 87   (d) 81

3.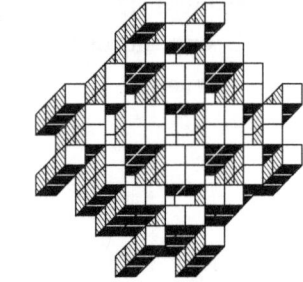
   (a) 150   (b) 168
   (c) 158   (d) 144

4.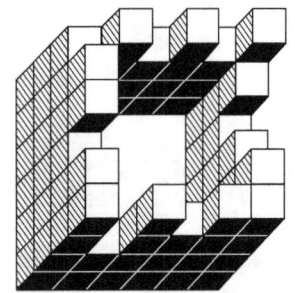
   (a) 71   (b) 70
   (c) 69   (d) 68

5.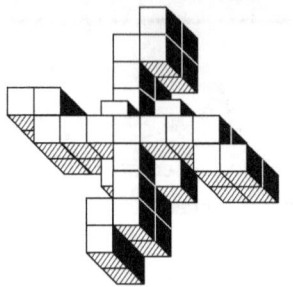
   (a) 45   (b) 46
   (c) 47   (d) 48

6.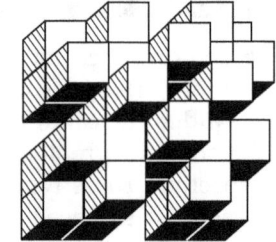
   (a) 36   (b) 38
   (c) 40   (d) 42

7. A cube painted blue on all faces is cut into 27 small cubes of equal size. How many small cubes are painted on one face only?
   (a) 6   (b) 4   (c) 8   (d) 12

8. A cube painted black on all faces and is then cut into 125 cubes of equal size, then how many cubes are not painted on any face?
   (a) 8   (b) 27
   (c) 36   (d) 64

9. A cube painted red on all faces is cut into 27 small cubes of equal size, then how many cubes are not painted on any face?
   (a) 1   (b) 6   (c) 2   (d) 4

10. 125 cubes of same size are arranged in the form of cube on a table and then a column of five cubes is removed from each of the four corners. All the exposed faces of rest of the cubes are coloured yellow. How many small cubes are there in the solid after removal of the column?
    (a) 100   (b) 105
    (c) 110   (d) 120

11. A cube of side 10 cm is coloured green with a 2 cm wide red strip along all the sides on all the faces. The cube is cut into 125 smaller cubes of equal size, then how many cubes are without any colour?
    (a) 4 (b) 8
    (c) 27 (d) 64

12. A cube is painted black on two adjacent faces, red on two faces opposite to the black faces and blue on the remaining faces. It is then cut into 64 smaller cubes of equal size, then how many cubes are painted on all faces?
    (a) 0 (b) 4 (c) 8 (d) 27

13. How many dots are there on the dice face opposite the one with three dots?

    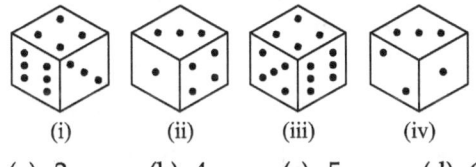

    (a) 2 (b) 4 (c) 5 (d) 6

14. Four usual dice are thrown on the ground. The total of numbers on the top faces of these four dice is 13 as the top faces showed 4, 3, 1, 5 respectively. What is the total of the faces touching the ground?
    (a) 15 (b) 16 (c) 13 (d) 12

15. Three positions of a dice are given. Based on them find out which number is found opposite the number 2 in the given cube.

    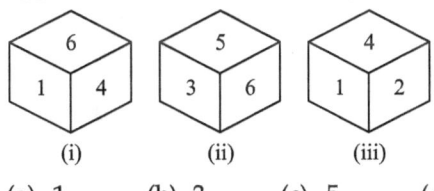

    (a) 1 (b) 3 (c) 5 (d) 6

16. The figure given below three different positions of a dice. Find the number of dots on the face opposite to the face with one dot.

    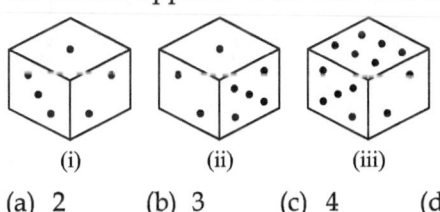

    (a) 2 (b) 3 (c) 4 (d) 6

17. In the given figure find the number of dots on the face opposite the face having 3 dots.

    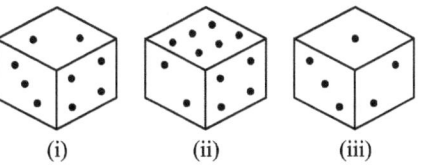

    (a) 4 (b) 5 (c) 6 (d) 2

18. In the figure given below. Find the number on the face opposite the face showing 4.

    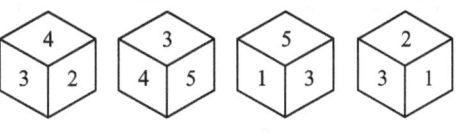

    (a) 1 (b) 2 (c) 5 (d) 6

19. Two positions of a dice are shown. When 4 is at the bottom, what number will be on the top?

    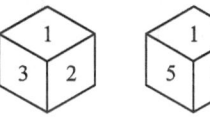

    (a) 1 (b) 2 (c) 5 (d) 6

20. A figure is given below. What is the number at the bottom, when the top is 3?

    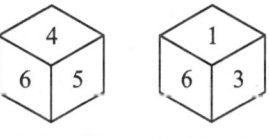

    (a) 2 (b) 4 (c) 5 (d) 6

21. In the given figure, when 4 is at the bottom, what number will be on the top?

    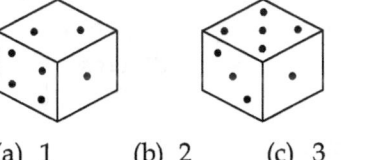

    (a) 1 (b) 2 (c) 3 (d) 6

22. In the given figure, when 2 is at the bottom, what number will be at the top ?

    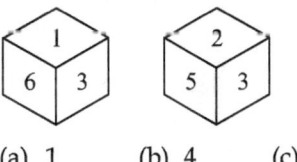

    (a) 1 (b) 4 (c) 5 (d) 6

Cubes and Dice

23. Two positions of a parallelepiped are given below. When the number 3 will be on the top side, which number will be at the bottom?

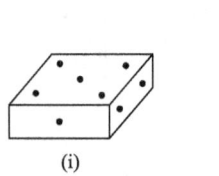

(i) (ii)

(a) 1 (b) 4 (c) 5 (d) 6

24. Two positions of a block are given below. When 1 is at the top, which number will be at the bottom?

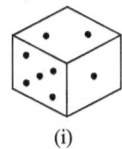 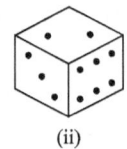

(i) (ii)

(a) 2 (b) 3 (c) 4 (d) 6

25. Three different positions X, Y, Z of a dice are as shown below.

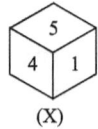 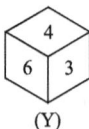 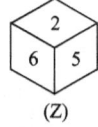

(X) (Y) (Z)

Which number lies opposite to 6?

(a) 1 (b) 2 (c) 4 (d) 5

26. In the given figure, which symbol is opposite to the dot?

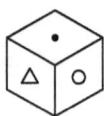  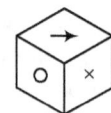

(a) triangle (b) arrow
(c) circle   (d) cross

27. In the given figure, which number lies at the bottom face in position B?

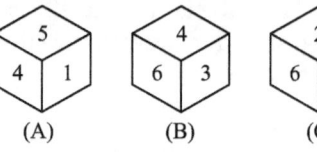

(A) (B) (C)

(a) 2 (b) 3 (c) 4 (d) 5

28. In the given figure, find the alphabet opposite to A.

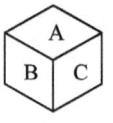  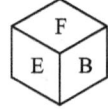

(a) C (b) D (c) E (d) F

29. In the following figure, which symbol is opposite to the arrow.

  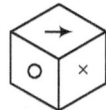

(a) Dot   (b) Triangle
(c) Circle   (d) Cross

30. A cube is painted red on the two adjacent faces and black on the surfaces opposite to red surfaces and orange on the remaining faces. Now the cube is divided into 216 smaller cubes of equal size. How many smaller cubes will have no surface painted?

(a) 36 (b) 64
(c) 60 (d) 54

SECTION 3
ACHIEVERS' SECTION

Achievers' Section

Some Thoughtful Questions

1. Explain why it is dangerous to jump out of a moving bus.

   Ans.

   While moving in a bus our body is in motion. On jumping out of a moving bus our feet touches the ground and come to rest. While the upper part of our body stays in motion and moves forward due to inertia of motion and hence we can fall in forward direction. Hence, to avoid this we need to run forward in the direction of bus.

2. Why do fielders pull their hand gradually with the moving ball while holding a catch?

   Ans.

   While catching a fast moving cricket ball, a fielder on the ground gradually pulls his hands backwards with the moving ball. This is done so that the fielder increases the time during which the high velocity of the moving ball decreases to zero. Thus, the acceleration of the ball is decreased and therefore the impact of catching the fast moving ball is reduced.

3. In a high jump athletic event, why are athletes made to fall either on a cushioned bed or on a sand bed?

   Ans.

   In a high jump athletic event, athletes are made to fall either on a cushioned bed or on a sand bed so as to increase the time of the athlete's fall to stop after making the jump. This decreases the rate of change of momentum and hence the force.

4. How does a karate player breaks a slab of ice with a single blow?

   Ans.

   A karate player applied the blow with large velocity in a very short interval of time on the ice slab which therefore exerts large amount of force on it and suddenly breaks the ice slab.

5. Give any three examples in daily life which are based on Newton's third law of motion.

   Ans.

   Three examples based on Newton's third law are:

   (i) **Swimming:** We push the water backward to move forward.

   action – water is pushed behind

   reaction – water pushes the swimmer ahead

   (ii) **Firing gun:** A bullet fired from a gun and the gun recoils.

   action – gun exerts force on the bullet

   reaction – bullet exerts an equal and opposite force on the gun

   (iii) **Launching of rocket:** action – hot gases from the rocket are released

   reaction – the gases exert upward push to the rocket

6. Camels can walk easily on desert sand but we are not comfortable walking on the sand. State reason.

   Ans.

   Camels feet are broad and the larger area of the feet reduces the force/ pressure exerted by the body on the sand. But when we have to walk on the same sand, we sink because the pressure exerted by our body is not distributed but is directional.

7. Two cork pieces of same size and mass are dipped in two beakers containing water and oil. One cork floats on water but another sink in oil. Why?

   Ans.

   The cork floats on water because the density of cork is less than the density of water, and another cork sinks in the oil because the density of cork is more than the oil.

8. A milkman sold his milk in the city and always carried lactometer with him. The customers trusted him and his business flourished.
   (a) What is lactometer?
   (b) What is the principle of working of lactometer?
   (c) What value of milkman is seen in this case?

Ans.
   (a) Lactometer is a device that measures the purity of milk.
   (b) The principle of lactometer is 'Archimedes' principle'. It states that when a body is immersed fully or partially in a fluid, it experiences an upward force that is equal to the weight of the fluid displaced by it.
   (c) Milkman is very honest and trustworthy.

9. Reeta was wearing a high heel shoe for a beach party, her friend told her to wear flat shoes as she will be tired soon with high heels and will not feel comfortable,
   (a) Why would one feel tired with high heel shoes on beach?
   (b) Give the unit of pressure.
   (c) What value of Reeta's friend is seen in the above act?

Ans.
   (a) The high heel shoes would exert lot of pressure on the loose sand of beach and will sink more in the soil as compared to flat shoes. Hence large amount of force will be required to walk with heels.
   (b) Unit of pressure is Pascal.
   (c) Reeta's friend showed the value of being helpful, concerned and intelligent.

10. In the school fair, there was a game in which one need to find the heaviest ball without holding them in hand. Three balls were given and few disposable glasses were kept. Tarun saw his friend struggling to win the game but he was unable to find the heaviest ball. Tarun helped him by dipping the three balls one by one in the glasses full of water upto the brim and finally they won the game.
    (a) Why did Tarun told his friend to dip the balls one by one in completely filled glass of water?
    (b) Name the principle used here.
    (c) What value of Tarun is reflected in this case?

Ans.
   (a) Tarun wanted to measure the amount of water displaced by each ball when dipped in water.
   (b) The principle used is 'Archimedes' principle'.
   (c) Tarun showed the value of being helpful, kind and intelligent.

11. When a force retards the motion of a body, what is the nature of work done by the force? State reason. List two examples of such a situation.

Ans.
The work done by the force is negative because the displacement is opposite to the direction of force applied.

Example:
   (i) Work done by the force of friction;
   (ii) Work done by applying brakes.

12. When is the work done by a force said to be negative? Give one situation in which one of the forces acting on the object is doing positive work and the other is doing negative work.

Ans.
Negative work: When the force is acting opposite to the direction of the displacement, the work done by the force is said to be negative. When we lift an object, two forces act on the
   (i) Muscular force: Doing positive work in the direction of the displacement.
   (ii) Gravitational force: Doing negative work opposite to the direction of the displacement.

13. Raj noticed that his pet dog was frightened and trying to hide in safe place in his house when some crackers were burst in the neighbourhood. He realized the problem

and he decided not to burst crackers during diwali or for any other celebrations.

(a) What must be the range of crackers sound?

(b) Name two health conditions that can be caused due to noise pollution.

(c) Name the values of Raj reflected in above act.

Ans.

(a) The range of crackers sound must be between 20 Hz to 20 kHz.

(b) Two health conditions that can occur due to noise pollution are heart attack and high blood pressure.

(c) Raj reflects the value of respecting sensitivity for animals and caring for animals.

14. It is not advisable to construct houses near airports, in spite of that many new residential apartments are constructed near airports. Sumit files RTI and also complains the municipal office about the same.

(a) Why one should not reside near airport?

(b) Name other two places where there is noise pollution.

(c) What value of Sumit is reflected in this act?

Ans.

(a) The landing and taking off of the airplanes causes lot of noise pollution which may lead to deafness, high blood pressure and other health problems.

(b) The other two places where there is noise pollution is, residing near the heavy traffic routes and railway stations or lines.

(c) Sumit shows participating citizen and moral responsibility values.

15. Explain why solids have fixed shape but liquids and gases do not have fixed shape. Liquids and gases can be compressed but it is difficult to compress solids. Why?

Ans.

Solids have fixed shape due to strong intermolecular force of attraction between them. The liquids and gases have molecules with less intermolecular force of attraction and hence they can flow and take shape of the container.

Liquids and gases have intermolecular space, on applying pressure externally on them the molecules can come closer thereby minimizing the space between them. But in case of solids there is no intermolecular space to do so.

16. A balloon when kept in sun, bursts after some time. Why?

Ans.

The balloon has air filled in it. The balloon when kept in sun gets heated and the air inside it also gets heated. The molecules of air get energy, and vibrate faster thereby exerting large force on the walls of the balloon. Due to this expansion of gases the balloon bursts.

17. On a hot sunny day, why do people sprinkle water on the roof or open ground?

Ans.

During hot sunny day, the surface of roof or ground absorbs large amount of heat and remains hot, on sprinkling water on these surfaces, the water absorbs large amount of heat from the surface due to its large latent heat of vaporisation thereby allowing the hot surface to cool.

18. On a hot sunny day why do we feel pleasant sitting under a tree?

Ans.

Tree has lot of leaves which constantly show transpiration. Transpiration is the loss of water through small tiny pores of leaves called stomata. When this water comes on the surface of leaf the water evaporates thereby causing cooling effect. Therefore we feel pleasant sitting under the tree on a hot sunny day.

19. Adil parked his bicycle on a sunny day in a parking stand of his school campus. When the school got over Adil saw his cycle tyre burst. Thereafter he kept less air in his cycle tyres and did not inflate them fully.

(a) Why did the tyre burst?
(b) Why is air compressible?
(c) What value of Adil is reflected in the above act?

Ans.
(a) The tyre burst because the air inside the tyre got heated and therefore exerted pressure on the walls of the tyre.
(b) Air is compressible because it has large intermolecular space.
(c) Adil showed the value of intelligence, awareness and self responsibility.

20. Akshay's friend visited his house in Mumbai and he was surprised to see air conditioners installed in all of his rooms. His friend advised Akshay to use water-coolers and save electricity. On this Akshay told him, that the water-cooler is not at all effective in coastal areas.
(a) Why are water-coolers not effective in coastal areas?
(b) What are the other two factors on which evaporation of water depends?
(c) What value of Akshay's friend is seen in this act?

Ans.
(a) Water coolers are not effective in coastal areas due to high rate of humidity.
(b) The other two factors on which evaporation of water depends are temperature and surface area.
(c) Akshay's friend showed the value of concerned citizen, morally responsible and friendly in nature.

21. Sita lived in a village and could, not afford refrigerator in her house. She knew how to keep water cold and preserve all perishable items in her house. She kept wet cloth surrounding the earthen pot to keep water cool, she also kept vegetables fresh by keeping them in wet gunny bag and timely sprinkled water over it.
(a) Why did Sita keep wet cloth surrounding the earthen pot?
(b) Suggest one more method of keeping the house cool in summer.
(c) What value of Sita is reflected in the above case?

Ans.
(a) The wet cloth gave the cooling effect to the pot, as the water in the cloth evaporated and evaporation causes cooling effect.
(b) By sprinkling some water on the lawn/veranda of the house can keep the house cool.
(c) Sita showed the value of responsible behaviour.

22. Anil's sister accidentally added some water into the bottle containing olive oil and she was afraid of the scolding. Anil helped his sister and separated the water from olive oil using bottle as separating funnel.
(a) What is the principle of using and working of separating funnel?
(b) Suggest two separation techniques used to separate liquid mixtures.
(c) What value of Anil is seen in the above case?

Ans.
(a) The principle of separating funnel is difference in the densities of two liquids.
(b) Liquid mixtures can be separated by distillation and fractional distillation.
(c) Anil showed the value of helping, caring and responsible behaviour.

23. Preeti saw a labour entering into the sewage manhole immediately after removing the lid. She promptly stopped the labour from entering into the manhole and told him to wait for some time before he enters into it.
(a) What will happen if the labour immediately enters into the manhole for cleaning) after removing the lid?
(b) Name main gases that are released from the manhole.
(c) What value of Preeti is seen in the above act?

Ans.
(a) If the labour immediately enters the manhole on removing its lid he would die due to suffocation and inhalation of

Achievers' Section

poisonous gases which are compressed and released by sewage.

(b) Gases released from the sewage manhole are methane, carbon dioxide and hydrogen sulphide.

(c) Preeti shows the value of moral responsible behaviour and aware citizen.

24. Prasanna wanted to buy a deodorant from the shop. While buying a bottle he felt that it was slightly heavier than usual deodorant bottle that he purchased everytime. He read the weight mentioned on the bottle and told the shopkeeper to weigh the same. He found the bottle was heavy and on opening the deodorant bottle he found it half-filled with water. He complained the matter to the consumer authority.

(a) Define density.

(b) Apart from water what is the other substance that some shopkeepers add into the deodorant.

(c) What value of Prasanna is reflected in this act?

Ans.

(a) Density of any substance is defined to be the mass of the substance per unit volume.

(b) One can add some cheap gases or compressed air in the deodorant bottles.

(c) Prasanna showed the value of being having leadership quality, rightful, aware and responsible citizen.

25. Rita's father always got his vehicle checked for pollution control. He got it tested for the aerosol if released by his car. He also uses unleaded petrol and makes use of public transport wherever possible. He sparingly use his car.

(a) What is aerosol?

(b) What happens when smoke released from vehicle mixes with fog?

(c) What are the values of Rita's father is reflected here?

Ans.

(a) When the solid or liquid is dispersed in a gas it is called aerosol e.g. smoke.

(b) When smoke mixes with fog it forms smog.

(c) Rita's father is an aware citizen, environmentally concerned and dutiful.

26. Many medicinal plants every year are getting extinct. A group of students who had gone for educational trip clicked photographs of endangered plants. These photograph were used by the school laboratory to study these plants.

(a) Name two endangered plants.

(b) Name any one medicinal plant and give its medicinal use.

(c) What value of students is reflected in the above act?

Ans.

(a) Two endangered plants are:
 (i) Euphrasia
 (ii) Ubnus rubra

(b) Aloe-vera. Juice of Aloe-vera is used in case of indigestion, treating dkin infection etc.

(c) Students are caring citizens, shows responsible behaviour.

27. Due to global warming coral is getting diminished in all the oceans/water bodies. People in Lakshadweep island protects their corals by not allowing people/tourist to scape take few pieces away.

(a) Name the phylum of coral.

(b) What is coral made up of.

(c) What values of people in Lakshadweep island is reflected?

Ans.

(a) Phylum of coral is coelenterata.

(b) Coral is made up of calcium carbonate.

(c) People in Lakshadweep island reflect the value of-being-responsible (Citizen, respecting environment and nature.

28. Sudha's brother who is 5 years old had high fever for two days, doctor prescribes him antibiotics. Sudha hesitantly asks for the name of the disease his brother had and why was he advised to take antibiotics without any diagnosis?

(a) Is fever a disease?
(b) What is the role of antibiotics?
(c) What value of Sudha is reflected in the above act?

Ans.
(a) Fever is not a disease it is a symptom.
(b) Antibiotics are medicines advised to be taken only when the immune system of a patient is unable to fight against the microbes.
(c) Sudha showed moral responsibility, general awareness.

29. Malaria was on the outbreak in a locality of a town. People thought that the bite of mosquitoes cause malaria and started killing mosquitoes. Anita told the masses to clean the breeding grounds of mosquitoes, to add oil on the water bodies and clean all the areas, where stagnant water was present.
    (a) What is the cause of malaria?
    (b) Give two ways to prevent it.
    (c) What value of Anita is reflected in this act?

Ans.
(a) Malaria is caused due to the protozoa named Plasmodium.
(b) Two ways to prevent malaria are:
    (i) Clear all breeding grounds of mosquitoes i.e., stagnant water.
    (ii) Use mosquito repellents.
(c) Anita showed the values of social responsibility and self-awareness.

30. (i) Sheela saw blue-green algae forming bloom in the village pond.
    (ii) Fish, which were previously abundant wwer no where to be seen.
    (iii) The pond started giving stink. Water of the pond is not even fit for cattle. Some of the cattle who were taken to the pond for drinking and bathing have fallen sick.
    (iv) What explanation will Sheela give for this to the villagers?

Ans.
(i) Bloom forming algae occur in a pond only when the quality of pond water has deteriorated due to pollution. Blue-green algae secrete toxins that are harmful to animals and humans,
(ii) Fish must have died due to deficiency of oxygen in pond water. Oxygen deficiency occurs when there is excess of organic matter (organic loading). The aerobic decomposers consume the dissolved oxygen. This is followed by anaerobic decomposition of organic matter. It produces sulphides and other sludge producing substances. Blue-green algae can grow under such circumstances.
(iii) Stink comes from anaerobic breakdown products of organic matter. The toxins released by blue-green algae further deteriorate the quality of water causing sickness and skin rashes in animals and humans.
(iv) Sheela could explain to the villagers that deterioration of pond has been due to excess fertilizers used by them in their fields. Rain wash brought these fertilizers into the pond. There was initial spurt in the growth of plants due to this. The phenomenon is called eutrophication. Excess plant matter slowly caused organic loading of water that reduced its oxygen content, killing the fish and other aquatic animals. So fertilizers should be used very judiciously in the fields.

Model Test Paper 1

1. Gravity is related to Pull in the same way as Magnetism is related to _____.
   (a) Repulsion
   (b) Separation
   (c) Attraction
   (d) Push

2. Choose correct mirror-image of the Fig. (X) from amongst the four alternatives (a), (b), (c) and (d) given along with it. The miror may be represented by a line MN or M_1M_2.

   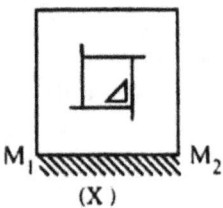 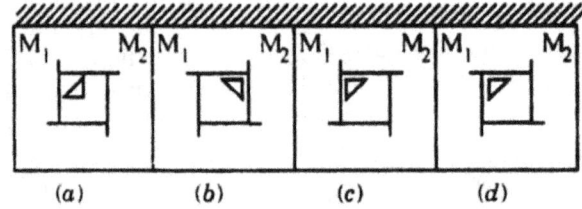

3. In the given problem figure, a square transparent sheet with a pattern is given. Figure out from amongst the four alternatives as to how the pattern could appear when the transparent sheet is folded at the dotted line.

   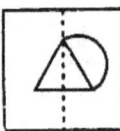 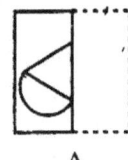 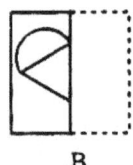 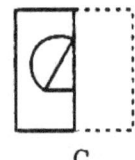 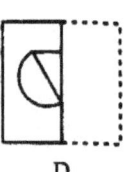

   A   B   C   D

4. The figures X, Y and Z are showing sequence of folding of a piece of paper and Fig. (Z) shows the manner in which the folded paper has been cut. There three figures are followed by four answer figures from which you have to choose a figure which would most closely resemble the unfolded form of fig (Z).

    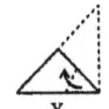 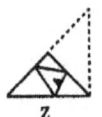
   X   Y   Z

   A   B   C   D

5. A man is facing south. He turns 135° in anti clockwise direction and then 180° in clockwise direction. Which direction is he facing now?
   (a) North-East
   (b) North-West
   (c) South-East
   (d) South-West

6. One morning after sunrise, Raghav was standing facing a pole. The shadow of the pole fell exactly to his right. Which direction was he facing?
   (a) South
   (b) East
   (c) West
   (d) Data inadequate

7. Pointing to a man on the stage, Shaly said, "He is the brother of the daughter of the wife of my husband." How is the man on the stage related to Shaly?
   (a) Son   (b) Husband
   (c) Cousin   (d) Nephew

Direction (8-10): Study the information given below and answer the questions that follow:
'A + B' means 'A is the daughter of B'
'A − B' means 'A is the husband of B'
'A × B' means 'A is the brother of B'

8. If A + B − C, which of the following is true?
   (a) C is the mother of A
   (b) C is the sister-in-law of A
   (c) C is the aunt of A
   (d) C is the mother-in-law of A

9. If A × B + C, which of the following is true?
   (a) A is the brother of C
   (b) A is the uncle of C
   (c) A is the son of C
   (d) A is the father of C

10. If A + B × C, which of the following is true?
    (a) A is the niece of C
    (b) A is the daughter of C
    (c) A is the cousin of C
    (d) A is the daughter-in-law of C

11. The numerical ratio of displacement to distance for a moving object is ———.
    (a) Always less than 1
    (b) Always greater than 1
    (c) Equal to 1 or greater than 1
    (d) Equal to 1 or less than 1

12. A car of mass 1000 kg is moving with a velocity of 10 ms⁻¹. If the velocity-time graph for this car is a horizontal line parallel to the time axis, then the velocity of car at the end of 25s will be ———.
    (a) 250 ms⁻¹   (b) 10 ms⁻¹
    (c) 250 ms⁻¹   (d) 400 ms⁻¹

13. Which would require a greater force − accelerating at 10 g ball at 5 m/s² a 20 g ball at 2m/s²?
    (a) 10 g ball
    (b) 20 g ball
    (c) both requires equal force
    (d) none of these

14. A fielder pulls his hands backwards after catching the cricket ball. This enables the fielder to ———.
    (a) Exert larger force on the ball
    (b) Reduce the force exerted by the ball
    (c) Increase the rate of change of momentum
    (d) Keep the ball in hands firmly

15. An object is thrown vertically upwards with a velocity u, the greatest height h to which it will rise before falling back is given by ———.
    (a) $\dfrac{u^2}{2g}$ (b) $\dfrac{u}{g}$
    (c) $\dfrac{2u}{g^2}$ (d) $\dfrac{u}{2g}$

16. The gravitational force of attraction between two objects is x, keeping the masses of the objects unchanged, if the distance between the objects is halved, then the magnitude of gravitational force between them will become ———.
    (a) $\dfrac{x}{4}$ (b) $\dfrac{x}{2}$
    (c) $2x$ (d) $4x$

17. The momentum of a bullet of mass 20 g fired from a gun is 10 kg ms⁻¹. The kinetic energy of this bullet in kJ will be ———.
    (a) 1.5   (b) 1.75
    (c) 2.5   (d) 25

18. A stone is thrown upwards as shown in the diagram. When it reaches P, which of the following has the greatest value for the stone?

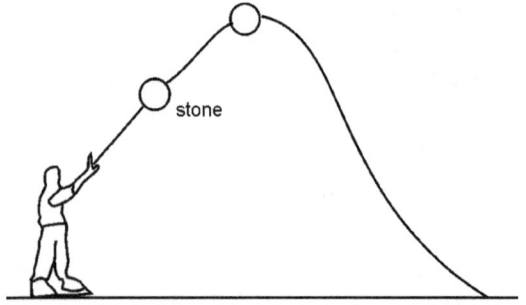

(a) Its acceleration
(b) Its potential energy
(c) Its kinetic energy
(d) Its weight

19. Which one of the following does not consist of transverse waves?
    (a) Light of a CFL
    (b) TV signals from a satellite
    (c) Ripples on the surface of a pond
    (d) Musical notes of an orchestra

20. Which of the following frequency of sound can be generated by a vibrating simple pendulum as well as by the vibrating vocal cords of a rhinoceros?
    (a) 5 kHz   (b) 25 Hz
    (c) 10 Hz   (d) 15 kHz

21. The Kelvin temperature for 373°C is _____.
    (a) 373 K   (b) 646 K
    (c) 298 K   (d) 479 K

22. When heat is constantly supplied by a gas burner with small flame to melt ice, then the temperature of ice during melting _____.
    (a) Does not increase at all
    (b) Increases very slowly
    (c) Increases to form liquid water
    (d) First remains constant and then increases

23. In which of the following conditions, the distance between the molecules of hydrogen gas would increase?
    (i) Increasing pressure on hydrogen contained in a closed container
    (ii) Some hydrogen gas leaking out of the container
    (iii) Increasing the volume of the container of hydrogen gas
    (iv) Adding more hydrogen gas to the container without increasing the volume of the container
    (a) (i) and (ii)
    (b) (ii) and (iii)
    (c) (iii) and (iv)
    (d) (i) and (iv)

24. A solution is prepared by dissolving 80 g of salt in 500 g of water. Find the concentration of the solution.
    (a) 14.2%   (b) 13.8%
    (c) 12.6%   (d) 10%

25. Glowing of an electric bulb and breaking of a glass tumbler, making a solution are the examples of _____.
    (a) physical changes
    (b) chemical changes
    (c) both of these
    (d) none of these

26. One of the following does not undergo sublimation. This one is _____.
    (a) iodine   (b) dry ice
    (c) camphor   (d) silica

27. The molecular mass of sulphuric acid (H_2SO_4) will be _____.
    (a) 49 u   (b) 98 u
    (c) 32 u   (d) 64 u

28. Find the number of moles in 128 g of oxygen molecules _____.
    (a) 4   (b) 8
    (c) 12   (d) 16

29. An element E has a valency of 4. What will be the formula of its chloride?
    (a) E Cl   (b) E Cl_2
    (c) E Cl_4 (d) E_4 Cl

30. Calculate atomic number of an element whose atomic nucleus has mass number 23 and neutron number 12.
    (a) 35   (b) 23
    (c) 12   (d) 11

31. There are two species represented as ^{35}Cl and ^{37}Cl. Which of the following statements is correct regarding these species?
    (a) They have the same number of protons
    (b) They have different chemical properties
    (c) Their physical properties are the same
    (d) They are isobars of the same element
32. The e/m for proton depends on which one of the following?
    (a) Cathode
    (b) Anode
    (c) Potential of electricity
    (d) Nature of gas taken in discharge tube
33. Red wood tree of California reaches a height of ———.
    (a) 100 m (b) 75 m
    (c) 50 m   (d) 25 m
34. 'Taxa' differs from 'taxon' due to ———.
    (a) This being the lower taxonomic category than taxon
    (b) This being the higher taxonomic category than taxon
    (c) This being the singular of taxon
    (d) This being the plural of taxon
35. Which one is an acute disease?
    (a) Hypertension   (b) Typhoid
    (c) Tuberculosis   (d) Diabetes
36. Health deals with ———.
    (a) Mental fitness
    (b) Physical fitness
    (c) Social well being
    (d) All of these
37. Rinderpest disease of poultry is caused by ———.
    (a) Virus   (b) Bacteria
    (c) Insects (d) Protozoa
38. Which of the following is the high milk yielding variety of cow?
    (a) Dorset   (b) Holstein
    (c) Red sindhi (d) Sahiwal
39. Human cheek cells are commonly stained with ———.
    (a) Acetocarmine
    (b) Methylene blue
    (c) Eosine
    (d) Safranin
40. Coverslip is put on the mounted material on a slide very gently to ———.
    (a) Avoid oozing of stain
    (b) Avoid the crushing of mounted material
    (c) Avoid the entry of air bubble
    (d) Avoid oozing of glycerine
41. Contractile vacuoles take part in ———.
    (a) Osmoregulation
    (b) Excretion
    (c) Absoption of water from outside
    (d) Both (a) and (b)
42. Permanent tissue differs from meristematic tissue in ———.
    (a) Performing a distinct function
    (b) Inability to divide
    (c) Attainment of definite shape and size
    (d) All of these
43. Cartilage is not found in ———.
    (a) Nose   (b) Ear
    (c) Kidney (d) Larynx
44. The ozone layer of the atmosphere blocks ———.
    (a) UV radiation
    (b) Sunlight
    (c) Infrared radiations
    (d) Both UV and infrared radiation
45. Air is ———.
    (a) Good conductor of heat
    (b) Bad conductor of heat
    (c) Neither good or bad conductor of heat
    (d) Sometimes good and sometimes bad conductor of heat

Model Test Paper

46. The quantity of matter present in an object is called its ———.
    (a) Density
    (b) Mass
    (c) Vapour pressure
    (d) Volume

47. Match the column I (symbols of different elements) with column II (atomic mass of different elements) and choose the correct option.

Column I	Column II
(A) Na	(i) 12u
(B) C	(ii) 27u
(C) Al	(iii) 23u

    (a) (A)-(iii), (B)-(i), (C)-(ii)
    (b) (A)-(ii), (B)-(iii), (C)-(i)
    (c) (A)-(i), (B)-(ii), (C)-(iii)
    (d) (A)-(ii), (B)-(i), (C)-(iii)

Direction (48 – 50): Fill in the blanks with the correct option.

48. Atomic number of an element is the number of _____ in one atom.
    (a) Molecules
    (b) Valence electrons
    (c) Protons
    (d) None of these

49. Atoms of the same element having the same _____ but different _____.
    (a) Atomic number, mass number
    (b) Mass number, atomic number
    (c) Valency, atomic number
    (d) Atomic number, valency

50. The _____ present in the outermost shell of an atom are known as valency of the atom.
    (a) Electrons
    (b) Protons
    (c) Molecules
    (d) None of these

Model Test Paper 2

1. If the sum of four consecutive odd numbers is 40, the smallest number is _____
   (a) 7
   (b) 9
   (c) 11
   (d) 13

2. In the given figure, ABCD is a parallelogram. $DL \perp AB$ and $DM \perp BC$.

   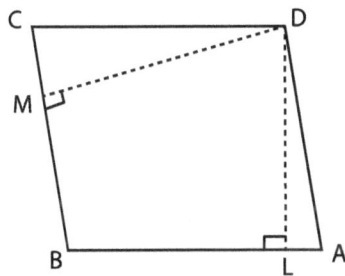

   If $AB = 18$ cm, $BC = 12$ cm and $DM = 10$ cm. Find DL.
   (a) 6 ½
   (b) 6 cm
   (c) 6 cm
   (d) None of these

3. Given that $4^{n+1} = 256$, find the value of n.
   (a) 2
   (b) 3
   (c) 5
   (d) 63

4. In the given figure, $AB \parallel CD$. Find the value of x.
   (a) 110°
   (b) 120°
   (c) 130°
   (d) 140°

5. The mean of 8 numbers is 25. If 5 is subtracted from each number, what will be the new mean?
   (a) 10
   (b) 20
   (c) 30
   (d) 40

6. In an examination, 96% of the candidates passed and 50 failed. How many candidates appeared in the examination?
   (a) 1240
   (b) 1250
   (c) 1260
   (d) 1270

7. In the given question, three classes are given. Out of the four figures that follow, you are to indicate which figure will best represent the relationship amongst the three classes.

   "Boys, Students, Athletes"

   (a)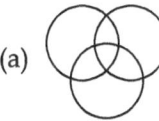
   (b)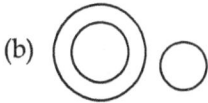
   (c)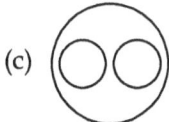
   (d)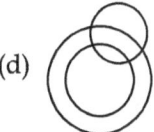

8. Thirty six vehicles are parked in a parking lot in a single row. After the first car, there is one scooter. After the second car, there are two scooters. After the third car, there are three scooters and so on. Then the number of scooters in the second half of the row, is _____
   (a) 16
   (b) 14
   (c) 15
   (d) 13

9. Find the missing number in the given figure.

   (a) 10
   (b) 11
   (c) 12
   (d) 13

10. Count the number of triangles and squares in the given figure.

    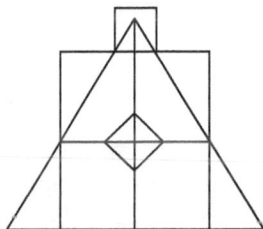

    (a) 21 triangles, 7 squares
    (b) 18 triangles, 8 squares
    (c) 20 triangles, 8 squares
    (d) 22 triangles, 7 squares

11. Find the next term in the series:
    BMO, EOQ, HQS, ?
    (a) KSU   (b) LMN
    (c) SOV   (d) SOW

12. How many L's are there which do not have R preceding them and also do not have T following them?
    Z Q S T L R M N Q N R T U V X R L T A S L T Q R S L T
    (a) 1   (b) 2
    (c) 3   (d) 4

13. Eleven students A, B, C, D, E, F, G, H, I, J and K are sitting in the first line facing the teacher. D who is just to the left of F, is to the right of C at second place. A is second to the right of E who is at one end. J is the nearest neighbour of A and B and is to the left of G at third place. H is next to D to the right and is at the third place to the right of I. Who is just in the middle?
    (a) I   (b) B
    (c) J   (d) G

14. A new museum has two circular display rooms. The radius of the large circular room is 6 yards. The radius of the smaller circular room is 3 yards. What is the area of the smaller room in relation to the area of the large room?
    (a) 1/6 of the large room's area
    (b) 1/4 of the large room's area
    (c) 1/3 of the large room's area
    (d) 1/2 of the large room's area

15. If RAB = 36 and MEC = 195, then REG = _____.
    (a) 240   (b) 160
    (c) 40   (d) 630

16. Two bodies of equal masses (m) moving with equal velocities (v) in opposite directions collide. The resultant velocity of the combination is
    (a) v   (b) 2v
    (c) –v   (d) Zero

17. Which of the following distance time graphs does not represent a real situation?

    (a)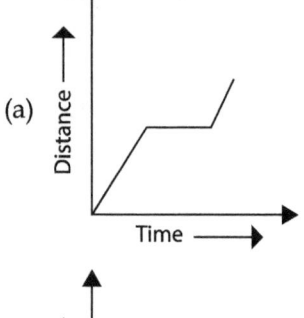

    (b)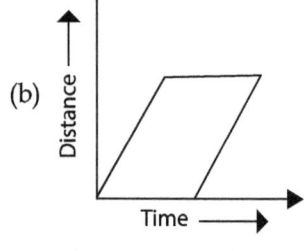

    (c)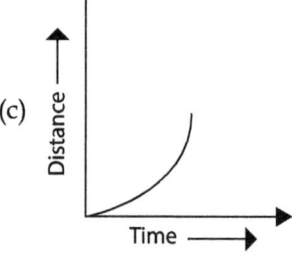

    (d)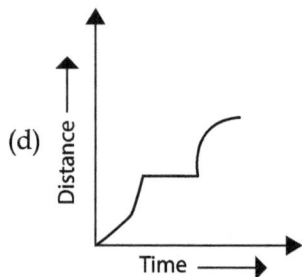

18. Which of the following is not an effect of inertia?
    (a) A person in a bus tends to fall backwards, when it starts suddenly.
    (b) When a tree is shaken vigorously, some of its leaves fall down.
    (c) A gun recoils back, when a bullet is fired from it.
    (d) None of these

19. A car and a motor cycle are moving with the same momentum. When equal retarding forces are applied, the car comes to halt in t_1 seconds and the motor cycle in t_2 seconds. If the mass of the car is five times more than the mass of the motor cycle, then _____
    (a) $t_1 = t_2$
    (b) $t_1 = 1/5 t_2$
    (c) $t_1 = t_2$
    (d) $t_1 = 25 t_2$

20. Read the given statements and choose the correct option.
    Statement 1: Acceleration due to gravity at a place on earth remains constant for all objects.
    Statement 2: Acceleration due to gravity doesn't depend on the mass of the object, but only on mass of earth.
    (a) Both statement 1 and statement 2 are true and statement 2 is correct explanation of statement 1.
    (b) Both statement 1 and statement 2 are true, but statement 2 is not correct explanation of statement 1.
    (c) Statement 1 is true but statement 2 is false.
    (d) Statement 1 is false but statement 2 is true.

21. Read the given statements and choose the correct option.
    Statement 1: There can be displacement of an object even in the absence of any force acting on it.
    Statement 2: An object in uniform motion in a straight line shows displacement even when the net force acting on it is zero.
    (a) Both statement 1 and statement 2 are true and statement 2 is correct explanation of statement 1.
    (b) Both statement 1 and statement 2 are true, but statement 2 is not correct explanation of statement 1.
    (c) Statement 1 is true but statement 2 is false.
    (d) Statement 1 is false but statement 2 is true.

Direction: Read the passage carefully and answer question numbers 22 and 23.
The relative density of a solid with respect to a liquid is 4/5 and relative density of the liquid with respect to water is 10/9. The buoyant force exerted by a liquid on a solid immersed in it is equal to the weight of the liquid displaced by the solid.

22. Specific gravity of solid with respect to water is
    (a) 18/25
    (b) 8/9
    (c) 0.56
    (d) 1.8

23. When 4 kg of this solid is immersed in water, the buoyant force experienced by it is (given g = 9.8 m s^{-2})
    (a) 4.5 g
    (b) 4 g
    (c) 5 g
    (d) 10 g

24. Match the following:

Column I	Column II
1. Paraffin wax	(p) Domestic fuel
2. Petrol	(q) Used for manufacturing steel
3. LPG	(r) Candles
4. Coke	(s) Aviation fuel

    (a) 1 – (p); 2 – (q); 3 – (r); 4 – (s)
    (b) 1 – (q); 2 – (p); 3 – (r); 4 – (s)
    (c) 1 – (s); 2 – (r); 3 – (p); 4 – (q)
    (d) 1 – (r); 2 – (s); 3 – (p); 4 – (q)

25. A spoon was kept in contact with ice cubes for some time. Later, the same spoon was held over the flame of a small candle. The figure shows the observation. What do you infer from the given figure?
    (a) Spoon is an inflammable substance.
    (b) Burning of candle is a spontaneous process.
    (c) CO_2 is a product of combustion.
    (d) Water vapour is a product of combustion.

26. Identify the incorrect statement from the given definitions of solids, liquids and gases in terms of melting and boiling points.
    (a) A substance is said to be in solid state if under normal pressure, its melting point is above the room temperature.
    (b) A substance is said to be in liquid state if under normal pressure, its melting point is below the room temperature.
    (c) A substance is said to be in gaseous state if under normal pressure, its boiling point is below the room temperature.
    (d) A substance can exist in solid, liquid and gaseous state under normal pressure and room temperature.

27. Membrane biogenesis is associated with which of the following cell organelles?

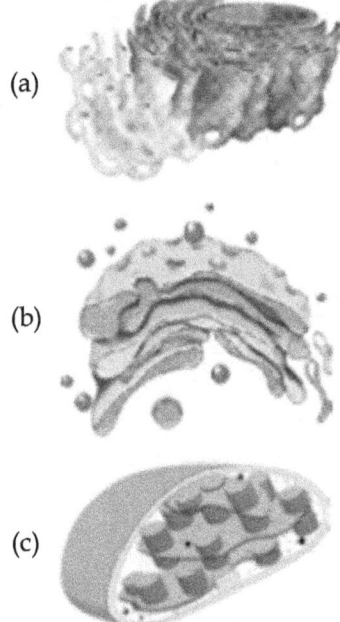

(a)

(b)

(c)

(d) Both (a) and (b)

28. Several microorganisms cause diseases in plants and reduce their yield. Which of the following plant diseases is incorrectly matched with its causal microorganism?
    (a) Citrus canker   Bacteria
    (b) Tobacco mosaic   Virus
    (c) Rust of wheat   Fungi
    (d) Yellow vein mosaic of bhindi   Bacteria

29. _____ was the first one to observe free living cells. The term cell was given by _____. Cell theory was proposed by _____ and _____. All cells arise from preexisting cells was suggested by _____.

    Select the correct sequence of names to complete the above paragraph.
    (a) Robert Hooke, Virchow, Anton Von Leeuwenhoek, Schleiden, Schwann
    (b) Anton Von Leeuwenhoek, Robert Hooke, Schleiden, Schwann, Virchow
    (c) Robert Hooke, Virchow, Schleiden, Schwann, Anton Von Leeuwenhoek
    (d) Anton Von Leeuwenhoek, Virchow, Schleiden, Schwann, Robert Hooke

30. Which of the following diseases is not transmitted by the vector shown in the figure?
    (i) Malaria   (ii) Yellow fever
    (iii) Typhoid   (iv) Sleeping sickness
    (v) Kalaazar
    (a) (ii), (iii) and (iv)   (b) (i), (iii) and (v)
    (c) (i) and (ii)   (d) (iii), (iv) and (v)

31. A __(i)__ is a nonliving, elongated cell with tapering ends. Its walls are highly thickened with __(ii)__ except at certain circular spots known as __(iii)__. A __(iv)__ is a cylindrical tubelike structure placed one above the other end to end. __(v)__ is a nonliving, thick walled cell providing mechanical support.

    Select the correct sequence of words to complete the above paragraph.

	(a)	(b)	(c)	(d)
(i)	Vessel	Tracheid	Vessel	Tracheid
(ii)	Lignin	Suberin	Suberin	Lignin
(iii)	Stoma	Pits	Stoma	Pits
(iv)	Tracheid	Vessel	Tracheid	Vessel
(v)	Xylem fibre	Parenchyma	Sclereid	Xylem fibre

32. Which of the following are threatened wild animals?
    (i) Golden cat   (ii) Pink hued duck
    (iii) Dinosaur   (iv) Dodo
    (v) Passenger pigeon   (vi) White tailed mongoose
    (vii) Gharial   (viii) Marsh crocodile
    (a) (i), (ii), (iv) and (v)
    (b) (v), (vi), (vii) and (viii)
    (c) (ii), (iv), (vi) and (vii)
    (d) (i), (ii), (vii) and (viii)

Direction: Refer the given experiment and answer Q. nos. 33 and 34.

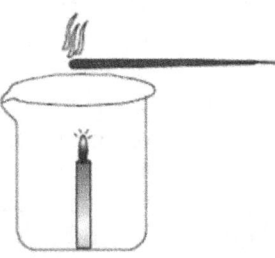

Place a candle in a beaker or a widemouthed bottle and light it. Light an incense stick (agarbati) and take it to the mouth of the beaker as shown in figure. Note the way in which the smoke flows when the incense stick is (i) near the edge of the beaker, (ii) kept a little above the candle, and (iii) kept in other regions.

33. In which case, the direction of flow of smoke will be towards the candle first and then upwards?
    (a) (i) (b) (ii)
    (c) (iii) (d) Both (i) and (iii)

34. What does the above experiment show?
    (a) The direction of movement of hot and cold air.
    (b) Oxygen is present in the air and is necessary for burning.
    (c) The temperature of air inside the bottle is more than the temperature of open air.
    (d) The direction in which the maximum smoke is produced & pollutes the environment.

35. This implement is made of wood and is drawn by a pair of bulls or other animals. It contains a strong triangular iron strip called share. The main part of it is a long log of wood which is called a shaft. There is a handle at one end of the shaft. The other end is attached to a beam which is placed on the bulls' necks.

    Which implement are we talking about and for what purpose is it used?
    (a) Plough Tilling the soil
    (b) Hoe Removing the weeds
    (c) Cultivator Sowing the seeds
    (d) Seed drill Tilling the soil

36. In honey bee the drones (males) are produced from
    (a) Unfertilized eggs
    (b) Fertilized eggs
    (c) Larvae from unfertilized eggs, which are fed on royal jelly
    (d) Larvae from unfertilized eggs, which are not cared by the workers at all

37. A sonic 'tape measure' is used to measure the length of a room. It measures a time interval of 0.06 s between transmitting a sound pulse and receiving the echo. The speed of sound in air is 330 m/s. How far is the reflecting wall from the tape measure?
    (a) 5.5 m (b) 9.9 m
    (c) 11 m (d) 20 m

38. A person exerts a horizontal force of 500 N on a box, which also experiences a frictional force of 100 N. How much work is done against friction when the box moves a horizontal distance of 3 m?

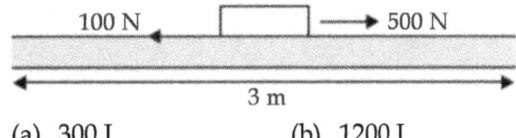

    (a) 300 J (b) 1200 J
    (c) 1500 J (d) 1800 J

39. Thermometer X at 20°C is placed in some water at 50°C in beaker Y. After some time, thermometer X will show a maximum temperature of _____.

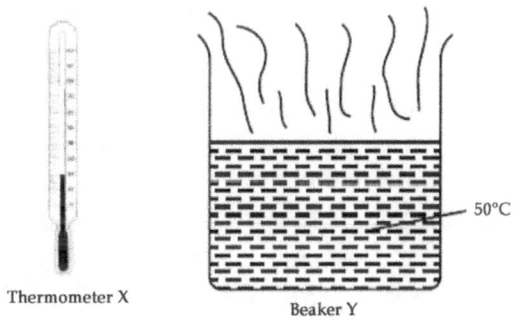

    (a) 20°C (b) 35°C
    (c) 50°C (d) 30°C

40. The experiment given below shows that light _____.

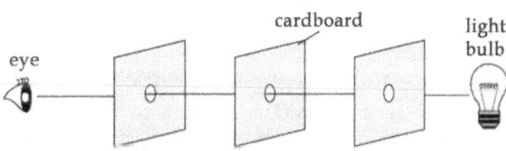

    (a) Can be reflected
    (b) Is a form of energy
    (c) Travels in straight line
    (d) Can pass through all objects

41. When we remove polyester or woolen cloth in dark, we can see sparks and hear a cracking sound. These are due to _____.
    (a) Static electricity
    (b) Current electricity
    (c) Reflection of light
    (d) Refraction of light

42. A car starts from rest and is uniformly accelerated to a speed of 30 m/s in 6 s. What is the distance travelled by the car?
    (a) 5 m   (b) 30 m
    (c) 90 m   (d) 180 m

43. A crane uses a petrol engine to lift a heavy girder. What is the overall energy conversion in the system when the girder is moving at a steady rate?
    (a) Chemical into kinetic
    (b) Chemical into potential
    (c) Kinetic into potential
    (d) Potential into kinetic

44. Solids cannot be compressed because _____.
    (a) The constituent particles are closely packed
    (b) The movement of the constituent particles is restricted
    (c) The intermolecular attractive forces are very strong
    (d) None of these

45. X and Y are miscible liquids. Boiling point of X is 56°C and that of Y is 100°C. Which separation technique can be used to separate X and Y from the mixture?
    (a) Separating funnel
    (b) Distillation
    (c) Evaporation
    (d) Condensation

46. The solubility of potassium chloride at 20°C is 34.7 g in 100 g of water. The density of the solution is 1.3 g mL^{-1}. What is the w/V percentage of potassium chloride in the solution?
    (a) 25.76   (b) 32.98
    (c) 33.49   (d) 22.56

47. What will be the number of aluminium ions in 0.051 g of aluminium oxide?
    (a) 5.0×10^{-4} ions   (b) 6.0×10^{23} ions
    (c) 12×10^{23} ions   (d) 6.0×10^{20} ions

48. An ion M^{2+} contains 10 electrons and 12 neutrons. What is the atomic number and mass number of element M?
    (a) 10, 24   (b) 10, 22
    (c) 12, 24   (d) 12, 22

49. Microorganisms are our friends and foes. Some of them are useful for us while some of them are harmful. From the given list sort out useful and harmful actions of microorganisms. Production of antibiotics, food spoiling, curd preparation, vaccine production, citrus canker.
    (a) Useful: Curd preparation, citrus canker, production of antibiotics.
        Harmful: Food spoiling, vaccine production.
    (b) Useful: Production of antibiotics, curd preparation, vaccine production.
        Harmful: Food spoiling, citrus canker.
    (c) Useful: Citrus canker, vaccine production, curd preparation.
        Harmful: Food spoiling, production of antibiotics
    (d) Useful: Vaccine production, curd preparation.
        Harmful: Food spoiling, citrus canker, production of antibiotics.

50. A layer of air known as the atmosphere surrounds the earth. The composition of the atmosphere can be changed by air pollution. Which of the following statements about air pollution are correct?
    (i) It affects the weather.
    (ii) It covers the leaves of plants and limits photosynthesis.
    (iii) It may cause breathing difficulties and diseases of the respiratory tract.
    (iv) It is mostly caused by the burning of fossil fuels.
    (a) (iii) & (iv)   (b) (i), (ii) & (iii)
    (c) (i), (iii) & (iv)   (d) (i), (ii), (iii) & (iv)

Answer Keys

Scan the QR Code to see the Hints and Solutions

Access Content Online on Dropbox: https://www.dropbox.com/scl/fi/x1il8nzpuzwm1qyz8yycu/NSO-01-Science-Olympiad-Hints-and-Solutions.pdf?rlkey=kzkx1753ie7dfs4rlkt3yo4pa&dl=0

SECTION 1: SCIENCE

1. MOTION

Answer Key

1. (a)	2. (b)	3. (c)	4. (a)	5. (b)	6. (d)	7. (c)	8. (d)	9. (b)	10. (c)
11. (a)	12. (c)	13. (b)	14. (b)	15. (d)	16. (a)	17. (a)	18. (b)	19. (c)	20. (b)
21. (a)	22. (b)	23. (b)	24. (b)	25. (c)	26. (a)	27. (c)	28. (c)	29. (b)	30. (d)

HOTS

1. (d)	2. (c)	3. (c)	4. (a)	5. (b)	6. (b)	7. (c)	8. (a)	9. (d)	10. (a)

2. FORCE AND LAWS OF MOTION

Answer Key

1. (b)	2. (d)	3. (a)	4. (c)	5. (c)	6. (c)	7. (a)	8. (b)	9. (a)	10. (c)
11. (c)	12. (d)	13. (b)	14. (c)	15. (a)	16. (b)	17. (a)	18. (d)	19. (d)	20. (c)
21. (a)	22. (c)	23. (d)	24. (c)	25. (a)	26. (c)	27. (b)	28. (c)	29. (b)	30. (a)

HOTS

1. (b)	2. (a)	3. (b)	4. (a)	5. (a)					

3. GRAVITATION

Answer Key

1. (b)	2. (b)	3. (a)	4. (c)	5. (d)	6. (a)	7. (a)	8. (b)	9. (d)	10. (b)
11. (c)	12. (a)	13. (b)	14. (c)	15. (b)	16. (a)	17. (d)	18. (d)	19. (a)	20. (c)
21. (b)	22. (c)	23. (c)	24. (c)	25. (b)	26. (c)	27. (a)	28. (b)	29. (c)	30. (d)

HOTS

1. (b)	2.(c)	3. (b)	4. (b)	5. (c)				

4. WORK AND ENERGY

Answer Key

1. (b)	2. (b)	3. (a)	4.(a)	5. (c)	6. (b)	7. (a)	8. (c)	9. (b)	10. (a)
11. (c)	12. (b)	13. (a)	14. (d)	15. (d)	16. (c)	17. (a)	18. (d)	19. (d)	20. (b)
21. (a)	22. (d)	23. (b)	24. (c)	25. (c)	26. (c)	27. (b)	28. (c)	29. (d)	30. (b)

HOTS

1. (b)	2. (b)	3. (d)	4. (c)	5. (a)				

5. SOUND

Answer Key

1. (b)	2. (b)	3. (c)	4. (b)	5. (c)	6. (b)	7.(b)	8 (a)	9. (a)	10. (c)
11. (d)	12. (b)	13. (a)	14. (b)	15. (a)	16. (c)	17. (a)	18. (a)	19. (b)	20. (a)
21. (c)	22. (a)	23. (d)	24. (a)	25. (b)					

HOTS

1. (c)	2. (a)	3. (c)	4. (d)	5. (b)	6. (a)	7. (a)	8. (c)	9. (a)	10. (d)

6. MATTER IN OUR SURROUNDINGS

Answer Key

1. (a)	2. (b)	3. (a)	4. (b)	5. (b)	6.(a)	7. (d)	8. (b)	9. (d)	10. (a)
11. (c)	12. (b)	13. (b)	14. (b)	15. (a)	16. (a)	17. (d)	18. (b)	19. (b)	20. (b)
21. (b)	22. (c)	23. (a)	24. (d)	25. (c)	26. (a)	27. (c)	28. (b)	29. (b)	30. (b)

HOTS

1. (b)	2. (b)	3. (c)	4. (a)	5. (d)				

7. IS MATTER AROUND US PURE

Answer Key

1. (b)	2. (b)	3. (a)	4. (c)	5. (b)	6. (c)	7. (b)	8. (b)	9. (b)	10. (b)
11. (c)	12. (a)	13. (a)	14. (c)	15. (d)	16. (a)	17. (b)	18. (a)	19. (c)	20. (b)
21. (a)	22. (d)	23. (a)	24. (b)	25. (d)	26. (b)	27. (a)	28. (c)	29. (d)	30. (a)
31. (a)	32. (d)	33. (a)	34. (c)	35. (b)					

HOTS

1. (c)	2. (c)	3. (b)	4. (d)	5. (c)					

8. ATOMS AND MOLECULES

Answer Key

1. (b)	2. (c)	3. (a)	4. (b)	5. (c)	6. (b)	7. (c)	8. (d)	9. (b)	10. (d)
11. (b)	12. (d)	13. (a)	14. (c)	15. (b)	16. (a)	17. (b)	18. (b)	19. (a)	20. (b)
21. (c)	22. (b)	23. (b)	24. (b)	25. (c)	26. (a)	27. (b)	28. (d)	29. (c)	30. (a)
31. (a)	32. (b)	33. (c)	34. (d)	35. (c)					

HOTS

1. (c)	2. (a)	3. (b)	4. (a)	5. (c)					

9. STRUCTURE OF ATOM

Answer Key

1. (b)	2. (b)	3. (d)	4. (d)	5. (c)	6. (c)	7. (d)	8. (c)	9. (c)	10. (b)
11. (b)	12. (b)	13. (a)	14. (a)	15. (d)	16. (b)	17. (b)	18. (d)	19. (d)	20. (b)
21. (c)	22. (a)	23. (c)	24. (a)	25. (b)	26. (d)	27. (c)	28. (b)	29. (a)	30. (b)
31. (a)	32. (c)	33. (a)	34. (c)	35. (a)					

HOTS

1. (c)	2. (b)	3. (b)	4. (c)	5. (a)					

10. CELL –THE FUNDAMENTAL UNIT OF LIFE

Answer Key

1. (c)	2. (b)	3. (a)	4. (a)	5. (c)	6.(a)	7. (c)	8 (b)	9. (b)	10. (b)
11. (c)	12. (a)	13. (d)	14. (a)	15. (d)	16. (d)	17. (a)	18. (c)	19. (b)	20. (c)
21. (b)	22. (c)	23. (c)	24. (d)	25. (c)	26. (c)	27. (b)	28. (c)	29. (a)	30. (d)
31. (a)	32. (b)	33. (b)	34. (d)	35. (b)	36. (b)	37. (c)	38. (d)	39. (a)	40. (d)
41. (b)	42. (a)	43. (a)	44. (b)	45. (c)					

HOTS

| 1. (d) | 2. (b) | 3. (d) | 4. (c) | 5. (b) | 6.(b) | 7. (c) | 8 (b) | 9. (b) | 10. (b) |

11. TISSUES

Answer Key

1. (b)	2. (c)	3. (b)	4. (c)	5. (b)	6.(c)	7. (c)	8. (a)	9. (a)	10. (c)
11. (b)	12. (c)	13. (b)	14. (d)	15. (c)	16. (c)	17. (b)	18. (a)	19. (c)	20. (a)
21. (b)	22. (c)	23. (b)	24. (a)	25. (c)	26. (c)	27. (c)	28. (a)	29. (a)	30. (a)
31. (b)	32. (a)	33. (b)	34. (c)	35. (a)	36. (d)	37. (a)	38. (b)	39. (a)	40. (c)
41. (c)	42. (d)	43. (c)	44. (b)	45. (a)					

HOTS

| 1. (a) | 2. (b) | 3. (b) | 4. (d) | 5. (d) |

12. DIVERSITY IN LIVING ORGANISMS

Answer Key

1. (b)	2. (a)	3. (d)	4. (c)	5. (b)	6. (c)	7. (a)	8. (a)	9. (c)	10. (b)
11. (a)	12. (c)	13. (b)	14. (c)	15. (b)	16. (b)	17. (a)	18. (d)	19. (d)	20. (b)
21. (c)	22. (b)	23. (a)	24. (c)	25. (a)	26. (c)	27. (d)	28. (b)	29. (c)	30. (a)
31. (c)	32. (a)	33. (b)	34. (d)	35. (d)	36. (a)	37. (b)	38. (b)	39. (a)	40. (b)
41. (b)	42. (c)	43. (b)	44. (a)	45. (c)	46. (b)	47. (d)	48. (c)	49. (b)	50. (b)

HOTS

| 1. (b) | 2. (d) | 3. (d) | 4. (d) | 5. (c) |

13. WHY DO WE FALL ILL

Answer Key

1. (d)	2. (b)	3. (a)	4. (b)	5. (c)	6. (d)	7. (d)	8. (a)	9. (b)	10. (b)
11. (c)	12. (b)	13. (a)	14. (d)	15. (a)	16. (c)	17. (b)	18. (a)	19. (b)	20. (c)
21. (b)	22. (a)	23. (c)	24. (d)	25. (b)	26. (d)	27. (b)	28. (c)	29. (d)	30. (b)
31. (c)	32. (b)	33. (c)	34. (b)	35. (c)	36. (b)	37. (c)	38. (a)	39. (a)	40. (d)
41. (b)	42. (d)	43. (b)	44. (a)	45. (d)	46. (a)	47. (b)	48. (a)	49. (d)	50. (b)

HOTS

| 1. (a) | 2. (b) | 3. (b) | 4. (c) | 5. (d) | | | | | |

14. NATURAL RESOURCES

Answer Key

1. (c)	2. (b)	3. (b)	4. (d)	5. (b)	6. (a)	7. (a)	8. (d)	9. (d)	10. (b)
11. (b)	12. (d)	13. (c)	14. (b)	15. (c)	16. (a)	17. (c)	18. (b)	19. (b)	20. (c)
21. (c)	22. (a)	23. (b)	24. (a)	25. (c)	26. (b)	27. (b)	28. (c)	29. (d)	30. (c)
31. (d)	32. (d)	33. (a)	34. (d)	35. (b)	36. (c)	37. (c)	38. (b)	39. (c)	40. (d)
41. (c)	42. (c)	43. (b)	44. (a)	45. (d)					

HOTS

| 1. (d) | 2. (a) | 3. (b) | 4. (d) | 5. (b) | | | | | |

15. IMPROVEMENT IN FOOD RESOURCES

Answer Key

1. (c)	2. (b)	3. (d)	4. (a)	5. (a)	6. (b)	7. (a)	8. (b)	9. (d)	10 (a)
11. (b)	12. (a)	13. (b)	14. (d)	15. (a)	16. (c)	17. (b)	18. (d)	19. (b)	20. (c)
21. (d)	22. (c)	23. (d)	24. (c)	25. (a)	26. (a)	27. (b)	28. (c)	29. (b)	30. (d)
31. (d)	32. (a)	33. (a)	34. (b)	35. (d)	36. (b)	37. (a)	38. (d)	39. (b)	40. (c)
41. (a)	42. (b)	43. (a)	44. (c)	45. (a)	46. (a)	47. (d)	48. (b)	49. (a)	50. (b)

HOTS

| 1. (a) | 2. (d) | 3. (c) | 4. (b) | 5. (d) | | | | | |

SECTION 2: LOGICAL REASONING

1. ANALOGY

Answer Key

1. (b)	2. (c)	3. (d)	4. (b)	5. (b)	6. (a)	7. (d)	8. (a)	9. (c)	10. (b)
11. (d)	12. (c)	13. (d)	14. (a)	15. (d)	16. (a)	17. (d)	18. (b)	19. (a)	20. (d)
21. (a)	22. (d)	23. (d)	24. (d)	25. (c)	26. (d)	27. (b)	28. (b)	29. (a)	30. (d)

2. CLASSIFICATION

Answer Key

1. (a)	2. (c)	3. (c)	4. (d)	5. (a)	6. (b)	7. (a)	8. (c)	9. (a)	10. (a)
11. (b)	12. (a)	13. (b)	14. (c)	15. (b)	16. (d)	17. (b)	18. (c)	19. (a)	20. (d)
21. (c)	22. (d)	23. (c)	24. (d)	25. (a)	26. (b)	27. (c)	28. (d)	29. (d)	30. (b)
31. (d)	32. (a)	33. (c)	34. (c)	35. (a)	36. (c)	37. (a)	38. (d)	39. (c)	40. (c)

3. SERIES COMPLETION

Answer Key

1. (a)	2. (c)	3. (b)	4. (d)	5. (c)	6. (b)	7. (d)	8. (b)	9. (c)	10. (b)
11. (a)	12. (c)	13. (d)	14. (a)	15. (a)	16. (c)	17. (a)	18. (b)	19. (a)	20. (c)
21. (a)	22. (a)	23. (a)	24. (d)	25. (b)	26. (b)	27. (b)	28. (a)	29. (a)	30. (b)
31. (a)	32. (b)	33. (a)	34. (a)	35. (d)	36. (a)	37. (a)	38. (b)	39. (c)	40. (c)

4. CODING AND DECODING

Answer Key

1. (c)	2. (c)	3. (c)	4. (c)	5. (c)	6. (b)	7. (d)	8. (a)	9. (a)	10. (a)
11. (a)	12. (a)	13. (c)	14. (a)	15. (a)	16. (b)	17. (b)	18. (b)	19. (c)	20. (b)
21. (a)	22. (b)	23. (a)	24. (a)	25. (c)	26. (c)	27. (c)	28. (b)	29. (c)	30. (a)

5. NUMBER, RANKING AND TIME SEQUENCE TEST

Answer Key

1. (a)	2. (b)	3. (b)	4. (d)	5. (a)	6. (b)	7. (b)	8. (c)	9. (c)	10. (b)
11. (b)	12. (d)	13. (d)	14. (c)	15. (b)	16. (b)	17. (b)	18. (a)	19. (a)	20. (c)
21. (b)	22. (b)	23. (a)	24. (c)	25. (b)	26. (c)	27. (c)	28. (b)	29. (b)	30. (c)

6. ALPHABET TEST

Answer Key

1. (b)	2. (b)	3. (d)	4. (c)	5. (a)	6. (d)	7. (b)	8. (c)	9. (a)	10. (c)
11. (c)	12. (a)	13. (c)	14. (b)	15. (c)	16. (c)	17. (c)	18. (d)	19. (b)	20. (d)
21. (b)	22. (b)	23. (a)	24. (c)	25. (a)	26. (c)	27. (d)	28. (d)	29. (a)	30. (d)
31. (d)	32. (c)	33. (b)	34. (d)	35. (a)	36. (b)	37. (d)	38. (c)	39. (c)	40. (c)

7. BLOOD RELATIONS TEST

Answer Key

1. (b)	2. (a)	3. (d)	4. (c)	5. (a)	6. (c)	7. (a)	8. (a)	9. (a)	10. (a)
11. (a)	12. (a)	13. (b)	14. (b)	15. (c)	16. (c)	17. (a)	18. (c)	19. (c)	20. (a)
21. (a)	22. (b)	23. (a)	24. (d)	25. (d)	26. (a)	27. (b)	28. (c)	29. (a)	30. (d)

8. MATHEMATICAL OPERATIONS

Answer Key

1. (c)	2. (a)	3. (b)	4. (b)	5. (b)	6. (b)	7. (b)	8. (c)	9. (b)	10. (a)
11. (a)	12. (d)	13. (a)	14. (a)	15. (c)	16. (b)	17. (a)	18. (d)	19. (d)	20. (d)
21. (c)	22. (a)	23. (a)	24. (c)	25. (a)	26. (a)	27. (c)	28. (b)	29. (a)	30. (c)

9. ARITHMETICAL REASONING

Answer Key

1. (c)	2. (a)	3. (b)	4. (b)	5. (b)	6. (a)	7. (d)	8. (c)	9. (a)	10. (d)
11. (c)	12. (b)	13. (b)	14. (c)	15. (c)	16. (b)	17. (a)	18. (a)	19. (b)	20. (b)
21. (a)	22. (c)	23. (c)	24. (c)	25. (a)	26. (c)	27. (a)	28. (c)	29. (b)	30. (a)

10. INSERTING THE MISSING CHARACTER

Answer Key

1. (a)	2. (a)	3. (c)	4. (b)	5. (c)	6. (a)	7. (d)	8. (b)	9. (c)	10. (b)
11. (b)	12. (b)	13. (b)	14. (c)	15. (d)	16. (c)	17. (c)	18. (a)	19. (b)	20. (a)
21. (b)	22. (d)	23. (b)	24. (b)	25. (b)	26. (c)	27. (a)	28. (b)	29. (a)	30. (c)

11. SERIES

Answer Key

1. (a)	2. (c)	3. (e)	4. (e)	5. (a)	6. (e)	7. (a)	8. (a)	9. (c)	10. (c)
11. (b)	12. (e)	13. (d)	14. (a)	15. (d)	16. (d)	17. (b)	18. (d)	19. (b)	20. (b)
21. (d)	22. (e)	23. (d)	24. (c)	25. (c)	26. (c)	27. (b)	28. (a)	29. (e)	30. (e)

12. PAPER CUTTING

Answer Key

1. (a)	2. (c)	3. (c)	4. (d)	5. (d)	6. (a)	7. (b)	8. (b)	9. (c)	10. (d)
11. (d)	12. (c)	13. (b)	14. (b)	15. (c)	16. (c)	17. (d)	18. (a)	19. (c)	20. (b)
21. (d)	22. (b)	23. (c)	24. (b)	25. (c)	26. (c)	27. (c)	28. (c)	29. (b)	30. (c)
31. (d)	32. (d)	33. (d)	34. (b)	35. (b)	36. (a)	37. (c)	38. (c)	39. (d)	40. (c)
41. (a)	42. (d)	43. (a)	44. (d)	45. (d)					

13. MIRROR IMAGES

Answer Key

1. (b)	2. (c)	3. (a)	4. (b)	5. (a)	6. (c)	7. (a)	8. (d)	9. (b)	10. (c)
11. (d)	12. (a)	13. (c)	14. (b)	15. (b)	16. (a)	17. (a)	18. (c)	19. (d)	20. (c)
21. (b)	22. (d)	23. (a)	24. (c)	25. (b)	26. (a)	27. (d)	28. (c)	29. (c)	30. (a)
31. (c)	32. (b)	33. (c)	34. (b)	35. (d)	36. (c)	37. (b)	38. (a)	39. (b)	40. (c)
41. (c)	42. (a)	43. (d)	44. (a)	45. (d)	46. (d)	47. (b)	48. (a)	49. (a)	50. (b)
51. (b)	52. (d)	53. (a)	54. (b)	55. (c)					

14. WATER IMAGES

Answer Key

1. (c)	2. (a)	3. (d)	4. (c)	5. (b)	6. (d)	7. (c)	8. (a)	9. (d)	10. (b)
11. (a)	12. (d)	13. (c)	14. (b)	15. (c)	16. (d)	17. (c)	18. (d)	19. (b)	20. (b)
21. (d)	22. (b)	23. (d)	24. (a)	25. (c)	26. (b)	27. (b)	28. (d)	29. (c)	30. (a)
31. (c)	32. (b)	33. (b)	34. (a)	35. (a)	36. (c)	37. (d)	38. (d)	39. (a)	40. (c)

15. CUBES AND DICE

Answer Key

1. (c)	2. (a)	3. (b)	4. (c)	5. (b)	6. (c)	7. (a)	8. (b)	9. (a)	10. (b)
11. (c)	12. (a)	13. (c)	14. (a)	15. (d)	16. (d)	17. (c)	18. (a)	19. (a)	20. (c)
21. (c)	22. (a)	23. (c)	24. (d)	25. (a)	26. (d)	27. (a)	28. (c)	29. (b)	30. (c)

MODEL TEST PAPER - 1

Answer Key

1. (c)	2. (b)	3. (c)	4. (d)	5. (d)	6. (a)	7. (a)	8. (a)	9. (c)	10. (a)
11. (d)	12. (b)	13. (a)	14. (b)	15. (a)	16. (b)	17. (d)	18. (b)	19. (d)	20. (c)
21. (b)	22. (a)	23. (b)	24. (a)	25. (a)	26. (d)	27. (b)	28. (b)	29. (c)	30. (d)
31. (a)	32. (d)	33. (a)	34. (d)	35. (b)	36. (d)	37. (a)	38. (b)	39. (b)	40. (c)
41. (d)	42. (d)	43. (c)	44. (a)	45. (b)	46. (b)	47. (a)	48. (c)	49. (a)	50. (a)

MODEL TEST PAPER - 2

Answer Key

1. (a)	2. (c)	3. (b)	4. (c)	5. (b)	6. (b)	7. (a)	8. (c)	9. (b)	10. (a)
11. (a)	12. (c)	13. (a)	14. (b)	15. (d)	16. (d)	17. (b)	18. (c)	19. (a)	20. (a)
21. (a)	22. (b)	23. (a)	24. (d)	25. (d)	26. (d)	27. (d)	28. (d)	29. (b)	30. (d)
31. (d)	32. (d)	33. (d)	34. (a)	35. (a)	36. (a)	37. (b)	38. (a)	39. (c)	40. (c)
41. (a)	42. (c)	43. (b)	44. (a)	45. (b)	46. (c)	47. (d)	48. (c)	49. (b)	50. (d)

Appendix

There are different organizations that conduct these examinations and covering all of them is not needed as the focus should be to understand the main type of exams conducted. They are similar for these organizations with the difference being the change in name of the exam.

\multicolumn{3}{c}{Science Olympiad Foundation (SOF)}		
S. No.	Name of Exam	Grade
1.	National Science Olympiad (NSO)	Class 1-10
2.	National Cyber Olympiad (NCO)	Class 1-10
3.	International Mathematics Olympiad (IMO)	Class 1-10
4.	International English Olympiad (IEO)	Class 1-10
5.	International Commerce Olympiad (ICO)	Class 1-10
6.	International General Knowledge Olympiad (IGKO)	Class 1-10
7.	International Social Studies Olympiad (ISSO)	Class 1-10
\multicolumn{3}{c}{Indian Talent Olympiad (ITO)}		
S. No.	Name of Exam	Grade
1.	International Science Olympiad (ISO)	Class 1-12
2.	International Math Olympiad (IMO)	Class 1-12
3.	English International Olympiad (EIO)	Class 1-12
4.	General Knowledge International Olympiad (GKIO)	Class 1-12
5.	International Computer Olympiad (ICO)	Class 1-12
6.	International Drawing Olympiad (IDO)	Class 1-12
7.	National Essay Olympiad (NESO)	Class 1-12
8.	National Social Studies Olympiad (NSSO)	Class 1-12
\multicolumn{3}{c}{EduHeal Foundation}		
S. No.	Name of Exam	Grade
1.	Eduheal International Cyber Olympiad (ICO)	Class 1-12
2.	Eduheal International English Olympiad (IEO)	Class 1-12
3.	National Interactive Math Olympiad (NIMO)	Class 1-12
4.	National Interactive Science Olympiad (NISO)	Class 1-12
5.	International General Knowledge Olympiad (IGO)	Class 1-12
6.	National Space Science Olympiad (NSSO)	Class 1-12

| \multicolumn{3}{c}{**Humming Bird Education**} |
S. No.	Name of Exam	Grade
1.	Humming Bird Commerce Competency Olympiad (HCC)	Class 1-12
2.	Humming Bird Cyber Olympiad (HCO)	Class 1-12
3.	Humming Bird English Olympiad (HEO)	Class 1-12
4.	Humming Bird General Knowledge Olympiad (HGO)	Class 1-12
5.	Humming Bird Hindi Olympiad (HHO)	Class 1-12
6.	Humming Bird Mathematics Olympiad (HMO)	Class 1-12
7.	Humming Bird Science Olympiad (HSO)	Class 1-12
8.	Humming Bird Aptitude and Reasoning Olympiad (ARO)	Class 1-12
9.	Humming Bird Spelling Competition (Spell BEE)	Class 1-12
10.	Humming Bird Language Olympiad	Class 1-12

International Assessments for Indian Schools (IAIS) (MacMillan and EEA Collaboration)

S. No.	Name of Exam	Grade
1.	IAIS Maths Olympiad	Class 3-12
2.	IAIS ScienceOlympiad	Class 3-12
3.	IAIS English Olympiad	Class 3-12
4.	IAIS Digital Technologies Olympiad	Class 3-12

SilverZone Foundation

S. No.	Name of Exam	Grade
1.	International Informatics Olympiad	Class 1-12
2.	International Olympiad of Mathematics	Class 1-12
3.	International Olympiad of Science	Class 1-12

Unified Council

S. No.	Name of Exam	Grade
1.	Unified Council Cyber Exam	Class 1-12
2.	Unified International English Olympiad.	Class 1-12
3.	Unified International Mathematics Olympiad (UIMO)	Class 1-12

Unicus

S. No.	Name of Exam	Grade
1.	Unicus Non-Routine Mathematics Olympiad (UNRMO)	Class 1-11
2.	Unicus Mathematics Olympiad (UMO)	Class 1-11

Appendix

S. No.	Name of Exam	Grade
3.	Unicus Science Olympiad (USO)	Class 1-11
4.	Unicus English Olympiad (UEO)	Class 1-11
5.	Unicus Cyber Olympiad (UCO)	Class 1-11
6.	Unicus General knowledge Olympiad (UGKO)	Class 1-11
7.	Unicus Critical Thinking Olympiad (UCTO)	Class 1-11
CREST (Online Mode)		
S. No.	Name of Exam	Grade
1.	Mathematics (CMO)	Classes KG-10
2.	Science (CSO)	Classes KG-10
3.	English (CEO)	Classes KG-10
4.	Computer (CCO)	Classes 1-10
5.	Reasoning (CRO)	Classes 1-10
6.	Spell Bee Summer (CSB)	Classes 1-8
7.	Spell Bee Winter (CSBW)	Classes 1-8
8.	Mental Maths (MMO)	Classes 1-12
9.	Green Warrior Olympiad (GWO)	Classes 1-12

How To Apply?

Anyone willing to participate in the Olympiad exam can follow these steps to apply for the exam:

- Log in to the official website of the conducting organization.
- Find the Registration Option to register
- Fill up the details such as Student Name, Parent Name, School Name, Class, Postal Address, E-mail Address, Password, etc.
- Select the subjects you want to apply for. Pay the necessary registration fees and you are done.
- You will receive necessary details on your email id.

There are no minimum marks required by the Olympiad conducting organizations to apply for the exam.

Awards

Based on the organization rules, students as well as schools participating in these exams are awarded with several recognitions based on the marks they score.

www.ingramcontent.com/pod-product-compliance
Lightning Source LLC
Chambersburg PA
CBHW082036230426
43670CB00016B/2675